T0307951

Praise for Cynthia Haven

In *Evolution of Desire: A Life of René Girard*, Cynthia Haven—a literary journalist and the author of books on Joseph Brodsky and Czesław Miłosz—offers a lively, well-documented, highly readable account of how Girard built up his grand "mimetic theory" over time.

—*New York Review of Books*

[Haven's] carefully researched biography is a fitting tribute to her late friend and one that will enlighten both specialists and non-specialists alike. . . . Haven's ability to interweave Girard's life with his publications keeps her narrative flowing at a lively pace.

—*Wall Street Journal*

Haven's *Evolution of Desire: A Life of René Girard* is exemplary in its sensitivity. She expresses openly her affection and admiration for her friend, who comes across as more of a teasing humorist than his public persona might suggest. Yet she recognizes the various intellectual arguments against Girard and the *girardiens*. Her readers are challenged but left free to make up their own minds. She fleshes out her material with rich digressions. . .

—*Times Literary Supplement*

It is the author's closeness to the man once described as "the new Darwin of the human sciences" that brings this fascinating biography to life. . . . At a time when religious fundamentalism, violent extremism and societal division dominates the headlines, Haven's book is a call to revisit and reclaim one of the 20th century's most important thinkers.

—*San Francisco Chronicle*

Girard, who died in 2015 at 91, ventured into many disciplines. Cynthia Haven's *Evolution of Desire* is an ingenious travelogue of his life and thought. . . . The result is an extraordinarily vivid portrait of a man admired not just for his intelligence and erudition, but also for his character, wisdom, and humor.

—*Philadelphia Inquirer*

Cynthia Haven's moving portrait inspires readers to look inward and scrutinize themselves, unsparingly yet forgivingly—just as Girard would have wanted.

—Los Angeles Review of Books

Cynthia Haven's mind-altering biography of this towering figure in 20th-century thought brings so much new information, and so many interpretive insights, that it's hard to imagine any full-service public library, not to mention any academic collection, without a copy. The book is alive.

—Tablet Magazine

While the relationship between biographer and subject can be risky—producing hagiography at one extreme, disparagement at the other—Haven balances her frank admiration with critical commentary . . . this is an ambitious and thought-provoking life portrait.

—Stanford Magazine

In this intimate but philosophically searching book, the author's writing is marvelously clear. She expertly unpacks Girard's ideas, making them unusually accessible, even to readers with limited familiarity. A penetrating account of an important thinker—and as agile, profound, and affecting as its subject.

—Kirkus Reviews

Evolution of Desire is one of the best biographies I have ever read.

—Books, Inq.

Evolution
of Desire

Evolution of Desire

A Life of René Girard

Cynthia L. Haven

Michigan State University Press · *East Lansing*

Michigan State University Press
East Lansing, Michigan 48823-5245

Printed and bound in the United States of America.

27 26 25 24 23 22 21 20 19 18   1 2 3 4 5 6 7 8 9 10

LIBRARY OF CONGRESS CATALOGING-IN-PUBLICATION DATA
Names: Haven, Cynthia L., author.
Title: Evolution of desire : a life of René Girard / Cynthia L. Haven.
Description: East Lansing : Michigan State University Press, 2018. | Series: Studies in violence, mimesis,
and culture | Includes bibliographical references and index.
Identifiers: LCCN 2017026391| ISBN 9781611862836 (pbk. : alk. paper) | ISBN 9781609175634 (pdf) |
ISBN 9781628953305 (epub) | ISBN 9781628963304 (kindle)
Subjects: LCSH: Girard, René, 1923-2015. | Philosopher—France—Biography. | Philosophy,
French—20th century. | Philosophy, French—21st century.
Classification: LCC B2430.G494 H38 2018 | DDC 194—dc23
LC record available at https://lccn.loc.gov/2017026391

Book design by Charlie Sharp, Sharp Des!gns, East Lansing, MI
Cover design by David Drummond, Salamander Design, www.salamanderhill.com.
Cover image of René Girard is ©2017 Michael Sugrue and is used with permission
of the photographer. All rights reserved.

Michigan State University Press is a member of the Green Press Initiative and is committed to developing
and encouraging ecologically responsible publishing practices. For more information about the Green
Press Initiative and the use of recycled paper in book publishing, please visit www.greenpressinitiative.org.

Visit Michigan State University Press at www.msupress.org

For René, with all my love
(but not the triangular sort)

Contents

CHAPTER 1

Introduction

Armed with a copy of the *Iliad* and a shovel, Heinrich Schliemann set out to find Troy in 1871. Two years later, he hit gold.

He was vilified as an amateur, an adventurer, and a con man. As archaeologists refined their methods of excavation in the subsequent decades, Schliemann would also be deplored for destroying much of what he was trying to find.

Nevertheless, he found the lost city. He is credited with the modern discovery of prehistoric Greek civilization. He ignited the field of Homeric studies at the end of the century. Most importantly, for our purposes, he broke new ground in a figurative, as well as literal, sense: he scrutinized the words of the text, and believed that they held the truth.

"I've said this for years: in the global sense, the best analogy for what René Girard represents in anthropology and sociology is Schliemann," said the French theorist's Stanford colleague, Robert Pogue Harrison. "Like him, his major discovery was excoriated for using the wrong methods. The others never would have found Troy by looking at the literature—it was beyond their imagination." Girard's writings hold revelations that are even more important, however: they describe the roots of the violence that destroyed Troy and other empires throughout time.

Like Schliemann, the French academician trusted literature as the repository of truth, and as an accurate reflection of what actually happened. Harrison told me that Girard's loyalty was not to a narrow academic discipline, but rather to a continuing human truth: "Academic disciplines are more committed to methodology than truth. René, like Schliemann, had no training in anthropology. From the discipline's point of view, that is ruthlessly undisciplined. He's still not forgiven."

I have appreciated Harrison's analogy, though some of Girard's other friends will no doubt rush to his defense, given Schliemann's scandalous character—but Girard scandalized people, too: many academics grind their teeth at some of Girard's more *ex cathedra* pronouncements (though surely a few other modern French thinkers were just as apodictic). He never received the recognition he merited on this side of the Atlantic, even though he is one of America's very few *immortels* of the Académie Française.

For Girard, however, literature is more than a record of historical truth, it is the archive of self-knowledge. Girard's public life began in literary theory and criticism, with the study of authors whose protagonists embraced self-renunciation and self-transcendence. Eventually, his scholarship crossed into the fields of anthropology, sociology, history, philosophy, psychology, theology. Girard's thinking, including his textual analysis, offers a sweeping reading of human nature, human history, and human destiny. Let us review some of his more important conclusions.

He overturned three widespread assumptions about the nature of desire and violence: first, that our desire is authentic and our own; second, that we fight from our differences, rather than our sameness; and third, that religion is the cause of violence, rather than an archaic solution for controlling violence within a society, as he would assert.

He was fascinated by what he calls "metaphysical desire"—that is, the desire we have when creature needs for food, water, sleep, and shelter are met. In that regard, he is perhaps best known for his notion of mediated desire, based on the observation that people adopt the desires of other people. In short, we want what others want. We want it *because* they want it.

Human behavior is driven by imitation. We are, after all, social creatures. Imitation is the way we learn: it's how we begin to speak, and why we don't eat with our hands. It's why advertising works, why a whole generation may decide at once to pierce their tongues or tear their jeans, why pop songs top the charts and the stock markets rise and fall.

The idea of mimesis is hardly foreign to the social sciences today, but no one had made it a linchpin in a theory of human competition and violence, as Girard did, beginning in the 1950s. Freud and Marx were in error: one supposed sex to be the building block of human behavior, the other saw economics as fundamental. But the true key was "mimetic desire," which precedes and drives both. Imitation steers our sexual longings and Wall Street trends. When a Coca-Cola advertisement beckons you to join the glamorous people at a beach by drinking its beverage, mimetic desire poses no immediate privations—there is enough Coca-Cola for all. Problems arise where scarcity imposes limits, or when envy eyes an object that cannot be shared, or one that the possessor has no wish to share—a spouse, an inheritance, the top-floor corner office.

Hence, Girard claimed that mimetic desire is not only the way we love, it's the reason we fight. Two hands that reach toward the same object will ultimately clench into fists. Think of *A Midsummer Night's Dream,* where couples dissolve and reassemble, tearing friendships asunder as the two men suddenly want the same woman. Whatever two or three people want, soon everyone will want. Mimetic desire spreads contagiously, as people converge on the same person, position, or possession as the answer to a prayer or the solution to a problem. Even conflict is imitated and reciprocated.

Eventually, one individual or group is seen as responsible for the social contagion—generally, someone who is an outsider, who cannot or will not retaliate, and so is positioned to end the escalating cycles of tit-for-tat. The chosen culprit is therefore a foreigner, a cripple, a woman, or, in some cases, a king so far above the crowd that he stands alone. The victim is killed, exiled, pilloried, or otherwise eliminated. This act unites the warring factions and releases enormous social tension, restoring harmony among individuals and within the community. First the scapegoat is a criminal, then a god—more importantly, the scapegoat is both, since the single-handed power to bring either peace and harmony or war and violence to a society is seen as supernatural. Oedipus is deified at Colonus, Helen of Troy ascends Mount Olympus, and even as Joan of Arc is burned at the stake, the mob begins to murmur, "We have killed a saint!" Archaic religious sacrifice, Girard argued, is no more than the ritual reenactment of the scapegoat's killing, invoking the magical powers that preempted a societal catastrophe previously. He offered a complete deconstruction of religion, just as he had deconstructed desire.

He not only replaced Freudian desire with a more streamlined notion of mimesis, he also reconsidered Freud's *Totem and Taboo,* the psychoanalyst's ventures into archaeology and anthropology, at a time when the book was largely rejected. Girard took its notions of collective murder, and its insight that the foundation of culture is murder, one step further. He reaffirmed the book's importance, but ultimately refuted it with his daring, erudite argument.

His next step was to prove the most provocative of all: he describes how the Judeo-Christian texts are unique in revealing the innocence of the scapegoat, thus destabilizing the mechanism that allowed the victim to be both criminal and redeemer, the violent solution to social violence. We can no longer have clean consciences as we murder. Individuals and groups even compete for the cachet of being a victim in the Oppression Olympics, as the power-holders play defense. Wars continue, but end with no clear resolutions. International rivalries still escalate toward uncertain ends. The stakes are higher than ever today: we teeter on the nuclear brink.

For the reader meeting René Girard for the first time in these pages, the obvious question is why, in a world flooded with new information daily, we should care about the books, interviews, articles, and life of a man who died quietly in his early nineties in late 2015. I would begin by noting that he is a champion of the long thought, in a world that favors increasingly short and trivial ones. He is one of the few real thinkers we have had in our times.

Many have attempted to compartmentalize him according to his various interests (literature, anthropology, religions) or according to the distinct phases of his work (mimesis, scapegoating, sacrifice). However, Girard cannot be parsed into segments because the phases of his work are not diverse moments in one person's episodic life. They show the substance of his intellectual, emotional, and spiritual involvement with twentieth-century history, and his personal effort to come to grips with it. More often, journalists and others marshal one piece of his thought to support the discussion at hand, while failing to consider the context of the whole. But attempts to put him in a box reveal something about our own need to comfort ourselves.

Compartmentalizing his ideas is a mistake, obviously. It cannot and should not be done, for the simple reason that if you do so *you* won't be changed. That, in the end, is the real core of Girard's thought: change of being.

"All desire is a desire for being," he wrote, and the formulation, stunning in its implications, is an arrow that points the way out of our metaphysical plight. We want what others want because we believe the "other" possesses an inner perfection that we do not. We become consumed by the wish to *be* the godlike others. We hope that by acquiring their trappings (their cars, their couturiers, their circle of friends), we will acquire their metaphysical goods—authority, wisdom, autonomy, self-fulfillment—which are largely imagined, anyway.

The imitation puts us in direct competition with the person we adore, the rival we ultimately come to hate and worship, who responds by defending his or her turf. As competition intensifies, the rivals copy each other more and more, even if they're only copying the reflected image of themselves. Eventually, the *objet du désir* becomes secondary or irrelevant. The rivals are obsessed with each other and their fight. Bystanders are drawn into "taking sides," and so the conflict can envelop a society, with cycles of retaliatory (and therefore imitative) violence and one-upmanship.

That's why Girard's theories must explode inward rather than outward. If you use these tools to castigate the defective "other," you miss the point. Desire is not individual but social. The other has colonized your desire, long before you knew you had it. And the phantom being that you covet recedes as you pursue it. Girard asks you to ask yourself: who do I worship?

The flashpoint of his oeuvre is not ancient Mesopotamia, Greek texts, or a handful of writers he favored. His work invites you to set fire to the chair you are sitting on. It is a process he went through himself. One of Girard's most beloved authors, Marcel Proust, wrote in his own magnum opus:

> I had a more modest view of my book and it would be incorrect to say even that I was thinking of those who might read it as 'my readers.' For, to my mind, they would not be *my* readers but the very readers of themselves, my book serving only as a sort of magnifying glass, such as the optician of Combray used to offer to a customer; my book might supply the means by which they could read themselves. So that I would not ask them to praise me or to speak ill of me, but only to tell me that it is as I say,

if the words which they read within themselves are, indeed, those which
I have written.[1]

Clearly, Girard is tenaciously loyal to a heritage that has been abandoned
in the last century and a half: the *grand récit*—that is, a meta-narrative that
offers a sweeping, teleological worldview. He is working against a Western
philosophical tradition that has increasingly limited what philosophers can
describe. With an intellect and ambition to challenge the major thinkers of
our time, Girard is among the last of this breed, giving elegant expression to
vast swaths of human reality with a kind of exposition and style not commonly found in the social sciences.

Today we are talking about war, rivalry, violence, and conflict while
once-trendy preoccupations with sign and signifier are passé, and may soon
be largely forgotten. In fact, one could argue that the prominence of the
words "scapegoat," "sacrifice," "social contagion," and certainly "mimesis"
in our culture comes from Girard. He did not coin these terms, of course,
but their widespread usage may owe something to their repeated emphasis
in his work. Our sensitivity to the phenomenon of scapegoating itself may
pay homage to his thought. Girard is, by any measure, a giant of twentieth-
century thought.

All that sounds very grand, but my perspective differs from most of
Girard's admirers. I encountered René Girard not through theory or books,
but through the man himself. Unlike many who have written about him, I
came to his work through his kindness, generosity, and his personal friendship, not the other way around. I have tried to keep in mind that not all
readers will delve deeply into his works, but will still find the ideas he promulgated to be important ones.

This book is above all a presentation of the man, in the context of his
life and times, with the intention that his ideas will not only be thought but
felt, as a working dynamic in human society, rather than a scientific formula
to be rigorously imposed. In doing so, I hope to create a larger tent—not of
true believers, but of educated nonspecialists who are likely to find themselves
drawn to the questions Girard asked, and wish to become familiar with the
contours of his thought, whether they ultimately agree with his answers or not.

These readers will not approach his work as a theory to be confirmed or
repudiated but as a heuristic framework to describe more effectively what

we see around us. For myself, I am convinced of the applicability of Girard's ideas to a wide range of situations and its importance to a general audience. Their explanatory power roams from international politics to the memes on the daily Twitter feed. I do not think, however, that his theories are the only lens that resolves these issues—nor did he. A telescope is a very useful instrument for gazing at the stars, but it cannot detect microbes—a microscope would be far handier. Nor can we use a microscope to admire a landscape rather than binoculars. We use whichever tool helps us *see* better.

The discursive and conversational nature of much of his oeuvre (his major work is a book-length Q&A, for example) discourages a dogmatic approach. "I make it as systematic as possible for you to be able to *prove* it *wrong*," he admonished his critics,[2] yet I think he was as intuitive as he was rational. Though he prided himself in his role as a French intellectual, he was also a visionary, *malgré lui.*

As he once indicated in a characteristically roundabout way: "This irreducible personal involvement of the questioner as well as, at the other end, the all-embracing nature of the question, gives to my research a 'philosophical' and even a 'religious' twist that may forever prevent it from becoming 'scientific' in the eyes of the scientist. Does it mean that our scientific culture can ignore this question? Can it really afford to?"[3]

Throughout this book, I have indulged a personal prejudice of my own, and one shared by one of Girard's favorite authors. A professor from my University of Michigan days, the Slavic scholar and publisher Carl Proffer of Ardis Books, put it this way: "Dostoevsky insisted that *life* teaches you things, not theories, not ideas. Look at the way people end up in life—that teaches you the truth."[4] Girard himself is the best endorsement of his oeuvre. He pretty much practiced what he preached, and got better as he practiced. I observed his immense personal dignity, his remarkably serene and devoted marriage of six decades, his industriousness, his lifelong loyalties and friendships, his unfailing courtesy to newcomers, such as this one. Some have claimed that the gentleness and affection were the by-product of advanced age, but one could have argued equally that old age brings stagnation, crotchetiness, and rigidity. At least for this visitor, he maintained his cheerfulness, curiosity, and good humor to the end. He was a great man, and a wise one—I have known others, but none with his personal qualities, which recommended themselves before I even encountered his work.

He wasn't anxious to be a hero, however, and went to some pains to downplay his personal story. "I left France for the United States at twenty-three. I taught in various universities, I married, I had children. With my family, I went to France and Europe for many summer holidays as well as several years of sabbaticals," he wrote. "In sum, a banal enough existence for the second half of the twentieth century."[5]

I found that that wasn't entirely the case, as I suspected it wasn't from the outset. Although his life was outwardly placid, he had his share of perturbations and suffering. In his remarks to me and others, Girard showed a stoic consistency in minimizing events, or his reaction to them, even when eyewitnesses to events remembered otherwise. Those who have chided his hubris might take note of his modesty: "I'm not concealing my biography, but I don't want to fall victim to the narcissism to which we're all inclined."[6]

It is commonly said that to write of a life is to become disillusioned with one's subject. I am happy to say that was not so. In his study of the greatest literature, Girard always maintained that the story of the novel was the story of the author as well. We could say the same about Girard and his oeuvre.

But Girard expressed himself in the human sciences rather than fiction. His language is eloquent, lively, and persuasive. Until now, however, the experiences behind his theories remained in shadow. We have his books; here are the outlines of the life.

CHAPTER 2

Magnetic North

As if his whole vocation
Were endless imitation.
—William Wordsworth, "Ode: Intimations of Immortality"

The city is small and the traffic fast. I had to negotiate the turn quickly and decisively, or swing outward from the still center of Avignon, my rented silver Citroën pulled centrifugally by the mid-day traffic toward either the Rhône or Le Pontet and Barbentane.

The ring of modern highway hews to the old ramparts, which wrap the city in a tight embrace. It's easy to be distracted from the road signs while driving along the tall white walls, seven centuries old, with their thirty-nine massive towers and machicolated battlements. "Let peace be in thy strength: and abundance in thy towers," sang the Psalmist, and indeed the earlier denizens of this Provençal town seemed to depend on the towers for protection and power. Now, however, the same landmarks look like the rooks in a giant chess game that endured for centuries and is now paused, awaiting the next move.

Take the turnoff into the city, and suddenly you are *there*: right in front of you, the Palais des Papes, the largest Gothic edifice in Christendom, and one of the most architecturally spectacular, rises impregnably, majestically from the rock of Doms. The sun-bleached fortress is an overwhelming presence in the town, so it's natural that traffic comes to a halt here, where the most effective mode of transportation is usually walking.

Today's Avignon is a small provincial city of ruins and museums, schools and shops—a place with its glorious face turned resolutely toward the past. It was, however, once the avant-garde—the hub of medieval Christendom, a city of popes and antipopes in a region of saints and heretics. For René Girard, Avignon was the site of his most formative years, and it left an indelible stamp. His father was curator of the Palais and an eminent historian of the city and region, so its long past would have been sealed into the young Girard's psychological makeup—though he would later downplay its charm.

"If you are from Avignon, it is not that romantic. In some ways, it's more like Italian cities than French," he said one afternoon. "It's really the south, and people tend to live more outside than they do in northern France. There is quite a bit of difference between northern France and southern France. . . . It is less than 50 miles from the sea. But it's not the Riviera, it's a small provincial town."

Yet Avignon would pop up frequently in conversations. I always suspected it gave him extra insulation against intellectual fads and the prejudices of the Parisian intelligentsia. He never quite lost all traces of the slower, softer, slightly lilting Avignonnais accent. Girard was amused at my interest in the city of his birth—but beneath its placid surface it had a turbulent history, and I sensed he had a secret, regional pride in the place he disparaged as a provincial town.

Girard did not often talk about his life unless I prodded him, but this place had a story to tell me. The city itself was eager and eloquent—a place impossible to silence.

He explained to me that the fierce and turbulent Rhône that runs round the city divides France between the influences of Spain to the west, and Italy to the east. The east played the decisive card in Avignon's medieval destiny.

Avignon and Rome. For a century, the rivalrous locked embrace of these two powers tore Europe asunder, splitting church and state, spiritual and temporal power. It's not mere chance that the man who developed a theory of imitation, rivalry, and conflict began here.

In those days, the mysterious chess game was in full play. There was only one papacy, a single, tantalizing prize. Who would own it? And the supernatural sovereign would preside under which earthly king's sway? The ceaseless conflict, corruption, and bickering within the medieval Church, and among the nations dealing with it, made the Eternal City an unpleasant, even dangerous, place for a pope to unpack his horse. Hence, Pope Clement V took up residence instead in Avignon, which was then in the kingdom of Arles, in 1309.

The decision had some precedent. The popes of the Middle Ages had fled Rome before. But Clement V upped the ante, refusing to budge from France, after his 1305 installation as pope in Lyon.

A few years later, he set up shop in this city, which had endured occupation by the Romans, Saracens, Franks, Burgundians, Ostrogoths, and Moors. Something of a quiet backwater at the time—but interesting things often happen in backwaters.

Dante condemned Clement V as "a lawless shepherd from the west, of uglier deeds."[1] A series of French popes followed, and their friends and relations were made cardinals, further undermining any attempt to return the papacy to Italy. Clement's successor, John XXII, continued building Avignon into one of the mightiest and most heavily fortified cities in Europe.

To us, the Avignon papacy may seem like a footnote in history, but that only shows the tilt of our times. Two of the greatest geniuses of the Late Middle Ages flourished during this era. Dante began the *Divine Comedy* about the time the Avignon Papacy began, and his masterpiece may have been partly motivated by the upheaval. Because he sets the *Commedia* five years before Clement V became pope, in the year 1300, we can easily forget that the Church was centered in France, not Italy, during the most creative period of the poet's life.

Meanwhile, Petrarch's family followed Pope Clement V from Incisa, near Florence, to Avignon at the beginning of the Babylonian Captivity— the poet's father was Dante's close friend and, like him, had been banished from Florence. In Avignon, Petrarch encountered Laura, his beloved, who was born there in 1327. They met on a Good Friday and she died on another, twenty-one years to the hour after Petrarch first saw her. Were it not for Laura of Avignon, we would not have Petrarch's *Canzoniere*. It took the intervention of a saint, Catherine of Siena, to persuade the pope to return to Rome—but years of Western Schism followed, with popes in Rome and antipopes in Avignon battling for supremacy. Europe was bled dry as it supported two papal residences, and two papal administrations. By that time, the backwater had been transformed into a sophisticated city seeking to displace Rome. The Palais des Papes had appeared, along with the Petit Palais, the Church of Saint-Didier, and the circular white ramparts.

Girard's father would have told him these tales, for the family was entwined with Avignon's history. And his son would return to this time and place for his thesis for the École des Chartes on the second half of the fifteenth century, beginning where the Schism leaves off—the choice certainly underscores how much the story was in his essence.

.   .   .

René Noël Théophile Girard was born on the evening of Christmas day, 1923, in a room watched over by a painting the color of dark honey, featuring a half-dozen or so goats. The same painting would later hang in the Girards' living room in Palo Alto: a nineteenth-century pastoral idyll on the stock theme of a shepherd courting a shepherdess, with other young people to the side, absorbed in country labor among the frolicking goats. Not "scapegoats," exactly, but the close-enough augury was occasionally pointed out to visitors, with a whimsical smile.

Although his second name suggests a prescient sense of timing, in fact the "Noël" was borrowed from a grandfather or great-grandfather, perhaps on the maternal side. His mother was from Bouchet in the Drôme département of the Rhône-Alpes. Her family had lived in Provence for centuries and once owned silk mills in Sérignan-du-Comtat. The family name, de Loye, is still associated with silk-making in that part of the world. Girard referred to his family as "the old, impoverished bourgeoisie."[2] The family, on both sides, had seen better days, and had failed to make a success of several businesses, though its members were leaders of their communities and highly respected.

Girard remembered learning only a smattering of the residual Provençal language that recalls how much this region was a separate people at the time of the Avignon papacy, and how it remained so in the centuries since.

A trip to the archives for the of Vaucluse, carved out in the side of the cliff that holds the Palais, shows what a small, tight-knit society Avignon still is. The slender and serious archivist, Blandine Silvestre, had her own ties to the Girard family: she had lived at the former family address at 12 Rue de la Croix. That would not have been René Girard's home, as she had thought, but rather the family home of his father and paternal grandparents. Madame Silvestre pulled out an old-fashioned wooden file drawer for Girard's father, Joseph Frédéric Marie Girard (1881–1962), with about sixty file card entries under his name for books and articles. The archivist paleographer was known not only for his scholarship, however. He was the curator of the Palais des Papes, and before that, from 1906 to 1949, the curator for Avignon's little jewel, the Calvet Museum, a fine arts institution housed in a magnificent eighteenth-century mansion.

Girard described his mother as a very intelligent woman and something of a free spirit. Marie-Thérèse de Loye Fabre (1893–1967), had some local renown as one of the first women in the region to get a baccalauréat (secondary school) degree. In 1808, the first year Napoléon established the "bac," only thirty-one received the degree; in 1931, only 2.5 percent of the nation's age cohort passed the bac;[3] it certainly remained a mark of distinction.

Although we seem to know much more about the father's side of the family now, one senses that Mademoiselle Fabre was taking a slight step down with her marriage in 1920, and that Joseph Girard was lucky to marry into the old family of the Comtadine, the wine-growing region around Avignon that produces the ruby red vintages of Châteauneuf-du-Pape, initially made for the bibulous Avignon popes. Shortly after their marriage, the bride's parents let the young couple move into their home at 7 Chemin de l'Arrousaire, with its large garden and plane trees, on the south of the ramparts. René Girard's wife Martha recalled a remark that revealed some of the changes that marriage brought for Girard's mother: Martha had learned cooking from her mother-in-law, who told her that she had not been brought up to cook. Understandably, then, the elder Madame Girard's cuisine was simple and straightforward.

His mother's family was well-born enough, in any case, to have feared persecution during the French Revolutionary times. In recent years, a relative sent Girard the certificate restoring the De La Loye name, which had been shortened to Deloye to look and sound less dangerously aristocratic during Robespierre's Reign of Terror.

Joseph and Thérèse Girard were married at Bouchet, but Auvergne also figured in the new family's life, for Joseph's father was born there. For many years, the extended Girard family spent their long summers in Viverols in the Puy de Dôme département, with its eponymous dormant volcano, the tallest in a region full of them. Girard told me it's the part of France he loves most—known for its mountains, maars, cinder cones, and lava domes, the dark, mounded hills that are the "puys" that figure so prominently in the local names.

Descriptions of Joseph Girard sometimes make him sound a bit forbidding, an adamant disciplinarian. But that's far from the whole story. He lost his father at five and, with his two brothers, was sent to the Jesuit Collège St. Joseph in Avignon. In 1899, he went on to the École Nationale des Chartes, the national training ground for archivists, librarians, and paleographers—only a year after leading figures in the École had unanimously concluded that the "bordereau" was not in the handwriting of Alfred Dreyfus. Though the Dreyfus Affair would continue for some years more, it was the École's finest moment. "My father often spoke of that Chartist exploit," said Girard. "He was a Dreyfusard, a bit of an old-school radical-socialist."[4]

Joseph Girard was a lieutenant in World War I, and received a shrapnel wound in his head at Reims, a city under heavy German bombardment in the far north of France. The injury could easily have been treated with modern antibiotics, but in that era the medical adjunct simply put a bandage on it and sent him home to recover. By the time he reached Avignon, he was near death and required surgery and a long hospitalization. He was solidly anti-war for the rest of his life. "He was aware of the stupidity of it all," Girard told me. Joseph's older brother Henri—a captain leading the youngest, greenest soldiers—would be killed in the final offensive at the Battle of the Somme, one of humanity's bloodiest battles. His younger brother Pierre would survive to be a successful doctor in Avignon. Joseph, too, remained in Avignon.

Girard said his father was a "typical archivist." He had several people working for him, and would head into town on a mobylette from the family home on Arrousaire, just outside the old city walls, near the train station. He was a highly respected man and historian, but the military experience left its imprint. Some accused him of being obdurate and fixed in his ways. Martha recalled him as "very nice, not an icy person." In his years of authority, she said, she was told about him once breaking a plate in anger. The plate has long since been swept up, mourned, and deposited in a dustbin—but the moment was uncharacteristic enough to linger in family memory. As for

Thérèse, "She had had some skepticism, quite a lot, in fact," recalled Martha. "She'd often say, 'Les gens sont mauvais'—'People are wicked.'"

Yet Madame Girard was a good Catholic who took the children to various churches around town on Sundays and holy days, including the twelfth-century Cathédrale Notre-Dame next to the Palais. In his communion photo, the dark-haired son is serious and ramrod-straight, aware of the importance of the occasion. By twelve or thirteen, however, he had stopped attending mass. Later, however, he was enrolled in the optional catechism classes at the lycée—perhaps his mother's influence.

"I tend to have the taste of my mother, you know, who was classical," he once said in his living room on the aptly named Frenchman's Road. "In France, middle-class families of academic upbringing tended to be very classical in music, and totally German. They paid no attention to French music, curiously, because the historical line of music begins with the predecessors of Bach and ends up with Schubert. Now the really daring guys, they go on to Stravinsky and Mahler," he said, laughing.

Girard described a childhood that centered on a "serene and comfortable environment, in a very normal family life."[5] The husband and wife were a dozen years apart in age, however, and of different temperament and tempers. Girard's memories are threaded with the inevitable, though not serious, discord between the two. He inherited a good deal from each of them, and both sides were to play out in his nature. And the deeply Catholic mother and anti-clerical, republican father reflected much in the history of Avignon itself. Catholicism was a negative-to-positive, positive-to-negative current running throughout the lives of this region, leaping over the centuries. It was always a highly charged topic. Whether for or against it, no one was indifferent. And so it played out in the Girard household.

Girard himself once said, "I was raised in the double religion of Dreyfusism and Catholicism (on my mother's side), although I didn't learn about Péguy until much later."[6]

.   .   .

What did René Girard remember most about his childhood? The books. His mother, who loved the arts and literature, read Alessandro Manzoni's *The Betrothed* to all the children.

For the most part, however, he found his own tastes. At a young age, he showed a lifelong penchant for taking his own path, a solitary education formed by his own enthusiasm and intuitions. Girard's anti-institutional bias surfaced when he was very young. "I began working on my own very early. When I was a child, I could not stand the atmosphere of the schools. So my mother withdrew me from the small lycée to take lessons at home."

When his interlocutor Mark Anspach asked what exactly he disliked, his condemnation was categorical: "Everything! The teacher was for me a terrifying lady. I couldn't stand the class, I couldn't stand the recess, all the kids . . . In fact, I couldn't stand foolishness. So my mother enrolled me in this private course where there were only two other students and me. My father called this a 'school for the spoiled.' Thus, up to the age of ten, I didn't have a real school. My class hours were very limited, and I read whatever I wanted."[7]

"I had, and still have, a very strong sense of belonging to my childhood," he once said. "I had a very happy childhood and I have always tried to surround myself with the things of my childhood. Simple things like food or the books I read as a child, such as my abridged version of *Don Quixote*, or the Comtesse de Ségur's novels.[8]

What is surprising is how much three of the books read in his youth formed a ground plan for his lifetime's work. First and foremost was *Don Quixote*, which he read at ten, in an adapted children's version with pictures that were as memorable as the text. Cervantes's satirical side was emphasized, and he found the illustrations very funny. "When I spoke about *Don Quixote* in *Mensonge romantique* [*Deceit, Desire, and the Novel* in English] these were the images I had in my head," he said.[9] Hence, Girard didn't identify with the benighted knight or see him as a particularly sympathetic character—that would come later. The book would remain a cherished volume in his library, and he regularly revisited it throughout his life.

Undoubtedly, the book influenced his anti-romantic mind-set, an enduring distaste that extended long beyond the last pages of *Deceit, Desire, and the Novel*. He would smirk politely when I told him I loved Victor Hugo's *Les Misérables* as a girl.

The second book was Rudyard Kipling's *Jungle Book,* which he read at about the same age. He found it an impressive description of scapegoating with pervasive themes of mob violence, imitative monkeys, and the lynching of a lame tiger. Within Kipling's pages, he began to discover how we rewrite our stories to make the victim guilty, and so conceal our collective guilt.

Kipling does not make much of an appearance in Girard's writings—a curious omission, given that he was to say of Kipling's *Jungle Book*, "I have come to realize that it contains all the mimetic theory within it, which is rather extraordinary." The third book would come a few years later.

Meanwhile, his favorite game was a solitary one: with toy soldiers, he reenacted France's major battles, taking all the roles himself. Sometimes he modeled whole parliaments and parliamentarians out of clay. He recreated the medieval wars, the Napoleonic wars, Austerlitz, and Waterloo. "I also read books about Napoleon," he said. "I learned all the clichés, such as: 'It is only the first and last battles that count.'" He indicated a bookshelf with his hand. "You see this library on the Louis XVI bookcase? It belonged to my father, who was a historian. It contained books that interested me, for example, Louis Madelin's history of the Revolution. That really grabbed me."

As Hitler was consolidating his power in Germany, Girard succumbed to the popular craze for another of Avignon's historic neighbors—Nostradamus was born about twenty miles away and had attended university in Avignon in the sixteenth century. Although Girard was dismissive ("some kind of crazy guy"), he and his peers puzzled over the references to "Hissler," and read his remarks as presaging the rise of the Führer.

"From a very early age, twelve years old, I was fascinated by politics. One sensed the war was coming, already by 1932–1936," he said. "I felt an odd kind of political excitement, a sense of danger and, despite everything, something enthralling."[10]

.   .   .

He was the second of five children. The eldest brother, Henri, three years older, would follow his Uncle Pierre into the medical profession. A younger sister, Marthe, eventually settled in Paris, and another sister, Marie, a decade younger, moved to Marseille. The last child, Antoine, was born more than fifteen years after René—another generation, really.

Girard was the sickly one. He said he was the last person in Avignon to have typhoid fever when he was about ten or eleven. He was treated by his Uncle Pierre. "It was a drawn-out affair," he explained, with an elegant wave of the hand. Typhoid is not endless, though it may feel so to the patient; it usually lasts about a month, leaving the victim exhausted and emaciated. The disease, caused by contaminated food or water, and then transmitted from person to person, is characterized by high fever, diarrhea, headache and coughing, chills and sweating, pain, delirium. In those days, two decades before it was treated with antibiotics, it was still very much a killer, and his mother had every reason to be frightened.

He was saved several times from serious illnesses. Certainly it helped to have a doctor in the family. He recalled an infection in his right leg, and a flurry of other ailments. He added dismissively that that is the way it is in the South of France—"things deadly turn out to be nothing." He was a frail boy, then? "That was my mother's belief, not entirely unjustified," he said. Martha added, "She tended to pamper him."

One family photograph tells the story: the dark-haired boy in sweater and shorts is smiling contentedly in the center; he knows that he is adored. He has slipped his arms familiarly through those of the protective grand-mothers who flank each side, enveloped in dark, Old World dresses. The other adults and children arrange themselves around this central motif. The pampering continued, obviously, with home schooling and later, in Lyon, and then Paris, when he would plead to come home to the familial hearth.

.   .   .

In their living room on Frenchman's Road, Martha and René relax over tea, which Martha had poured into bone china teacups. Martha thought his characterization of Avignon a bit unfair, and recalled the charms of the old city, which she called "a marvelous place."

But on one point Girard seemed adamant that particular afternoon: "I should have gone to the Jesuit school," he said with unexpected vehemence, as we were discussing his education so long ago. His father had vigorously opposed it. Girard later shrugged and laughed when he recalled his father's anti-clerical side, manifested in a strenuous antipathy to the Jesuits.

The Jesuit school in Avignon was the one his father attended, and it had a certain élan. After all, Athanasius Kircher had graced the college with his fascinating presence in the 1630s. Petrarch's Laura is buried somewhere beneath the courtyard, which marks the site of a demolished Franciscan church. One wonders if the brilliant son of Avignon might have fared better in the Jesuit school, or whether his taste for high jinks might have started even earlier.

The alternative was the Lycée Collège Frédéric Mistral—pretty enough today on one of Avignon's sidestreets, with a covered bridge arching overhead.

But Girard told me it had moved since his school days. Some bragged that they were learning "in the classroom of Stéphane Mallarmé"—though, in 1864, the twenty-two-year-old poet was only visiting his friend who taught at the lycée. The legend lingered, nonetheless.

Either would have offered a superb education. Most Americans today don't appreciate what a top-notch educational system was available to the children of France in that era. The best of the best, from the École Normale Supérieure and other elite schools, were sent to the provinces to teach—Simone Weil was among them during those years, serving a stint at a school in Le Puy-en-Velay, in Girard's beloved Auvergne, where she taught Latin, Greek, philosophy, the sciences, and grammar.

Girard never worked well in a pen, however, and had to repeat his sixième after the "School for the Spoiled" ended—clearly, the shock of reentry was too great. Nevertheless, he seems to have a few fond memories of the lycée, and found several fellow travelers: "I had some friends who were greatly interested in literature, but their taste was typical of the late-surrealist era. Majestically circling above our heads, there was René Char, the famous poet who later invited Heidegger to the 'Séminaires du Thor.'" The poet was "very nice to his younger friends who idealized him, although I never managed to become interested in his poetry."[11]

Girard often said he had been an outstanding student until his later years, about the time puberty would have set in with all the usual ramifications. He described himself as an undisciplined cut-up—not exactly the ringleader, perhaps, but a known troublemaker and instigator, and therefore the one most likely to be held responsible. He was penalized by detention on Saturdays. An unexpected benefit: he met Paul Thoulouze, Jacques Charpier, and others who would become close friends.

Some of his report cards tell a slightly different story: after a very bad sixième, he received an award for excellence the second time around, and also in the subsequent two levels. Though he was dropped from the honor roll in the rowdy years, his grades still maintained a fairly consistent "très bien," "assez bien," and "bien." He excelled in English, on at least two occasions top in the class, and also in history. By the troisième, his formerly "irreproachable" conduct began to crumble, with teachers noting that he was far too easily distracted and jittery. According to one teacher, he was a good student when he held his tongue. In math, he was rated "insufficient" by his premier

20

Chapter Two

year, and was told he "must decide to be more serious," though he was "very gifted" in Latin. Critical reviews, but hardly catastrophic.

He was fifteen by then, and other aspects of adulthood were coming into play. He spoke of the young swains strutting their stuff along the Rue de la République, and perhaps he was one of them, dressed to please, dying to impress the girls. But a more important factor was taking shape during these high-spirited years: the distant war was becoming a reality in France. In September 1938, during the Sudeten crisis, the French called up half a million reservists to join the half million men already under arms. The effect on schools was chaotic: male instructors were drafted, and the teachers who replaced them were less experienced and often female. The boys inevitably took advantage of the situation, and the disorder spread like a contagion.

Girard still relished the memory of the pranks: on one occasion, he and his cohorts removed a door completely from its hinges and, turning it sideways, reattached it to serve as a barricade to block the doorway. Other students had to clamber over it to enter the classroom. Fortunately, the much-mocked older teacher, an early animal rights activist and, at bottom, a courageous man, Girard later admitted, had mercy on his unruly charges. He didn't report the incident.

At this point, history intersected Girard's life in a devastating way. After the Battle of France, the French surrendered to the Germans in June 1940. What has been called France's "strange defeat" would haunt Girard for the rest of his life, though its consequences didn't immediately affect his teenage horseplay. Avignon was initially in the *zone libre*, the two-fifths of France under the Vichy regime and Maréchal Pétain. Democracy had already vanished, however, and the *zone libre* was cooperating with Germany, though it wouldn't be under full occupation for another two years. The citizenry was on edge. So the next prank, in October 1940, would have more serious consequences.[12]

Girard and some friends telephoned the lycée principal, pretending to be the national Ministry of Education in Vichy. Calling from the Avignon post office—many Avignon homes still didn't have telephones—with a handkerchief over the mouthpiece, they announced a program to put full professors into retirement. It was Friday; arrangements had to be made quickly, because the event would begin with a solemn flag ceremony first thing on Monday morning at the opening of the lycée.

"After we made our calls for laughs, we had no sooner left the post office when the police came to arrest us. They knew what we had done. The phones were under surveillance. There were switchboard operators at the post office at that time. It was not 'high-tech.'" Girard added that "when the police came looking for us at the post office, I was really scared. If it had escalated beyond the level of the Lycée to reach the level of the city of Avignon, the case would have been a much more serious matter."[13] He lived in a conquered country, under new rules. Particularly in the early, testy days of the new government, school officials were far less likely to be indulgent. It was the last straw.

His accomplices may have disappeared or been too discreet to get caught, or perhaps they were let off more lightly because their classroom record was better. Girard had the distinction of being a prankster both in the classroom and out, and his studies were also suffering. His father had a conference with the school.

He wasn't exactly "sent down," as the British say, during his *terminale* year. Perhaps because his father was a municipal official and local dignitary, there was an amicable arrangement with the school that Girard would withdraw and not finish his final year at the lycée. Instead, he would study for his baccalauréat at home on his own. Girard liked to say he was kicked out, and in effect, that's true.

"My father was a member of the board, so I was not officially expelled. My father withdrew me from the school. But obviously, he was not thrilled."[14] He added, "It would be too much to present me as a true scapegoat, a true *bouc émissaire*. Or else it would have to be a comic scapegoat."[15] The repeated incidents gave him a rebellious, slightly heroic cachet among his comrades, while, in typically mimetic fashion, others resented his academic gifts coupled with high-visibility shenanigans.

He needed to find the jokes where he could. Among the Vichy regime's new initiatives was the "Chantiers de la jeunesse française," a military-style youth camp designed to instill new national values, including the veneration of Pétain. The activities were akin to scouting, with teenagers living in the woods and performing manual labor. Unlike scouting, however, the service was obligatory and lasted for six months or so. Radios and political discussions were forbidden. Girard disliked the boot camp from the moment he set foot in the woods. He enlisted his older brother Henri, a medical student, for an early release due to an invented "heart murmur"; he was even willing to experiment with medications to make the invented disorder a reality, as long as he could go home. His father took watchful note of his son's nature, and was anxious to see Girard avoid the next step, STO, the *Service du Travail Obligatoire*, mandatory labor for young and able Frenchmen in German factories and farms to replace the men who had been drafted into the military. This provided another reason for Joseph Girard to encourage his son to put more steam into his studies as Girard prepared for "le bac" on his own.

Although the bac has fallen under criticism for being too lax in recent years, at that time it was unquestionably a traumatic rite of passage with a daunting amount of rigor. It would have left most of today's American students reeling: candidates were expected to comment intelligently on a complex twelfth-century text by philosopher-theologian Saint Anselm or a page by Schopenhauer on desire and privation. Essay prompts included such questions as "What do we owe the state?," "Does the objectivity of history imply the historian's impartiality?," and "Is language just a tool?" The grueling series of exams takes hours and hours, and can be oral or written. The stakes are high: the winnowing shuffles the failures to the job market and the crème de la crème to the *grandes écoles*. These small, selective, well-funded institutions train the nation's future elites—*hauts fonctionnaires*, leaders of industry, top military brass, leading politicians, engineers, physicists, and so on.

Different sources list Girard receiving his *baccalauréat* in either 1940 or 1941. Both are correct, because he would have received two. The first was the general one common to all students, a prerequisite to applying for more specialized recognition. He exceeded expectations, however, when he received his second *baccalauréat* in philosophy at the Lycée Mistral of Avignon—with distinction. "From that moment, my father gave me his renewed confidence. It was getting my own back, but something of a vindication for him, too."[16]

His whole time at the lycée and at home showed a pattern that was to recur in future years—a precocious, playful and mischievous child, Girard balked at institutional strictures and worked best when given free rein for his creative intelligence, and when allowed to be alone with his books. The child is father to the man.

As the war deepened, Girard recalled his well-born mother struggled heroically to provide for the family on meager rations. She was clever at finding food, and the Girards never faced hunger. Gardens provided the only fruits and green vegetables in town—and olive oil was readily available. The family could still keep the war at bay, and gathered around the radio to listen to the French broadcasts from the BBC.

"In France, in the first few years of the occupation, food was getting scarce, but there was nothing tragic about the situation," he explained to me. "The BBC was the big ceremony of the day, at eight o'clock. It was jammed by the Germans, and the French, maybe, but you could still get it. Everybody did. You could hear the jamming from a great distance. There was no danger. France, during the occupation, was not like Poland."

He downplayed collaboration, commenting that 95 percent of the people were in total sympathy with the Allies, and were waiting for the landing, though he conceded that their support was not very active. Elsewhere, he said, "It is often repeated that the south of France was very pro-Vichy, but that is exaggerated. Of course, *Maréchal nous voilà*[17] was composed in Avignon, by an Avignonnais author. But in cinemas, there was actually a lot of heckling of the Nazis. I think *The Sorrow and the Pity* is misleading in this regard. At the cinema, people openly applauded England and, later, the Russians. They didn't actively resist, but they wished the Allies victory, too passively, no doubt, but with much ardor. Our jokes about saluting the flag were obviously meant to mock the regime. All the members of my group were anti-Vichy."[18]

Few had a presentiment of impending catastrophe. Perhaps Girard explained it best a few years later, when he said that no one viewed 1940 as the final chapter, the last word of the Franco-German feud: "It was impossible for these people to believe that the mad men from Nuremberg could model Europe according to their caprice. When France, which they had thought allergic to the Nazi disease, surrendered to Hitler, they refused to consider this surrender as final," he wrote. It was perhaps a way to conquer the victors and deny Hitler a victory: "The type of intelligent living represented by France was judged by them to be so superior to Nazism that they refused to admit that Fascist brutality could ever stamp it out or be won over to it."[19]

Girard's future still hung in the air. In 1941, he wanted to take the entrance exam for the École Normale Supérieure, the foremost among the *grandes écoles*. "So I went to Lyon for a hypokhâgne [the first year of a preparation course for the École Normale Supérieure entrance exams]. But I left after a few weeks. It was the beginning of the occupation, there were material problems. We ate badly. Hazing was especially unbearable. I rediscovered my terror of school that I had felt as a child. I went home, telling my mother, 'It's impossible, I can't do it.' So I gave up the idea of going to the École Normale."

His father then suggested that he could prepare for admission at the École des Chartes, alone at home, as he had done for the bac. "To prepare for the École des Chartes on my own, I invented all sorts of exercises. I did countless compositions in Latin without a dictionary," he said.[20]

"My only concern at that time was to postpone my exit from the familiar 'nest,' so I accepted and spent one more year at home."[21] It wasn't a bad idea: Provence was part of the *zone libre,* and many from the north were fleeing to southeast France, which remained comparatively free under the Vichy regime. Staying at the family home in Avignon must have seemed very prudent indeed.

In November 1942, however, the Germans extended their full occupation to the south of France, with the Italians occupying the small portion of France east of the Rhône.

•   •   •

On the Rue de la République in this slightly seedy little city, bakeries and pastry shops sell chocolate and regional treats. In the mornings, they fill the biscuit bins in rows as they prepare for the off-season tourists. Only with a sort of double vision can one see beneath the town's modern patina to the land where popes once ruled over the medieval world, to a city where churches were later ransacked and blood ran in the streets. The man who was to write about violence, scapegoating, lynchings, and mobs never really had to look farther than the earth of his native realm for examples—in fact, he never had to go farther than the Palais des Papes itself.

A tour through the Palais leads one to a wall of illustrations from the palace's history, including an engraving of a massacre that occurred within these old white walls. The history gives a local context for anti-clericalism, and the extremes to which it was taken a few centuries ago.

"The French Revolution was the most amazing event," Girard said with excitement. "It was the best anticipation of the Russian Revolution. France was the first of the great countries to turn atheist."

In June 1790, the revolutionary Avignonnais expelled the papal representative of this city, which had been a papal state for more than four centuries, and demanded the city's unification into France. The following month, the French government nationalized the church, dissolving monasteries and orders. The annexation of Avignon was ratified by the National Assembly a little over a year later, in September 1791. In early October, the secular municipal authorities of Avignon decided to melt the church bells to provide ready cash—and that paved the way for an orderly, secular looting of church property. That, with some local apparitions of the Virgin Mary, led to a mob murder of Lescuyer, the secretary-clerk, in the Franciscan chapel. Troops intervened, and dozens of suspects were detained, including two pregnant women. About sixty were incarcerated in the Palais des Papes. They were clumsily executed, one by one, and the bodies tossed into the palace cooler. The executioners worked well into the night, with twenty bottles of liquor to inspire and numb them to the task.

The events of 16–17 October 1791, known as the massacres of La Glacière, signaled Avignon's last bid for independence from the state, and a chilling foreshadowing of the Reign of Terror.

The reaction to the atrocity reverberated for decades—Jules Michelet devotes two chapters of his 1847 *History of the French Revolution* to the events. But more turmoil was to come. Although calm was finally restored under the Consulate of Napoléon Bonaparte, and the pope accepted the absorption of Avignon into France in 1797, the emperor and his regime remained unpopular. En route to Elba, Napoléon stopped in Avignon on 25 April 1814, and narrowly escaped being torn to pieces by the mob. His supporters weren't always so lucky. At the beginning of the Bourbon Restoration's "White Terror," Napoléon's Maréchal Guillaume Brune, hero of the Empire, was lynched by the Avignon mob and his body thrown into the Rhône. In his Napoleonic-era portraits he is handsome and dashing, with a strong jaw and bold gaze, his uniform adorned with his sashes and medals, ribbons and epaulettes. As with many old portraits, however, we know the dark destiny of the gallant man who breathes from the canvas; we see the resolute, intelligent face disappearing under the cold and turbulent waves of the Rhône. He was staunchly republican, arousing Napoleon's suspicions, a successful military leader and diplomat—but he wasn't a match for the royalist mob that had already triumphed on the wider stage of France.

Curious about this history, I turn the pages of Joseph Girard's thick volume, *Évocation du vieil Avignon*. The book gives scant mention of the havoc wrought during the Revolutionary era, with its local massacres and lynch-ings. The few stories nestle among the anecdotes of cardinals and kings. The violence, however, was something his son would understand well, and write about in the decades to come from a distant country.

But even in faraway America, Avignon would remain his magnetic north, its influence apparent in his commonsense, his psychological independence, his allergy to cant, his sense of the ridiculous, his adamant resistance to intel-lectual fashion.

On his patio on Frenchman's Road, among the hummingbirds and flow-ers, he mused, "Do I live in California, really? Today people can live in a place all their lives, and not be of that place. So I'm probably more French than I'm anything else. Not that it's too different from America in many ways—but in some ways it's different. It's different because it has a different relationship to the Christian past." The Rhône Valley, after all, was Christianized in the first or second century.

Provence was his bedrock, although his delicate health after 2008 would keep him from returning to France again. He reminisced about his father while sitting in the rose-colored velvet Louis Quinze chair with pale, worn wood that had belonged to Joseph Girard. And he reminded me, as he always did, that his father had been curator of the Palais des Papes.

CHAPTER 3

Dark Times in the City of Light

I will always remember that I have been cast out of the Pack.

—Rudyard Kipling, *The Jungle Book*

The Girard family lived within sight and sound of the railroad tracks on Chemin de l'Arrousaire—and trains became the backdrop and subject of the children's games. During the dark years of German occupation, however, the railroad took on a more ominous aspect. The Allies had bombed Avignon as the Germans were leaving the region, since the tracks were a critical target. Some of the bombs landed near the Girard home. This was hidden from Martha when she visited a decade later—her new in-laws thought she might be offended by any mention of American bombing.

Recalling the war years, Girard said with a marked emphasis: "I was not affected the way I should have been." It figured among many comments about his affectless reaction to events around him, as if he were puzzling over his own detached nature. But I came to wonder whether, in such cases, he simply was not feeling what he expected to be feeling, or as others claimed to have felt. But whose emotions run according to preconceptions? "Occupied Paris had paralyzed me," he once declared.[1] That says it all.

.   .   .

Paris can be a bitter, miserable place in the wintertime, and especially for one navigating his way through the friendless city among German officers, Nazi functionaries, and, to a greater or lesser extent, a collaborating population. Girard was a provincial student in this wartime city, and he was living on a shoestring budget. He recalled a hungry Paris.

From 1943 to 1947, he studied at the École des Chartes. It was, he said with vehemence, "the worst experience in my life." He was finally admitted to the school, though he was among the last applicants to be accepted for that class. "I hated it. I hated Paris. I hated Paris more than any other city." He was an outsider here, and said he experienced some prejudices towards him as a provincial "Southerner." As always, he wanted to "scuttle back to Avignon," but travel under German Occupation was tricky—it was easier to go to Paris than to return to Provence. For the first year he shivered in an unheated room in the Hôtel du Square Monge, and his life seemed largely confined to metro stations. And, of course, the occupying Germans cast their own emotional layers of denial, fear, and contradiction over the city.

"All my life, I've never been able to work except outside institutions and so, subconsciously, I worked against them. And once more, of course, the same scenario began again," he said. "Once installed in the cold and hungry Paris of 1942,[2] my only desire, as usual, was to go home. Fortunately, it was impossible because of what was called the demarcation line between occupied France and Vichy France. In sum, it is thanks to the German occupiers that I managed to finish my studies in the École des Chartes."[3]

The second year was better, though his gift for high-spirited mischief and attracting accomplices, or simply friends, was in abeyance during these years. He was dependent upon the kindness of strangers, and eventually took up residence on the longest road in Paris: "Fortunately, the second year, thanks to a charitable Chartiste, I was admitted to the Maison des Étudiants, 104 Rue de Vaugirard. It counted among its alumni people like François Mauriac and François Mitterrand. There were the sons of the great landowners of Normandy or Île-de-France, who sent us tons of potatoes. I got little to eat from Avignon. My family was very poorly placed for the black market because my father, a museum curator, had nothing to barter to get food."[4]

In these years, ill health would continue to dog him. He suffered a primo infection, considered a precursor to tuberculosis, while at the École des Chartes. The correspondence between René, Joseph Girard, and the École during those years shows how frequently his studies were interrupted. He was out of school during much of 1944 (his illness also made him ineligible for military service), and pneumonia pulled him back to Avignon again in 1946. Certainly that is one reason his thesis, "La Vie privée à Avignon dans la seconde moitié du XVe siècle," focused on his hometown. It was, of course, straight out of his father's playbook (his father's thesis had focused on local history to the end of the fourteenth century)—in fact, his father helped with his thesis, not only in design but in its realization. He would continue his studies within the archives of Avignon during his recovery.

It's hard to determine whether illness was the cause or effect of his misery during those depressing years. Historian Eugen Weber listed his own acrimonious memories of the Occupation, which give a taste of what Girard endured:

> the archaic dottiness of Vichy claptrap, all clean living and fuzzy thinking; the use of 'National' to designate the least smokable, drinkable, eatable, or wearable products; the appeals to energy, vitality, virility; the power cuts and lack of heat; the shortages of paper (so painful to pullulating bureaucrats), real coffee, sugar, and tobacco; the stews of cat, crow, or pigeon; the winds of virtue blowing furiously to prohibit dancing, Pernod, Dubonnet, and 'Judeo-American' music; the concomitant vogue of jazz, of swing, of clandestine hops, and of the slang connected with them (to be 'swing' was to be 'cool'); the rage for wearing berets, preferably capacious ones 'practical to cover your ears,' and their abandonment after the Liberation, when they were tarred with the brush of Vichy; the doubletalk, the humorlessness, the creeping seediness; the shabby, shiny, stained, and greasy clothes, threadbare and stinking with sweat.[5]

But the first year had been the worst. Years later, when he was safely ensconced in America, Girard would return to Paris with Martha. One time, she recalled, she had been in the grips of a postpartum blues and feeling miserable. Girard took her to 12 Rue des Écoles and they stood before the building at the address. This, *this,* he told her, for purposes of comparison, was truly hell. I imagine Girard rapt in silent contemplation after his statement, casting a lingering, melancholy gaze at the severe gray lines of the Hôtel du Square Monge.

.   .   .

On the bookshelves of the Girards' apartment near the Eiffel Tower, I noticed a few titles by a man Girard had mentioned with pride as an acquaintance, the brilliant, charismatic, and enormously popular "Jewish Cardinal," Jean-Marie Lustiger, who, like Girard, was an *immortel* in the Académie Française. The Sorbonne intellectual and convert had been born in Paris of a Polish Jewish family; his mother died at Auschwitz while her son was in hiding in Orléans. As a Jewish teenager, he had been both witness and victim.

Lustiger offered a poignant testimony to the contradictions of wartime France: "Who could understand what was happening? A world was crashing in upon us. . . . A world was destroyed, and its values held up to ridicule. . . . How could you be faithful to France against the French? Where were the traitors?"[6] Elsewhere, he noted, "In occupied France there were many people who no longer knew the difference between what was good and what was bad, between what you should or should not do."[7] Yet he said he also found considerable charity: strangers who provided him with forged documents, those who helped him get across the demarcation line, those who warned him that he might be arrested soon, those who sheltered him without questions. Others quietly left railroad cars unlatched.

The situation was a conflicted one, and morally compromised in all directions. "It has to be said that France, by large, was Pétainist," said Lustiger. "At the same time, among the people I saw, all—or almost all—were hostile to the Germans. Some of them, including comrades from the lycée, were already in the Résistance . . . those whom I had known the previous year, were heaven knows where doing heaven knows what. Underground activities? The *Résistance*? In the STO? There was a lot of talk about the STO."[8]

The prospect of the STO—Service du Travail Obligatoire—provided Girard with his most terrifying moments during the war. Like many young Frenchmen, he had a forged identification card. He narrowly escaped arrest. He explained it to me, years later:

You had a brush with the Germans in Paris . . .

Oh, it's the only time I was really in danger during the war. Have you been to the Luxembourg Gardens? Anyway, Marie de Medici, one of the queens of the sixteenth century, built that big palace, which now is the French Senate. It has a library, a lot of art, too. It's a beautiful building, with a public garden. But during the Occupation it was the headquarters of the German air force. Every day when I went to class, I passed next to the gate there, the entrance. Not long before the landing in Normandy, I was paying no attention as I was walking there, and suddenly I saw a huge French cop in front of me. He stopped me, and asked me for my identification card. He was alone, asking me . . . I saw that behind there was another line. There were some Germans there, some civilians and some military people, who were checking identities like he was doing. I would have reached them if I had continued. I had two identification cards. So I really lost my balance, and the cop immediately saw it. So, I gave him one of the two. But he said, "You have another one." And I had.

How did he know? Just because . . .

Because he saw that I had suddenly lost my composure completely. The people of my age very often had two cards. If I had been called for work in Germany, which was quite a possibility at the time, I would have gone to the underground. . . . Anyway, I don't really remember how it happened, but he had the two cards and he compared them, with the same picture, different names. That was the only time I saw myself finished. Tortured by the Germans to know where I had gotten it.

There was a little street to the right. So he insulted me, he said, "Little fool!" Real mad. He said, "Take to the right quickly!" He *ordered* me to run away. So he saved my life.

When I was ten steps beyond, I realized what had happened, how close I had been to being caught. The people behind were Gestapo people or German policemen . . . it happened like lightning. I thought, "Whew! What a narrow escape." Five minutes before, I didn't even know I was in danger.

.   .   .

Adolf Hitler's original plan had been to flatten Paris, as he would do to Warsaw a few years later, but then he had a better idea. His propaganda chief, Joseph Goebbels, declared in July 1940 that Paris would be a showcase city, animated and gay, so that life under the Nazis would appear attractive to Americans and other neutral parties. The Germans made Paris a luxurious playground for their soldiers and officials. Theaters reopened soon after the occupation began to capacity crowds of both French and German theatergoers. Cabarets were launched and flourished. Paris concerts that had traditionally attracted hundreds were drawing more than a thousand. Record sales increased, featuring American swing and most of all jazz, the last gossamer thread to the free world.

In 2008, an exhibition opened in Paris that shocked France: it included 270 color photographs of wartime Paris, snapped by André Zucca, a collaborationist French photographer who worked for the pro-Nazi magazine *Signal*. According to a British newspaper: "The photographs portray, for the most part, a remarkably familiar city, calm, chic, content and pleasure and fashion-loving. The exhibition has stirred discontent and unease in Paris, precisely because it shows Parisians being Parisians, and getting on with life, under the Nazi heel. They sit at sunny café terraces on the Champs Elysées. They self-consciously wear their newly fashionable dark glasses with white rims. They fish in the river Seine. They go shopping. . . . Nazi propaganda posters, swastikas and strutting officers in German uniform occasionally intrude. Otherwise, people chat gaily at terrace cafés; children roller-skate and watch puppet shows; lovers sit beside the Seine."[9]

Nothing appeared to have changed, except for the profusion of flags with black swastikas along the colonnade of the Rue de Rivoli. Girard recalled, on that same daily trip to the Sorbonne, passing by the Luxembourg Palace and seeing Hermann Göring, *Reichsmarschall* of the Greater German Reich and second in command, pass in a grand car, with a huge German flag at the front of it. Daily life in wartime Paris, circa 1940, was a preemptive defeat of the spirit and will, even more than a conquest.

Jean-Paul Sartre, in a 1945 essay, refuted his fellow Parisians who were already recasting the Nazi occupation as a time of misery, oppression, and defiance. He dismissed the simplistic images of Germans running up and down the streets with guns in their hands. He said the most troubling thing for most wartime Parisians was a sense of "bad conscience" and a queasy recognition of how easily they had acquiesced to the new rulers. Girard would later describe such conditions of societal meltdown, blurring the necessary distinctions that maintain social order and keep a community from descending into a rivalrous mob: "Institutional collapse obliterates or telescopes hierarchical and functional differences, so that everything has the same monotonous and monstrous aspect."[10] In this case, however, the crisis was not only within various elements of society, but within each individual, where collaboration and resistance cohabited uneasily.

The curator of the 2008 exhibit, the documentary filmmaker Jean Baronnet, recalled as a child seeing Pétain driving through Paris in an open-topped Renault. "I noticed how pink his face was and how white was his moustache. At the windows and on the pavements, people applauded and shouted 'Vive le Maréchal.'" It was a month before D-Day.

. . .

The École des Chartes shares its façade with the Sorbonne. The heavy black door, encrusted with escutcheons and furbelows, is a little to the left of the world-famous school, embedded within the gracefully arched stone entrance about four times the height of a man. The École seemed to be living perennially under the shadow of the Sorbonne—even the windows overlook its neighbor's slate-colored mansard roofs, once you climb the wooden stairs and look out over the bookshelves that line the narrow passageways.

Yet the orderly and slightly stuffy École that Girard found so dispiriting was born of chaos. During the French Revolution, thousands of libraries, archives, and churches had been ransacked. Revolutionaries are not preservers, by definition, so they were at a loss about what to do with many millions of books and documents, ranging from Montesquieu's *Persian Letters* to proclamations signed by Charlemagne. A preponderance were medieval— for many, a vestige of feudalism and tyranny. What to do? By 1800 most of the collections were moldering in warehouses.

The École, originally based at the Bibliothèque Nationale de France (then called the Bibliothèque Royale) on the Rue de Richelieu, was founded in the 1820s to train archivists to sort, analyze, catalogue, and preserve the pilfered documents. The École gave a new cachet to the profession and to the national history it studied. It relocated to its current site in 1897; Joseph Girard arrived to begin his studies there two years later.

Girard often impressed upon me that he was essentially a librarian by training—at various times, however, he also described himself as an historian or a literary theorist, and all were true, in different ways. He rarely mentioned the first credential without cautious qualification, sometimes disparagement: "I am an *archiviste-paléographe,* in other words, a graduate from the École des Chartes in Paris, a school entirely dedicated to the most technical aspects of French medieval studies," he once said. "When I was a student there, I was dissatisfied with the dry positivism of the school, but I was too young and ignorant to understand why I was such a mediocre student, and I wasted a lot of time."[11] "Some courses were of an archaism that was extremely old-fashioned. Bibliography of medieval history, bibliography of the fifteenth century, bibliography of the sixteenth century . . . The truth is that I did very little work because of the moral and material conditions of existence of that time. At the École, however, the working conditions were very good: there was plenty of space, all the books we needed were at our disposal, we could work in isolation or work in groups as one chose."[12]

Girard was already on a parallel path, one that recalls those fairy-tale plots in which the younger son turns every mishap that befalls him into a backhanded good. The piece of moldy cheese and the rusty nail in his pocket turn out to be precisely what he needs to enter the castle and win the princess. In this case, Girard would make his lifetime study the close reading of well-known texts that provide direct anthropological evidence of a hidden story of lies and violence. One could argue that he began to find his vocation in these otherwise barren years. He offered this telling comment on his work at the École: "One learns, in particular, to be wary of documents that can easily be false, and it is this work which is the true foundation of real historical knowledge."[13] He not only saw how texts are rewritten, but he had an unusual opportunity in Paris to observe firsthand how history itself could be rewritten, to disguise ugly truths, propagandize, or promote cultural unity.

.   .   .

At the height of the war Albert Camus and Jean-Paul Sartre finally met in Nazi-occupied Paris. Both were already public figures, and they had already reviewed each other's books. The occasion was the June 1943 dress rehearsal for Sartre's play, *The Flies,* recasting the Orestes revenge story with a new twist: in Sartre's ending, Orestes is freed from the effects of other people, of dogma, of the dichotomies of good and evil, which he had surpassed. It was an important rendezvous, for both thinkers would dominate postwar French thought. Both would be influential for Girard, too.

The 1943 meeting began a friendship that would become a legend. They met, and met, and met again, in cafés till 2 or 3 or 4 a.m. Sartre was clearly the more influential, but the younger writer was on the rise. Sartre's *Being and Nothingness* was about to be released. Camus published *The Stranger* and his *The Myth of Sisyphus,* to amazement and acclaim in 1942, calling for revolt against the meaninglessness and absurdity of a life without eternal values or truths. All were published with the approval of German censors.

The two were kindred souls with very different spirits. While even Camus conceded that Sartre was the superior mind (and a far fiercer prankster than Girard had ever been), the Algerian-born Camus was altogether a warmer and fuller human being, and better looking, too.

Girard would eventually write of such rivalries, which often begin in friendship: "When all differences have been eliminated and the similarity between two figures has been achieved, we say that the antagonists are *doubles*."[14] Camus and Sartre, those *doubles par excellence*, had a very public split. The breakup occurred after Camus's 1951 *The Rebel*, in which he rejected communism and, sin of sins, mentioned the concentration camps in the Soviet Union. Camus was seen to be turning away from the Great March Forward. Parisian intellectuals, many of whom were party members and almost all of them pro-Communist, were unforgiving. Camus confessed to loneliness and isolation in the years that followed, but Sartre's condemnation in particular was a sharp blow. The rift between the two tore the French intelligentsia asunder. Everyone took one side or the other. At the time, according to friends who knew him, Girard was on the Sartre side. The young Girard found he had more affinities with the more rigorous and systematic philosopher rather than with the intuitive novelist. His first book, *Deceit, Desire, and the Novel*, bears clear marks of Sartre's influence. Yet Girard was both a systematic thinker and a visionary, and both sides would play out in years to come, sometimes each to the detriment of the other.

.   .   .

In the early hours of 6 June 1944, Girard tapped on doors around the Maison des Étudiants, waking up his fellow students with the electric news: the Allies had finally landed on the shores of Normandy to liberate France. He heard the news first, and must have relished his pre-dawn mission to rouse the others.

A few months later, Paris was free. On 25 August 1944, the day the city was liberated by French and American tanks, General Charles de Gaulle spoke to the crowd in front of the city hall, as German and collaborationist snipers were still manning the rooftops. His improvised words began to remake history: "Paris outragé! Paris brisé! Paris martyrisé!" [Paris ravished! Paris smashed! Paris martyred!]

According to Lustiger, "What happened at the liberation—that is, what de Gaulle did—I called a masterstroke. I did not use the word *lie*. It was not at all the same thing! Perhaps it was simply a bandage, but it was a necessary bandage because the shame was unbearable, because it was essential to restore the people's honor—the characteristic of the Vichy regime having been to play on shame and to have consented to the unacceptable. If one wanted France to regain a certain face, it was crucial, at least for a time, to put a bandage over that shame; otherwise, the nation was going to tear itself apart again."[15]

Under the bandage, maggots festered nevertheless. Thousands of collaborators were killed without trial by the Résistance. Vichy leaders fled or were put on trial, and some were executed for treason. Pétain, the demi-god who was nearing ninety, was sentenced to death, but the sentence was commuted to life imprisonment. Four officials were tried for crimes against humanity—against Jews particularly, but also against prisoners and members of the Résistance, which now had the upper hand.

What Girard saw then would play out in his later writings, for the young René was undoubtedly as keen an observer of his society then as he would be years later. It was precisely the kind of situation Girard would describe again and again: a torn society where the necessary differences have melted away, which seeks a scapegoat to explain the disorder: "Ultimately, the persecutors always convince themselves that a small number of people, or even a single individual, despite his relative weakness, is extremely harmful to the whole of society. The stereotypical accusation justifies and facilitates this belief by ostensibly acting the role of mediator. It bridges the gap between the insignificance of the individual and the enormity of the social body." The cause appeases and justifies the crowd's appetite for violence: "Those who make up the crowd are always potential persecutors, for they dream of purging the community of the impure elements that corrupt it, the traitors who undermine it."[16]

More than twenty thousand women across France had their heads shaved by *tondeurs* in a time-honored ritual for shaming women. These *tondues* were accused of collaboration and assaulted by mobs. According to British historian Antony Beevor, "Women almost always were the first targets, because they offered the easiest and most vulnerable scapegoats, particularly for those men who had joined the resistance at the last moment ... Revenge on women represented a form of expiation for the frustrations and sense of impotence among males humiliated by their country's occupation. One could almost say that it was the equivalent of rape by the victor."[17] They were not necessarily innocent of the charges of collaboration, but they were noncombatants, and the blame heaped on them was disproportionate and symbolic.

As Girard would explain years later, "Men feel powerless when confronted with the eclipse of culture; they are disconcerted by the immensity of the disaster ... But, rather than blame themselves, people inevitably blame either society as a whole, which costs them nothing, or other people who seem particularly harmful for easily identifiable reasons. The suspects are accused of a particular category of crimes."[18]

Who were they? According to Girard, "In order to blame victims for the loss of distinctions from the crisis, they are accused of crimes that eliminate distinctions"[19]—hence, many were simply accused of *collaboration horizontale*, perhaps no more than succumbing to dinners with some lonely Franz far from home, eager to return to his studies at Tübingen. Some of them were young mothers with no means of support, motivated by hunger and need rather than by treason or even desire. Some were unmarried schoolteachers who were forced to billet German soldiers in their homes. Others were restless teenage girls who flirted with the foreign soldiers. One was a charwoman who cleaned the German military headquarters. There were no trials—only stylized rituals of retribution, a shameful carnival that often included stripping the women to their underwear and loading them onto trucks to drive through the town. They were exhibited to the sound of drumrolls, shouting, and catcalls, as if the trucks were tumbrils and 1789 had come alive again.

Girard, in his writings, has referred to "persecution texts." Did photography, in this case, serve as a twentieth-century persecution text? The persecutors seem so naive and sure of their rightness that they could not envision the revulsion this record would elicit in their descendants. "The perspective is inevitably deceptive since the persecutors are convinced that their violence is justified; they consider themselves judges, and therefore they must have guilty victims, yet their perspective is to some degree reliable, for the certainty of being right encourages them to hide nothing," Girard wrote.[20]

In one of the photos that has come down to us, two young women face the accusations of an older neighbor. In a subsequent photo, a mother of one of the women blocks the vigilantes from entering her home. In many, the women are being manhandled by smiling men, who are smoking cigarettes and carrying rifles, as they snip hair or daub women with tar or paint—sometimes other women help, vicious glee in their smiles and laughter. Photographer Robert Capa's shocking photo shows a shorn woman shielding her tiny, half-German infant from a jeering, hectoring mob, which extends all the way down the Rue du Cheval Blanc in Chartres.

American historian Forrest Pogue wrote of the victims that "their look, in the hands of their tormentors, was that of a hunted animal." One American colonel recalled: "The French were rounding up collaborators, cutting their hair off and burning it in huge piles, which one could smell miles away. Also, women collaborators were forced to run the gauntlet and were really beaten."[21] In Paris, prostitutes had been kicked to death simply for accepting German clients.

The captions to the photos show the persecutors' biases and assumptions. For example, this one: "Members of the French resistance party deal out punishment to all known Axis collaborationists, on the morning of Bastille Day. Housemaids, servants, etc., of the Germans were gathered together, shorn of all their hair, and paraded through the streets of Cherbourg, France, on July 17, 1944, their hairless heads the emblem of their violations of the rules of the party." There were no trials, so how were they to establish "known" collaborators, except by individual accusers, with perhaps motives of their own?

The United States has not suffered a vicious occupation, but mob hatred nevertheless has its own history in America. One 1957 photo comes immediately to mind: the slender and somber fifteen-year-old Elizabeth Eckford, holding her books and her silence, pursued by a mob of glaring, catcalling, jeering white classmates as she walks with ferric stoicism to the newly desegregated school in Little Rock. Hatred twists the faces of the girls, in particular, who dog her footsteps every step of the way. The emotion of the mob is always the same.

Girard may not have seen firsthand the work of the *tondeurs*, but one instance of retribution did not pass his notice: members of the Girard family were accused of collaboration. Given the ugliness of what was happening throughout France, Girard's discussion of the family trouble showed characteristic restraint. His parents had been Gaullist and not Pétainist, but it was not entirely so for his extended family.

Envy had reared its head in Avignon: the comparative wealth and social standing of Uncle Pierre's family—his father's brother, the doctor—had attracted attention and resentment. Pierre's wife, who came to the marriage with her own financial resources, was a "patron of the town's music"—and here Girard chuckled, as he clearly doesn't think much of the cultural level of wartime Avignon. His aunt was not exactly friendly to German officers, but she didn't cold-shoulder them, either. Perhaps she entertained them at her locally renowned cultural events. The uncle and aunt were thought to be supporters of the Vichy regime. At war's end, it took a lot less to attract the furies of revenge. Thanks to the intervention of Joseph Girard, the family was spared the ignominy of a possible stint in jail, said Girard.

Lustiger asked the same questions that would resonate for Girard in the coming decades: "I witnessed scenes of incredible cruelty. I saw women with shorn heads being flogged and dragged through the streets. They were collaborators, people said, whores who had been kept by the Germans. I saw men soaked in blood, their bodies torn to pieces, driven around the town on the hoods of automobiles draped with the French flag. . . . I was nauseated, and I kept repeating to myself, 'No, this is not France; it is not for *this* that friends died, it is not to see *this* that we are still alive.' I felt that we were falling into a trap; we were doing precisely what we had fought against. . . . the things I saw happening around me that posed a brutal question: How can violence be resisted without resorting to violence?"[22] These questions would haunt Girard to his last days.

Girard had two more penitential years at the École—perhaps not quite so penitential, as the darkness had lifted in the City of Light. Paris would have a different meaning when he returned as a scholar—and familiar Avignon would be the site of bold new challenges.

.   .   .

While in Avignon, I stayed at the Cloître St. Louis, a beautiful Zen-like renovation of a sixteenth-century Jesuit monastery; its new wing is designed by the famous French architect Jean Nouvel. The interior courtyard features a moss fountain shaded by ancient plane trees. There, by the biggest tree, a fluffy pale cat waits for visitors and their generous affection. The offices of the Avignon Festival are situated within the cloître complex. The festival is one of the greatest arts events in the world, and what the city is most known for today. It signaled France's postwar cultural revival when it began in 1947.

I queried one staff member after another about the origins of the festival. Like so many people I spoke to in Avignon, they'd never heard of René Girard. They looked puzzled when I mentioned his association with the festival. No, no, they said, the festival was founded by renowned French actor, director, and entrepreneur Jean Vilar (1912–71), whose museum, Maison Jean Vilar, is a few blocks away from the Palais.

Yet one could argue that Girard was a key player in creating the Avignon Festival, which began as the first major exhibition of modern art in the city, from 27 June to 30 September 1947. The argument begins with a small five by seven inch booklet of a hundred pages that lists the organizers as Yvonne Zervos, Jacques Charpier, and finally, René Girard. The festival committee included, in addition to Joseph Girard, Avignon's mayor, Georges Pons; Étienne Charpier, *beaux arts* delegate for the city; poet René Char; and Georges Antigue. Girard's disappearance from the festival's memory fits another pattern I began to see in his life—a willingness to release an idea fully when he is finished with it without looking backward, combined with an unusual indifference to maintaining his own reputation. So much so that he is often overlooked as one of Avignon's most venerable sons.

The achievement wasn't small: the festival had been a very necessary shot in the arm not only for Avignon, but for France. The nation was still a long way from recovery in 1947. "France was still a little bit hungry—not serious, but it was real," Girard recalled in the comparative affluence of Palo Alto. While the hunger he was referring to was literal, it certainly had a psychological component as well.

Art impresario Christian Zervos planned the exhibition in the main chapel of the Palais des Papes, thus taking advantage of the most spectacular setting the city had to offer. Girard and Jacques Charpier, his sidekick from the lycée's penitential hours of detention, had the encouragement of their influential fathers for the project. "My friend and I were hugely impressed, of course," recalled Girard. "At the time Zervos was eager to have an exhibition of paintings in that very castle. Thus, he found it useful to enlist our youthful collaboration in the project, and we became the official organizers of the event. This exhibition needed the active support of our fathers and our involvement in it was a good way for Zervos to get them interested in his project."[23]

The Charpier and Girard parents were already friends, since Joseph Girard was the museum curator and Charpier's father was the top aide to the mayor, in charge of arts and culture. That wasn't Étienne Charpier's most prestigious credential at the time, however: the communist politician had been an officer for the Free French forces in North Africa, under the orders of the celebrated Josephine Baker. Moreover, he already knew Christian Zervos, the greatest art merchant and art critic in Paris, who sold paintings for huge sums. Zervos's wife Yvonne was also a friend of Char. So the group was closely intertwined.

Girard remembered Zervos as an amiable fellow, always happy to chat. He was very much in charge of the show, and enjoyed the role. Though Joseph Girard wouldn't become curator of the Palais until 1949, he seems to have had an active role in the proceedings at the Palais, and certainly his role at the Calvet Museum would have given his son something of a leg up in the art world.

Jacques Charpier wanted to become a famous poet, Girard recalled, but he also wanted to make his fortune, and the young man sensed that the two endeavors led in different directions. With the festival, he had a chance to explore both: he would be a disciple of the poet René Char, who was also enjoying enormous esteem as a colonel in the Résistance's National Front; in addition, he would have a chance to be a mover and shaker, "an operator," said Girard, which was perhaps the deeper calling at the time. Jacques Charpier may not have found fame as a poet, said Girard, but he was "really a clever man—he managed to get something out of nothing." Both had youth and energy to recommend them. "We were not good enough to be real operators—we were also operated *on*. But we had nothing to lose," he told me. Suddenly Girard's familiarity with Paris was not the reminder of an affliction, but a job recommendation and doorway into an exciting new world.

Zervos lured Jean Vilar to the project, suggesting that a single performance of his celebrated production of *Murder in the Cathedral* would draw new audiences to his work. T. S. Eliot's verse play was an apt choice, especially given the history of Avignon, but Vilar resisted, since moving the production

from a small Paris theater to an open and untested space presented insurmountable technical problems. Instead, he proposed "Une Semaine d'Art
Dramatique en Avignon." He directed three plays in the Cour d'Honneur of
the Popes' Palace, where the floodlit façade provided a dramatic backdrop for
simple sets. The works—Shakespeare's *Richard II,* the first production of the
play in French; Paul Claudel's *Tobie et Sara* (*Tobit and Sara*); and Maurice
Clavel's second play, *La Terrasse de Midi* (*The Midday Terrace*)—established
Avignon's reputation for modern and unfamiliar scripts from the outset. The
theater effort brought other attractions to town: "One of the main causes
of our excitement in those days was the fact that we were hanging around
daily with actresses such as Sylvia Montfort and Jeanne Moreau, who had just
finished acting school and were still largely unknown,"[24] said Girard.

It was all heady stuff for the two footloose young men. "My friend and
I were in a state of continuous mimetic drunkenness at the thought of being
involved in such important cultural events. I remember going to [Pablo]
Picasso's painting studio in Paris, on the Quai des Grands Augustins, and
picking out twelve paintings with my friend and others, which we then took
down to Avignon in a little truck," said Girard. "I also remember mishan-
dling paintings by Matisse, and the result was a noticeable hole in one of
the *Blouses roumaines*, which was quickly repaired"[25]—fortunately, because
the festival offered no insurance for the masterpieces loaded onto trucks. It
took a month for the duo to gather the twelve paintings from Picasso, Henri
Matisse, Georges Braque, and also works by Marc Chagall, Paul Klee, Max
Ernst, Wassily Kandinsky, and others for the exhibition.

In Palo Alto, Girard looked around his comfortably large living room,
and waved his arm to indicate the space—the art impresario Zervos, he said,
had "three times that full of famous paintings of the twentieth century." He
and his friend Jacques, he added, "were quite seduced by that."

Into this war-torn and threadbare country, the superstars arrived:
"Picasso came to Avignon during the summer, in his chauffeur-driven car.
He complained humorously but loudly that there was no advertising for the
exhibition along the road between Paris and Avignon."[26]

He had a hidden motive, according to Girard: he wanted to make sure
that Matisse and Braque had given the same number of paintings, and ones
of equal importance and value. For Girard, watching the painters jostle for
supremacy, or at least parity, was another early lesson in mimetic rivalry.

Picasso spent two months among them, and pulled out his easel and paints while in Avignon. "My impression was that he was a very clever man—and because of that, he was a lot of fun," he said. "Picasso was kidding all the time." In keeping with the spirit of rivalry, Georges Braque came to spend a month among the Avignonnais, too.

Who started the Avignon Festival? Girard whimsically credits neither Zervos nor Vilar, but rather the poor, little-known Spaniard, on his way to Paris before either of the world wars: "It is possible that the original idea for the exhibition came from Picasso himself, who enjoyed talking about his first visit to Avignon. It was on his way from Spain, when he first came to Paris. He stopped at the Castle of the Popes to see it and, being very poor, he had offered to paint the concierge's portrait for five francs. The offer was rejected. It was Picasso's desire at the end of his life to have his last exhibition in the Castle of the Popes, and that is what happened."[27]

Hence, in 1970, the reclusive and ailing artist exhibited 165 paintings and 45 drawings in the Palais des Papes. It was still not the last time, not quite. Ten days before his death in April 1973, the nonagenarian was preparing more than two hundred paintings for exhibition at the Avignon Arts Festival the following month, again at the Palais des Papes. His ties with this mysterious city ran deep.

In 1947, Picasso offered a subtle homage to his younger, hungrier self at the exhibition, remembering the concierge who refused to buy his portrait for five francs half a century before. At the entrance to the exhibition, a very pretty woman sold tickets. Girard recalled: "Picasso arrives, looks at her, takes from her an album of reproductions of his own work that she had been looking at. He opens the album, and on the cover page, he makes a pencil drawing in a few seconds—a typically 'picassesque' devil's head. He signs it and returns the book to the woman, bowing very low before her. A tribute to her beauty."[28]

By the time I found myself sitting with Girard in his living room, he was almost the age of Picasso at his last Avignon exhibition and older than Matisse at his death. Reflecting years later on what fun it had been to work with Picasso, Girard added that he feels the artist's reputation is not what it was. "I have a problem about the modern arts. I have a feeling that it is a conspiracy of merchants," he mused aloud. "All of them. They are dead, the arts today. There is no real music, if one wants to be pessimistic." He added,

"Modern music, modern art—what could they do? It seems that they've tried everything."

"Europeans tend to be Nietzschean, in considering the decadence of the present. This is another aspect of America's youthfulness—because it doesn't have that kind of *a priori* decision in favor of total decadence," he said. "Most Europeans would tell you 'art and philosophy are dead, finished.'"

He felt, toward the end of his life, that we are living in the long holding pen of apocalypse—not a catastrophic bang, but a prolonged period where the old solutions for human conflict no longer work, and new solutions haven't been found or tried. The wait is getting a little tiresome, he admitted, but then his thoughts returned to our own era. "But anyway, it's an instant in the ocean of time. Therefore it doesn't prove anything."

Vilar continued his association with Avignon until his death in 1971, widening its cultural basis, increasing the official theaters to four, and organizing a number of productions in other venues around Avignon, including, for example, the courtyard of the Jesuit school. The festival now features between thirty-five and forty different shows, many of them world or French premieres, totaling about three hundred performances for nearly two hundred thousand people annually. It is arguably the most famous and innovative theater in France. No surprise, then, that Vilar is honored as the founder.

.   .   .

In one of the brilliant futures that Girard left behind him, he would have stayed to reap the rewards in the art world, after creating an event that was a success beyond all imagining.

Within weeks, however, he would emigrate. Curiously, he seems to have been too young and green to see the opportunity when it was before him. It would have been enough, Girard said, for Zervos merely to mention his name in Parisian conversations, for a different future to have been forged. Only a year or two later, he realized he could have had an important career in the big business of art. But the only future he saw on the horizon was the life of a medieval archivist. "He had to be dragged kicking and screaming into the Middle Ages," said a future colleague, the Dante scholar John Freccero, who knew of Girard's lineage and his École years. By 1947, Girard was a man who couldn't wait to throw the Middle Ages behind him.

His father wisely did not push him toward his own profession. "He did not want to, because he saw that I was not at all cut out for that type of work. But my options at the time were very limited"—limited not only by the times, but by the rigid French professional hierarchies that predetermined the opportunities for a *Chartiste*. Meanwhile, America beckoned: the G.I. Bill had flooded the universities with veterans, and the relatively prosperous country was looking abroad for help, snapping up teachers where it could find them. "My first opportunity to move out was an offer to teach in the USA, and I took it immediately," he said.

"Initially, I got a job at the Library of the United Nations. It was certainly more prestigious, but I understood quite quickly that it was mainly the work of a documentarian, in the service of the UN national delegations, which did not involve any personal research. Moreover, the first person I met there was one of my fellow *chartistes*! That was enough for me to decide to take my second option and go to Indiana University, where I was supposed to teach French and do a PhD in history."[29]

Lander McClintock, who had been a professor of French at Indiana since the 1920s, was sent to vet the young provincial applicant. Girard understood that the "little job" with a scholarship could become a permanent position. When I asked what had impressed the Americans, he replied, "The cultural tradition was pretty strong from my parents. It was immediately exploitable."

"My main desire was to get a car," he insisted. The much-repeated comment has become one of the legends around Girard, and perhaps shtick, too. But another friend remembers him admitting that the brush with the Nazis had made a deeper impression over time, and was instrumental, though not determinative, in his decision to leave. For Girard, Europe seemed a shaky place to stake one's future. "I enjoyed greatly the idea of going to the U.S. Indeed, on the whole, it was the best thing I did," he said. "Teaching in America appeared the only solution."

.   .   .

Before we leave Girard's youth behind in France, we should visit a brief Proustian episode in his life, even before he encountered Marcel Proust. Girard said it occurred sometime in his early twenties, without noting whether the setting was Paris or Avignon. He had, of course, started dating women, but none of them seemed to have left much of an impression, except one. This wasn't a Laura or Beatrice—he certainly wasn't mesmerized by any beatific qualities she may have had. It was rather how her behavior affected him that was important. It was a time of life when men and women naturally begin to think about marriage, but he backed off when she suggested it. As she went her own way, however, he became more interested again—"just like Proust,"[30] he marveled years later. He would remark to colleagues in future decades that this was his first inkling about the nature of mimetic desire, that we long for what others long for, and that we grab harder as the object eludes us.

He often portrayed his life as existing entirely within his head, with ideas emerging like Athena from Zeus, but that was not entirely so. As for anyone else, they were grounded in experience and reinforced by reading. But the fabric they were embroidered onto was gossamer. Subtle perturbations made an impression on his spirit, even when young. He was no Raskolnikov who had to commit an axe murder to prod his conscience. That, perhaps, is where he differed from many of us: the quieter rhythms of his life were enough to leave a mark.

He was ready for Proust. Just before he left town for good, he finally encountered *À la recherche du temps perdu* in a library near Avignon. The *Combray* section impressed him the most. The discovery, he said later, was "my first real literary interest." Proust's masterpiece was the third book that was to be a major influence on him. With the childhood books that had lingered in his mind, *Don Quixote* and *The Jungle Book*, the scaffolding for his future thought was complete, from imitated desire to mob violence and sacrifice. The tinder was ready for the spark. His friends, however, did not share his newfound passion.

"This was the time when I plunged in Proust with delight. Char and his surrealist friends did not like Proust," he said, recalling the poet who had been a leading figure in the Résistance. Then he added wryly, "They were insufficiently revolutionary."[31] He added, "My friends disapproved, because the novel in general, and Proust in particular, was regarded as horribly *démodé* and *dépassé*.

"When I left for the USA—even though initially I was supposed to spend only two years there—René Char was quite critical. He regarded that move as some kind of betrayal, and up to a point he was right. The intellectual and aesthetic atmosphere in which I found myself was alien to me. Without admitting it, without really being aware of it, I wanted to get away from it all."[32]

CHAPTER 4

Everything Is Possible

For me it was like a breath of freedom, an opening in the prison.

—René Girard

once asked Girard what the biggest events of his life were. Oh, he assured me immediately, they were all events in his head. His thoughts were what mattered. Unconvinced, I pressed harder. Surely, *surely* there were external events in his life that proved pivotal. Thoughts, after all, don't occur in a vacuum, and they tend not to linger unless they resonate with what we see and experience in the world around us. Then he replied emphatically: "Coming to America." With that, he said, everything else became possible.

In September 1947, Girard booked the cheapest seat on the French ocean liner *De Grasse*, the luxury steamer that took nine days to cross the Atlantic from Le Havre to New York City. He found a congenial companion on the trip to pass the time, Étienne Bloch. Girard remembers mostly the fun—the two chased the girls together, he said. But there was a serious side to the friendship, also: Bloch was the son of the important historian Marc Bloch, who wrote about the 1940 surrender;[1] the author had been shot by the Gestapo in 1944. These were the days before commercial air travel was commonplace. It would be years before Girard made his first flight to Duke University in North Carolina.

The culture shock when he arrived at Indiana University must have been dizzying. Suddenly, the postwar privations and bitterness were behind him, and he found himself in a spacious, tree-filled campus with limestone nineteenth-century buildings—about six or seven thousand students, but the enrollment was about to get much larger thanks to the postwar G.I.s who were flooding the campus. He was initially housed in the faculty club, which he enjoyed—a luxury certainly preferable to the chilly hotel in wartime Paris. Other than the familiar limestone, however, it must have seemed like landing on the moon.

The isolation is difficult for Americans under, say, forty years old to understand, born as they are into a world that is interconnected through the Internet and Skype, smartphones, and a hundred thousand air flights a day. Bloomington was, in spirit, even farther away from the nation's cultural centers than it is today. Produce stands would have been at the roadside, not too far outside the city, offering stacks of corn on the cob, squash, and fresh tomatoes from local farms. For Girard, the tuna casseroles, the macaroni and cheese, the Spam, the Cheerios, the ketchup, and the peanut butter and jelly sandwiches would have been as alien as chewing betel nut or cracking coconuts on the limestone. The Avignonnais who had grown up with Châteauneuf-du-Pape from the neighboring villages was now in a nation that hadn't recovered from Prohibition, a piece of legislation incomprehensible to those not accustomed to the American psychological landscape.

The dissolution of social distinctions, which had unleashed such violent repercussions in postwar France, was the very fuel that fed the American engine, and that fed American universities, in particular. You could climb fast, Gatsby-like, but you could fall fast, too, and there would be nothing to break your crazy descent. And everyone was trying to climb. "Mimetic desire—it's the theory of American universities," said one of his later Stanford colleagues, Jean-Marie Apostolidès. He recalled the wild tug-of-war between Harvard and Stanford in which he himself had been the coveted *objet du désir*. The more unattainable the prize, the more fantastic the offers. Girard would be the prize in even more battles. "For the two of us, America was a second mother," Apostolidès added. "It allowed us to have much more success than we would have had in France." America is the land of restless self-invention and self-fashioning. It rewarded hard work, flexibility, and the ability to make it up as you go along—a natural for the Avignonnais who had already gone through several incarnations. Girard left behind a future that was circumscribed by being a "Chartist," that is, a graduate of the École des Chartes. Finally these professional hierarchies, class prejudices, and the stifling atmosphere they created were thousands of miles away.

Jean-Michel Oughourlian, the Paris psychiatrist who became a colleague and collaborator with Girard, was not surprised when I told him that Girard described the arrival of the *De Grasse* in New York City as his biggest life event. "Everything is due to his moving to America," Oughourlian said in 2013. "What René remembered from Avignon is petiteness, everything is small." He added that the French still refer to everything as "petite"—"my small wife, my small home, my small life. It's the exact opposite in America. Everything is big—vast ambitions. In Avignon, everything was closed. That's what pisses him off," he said. "He was Americanized. His tendency is to be wide open."

There was a trade-off: he faced privations of a different and more novel kind. As his future friend, the Czech author Milan Kundera, an émigré to France, wrote: "Being in a foreign country means walking a tightrope high above the ground without the net afforded a person by the country where he has his family, colleagues, and friends, and where he can easily say what he has to say in a language he has known from childhood."[2] Girard's English certainly wasn't up to snuff. He said to me that the only English he learned at the lycée was Wordsworth's "I Wandered Lonely as a Cloud"—but that's not quite true. His lycée reports showed that he had excelled in English, but Wordsworth may have been just about all he recollected in adulthood. He had trouble being understood, and his accent was a puzzlement to his early students.

But they rewarded his fractured English with devotion. Martha recalled that Girard's "spark" kept students in French, so teaching courses in literature was quickly added to language instruction. Already, then, he was a charming, charismatic young instructor. That was from the outside. The world from within Girard was more complex and troubled. Looking back at his "frivolity and inattention" during these years when he was generously remunerated for his "meager and mediocre services," he confessed to a nagging sense of doom and fear, "enough to erect in me a whole edifice of repression." His marketable talent was his native tongue, "a competence that owed nothing to personal talent, and gave to me, with respect to everyone around me, the impression of cultural superiority." Nevertheless, he enjoyed the cachet of being a European in what was then a very provincial university. Haughtiness cloaked his misgivings, the "agonizing doubts and the accumulated trauma of defeat, occupation, and especially the American victory, a liberating victory in all other respects but psychologically overwhelming for the liberated."

Girard considered himself "very French and even more a French intellectual," and likely his students did, too. It was a recipe for what he would later call snobbism. One acquaintance described Girard's manner at that time as adamantly atheistic, fiercely iconoclastic—in short, typically "French intellectual," and that carried some cultural prestige, especially in a place where it was so rare. He was alternately attracted and annoyed by "the American way of life"—in particular, its massive confidence in its own infallibility. Nothing could shake the complacency of the American Midwest, and as always, he was reading the newspapers, which were among the greatest irritants. The Marshall Plan was doing much to rebuild an exhausted Europe, though he suspected its motives were self-serving. "It is very difficult to talk about these things with justice, to find the right tone," he wrote years later. "I wanted to write avenging pamphlets, to electrify throngs, but the beings who obsessed me were too mediocre for my obsession not to be itself mediocre."[3]

These words from the unpublished 1979 memoir found among his papers are startling for their candor and excoriating self-knowledge. The young Girard resembles the Dostoevskyan Underground Man he would write about later; here, however, his recollections are sharpened by the double awareness of the older man viewing his younger self. Preoccupied with the opinion of men for whom they have no respect, the Underground Men fall into "the law of their own desire," maintaining an appearance to others that masks their own sense of deficiency: "He does not conform to social decorum and conventional morality; he does not follow some religious precepts. To the bitter end, he sticks to the lessons of his own subjective experience," he would write in a strikingly original and often overlooked 1963 study on Dostoevsky.[4] "As a result of giving up transcendence, individual pride increases, and the higher it rises, the less willing it is to humble itself, to yield any particle of self-sovereignty. Sooner or later, this pride must encounter the tiny little stone, the puny obstacle that will turn into a major stumbling block."[5] The comfort and paycheck, coupled with a sense of his superiority, were setting him up for a nasty fall.

.   .   .

"Martha McCullough." On the first day of his second term teaching at Indiana, he was stumped midway through roll call. "I'll never be able to pronounce this name," he announced wearily. Within a few years he would solve the problem by changing it. But none of that was apparent at first sight. She was a young student, and he was dating someone else, anyway.

Martha was born on April 1, 1929—five years younger than her instructor, but already with some tough life experiences that may have fostered her early maturity and down-to-earth practicality. She was from Union City—a small town of a few thousand, straddled between Indiana and Ohio, that had its beginnings as an important railroad junction in the mid-nineteenth century. Her father had died at fifty-three of a heart attack, when Martha was only seventeen. The small family, comprising a younger sister and a mother who was a high-school English teacher, faced real hardships. But Martha showed academic promise. At Indiana, she earned a 4.0 after her first semester. While the expenses of a sorority were normally beyond the reach of a fatherless student, the local chapters were eager to bolster their academic credentials, so she was recruited to Delta Gamma.

Colleagues who remember her from a few years later had strong first impressions. "When I met Martha, it was like meeting Grace Kelly. A strong combination of beauty and coolness," said John Freccero. Another future colleague, Lionel Gossman, remembered, "She was very handsome. Really a very good-looking woman. I had tremendous admiration for Martha and liked her a great deal. One hundred percent American Midwest. Full of common sense. Such a contrasting pair."

Were they such a contrast, really? Girard remembered hardships, too. One also recalls the unpretentious good sense of the Avignonnais: the mother, born a little higher than the family she married into, who made sure her family was never short of food during the worst of the wartime privations; the father who pushed his son through many rough patches. These traits evidently resurfaced in the stability and determination of the son. Neither Martha nor René indulged drama of any kind—both were deeply loyal, highly principled, and unfussy. I sometimes felt they could have watched a crime take place in their living room, and in their no-nonsense way, they would have cleaned up any mess, assisted the police, and overlooked mentioning it to any of their guests afterward.

Alike, too, in their hospitality and generosity. "He's incapable of being critical of people close to him. I have benefited from that generosity," said Freccero. In that way, as in so many others, Martha was a perfect complement. She was always gracious and hospitable to guests—no matter how many—and there was usually something good that had just come out of the oven, or was just about to go into it. He was the reliable paterfamilias. Said one longtime friend, Marilyn Yalom, who has known them both for half a century, "He spotted the right woman, and she grew with him. Part of it was the luck of the right draw, part was intuition."

The French class ended in spring 1948, and no doubt Martha quickly forgot the lively French lecturer in the round of studies and social life—and he was otherwise occupied, too. But when they encountered each other again her sophomore year, the meeting proved more consequential.

One of her sorority sisters had a French boyfriend who had helped her move some boxes. His friend René came to lend a hand. He met Martha again, and she was no longer his student, with any ethical barriers that might have imposed. Their first date was a movie.

I once asked Martha if dating a French lecturer carried some prestige with her set. No, she replied, it was considered a rather odd thing to do; her school friends were dating football heroes and getting pinned by fraternity boys. "It was not interesting or exotic to take up with a foreigner," she said. Some later claimed that courting the girl from Union City, including summer trips to that far-away town 150 miles away, was a big distraction from what should have been serious efforts to thrive in academia.

Oughourlian thinks Girard's determination to stay in the United States is, in large part, due to Martha. "When you fall in love you love the place." He likened it to the visual trope of *The Wizard of Oz*: "If you're in love, the black and white movie turns into Technicolor."

But Girard was clearly overwhelmed by much more than a pretty girl—he had a whole new world to master.

.   .   .

When René Girard's dissertation, "American Opinions on France, 1940–1943," arrived on interlibrary loan from Indiana University, it was in pristine condition. The onion-skin pages were ever so slightly yellowed at the margins, but otherwise unmarked by time. No coffee stains or lightly penciled marginalia, no dog-eared pages. Only the faded black cloth binding with faded gold lettering on the spine showed the passage of the years.

The volume is clearly an original, not a copy for circulation, and appears to have been rarely opened since the day it was put on a library shelf. Few have looked at the professionally typed thesis since it was presented to the university for a doctorate in 1950, despite the author's subsequent fame. Its condition indicated care as well as neglect: no typos or corrections, and no evidence of faded typewriter ribbons. Girard's inadequate English had been corrected and massaged by others.

The dissertation is polished, diligent, workmanlike, but never really leaps to life. It was, nevertheless, a substantial effort. Girard described it as a low-balled endeavor, but it's a massive work of 418 pages, a dutiful achievement for a twenty-six-year-old instructor.

Much of his future thought is anticipated in it, though not in a way that might be immediately apparent. The man who would become hooked on the daily news was already glued to that mimetic phenomenon—opinion. We are mimetic creatures, and preoccupied with what others think of us. French intellectuals, in particular, are always curious to know how they appear to their American counterparts, and worried that they may be suffering from a "decline." The two nations eyed each other across the Atlantic. As Girard himself noted, "Americans always liked to hear about 'the moral laxity of the French people' and Frenchmen to contemplate 'the American lack of taste.'"[6] And he, in turn, wondered what the "natives" might think of him and the language of which he was the guardian and teacher—as his dissertation noted, "a language of wonderful clarity, in a beautiful sense of logic and proportion, in delicate irony, humor and tolerance, in an idealism that was sometimes earthy and sometimes heavenly."[7]

His method of investigation was easy, he told me. He wrote to the French ambassador in Washington, D.C., who shipped a large box of newspapers and magazine clippings to Bloomington. *Voilà!* Girard said he had undertaken the project "totally not seriously." He simply needed the doctorate for his visa, and he was determined to stay in the United States.

But there's more to it than that: it's important that the war, which during our conversations he claimed hadn't greatly affected him, was the subject of his massive dissertation, as well as an enduring preoccupation during these years. He wrote of the French and their "national propensity of finding a scapegoat for their sins"—was his mind already turning toward what would be a lifetime study?

One close colleague told me all his conversations with Girard had touched on Franco-German relations, and certainly the topic frequently recurred in my own talks with him. France's "strange defeat"—it was Bloch's phrase—is still a matter of debate among the French intelligentsia today. Even more so then. Clearly, he was beginning to ponder the real nature of the struggle, as only the latest expression of the Franco-German feud, which would be the centerpiece of his final book, *Battling to the End*.

Although he said at different times that he was trained to be a librarian, or historian, or literary scholar—his initial profession would shift with the context of the conversation—the Indiana dissertation and the École thesis cemented his training and his standing as an historian. "Many people see literary criticism as my original field but, in an academic sense, literary criticism is no more 'my' field than anthropology, or psychology, or religious studies. If our 'real' field is the one in which we are not self-taught, my 'real' field is history. In everything that truly matters to me, however, I am self-taught."[8]

.　　.　　.

Martha and René married on the same day she graduated, 18 June 1951. She simply returned home and changed into a street-length white dress with matching bolero and hat for the afternoon wedding at the Methodist church in Bloomington. The wedding ceremony was intimate, attended by Martha's family and a few close friends—no one from the groom's far-away family. An Indiana colleague served as best man. In an era that invented Hollywood standards of weddings, with six identically dressed bridesmaids, mountains of floral arrangements, and a father of the bride in a tuxedo, the simplicity of the event was another step away from her sorority sisters, away from a life as an American 1950s housewife.

More than fifty years later, the French academician Michel Serres praised Martha during the ceremony for the investiture of Girard into the prestigious Académie Française. After the conventional comparison with the Biblical

Mary and Martha, the one a symbol of the contemplative life, and the other the active, he gave eloquent praise to the latter-day Martha as "steadfast, loyal, sweet, generous, modest, and reserved."

"You embody the virtues we admire over the centuries, in the culture of your country: faithfulness, constancy, strength, fair-mindedness, fineness in sensing the feelings of others, devotion, dynamically and lucidly facing the things of life. Few people know that without you, without your inimitable presence, the great theories that I have the heavy charge to praise this evening assuredly would not have seen the light of day,"[9] he said.

Serres became more fulsome and flowery, but his encomium fell short of the simplicity and immediacy of what I saw before me, in more quotidian moments. Even toward the end of their long lives together, René would turn to her, depending on her not only in his unaccustomed helplessness, but in perfect devotion. She would reach to him with encouragement, affection, and loving good cheer, after the most severe of his debilitating strokes— holding his hand, patiently coaxing him to clarify something he had tried to say, discreetly withdrawing a question when it was too difficult for him to speak. Often, when she didn't observe my observing, great *tendresse* prevailed, heartbreaking and miraculous.

She remembered the details of their wedding as I sat in the TV room next to the kitchen with René, as their sixty-third anniversary was approaching. After the wedding, the newlyweds shared their honeymoon with another French couple, piling into a car and driving southward to Mexico for several weeks of adventure. They had expected to stay at Tampico, but it wasn't the resort they envisioned—rather gritty and small-town industrial, from her description—so they retreated to Mexico City. Their car was stolen and retrieved. She remembers Teotihuacán—the pyramids that were the site of human and animal sacrifice, offered to ensure the ancient people prospered.

Having weathered the silver and gold anniversaries, what was the appropriate landmark for a sixty-third anniversary? Do friends surround the *entente cordiale* and pelt the couple with diamonds? Martha smiled and recalled how they had forgotten their fiftieth anniversary in 2001. Their offspring remembered, however, and reminded them several days later. Celebrations? René didn't go in for such things, she said matter-of-factly.

.   .   .

Time has not been kind to Saint-John Perse, at least in the Anglophone world, where he is largely forgotten. It was not always so. Born in the French Antilles, the anti-Nazi poet had had his possessions taken and his citizenship revoked by the Vichy government and had settled in American exile by the time Girard arrived in the United States. He received the Nobel in 1960.

To my knowledge, Girard's brief fascination with Perse was only one of two occasions when he became engrossed in the work of a poet—though the second encounter, with Friedrich Hölderlin, would be more profound and more lasting. The interest in Perse was brief, but signaled that Girard was beginning to turn his considerable energies to something more enduring than girls and cars.

In an essay published in 1953, Girard praised the "historical presence" in Perse's work, but characteristically, it is the ideas, not the use of memorable language or its music, that caught Girard's attention: "Civilizations appear as worlds that cannot communicate with one another. They come into being, live, and die, only to be replaced by others just as ephemeral and isolated as they were. . . . There is no more absolute; man is condemned to the relative."[10] Girard would return to these questions again in future years, with a very different understanding.

Malraux proved a more powerful early influence. Girard noted that historical relativism as a theme of despair had perhaps attained its most perfect literary expression in Malraux's *Walnut Trees of Altenburg*, the surviving part of a novel destroyed by the Gestapo in 1944. The book's claim would reverberate through Malraux's later works: "The greatest mystery is not that we have been flung at random between this profusion of matter and the stars, but that within this prison we can draw from ourselves images powerful enough to deny our nothingness."[11]

Malraux's thinking as an art theorist, rather than as a novelist, haunted Girard. Malraux's three-volume *La Psychologie de L'Art* (published 1947–49) was to be a catalyst for Girard's thinking, although he would later call it "luridly romantic."[12] Romantic, perhaps, and often obscure, as in a passage claiming "the devil, who always prefers to paint in two dimensions, has become the most eminent of the artists of the unknown past; nearly all that he has contributed to painting has come back to life." The series was republished in a single-volume format as *Les Voix du Silence* in 1951; Girard was quick to find a copy in remote Indiana.

The books are mammoth in scope and astonishingly ambitious, rather like Girard himself—a stunning compendium of art through time, across cultures civilized and primitive, famous and obscure. Pages of black-and-white plates show close-ups of works we may not have seen before, or, if seen before, never quite this way. The mysterious, opaque expression on the face of the cloaked woman who has risen from the dead in a thirteenth-century Rheims stone sculpture, the alert intelligence of the Teutonic queen by the Master of Naumburg, turning her collar up against an imaginary wind. The women jostle with a range of exquisite Gandhāra Buddhas with elegant, unreadable eyes and the bison cave paintings of Altamira.

For the son of an art museum curator, and the organizer of a famous art exhibition, it is noteworthy that this is perhaps the only time after leaving France he was to discuss the visual arts and their history. Girard claimed to have been profoundly shaken by a passage that claims that history is "no longer a chronology but an anxious interrogation of the past to try to discover the destiny of the world." Malraux wrote that Western civilization had begun to question itself, and that a range of devils, from war to psychological "complexes"—all of them present in primitive art—had reappeared. Mankind is aiming towards its own destruction: "the demons of Babylon, of the Church, of Freud and of Bikini Atoll all have the same face."

Malraux deplored our "phantom cities," and their ravaged concept of man: "What nineteenth-century state would have dared to systematize torture?" he asked. In his dark and knotty prose, Malraux saw the gutted cities of the West, now so much like the primitive world that gave them birth—"mingling their last thin wisps of smoke with those rising from the death-ovens."[13]

Years later, Girard still recalled the effect of Malraux's association of "the ravages of war in our time" with our art, "its dehumanization and the dehumanization of the world around us, the advent of absolute violence." It's a straight arrow from what he was reading in these early years, to *Violence and the Sacred*, and then to his final major work, *Battling to the End*.

He was also intrigued by Malraux's critical reception: "Aesthetes who are neither real artists nor real thinkers are terrified by the implications of this relationship. They want art to continue; they want their critical tempests in a teapot, the paltry and profitable agitation around art to be safely perpetuated. They wanted reassurance that there was something really unwonted and alarming in the way Malraux had posed the problem." Some of the criticism was deserved, Girard wrote, but out of proportion with the importance of the book. "After performing the execution, critics completely stopped talking about him and his work, practically until the time of his death. The intelligentsia performed one of these radical executions, one of those sacrificial expulsions which it knows how to do so well."

Malraux's vision was a shot in the arm for Girard, and the public censure galvanized him. "A general cry arose against the author, but for me it was like a breath of freedom, an opening in the prison." He was relieved "that someone could speak to the heart of our time without acting as if nothing were happening. It was as if someone had lifted slightly the huge tombstone placed over the horrible secret of our time. Most intellectuals sit on the stone, pontificating until they are out of breath. I discovered all at once a universe where only those who had the most insipid chatter had the rights to the city."[14] But in the midst of that world of chatter, he discovered that meaningful words are still possible.

He had found his motivation and inspiration, which was generously seasoned with contempt. "It seemed difficult, but not impossible, for me to publish in American academic journals," he wrote, "the indifference they had inspired in me made them more accessible." He began writing, but it was too late.

·   ·   ·

Why did Indiana let him go? The simple answer would be that the university chose to award a tenured position to another Frenchman, a Sartre scholar and author named Robert Champigny. The administrative move was spearheaded by Samuel Will, the chairman of the French and Italian Department, who would go on to make the department one of the top five in the nation. Tenure in those days, said Martha, "was not the heart-stopping process it has become." Nonetheless, for a young man who had felt himself culturally superior, a cut above, the thump must have been a rude shock. It was a rough introduction to the cutthroat nature of the academic process. According to Girard, "I no longer appeared to be a 'promising young man' and it was necessary to get rid of me."[15]

Publish or perish is a cliché, but the number and eminence of scholarly articles and books mattered enormously in academic advancement. Girard repented of his frivolous inattention to the demands of academia: "It is under this principle that I started to write, around 1950, after two or three years devoted essentially to female students and cars. I was too ignorant of the system and too disoriented to lend an ear to the warnings of my department chair, which became more and more direct, even brutal, as his patience ran out. I managed for a long time not to hear anything," he wrote. "Perhaps, programmed with French attitudes, I could only imagine that a teacher, once in place, must be impossible to remove."[16]

Now he was paying the price. He had to find another position quickly. "I narrowly avoided disaster, but the fact that some of my articles had already been accepted kept me from falling into the semi-cataleptic state that the mere prospect of failure had once been enough to provoke."[17]

A more interesting question might be: What would have happened if he *had* been given tenure? Apostolidès recalled Girard telling him that if he had not come to America, he would never have published a single book—"he would never have become René." Would he have published any book at all if he had kept his comfortable perch at Indiana?

Girard had made it clear that Indiana University was something of a miracle to him—a new world, attended by fun and happiness and love. Would he have stayed on? Would he have eventually retired at Indiana? The counterfactual isn't all that improbable. Buoyed by his easy classroom popularity and marital happiness, one could argue that there would have been no *Deceit, Desire, and the Novel*, no *Violence and the Sacred*, no 1966 conference bringing French intellectual thought to America—because the stimuli that produced all those efforts lay in the future, in other cities.

In the early 1960s, Freccero recalls Prof. Samuel Will greeting Girard at a conference with a handshake and a jocular question, "Aren't you glad we fired you?" He had a point.

·   ·   ·

Henri Peyre appears at several points in Girard's dissertation, and at this point he enters Girard's life as well. Peyre was considered the "mafia boss of French scholars" in the United States, according to one colleague; Martha referred to him as "the god of jobs in French teaching." Peyre, the chair of romance languages at Yale, moved and placed French scholars in major positions across the United States like pieces on a chessboard. He was a man of astonishing intellectual range and apparently infinite connections. He contributed regularly to the *New York Times*, wrote thirty books in English and French, and, almost until his death, he wrote witty, provocative articles and book reviews. After each lecture, he tore up his notes "so I won't repeat myself each year," he said.[18] Peyre was famous for his incessant correspondence, which he conducted using violet ink for his loopy, bold handwriting that filled every corner of the page. He even wrote letters sitting at the back of the class, as students studied or took tests. According to the former president of Yale, they were "letters that were tireless, passionate, precise, radically decent, ever caring for what the recipient cared for, capable of immense tenderness and a steely eloquence—letters impatient with cant, unafraid of sentiment—letters that in every way reflected the man."[19]

Peyre and Girard already shared an important bond: they both had roots in Avignon. Girard's uncle and brother were doctors in Avignon; Peyre had a brother who was a physician there, too. Girard wrote him a letter.

Yale University Press in 2004 published over 1,100 pages of Peyre's letters that have survived—but only two mention Girard. Peyre was also known to throw incoming letters out once he had responded to them. So we only have the Girards' recollection of Peyre's dumbfounded reaction to Girard's first letter: "How did you get here without me knowing about it?" he asked.

Girard's back-door entry into American academia via the École des Chartes (rather than the Sorbonne or the École Normale) had eluded the almost universal surveillance of Peyre.

His surprise makes another point: Girard had no mentors, no guiding hand steering him at any point—no one, in fact, to whom he owed any intellectual fealty. In future years, some would claim that Girard could be a little cavalier about the nurturing graduate students needed, and a little hard on those in his sway—perhaps he never realized how much of their hearts he held in his hand, for he himself had never been anyone's protégé, nor required any master. He was a rare bird in academia.

In 1952 Girard went to Duke University as an instructor. It was not then the world-class institution it has since become. "After many useless letters, one eventually bore fruit. I got a position as mediocre as that of Indiana. Still at the bottom of the scale,"[20] he wrote. Peyre finagled him an assistant professorship at Bryn Mawr for the following year—an indication of his influence.

Yet Girard's independence was not at all compromised by his appeal to Peyre, who helped him to an academic position, but didn't influence his work.

"René would never have experienced such a career in France," Benoît Chantre explained in an email. Chantre is president of Paris's Association Recherches Mimétiques, one of several organizations that have formed around Girard's work. He noted that French academic institutions would not have supported Girard's early writing and research. "That is why Girard is, like Tocqueville, a great *French* thinker—and a great *French* moralist—who could yet nowhere exist but *in the United States*. René 'discovered America' in every sense of the word: he made the United States his second country, he made there fundamental discoveries, he is a pure 'product' of the Franco-American relationship, he finally revealed the face of a universal—and not an imperial—America."

.   .   .

According to legend, René Girard came to America for a car—and he finally got one, though that would be years later. John Freccero told me the story of René and Martha buying their first new car while visiting Martha's mother back in Union City. The Midwestern salesman took a dim view of the French-American alliance that was in front of him. "The guy took Martha's mother aside and said, 'The mixing of races never works,'" Freccero recalled with a chuckle. He remembered the car—a 1956 Chevrolet, with dramatic fins in the back. Yellowish.

CHAPTER 5

Mankind Is Not so Kind

The past is never dead. It's not even past.

—William Faulkner

n March 1948, a French play created a small sensation when it opened on Broadway for its controversial nine-month run. Some called the drama "anti-American," and, in fact, it was flagged by censors in a number of cities, most notably Chicago. Although the play was born in Paris, its setting was America's South. Its action focused on a black man accused of a crime he didn't commit, and a lynching that was about to happen—themes that would become central to Girard's work, but in this case, expressed by another influential thinker, Jean-Paul Sartre:

> THE NEGRO: The streets are full of all kinds of white folks. Old ones, young ones; they talk without even knowing each other.
>
> LIZZIE: What does that mean?
>
> THE NEGRO: It means all I can do is run around until they get me. When white folks who have never met before, start to talk to each other, friendly like, it means some nigger's goin' to die.[1]

The woman is a New York hooker—the man called simply "The Negro" is begging for her protection. Both are the outliers of Southern society. The focus on social distinctions that would be a hallmark in Girard's work is prefigured here: "It's always bad luck when you see a nigger. Niggers are the Devil,"[2] says the senator's son, who is trying to frame the black man for the crime. The scapegoat assumes a totemic role—not merely a guilty mortal, but a supernatural harbinger of bad things to come, even the devil himself—and therefore the pretext for what unfolds in the drama.

In a sense, Sartre was biting the hand that was feeding him. From January to May 1945, he had toured America as a guest of the U.S. State Department, writing for Camus's Resistance newspaper, *Combat*, and also the leading Paris daily *Le Figaro*. But Sartre was revolted by the bigotry he observed in the South—for example, two black soldiers who were refused service in the dining car of a train. He published "What I Learned about the Black Problem" in *Le Figaro* a month after his return. The subject was one he had been mulling for awhile, since his reading of Faulkner. Both experiences shaped his play, *The Respectable Prostitute*.

"Men are running about with flashlights and dogs. Are they celebrating something?"[3] asks Lizzie at the play's denouement. Girard was a close reader of Sartre's works, and clearly the older existentialist writer was on a parallel path, reflecting on much of the same scenery. The Nobel laureate Faulkner was a common point of origin for both thinkers. But what they would make of their journey was startlingly in opposition.

·   ·   ·

"You can smell the lynching," Girard told me, after he had made a casual reference to Faulkner's writing. The comment was odd for its vehemence, and delivered with an uncommon level of disdain. He didn't elaborate, but a friend told me that his year, 1952 to 1953, deep in America's segregated South was purgatorial. Some say Girard's theories of scapegoating were born in the South—but that would go too far, selling him short for the intuitive genius that wove together a range of observations and research into a magisterial theory of mankind's condition, and its implications for our past, present, and future. These ideas weren't formulated until much later, after *Deceit, Desire, and the Novel* had made its mark on the literary world. "I spent a year in North Carolina, which wasn't the worst area in the South, but nevertheless completely segregated and quite conservative,"[4] he later remarked. Yet it wasn't all penitential: he was enchanted by the lush and verdant beauty of the place, too, which may only have increased the cognitive dissonance.

Girard was not prone to rhapsodize about nature in his writing, so his description of the South is a sharp departure. He confessed that the new appointment gave him more pleasure than Indiana, but the pleasure appears to be purely sensual, as he remembered "clay country surrounded by pine trees, in the heart of the vast region of tobacco, studded with large warehouses where the huge blonde leaves were carefully warehoused for drying."

> I have very vivid memories of this first stay in the South of the United States: the prodigious floral explosion of the spring, the paradisial aspect of its suburbs, houses as tidy as brand new toys, nestled in colorful bouquets and surrounded by foliage of a hundred years' standing; vast gardens behind the houses; a great bay window in the living room, overlooking sea-green tinted undergrowth ... It was like being in a science-fiction capsule, suddenly plunged into a dazzling world, with all the seductions of ours, but more intense and more ordered.

Yet his description of race relations is somewhat oblique and literary:

> But as soon as summer arrived, an overwhelming heat weighed on you like a curse, provoking an anguish that was not experienced as a purely physical phenomenon, and which I could not separate, in my mind, from the racial malaise that always hung over this country, and remained as it had been described by the great writers of the South, especially Faulkner. I am against the tendency of some critics to reduce everything to mere literary constructions: this literature was great because it captured a meaning that was really there, and which haunted everything precisely because the majority of men refused to come to grips with it. I remember the scandal of the Congress that never managed to ratify the law that would have automatically passed to the federal level, with the highest guarantees of real justice, for everything related to lynching.[5]

Had he arrived in North Carolina by train, Girard would have seen segregated waiting rooms and segregated bathrooms at the station. He would have heard the soft, Southern drawl of everyone, and the even more alien cadences of African Americans, with their extra layer of idiom and slang. The Indiana car salesman who warned about "mixed races" must have come to his mind with a renewed poignancy and less humor in a place where miscegenation was not only banned (as it was in much of the nation) but feared. He would not only have known about Jim Crow laws, but he would have had to cooperate with them. Jim Crow's reach was broad, and few public spaces were exempt from its rule.

How quickly everything disappears beneath the waves. Lynching is a told and untold story—well documented, but largely unknown to those born after the Civil Rights era, except in the roughest outlines. How many today remember? The violence that held a social order in place erupted occasionally to reveal the truth underneath the courteous and comfortable surfaces that Girard observed—as it did, for example, in the double lynching in Marion, Indiana, in 1930, only sixty miles from Bloomington, seventeen years before Girard's arrival. Foreigners had to accustom themselves to the bloody gash in American history that never healed, concealed by the conversations that could not happen, the silences that would not end.

Blacks were a ubiquitous presence in Durham, except in the academic life of Duke. In 1952, there were no black students, no black professors, no black trustees, no black administrators—only black maids, janitors, cooks, and other service personnel. Duke's Wallace Wade Stadium had separate bathrooms and a section reserved for "coloreds."

If you sat down to eat at the faculty club, you would be joined by white people, while black people cleared the dishes, fried the potatoes and cooked the beans, and showed you to your reserved table.

Duke was one of the last top-ranked universities to take down the walls of segregation. The first shake-up began in 1948, an era that was still marked by a virulent white supremacist movement, along with politicians who pandered to it or remained silent. Duke Divinity School students sent a petition to the administration for more inclusion, but it would be over a decade before the first black graduate student was admitted, and fifteen years before the first black undergraduates enrolled.

Why didn't he write or speak about it, other than in a few unpublished paragraphs? By contrast, Simone Weil spent only four months in her family's Upper West Side apartment on Riverside Drive, where New York City began to merge into black Harlem. She wrote to her friend, Dr. Louis Bercher, "I explore Harlem. I go every Sunday to a Baptist church in Harlem where, except for me, there's not a single white." She was fascinated by revivals, gospel preaching, spirituals—and she also attended daily mass at Harlem's Corpus Christi. Bercher claimed that "if she had stayed in America she surely would have become a black," not realizing, perhaps, that racial affiliation is not a voluntary club with fellow feeling as a *billet d'entrée*. But for the most part, Girard was as silent on America's racial divide, as he was on life in occupied Paris.

Girard once admitted that "this experience has assumed for me a primary importance. But that is another story."[6] Yet it's one he's never elaborated—except, of course, indirectly, in a series of books beginning with *Violence and the Sacred*, and continuing through *Things Hidden since the Foundation of the World, The Scapegoat, I See Satan Fall Like Lightning,* and others. Why the silence? One friend proposed a possible answer.

.   .   .

Girard once told me that Jean-Michel Oughourlian was his "best friend," and while I'm sure a number of people have held that title, the psychiatrist certainly played a unique role in his life, as a collaborator on one of Girard's major books, and as the person who extended Girard's work into the hard sciences.

I met him on an autumn day at his home in the sixteenth arrondissement, in an interview interrupted by an appointment in his office downstairs, and by a steady stream of phone calls from the clinic and patients. He's a neuro-psychiatrist and psychologist, formerly head of psychiatry at the American Hospital of Paris, among other prestigious positions at the University of Paris, the Sorbonne, Johns Hopkins, and others.

The apartment wasn't at all a bad place to wait as he attended to the various visitors and smartphone beeps. Its appointments are lavish, with red plush upholstery, chairs with delicate flowers embroidered on yellow satin, a gilded wood antique desk, green malachite tables, Oriental carpets, two Freudian-style couches, and silver, crystal, and *bibelots*. The glass-covered bookcases lining the walls are filled with leather volumes, including complete editions of Balzac, Stendhal, Voltaire, Gerard de Nerval, Saint-Simon's memoirs, and much else. Large mirrors in gilt frames multiply the effects.

As the apartment and the ongoing hubbub suggest, he's a larger-than-life extrovert, with a wide grin and slightly Asiatic tilt to his eyes. Tanned, solidly built, and energetic, he acknowledges the psychological perspective and privileges his seventy-plus years offer. "Everything I know I owe to René, I don't try to deny it," he said—typical of his sweeping, generous statements. A little later, he added, "I am virtually at the end of my active life, so now I can say whatever I want." It was an appropriate preamble for what followed.

Oughourlian said there were two pivotal moments in Girard's life—the second is well known, and will be addressed in a later chapter. The first, however, caught me off guard: he insisted that Girard told him he had witnessed a lynching in the South. According to Oughourlian, Girard had said point blank: "When I'm speaking about scapegoats, I know what the hell I'm talking about"—and he added that the context of the discussion clearly referred to a lynching. The occasion was remarkable and unique: "He mentioned it once—it's the only sentence he ever said." To my surprise, Oughourlian did not grill Girard more on the subject, and my own questions to the doctor quickly hit a dead end. On reflection, perhaps I understood why Oughourlian asked no follow-up questions: Girard's personality and natural reticence are such that most people find it easier to let the self-revealing moment slide. Surely he had misunderstood? Oughourlian was unequivocal and emphatic. It was part of his promise to "say whatever I want." Again, he stressed that this experience was absolutely *pivotal*, one of two such moments in Girard's life.

He would modify his position years later, saying he was less certain, while never explicitly denying his remarks, but I couldn't foresee that in 2012. His comment would send me on a journey through some very dark territory indeed. It began almost immediately that winter afternoon in Paris.

When I hinted at such a possibility to another of Girard's colleagues, Benoît Chantre, as we walked to a café from his office at the publishing house Flammarion, his face wrinkled with distaste, as if he had bitten into a lemon. No, not possible, he said, and I changed the subject quickly to distract from my apparent faux pas. Clearly, Chantre did not believe this story, yet I have often found a protective wall of admiring friends surrounds Girard, and no one wishes to pry into his private life—a deference shared even by those at much farther remove from him.

So I tried much later with another colleague, Sandor Goodhart of Purdue University, and he yelped with glee at the notion. There are no "observers" at lynchings, he told me, laughing. "If you're at a lynching, *you are one of the lynchers!*" By and large, true. Lynchers don't invite impartial bystanders. Lynchings are recounted by the lynchers, who excuse and exonerate themselves—or else they are not recounted at all. According to Girard's later writings, observers by their very presence break the necessary unanimity of the participants. Yet I remembered the photos of the *tondues,* and faces at balconies and windows of those not wholly caught up in the madness. Surely a few people happened to be at the wrong place, at the wrong moment. There were "observers," as well as participants.

Lynchings are not necessarily spontaneous events. In the United States, many happened by appointment, and no doubt attracted curiosity seekers, though it is still impossible to imagine Girard as one of them. These lynchings were ritualized events with a predetermined outcome, sometimes planned in advance and advertised in newspapers, drawing large crowds of white families, like the guillotine executions of the French Revolution. Men dressed up in their Sunday best for the celebration; children played and adults cheered as the drawn-out savagery continued with variations—dismembering the victims while they still lived, dousing their bodies with gasoline and setting them on fire, or otherwise torturing them to death. Grisly souvenirs were fashioned from the victim's body parts, and postcards were made from the photographs. Newspapers described the event afterward—the word "alleged," to indicate an accusation but not a proven legal judgment, appeared infrequently. The historical accounts make Sartre's "edgy" play about racism, *The Respectable Prostitute,* seem absurdly whitewashed and naive. The real-life accounts make for unspeakably depressing and repellent reading. But read I did.

I was still testing Oughourlian's comment about a "pivotal moment." He said it had happened in the South. I searched online for lynchings that occurred around the time that Girard had lived in North Carolina, or perhaps even later. The reading takes one back to a time when a black man was expected to remove his hat while talking to a white man, and direct eye contact was considered "insolent." Blacks had to step aside and bow their heads in the presence of whites. While white people were addressed as "mister," "sir," or "ma'am," the black man was addressed by first name, "boy," or even a slur. Any offense that blurred racial and class distinctions—the purchase of a new car perceived to be "above his situation," or an "uppity" salutation—could be grounds for almost anything. However, the violence had tapered off as society settled into an uneasy post-Emancipation stasis; during Girard's time in the South, from 1952 to 1953, it's unlikely he would have witnessed anything of this nature.

The occurrences of lynching and other racial violence rose again in 1954 after the *Brown vs. the Board of Education* decision, which scuttled "separate but equal" provisions for schools. A year later, a fourteen-year-old boy from Chicago, Emmett Till, was gruesomely tortured and murdered in Mississippi for whistling at a white woman. The case stunned the nation and mesmerized the international press. The child's bloated and mutilated body was found days later in the Tallahatchie River. The horror and pity evoked by the photos of the disfigured corpse at the funeral—his distraught mother insisted on an open casket—still affects us powerfully today, without our being direct witnesses, and at sixty years' distance. Women and African Americans were barred from the jury, which acquitted the case in an hour.

The men who murdered Emmett Till confessed to the killing in a 1956 *Look* magazine interview. They remained free and unrepentant until their deaths, decades later.

·   ·   ·

There's yet another reason to temper Oughourlian's claim, as he himself did in 2017. Girard himself denied that his strong intuitions about scapegoating began in the South. In a conversation with Maria-Stella Barberi in *Celui par qui le scandale arrive*, he said:

> RG: In the U.S., Fredric Jameson, a literary critic, thinks that my whole theory of lynching comes from my having spent a year in the American south.
> MSB: And do you also think so?
> RG: No, I don't think so. On the other hand, I recognize that a writer like Faulkner has amazing insights on this topic. I don't like to read Faulkner very much, his style is painful to me. But his great novels, like *Light in August*, contain a Christian symbolism that is also a symbolism of the emissary victim.[7]

I could find nothing that Jameson, a renowned Marxist political theorist as well as critic, had written on Girard, so I emailed him to ask. Jameson answered with a hasty one-line, lower-cased response: "sorry, i don't have any idea what he meant."[8] Yet Girard had brought up the topic, only to dismiss it—as he did on a second occasion as well. Within a year or so of the Barberi interview, Christian Makarian had asked a similar question in a *L'Express* interview,[9] and Girard had replied: "Some of my American friends say that I was influenced by my personal contact, during my younger days, with the racial violence in the United States," and then turned the conversation in a broader direction. Those anonymous "others" again—Girard keeps putting the suggestion in other people's mouths and minds, only to reject it, which I kept in mind as I pondered Oughourlian's "pivotal moment."

.   .   .

The post-Reconstruction South would seem to be a paradigmatic example of Girard's thesis about rituals and scapegoating, and about how lynchings bring people together when social distinctions are dissolving and conflict threatens to tear them asunder.

American lynching conforms in all details except one: no one is hiding these horrors. Girard typically describes mob murder as the hidden history of civilization, its archaic violence veiled by a thick layer of accumulated ritual and misty historic memory. If Girard's theory is true, why are these lynching stories so easy to recover? One obvious reason is that the stories are still fresh. Within a generation or two in a pre-literate society, almost everything may be mythologized or forgotten. Perhaps we shouldn't assume too quickly that it will be greatly different in our current technological era, marked by a dismaying historical amnesia and an almost willful ignorance.

While the story of American lynching has been documented by researchers, written in books, and featured on television, already the general public is largely ignorant of all but the most caricatured outlines of the history. Billie Holiday's "Strange Fruit" lyrics may be the most durable way a society remembers, after the books have turned to dust, after the archived film reels and cassettes disintegrate, and after all other exhausted technologies disappear:

Southern trees bear a strange fruit,
Blood on the leaves and blood at the root,
Black bodies swingin' in the Southern breeze,
Strange fruit hangin' from the poplar trees.

This history brought to light a prejudice of my own: I had assumed that the silence that often surrounds lynching throughout the ages was a symptom of shame and guilt. Girard's hypothesis about scapegoating makes a different suggestion: suppose the hiddenness simply reveals that the participants felt no need to explain or exonerate themselves? As Girard wrote, "the certainty of being right encourages them to hide nothing of their massacres."[10] Like the townspeople who heckled and jeered at the slender, silent Elizabeth Eckford clutching her textbooks and walking to the newly desegregated school, they had no idea how they would appear to future generations, in the photographs where their faces are forever frozen in hatred and malice.

These Americans are cast in the same accusatory mold as the leering participants who surround the humiliated *tondues* in liberated France—mob justice always seems to wear the same face. The assumption of guilt continues decades later: when I discussed these extrajudicial punishments for women in separate conversations with two French scholars, both women rebuffed my conclusions: "But they were really guilty!" said one, her eyebrows raised in surprise at my suggestion of injustice; "It's a matter of having standards," replied the other coolly.

Clearly, the story is far from over. The puzzling role of denial and self-justification in murder has been taken to new extremes in the last century. Historians note with astonishment the meticulous record-keeping in some of the most notorious regimes, whose functionaries had compartmentalized the meaning of their actions: the interrogators' detailed transcripts at the Lubyanka; the bureaucrats who logged the new arrivals into the Nazi concentration camps and listed their confiscated possessions with zealous precision. The scapegoat mechanism is breaking down, Girard would write—yes, but it still has a stronghold in the human heart, where the participants in great evils had no sense of wrongdoing when the reporters found them on their New World doorstep, where the former Nazi guards now live as pleasant housewives under different names."[11]

Similarly, the ability to form mobs has been exponentially boosted by technology. Of course, no one ever thinks that they are joining a mob—they are fighting to do what's right, they are standing up for themselves, they're keeping the riffraff out, protecting their families or the community. They are defending freedom, their rights, or the purity of white women. "It's always imitative behavior," Girard told me. "It's the formation of a crowd. Every time you add one, the move towards the unity of the mob becomes faster, it has more power and attraction." Girard is right, of course, that lynchers are pleased with their lynching and see no need for defense.

Perhaps ancient stories were "hidden" simply because these societies had no printing presses, newspapers, telephones, photography, or the World Wide Web—everything is exposed, not concealed, by modern technology with its tweet, its Instagram, its texting. Today our ad hoc lynchings don the most up-to-date technological disguises. The shaming of individuals for a casually tweeted aside or throwaway remark has resulted in lost reputations, lost jobs, bankruptcy, and violence[12]—a sort of symbolic lynching that is easier on the conscience. In our conversation, Oughourlian took the measure of the times: "People tend to lynch people easily—morally, symbolically, physically."

Much of the technological change occurred in Girard's lifetime—and it continues to accelerate us as we move into the twenty-first century. We live in an age where everything is preserved in an Akashic avalanche of images, sound recordings, and writings that are televised, texted, and live-streamed, coming to us 24/7. To delete anything is the new taboo. When everything is public, is there anything to hide? Is there any point to shame at all? To the Google generation, shame is as antique as five-inch floppy disks—paradoxically, even as we ritually shame each other on the social media, to the delight of a worldwide community.

Perhaps Girard was writing about the nature of such violence at the very point where it could no longer be hidden, regardless of the mind-set of the perps. Or will it find new and ingenious self-disguises?

.   .   .

On his parallel path through much of the same scenery of mob violence, Girard's French colleague in the Paris cafés took some of the same bricks to build an entirely different edifice. In 1960, Sartre wrote his second major philosophical treatise, *Critique of Dialectical Reason,* putting Marxism and existentialism in a lethal cocktail.

In apocalyptic and elevated language, Sartre deployed long, clotted sentences that, like a New Age promotional pamphlet, capitalize such words as "Other" and "Terror." He praised a "fraternity-terror" that originates in violence and *is* violence—even violence extolled, with "violence affirming itself as a bond of immanence." All served to enhance the fusion and power of the "group," in language ominously stripped of values; violence seems to have become an end in itself. His new thinking seemed to endorse and legitimate murder—even lynching, which he saw as "a *praxis* of common violence for the lynchers in so far as its objective is the annihilation of the traitor" who is suspected "rightly or wrongly." The traitor remains a member of the group, bound to it, as it "reconstitutes itself by annihilating the guilty member, that is to say, by *discharging all its violence* onto him." The traitor is, in fact, a sacrifice *to* the group, and the murder is a sort of secular sacrament.

Sartre also claimed that a lynching requires unanimity among the lynchers—"it is clear that anyone who shunned this fraternity would be suspect," he writes. But he does not observe, as Girard does, that individual conscience is diminished when people enact the will of a group. In fact, Sartre seems to side with the lynchers, and sees the violence as an actual good. It is not only "Terror against the traitor" but "a practical bond of *love* between the lynchers."

Murder as described by Sartre also has ritual elements. For example, the accused is "abused in the name of his own pledge and of the right over him which he acknowledged in the Others." Even more, the action is "a brutal re-actualization of the pledge itself and in so far as every stone that is thrown, every blow delivered, is a new affirmation of the pledge: whoever participates in the execution of the traitor reaffirms the untranscendability of group-being as a limit of his freedom and as his new birth, and he affirms it in a bloody sacrifice which, moreover, constitutes an explicit recognition of the coercive right of all over every individual and everyone's threat to all."[13]

In short, Sartre reflects on the same dynamic that had dismayed Girard—but he celebrates, rather than renounces, it.

.   .   .

Oughourlian's remarks preoccupied the rest of the visit to Paris. I was still not persuaded by Girard's contention that his theories came solely out of his reading and his head. If they had, they would not have resonated with so many people—people who may not have witnessed a lynching, but had experienced their own daily versions of scapegoating and expulsion, and may have been firsthand witnesses of violence in their communities. I suspected something in Girard, too, had been swayed by his observations and experiences of racial injustice in America, whatever form they took, and notwithstanding his demurrers.

But of course any opposition between Girard's theory originating "in his head" and in his firsthand or general experience is a false one. Even an abnormal sensitivity to violence could not explain the development of his theory. He studied human behavior as reflected in the greatest works of literature, and found in them a recurring analytical observation of the serious consequences of mimetic behavior. This discovery opened his eyes to the hidden dynamic of group violence. That's not to say, however, that what he observed in the world around him didn't sway the direction of his thinking.

Although he would begin his career with a book on a different subject, *Deceit, Desire, and the Novel,* scapegoating and sacrifice had already left its mark on him. Years later, Girard would say in an interview, "All that I did in *Violence and the Sacred* was to retrace, with hesitations, my own intellectual journey, which eventually brought me to the Judeo-Christian writings, though long after I had become acquainted with the victimage mechanism. In the course of the journey, I remained for a long period as hostile to the Judeo-Christian texts as modern orthodoxy could wish."[14]

At least one detractor has pounced on this as evidence of duplicity, since 1961's *Deceit, Desire, and the Novel* was clearly written under a Christian star and shows an authorial attitude that was not at all "hostile," years before *Violence and the Sacred.*[15] A more careful examination of Girard's life, however, shows that the sequence of his thinking did not follow the sequence of his publication. In other words, the passage from the interview suggests that something had stirred his thinking about the sacred, sacrifice, and scapegoats years before anyone knew of it, years before his conversion, too—perhaps before he himself was aware of the forces at work within him. (One might even note Girard's early discussion of the expulsion of Swann from the Verdurin salon in Proust's *Swann's Way*—linking the salon's behavior to the Inquisition and witch hunts.)[16]

When asked as recently as 2007 if spontaneous lynchings in the South might be examples of archaic sacrifice, Girard replied at length, again referring to Faulkner: "Yes, of course. You have to go to Faulkner to find the truth about this—to a novelist. Many people believe that Christianity is embodied by the South. I would say that the South is perhaps the least Christian part of the United States in terms of spirit, although it is the most Christian in terms of ritual. . . . there are many ways to betray a religion. In the case of the South, it is very obvious, because there is such a return to the most archaic forms of religion. You must define these lynchings as a kind of archaic religious act."[17] Flannery O'Connor may have sensed the same when she wrote, "I think it is safe to say that while the South is hardly Christ-centered, it is most certainly Christ-haunted."[18] She had been born and reared in Georgia, so its ways were bred in her bones; Girard was a Frenchman whose time in the South must have been as alien as life among the Amungme animists of Indonesia.

"The art of the novel is anthropology." Milan Kundera, the renowned Czech writer who was enthusiastic about Girard's work, agreed with Girard's thesis—and in a radio conversation Girard added another layer to Kundera's understanding of how we recognize lynching as lynching, underscoring the importance of texts, especially novels. A thousand years hence, he said, historians will believe the archival evidence as authoritative, not the record of literature—at least if they think the same way as historians today. "If a Faulkner novel survived, telling the truth that is not in the archives, but rather the truth as it is in the Faulkner novel—nobody would believe it," he said. "They would all be wrong, obviously. They would lack the essential thing, the social scheme, the psychological scheme, in terms of everyday life, which determined the country at this time. Then we would be able to prove in a very concrete way that the novel is the truth, and the rest is lies."[19]

Girard excavates beneath the text to find the truth, a process the social scientists viewed with skepticism. In the works he examined, patterns come to light that aren't immediately apparent, akin to the photographer whose developed photos reveal a murder in Antonioni's 1966 *Blow-Up*. As always, the relevant question is: do we see something this way that we hadn't seen before? Consider Margaret Mitchell's 1936 Pulitzer prize-winning bestseller, *Gone with the Wind*, an unintended homage to a South that *might have been*, in an alternative universe. Her stories of the nineteenth century, drawn from the memories of the oldest members of her Georgia community, portray a world in which the "darkies" are faithful, docile, second-class members of benevolent white families, and the "field hands" are the shiftless poor relations. The white women are pure, the black women are unmolested, the slaves not tortured or beaten, and the post-war Ku Klux Klan a force for justice. In the world Girard described to Kundera, with researchers a millennium or two hence poring over the American archives, one wonders how they would square Mitchell's account with the novels of Faulkner.

.   .   .

Oughourlian mentioned his cosmopolitan origins several times in those few hours we met in Paris. "I could never be a racist or a fanatic," he said. "I have a complex heredity—South America, the Caucasus." Exotic, even for Paris, a city that has no shortage of colorful backgrounds. He was born in Beirut and came to France at ten. His mother was from Bogota, his father a refugee. As a consequence, Oughourlian speaks six languages, including Spanish, English, French, Arabic, and Armenian.

The "Armenian" on the roster of languages reminded me of the question I hadn't yet asked: surely, I asked, the name "Oughourlian" is Armenian? Did the Armenian genocide have anything to do with his family's wanderings? His face darkened slightly, momentarily, and his voice dropped in pitch and shifted in timber. It was an astonishing turn in the conversation, as if an invisible abyss had opened in the elegant room, beneath the malachite tables and the Oriental carpets.

His grandfather and most of his family were massacred by Turks in the genocide—his grandfather, I was told later by a mutual friend, with particular savagery. The French Red Cross took in his grandmother as a refugee. Hence, his father grew up in Lebanon, which was French territory. It was, he said, a case of a contagion of violence, akin to the Jews and the Nazis.

He answered a question he had skirted earlier, during a discussion of Girard's conversion. Oughourlian added that he is Catholic, too, but his explanation was unexpected: "Seventeen members of my family were killed because they were Christians. I cannot betray them."

Is the absence of evidence itself evidence? Oughourlian's own life exemplifies this principle—for this story and these people appear nowhere in his anecdotes, articles, and books. Why? "Each and every one of us hasn't written about the things that are most important," he said. "Mankind is not so kind."

While he had been out of the room, responding to one of the smartphone beeps, I had thumbed through one of his recent books on a table and found this: "The death of the victim creates a silence of unusual intensity because it follows the shouts of the lynch mob and the screams of the victim. This silence, it seems to me, is the beginning of consciousness."[20] It was a remarkable passage, and I remembered it. I bought the book when I returned to the United States.

You scratch the surface of a life, and it bleeds. Violence is everywhere and we don't see it, on the bus, at the workplace, in the family. Ask a few questions, and the stories surface. I remember visiting Argentina, when everyone I spoke to seemed to have a relative who had been tortured or "disappeared." One in six people in Poland were killed during World War II—in Warsaw, death and violence are beneath every step you take in the reconstructed city. Girard did not get a special exemption—he, too, is a witness of violence, whether in wartime France or in the Jim Crow South, whether as a direct witness or as a reader of newspapers, or simply as a listener to the stories of others. Just like the rest of us. I suspected that Oughourlian's contention was a vestige of his own family history, rather than a clue that reveals anything about Girard's experiences. What is unthinkable to most of us was not only "thinkable" in his family—it had happened. As it had happened to so many people, in many societies, throughout time.

In the years after the visit, I emailed Oughourlian twice, allowing him the opportunity for clarification or even denial, if he wished. I received no answer, and expected none, really.

Finally, I called his cellphone. By that time, he had retired and was serving as the ambassador of the Sovereign Military Order of Malta to the Republic of Armenia. By that time also, Girard had been dead for over year, which changed the landscape he had left among the living. Yes, Oughourlian said, he had received my emails, but wasn't sure how to respond anymore. "I'm not 100 percent sure. It was 47 years ago," he explained. Did Girard say that he had actually seen a lynching, or merely that he had read about them, that he felt lynching was in the air in this alien and racially paralyzed country? ("You can smell the lynching," Girard had told me.) Oughourlian was hesitant, and couldn't pin down his memory. He said he didn't want to appear to be exploiting Girard's memory after his death.

We tailor our memories to time and to audience. As Girard would argue, this also holds true for the crime of lynching itself. The lynchers, after all, tell the story to exonerate and even ennoble themselves. But it's true for all of us, in all circumstances surrounding elusive memory. Time softens, distorts, and sometimes exaggerates memory—but was the "true" memory his ambiguity, or the unambiguous statement of a few years earlier?

I had wondered over the years if Oughourlian's own family history had inclined him to read into Girard's comment something that wasn't there—if his interpretation wasn't, subconsciously, a way to honor his own. If so, with these pages may I honor them, too, even in the absence of evidence.

I finally found the lynching incident Oughourlian may have been talking about—almost accidentally, when reading a *Der Spiegel* interview with Girard. He was asked if he, personally, had been a victim of violence. He replied, "Just once in my life, I experienced such a thing as violent threat, in the days when there was still segregation in Alabama. We took a picture of blacks and whites together at a bar counter, and suddenly the people ganged up against us."[21] While the German phrasing in the article is very strong, I doubt Girard meant more than that the people became hostile and confrontational. To my knowledge, this was the only time he mentioned such an incident, and no one else seems to have mentioned it, either. Given the Jim Crow laws of the era, the mixed gathering may have been illegal, and the group might have been terrified.

.   .   .

Girard had quickly rectified his misstep at Indiana: after receiving his PhD, he had started writing articles about literature and historiography. But the slow wheels of academic publication meant that the publication of "L'histoire dans l'oeuvre de Saint-John Perse," in *Romantic Review* (1953), "Franz Kafka et ses critiques," in *Symposium* (1953), and "Valéry et Stendhal," in *Publications of the Modern Language Association of America* (1954) occurred long after he had left Indiana.

Girard's fellow Avignonnais Henri Peyre came to his rescue, as he did for so many others. After Girard's single year as an instructor at Duke, Peyre helped him to an appointment as assistant professor at Bryn Mawr in Pennsylvania. Girard held the post until his offer from Johns Hopkins in 1957, which began one of the catalytic periods of his life, as we shall see in the next chapter. For some perspective on racial relations in the era that many have forgotten or are too young to remember, here's a letter that Peyre wrote a year after Girard left for Bryn Mawr, to a colleague, Whitney Griswold:

My dear Whit: We have appointed, as assistant-in-instruction in the French Department, a negro, Alvis Tinnin, who has lived in France, studied French thoroughly, then been admitted to our Law School here, changed to MAT in French, received his MAT, then started his studies for a Ph.D. in French.

He is a fine man & a gentleman, tactful, dynamic. . . . I wanted, however, to say a word to you about this appointment, in case you are questioned on it. I also wanted to be sure there will be no embarrassment to anyone or to you & Mrs. Griswold if we bring Tinnin & his wife to your tea for the new members of the Faculty on October 24th. If you foresaw any embarrassment, just let me know & of course I'll be discreet on it & find a subtle way to leave that new colorful colleague out.[22]

CHAPTER 6

The Pleasure of His Company

All desire is a desire for being.

—René Girard

In those days, they called it "*the* Hopkins." Girard's first home in the United States had been in America's heartland, Indiana, but Johns Hopkins University was the place where he was to leave a permanent intellectual mark on the century with his provocative and seminal debut book, *Deceit, Desire, and the Novel.* The 1961 book, published initially as *Mensonge romantique et vérité romanesque* in France, was hardly the only attempt to study the nature of desire, but Girard was the first to insist that the desire we think is original and objective is, in fact, borrowed from others, that it is "mimetic." In this, he was giving a strong reading of Plato, Aristotle, and Hegel, but with a new twist.

Girard had an enduring affection for Johns Hopkins—indeed, everyone who was there during that golden era seems to recall the place with fondness—and returned even after he had been lured away to Buffalo for seven years. He arrived as associate professor in 1957, left in 1968, and came back to an endowed chair at Johns Hopkins in 1976.

"Johns Hopkins had a great tradition," Girard said. "It had been created following the German model of a graduate school. It was there that I met Leo

Spitzer and French literary critics such as Georges Poulet and Jean Starobin-
ski, as well as the Spanish poet Pedro Salinas."[1] Milton Eisenhower, a brother
of the U.S. president, had assumed the presidency of the university in 1956,
the year before Girard's arrival, and would hold the post through much of
Girard's stay.

The humanities at Johns Hopkins had been a haven for refugee scholars
fleeing war or impending war in Europe. It welcomed Nathan Edelman of
France, Ludwig Edelstein of Germany, and influential literary critic Leo
Spitzer of Austria.

One would have thought it was heaven. Consider the impression the
university and the city made on Girard's Scottish colleague, Lionel Gossman,
in 1958:

> As we drove into Baltimore, I immediately took to this city with its
> human-scale row houses and its luxuriant semi-tropical vegetation burst-
> ing through every available crack in brick or concrete. I was surprised and
> delighted by the elegant sweep of Charles Street as it rises northward from
> the harbor toward Mount Vernon Square, with its handsome monument
> to Washington and its ornamental Barye sculptures, and then further on
> to Homewood and the Johns Hopkins campus.
>
> That first impression never left me and very soon I was showing off
> Baltimore architecture to visiting colleagues—the superb galleried Library
> of the Peabody Institution, a miracle of cast iron, the orderly splendor of
> Latrobe's Cathedral, the idyllic landscaping of Olmsted's planned suburb
> of Roland Park, the simple good taste of the acres and acres of modest
> brick row houses, with their scrubbed front steps (or stoops) and their
> luxuriant back gardens. I remember in particular Sir Nicolas Pevsner's
> delight when I showed him the elegant industrial design of the Baltimore
> and Ohio Railroad's round house and the silence that came over the poet
> Yves Bonnefoy as we stood before the modest grave of Edgar Allan Poe on
> which the famous verses of Mallarmé are inscribed.[2]

Gossman told me that for him, Johns Hopkins meant "getting away
from the grayness of war and postwar period"—just as Indiana had rescued
Girard. "That's perhaps why I responded to it so much, it was exciting and
what I longed for. I still think of these Johns Hopkins years," he said. "It was

an institution willing to take risks. Tremendously open. The emphasis on intellectual things was overwhelming."

The struggle to keep Johns Hopkins in top rank was daunting. The Romance Languages department was so small that no PhD was granted in the five years between John Freccero's in 1958 and Marilyn Yalom's in 1963. The department had five faculty members, compared with Yale's thirty-five. "The dedication to our work was, for me, beyond anything I had experienced at Wellesley or Columbia or the Sorbonne," said Yalom, who would arrive in 1957 and become René's first graduate student (Eric Gans, who would write extensively about Girard's work, would arrive a few years later in 1961). "We were true believers. The life of Johns Hopkins was the life of a scholar," she told me. You couldn't go out to see the latest Doris Day flick—if you took time off from your studies, the film had to have the gravity of Ingmar Bergman, she explained; anything less serious was irresponsible. She was only half joking. Despite the customary chasm between students and faculty in that era, she recalls a cordiality and an *esprit de corps,* with students regularly invited to faculty homes. The friendship with Girard would continue at Stanford, where Yalom became one of the founders of feminist studies.

Girard was wound through her experiences and memories, as a presence, as well as a friend: "There's a depth in René—a depth of loyalty, a capacity for love, that goes along with his being all of a piece," she recalled. "I knew him when he wasn't a big star. I felt within him—we all did—a special intelligence, a privilege to be in his company." Marilyn Yalom is now a popular and acclaimed author, but back then she was a harried graduate student and mother of several children, living in the housing assigned to young psychiatrists doing their residencies at Johns Hopkins Hospital. (Her husband Irvin Yalom would eventually become one of the nation's leading psychotherapists and a lauded author in his own right.) In those days, she longed for her mentor's guidance and attention, and she didn't always get it. "He was so intense and seemed to have so many ideas floating in his head. He was pretty formidable," she said. "It's not an accident he has a large, leonine head. It's symbolic of a lot going on inside."

At one point Girard told Yalom he was discouraged in his teaching because his students "didn't throw the ball back" in discussions. She suggested his students found him intimidating, though he was never harsh. She described his manner as "courtly" and "gentlemanly," though he was not heavily involved in her scholarly work. Perhaps because his own path through academia had been unconventional, he simply didn't understand how much help others might welcome, or perhaps, as others commented, he never took academic rituals to heart. "He's delightfully but unshakably ironic," said John Freccero. "He doesn't take anyone seriously. Is there anyone he takes seriously?"

Students at considerable distance could feel the heat. One faculty member recalled a revealing anecdote: Girard was going down the stairs, while two graduate students were climbing up. Girard had absentmindedly forgotten the name of his student, but nevertheless politely stopped for a moment to ask in a friendly sort of way, "Comment va la thèse?" The student mumbled a reply, but as he continued walking with his friend, he muttered to her, "Girard is crowding me." Crowding him, although Girard couldn't even recall the name.

The story was told by Richard Macksey, who had just gotten his PhD when Girard arrived and would begin teaching at Hopkins the following year. He went on to become a legendary polymath and bibliophile at Hopkins. (He has one of the largest private libraries in Maryland, with well over seventy thousand books and manuscripts, many of them very rare indeed.) The student in the anecdote was his wife Catherine. Both the Mackseys would become close friends of the Girards. "René frightened people. It seems odd to me," he recalled. "I think they felt he would take over." The impression was not entirely unfounded: "The department was a hotbed of change, with visitors who did disturb the peace a little. And many of them because of René."

Freccero reminisces dreamily about the camaraderie and the lunchtime get-togethers with Girard and others several times a week—he and Girard discovered buttermilk, a novelty that seemed to amuse both of them. Together they found the only restaurant in Baltimore that served snails. "I loved René so much I learned to drink buttermilk," he repeated. "God, I love Johns Hopkins—I can see and taste and smell it. We had so much fun there."

The close-knit friendship over sandwiches and buttermilk became a wider fraternity. Freccero said they intended to "puncture the balloon of right-wing pomposity." Gossman told me the group enlarged to include "the younger Turks in the department," and he was among them. "We laughed our heads off—we thought we were kings of the castle." Girard was at the center of it all, the ringleader again: "He exuded a kind of joy, he was often

laughing and smiling . . . We made fools of the old timers, laughed the posi-
tivists out of town. *It was all very joyful.* Young people in revolt. This was long
before 1968. We were going to throw off all this old stuff." Among the targets
for their revelry was Girard's own École des Chartes, which "stood for all this
positivist scholarship that he had no time for."

The sensible and generous Nathan Edelman chaired the Romance Languages department, but Girard was already its driving force with his restless
daemon and high-octane exuberance. While most think that Girard was
thrown into the limelight by his first book in 1961, *Deceit, Desire, and the
Novel,* Gossman said he was in ascendency long before its publication. "Yes,
we were all tremendously attracted to René before the book came out," he
recalled. "I thought of him as fearless. He had a tremendous self-confidence,
in the best sense. He knew what he was, what he wanted, and what he
thought. He never felt threatened by people who had different ideas. . . . He
was a very powerful intellectual presence. Not in a dried-out way—but a very
lively physical presence, a big guy with a big head."

"We were so enthralled by him. We desperately wanted his approval."

.   .   .

The Girards eventually settled in My Lady's Manor just before Christmas
in 1961—a charming eighteenth-century historic district that developed
around a water-powered grist mill. The district, with its horse farms and old,
stately homes set back from the country roads, is about twenty minutes' drive
from Baltimore, just north of the city. "The Baltimore countryside is very
lovely," Gossman recalled. "It was not a big fancy house, a modest house, but
very pleasant." He recalled that invitations to visit were "such a tremendous
honor that when somebody else started getting invited and you weren't, it
was painful."

The Girards' children look back on My Lady's Manor fondly—especially, said son Daniel, after the more gritty urban experience of living in Baltimore itself. He recalled the parents of his Baltimore friends, some of them
World War II veterans, wearing white undershirts, smoking, and drinking
beer. My Lady's Manor, by comparison, was a rustic idyll. It hadn't yet been
subdivided, so hundreds of acres of undeveloped land provided seclusion
and places for children to explore. Spring was marked by the first croak of
a bullfrog in nearby Gunpowder Creek; daughter Mary recalled watching

pollywogs morph into frogs, and Daniel recalls taking care of animals in the neighborhood—pigs and basset hounds.

The link with Avignon continued: for a dozen years or so, Girard taught an accredited summer school program that he had launched with Michel Guggenheim in 1962, under the sponsorship of Bryn Mawr. The teachers in the school were not necessarily Bryn Mawr or even American faculty, but included their counterparts at French universities.

Martha showed me a photo of the cottage they had rented for some months on Villeneuve-lès-Avignon, across the Rhône from the old city, a charming stucco home with sea green shutters and a tile roof. The seasonal *mistral* was so strong, she recalled, that the curtains trembled even when the doors and windows were shut. In the photo the two sons—Martin, born in 1955, and Daniel, born in 1957—huddle together on the front doorstep. Their sister Mary was born on that island and joined them in the small home in 1960. The family was complete.

In another photo, the paterfamilias, Joseph Girard, sits in a chair on the patio outside the house. He is eighty in the photo, said Martha. The resemblance with his son is striking—unlike the photo I had seen earlier in the Vaucluse archives, where the head is in profile. Here, the dark, deep-set, cavernous eyes recall the son's, but they are set in a face that is solidly square, rather than the long rectangle of Girard's. He seems happy in the sunshine, amid the growing family. He would be dead within two years.

.   .   .

I met John Freccero at Stanford decades ago, when I attended his lectures on Dante—I remembered a potent concoction of urbanity, insight, and endless erudition. He assigned the multi-volume Charles Singleton prose translation of *The Divine Comedy,* urging us to buy the epic poem and commentary by Singleton as the definitive translation in English. Because of him, I still regularly refer to the thick gray volumes I found secondhand at Black Oak Books in Berkeley. "Why not a *poetic* translation?" a plaintive voice had queried from somewhere at the back of the large lecture hall. Freccero volleyed back with an appealing smile, "Because you should never give up on learning the Italian."

He disappeared from my life after the course was over, and returned when I realized that he had been a friend of Girard's for nearly sixty years. He was a pivotal figure during Girard's time at Johns Hopkins. Years later, Freccero helped bring Girard to Stanford. His observations were persuasive, and helped shape my understanding of the theorist I knew only in his last decade.

Girard acknowledged the role of two *Dantisti* in his life during these years: Freccero was finishing his PhD with Singleton, who had just returned from Harvard to Johns Hopkins. Singleton helped advance Girard's promotion after the publication of *Deceit, Desire, and the Novel* and Freccero introduced Girard to Dante. The influence went both ways: Freccero had just finished his dissertation on angelology in Dante, and was very interested in Girard's new book. Both found a lot to discuss in each other's academic endeavors. While no one, to my knowledge, has commented on Dante's hold on Girard, I sense a thin thread of Florentine gold running through Girard's life and his work. Certainly Freccero would have had a hand in making it so.

By the time I met Freccero again, the urbane and dapper man who had given polished presentations of *The Divine Comedy* had given way to the harsher realities of time. A quarter-century later, during his summer sojourn in Palo Alto, the octogenarian was recovering from hip surgery, his fifth, and moved carefully and uneasily around his pleasant and spacious home. The College Terrace dwelling is typical of the many houses built here in the 1960s and 1970s: full of light from the large windows and glass doors leading to the patio. A photo of his late wife Diane, who had been on the dance faculty at Stanford, is in the entryway—a Californian with long wavy blonde hair and a dancer's black leotard. He still grieves. But the voice is the same, though it strikes a more tragic note than I recall. Age, perhaps, and the depredations of recent surgery.

As we settled on the couch, next to the wall of glass looking out onto a patio, he pensively observed the hummingbirds. They always return to the same branch on the same tree, he said—"faithful, in their way."

John Freccero is an endearing and spellbinding presence; the younger cockiness has mellowed to a mélange of immense passion, unbearable personal charm, and an unfathomable, unassuageable anguish—all three teetering in each moment in a precarious balance. Our conversations were fueled with his weapon of choice, Bombay Sapphire gin martinis in the late afternoon.

He was eager and enthusiastic to talk about Girard, a colleague and friend, and insisted he could talk about him for weeks and weeks: "I remember when he was an assistant professor . . . We got word that there was a hot-shot guy from Bryn Mawr, snapping the whip." He repeatedly referred to his love for Girard. "I think of him constantly," he said. "He's a wonderful man. No man in my life has been more important. It's embarrassing to love René—what the hell, everybody loves René."

Friends say that nine-tenths of Freccero's conversations are about Dante, and the same could be said for his mentor Charles Singleton, a towering and inescapable presence at Johns Hopkins in that era. He tends to be overshadowed in people's memories by the tsunami of postmodern superstars and theorists who came after—though he was perhaps a more durable giant, commonly considered the father of Dante studies in America, so that by the mid-1980s, nearly all *Dantisti* belonged to the Singletonian school. The Oklahoma-born professor was an unlikely Dante scholar—"a farm guy at heart," said Macksey, adding that Singleton possessed a shyness that was sometimes mistaken for arrogance. Moreover, he was an atheist drawn to Dante's message of spiritual reclamation, which reverberates even in a secular world, centuries later. Girard's friend, Robert Harrison, who had also studied with Singleton, said that the maestro had insisted that "the fiction of the comedy is that it is not a fiction." Harrison recalled St. Peter grilling Dante on faith in the twenty-fourth canto of the Paradiso. "When it comes to the Christian faith, Singleton could tell the alloy and weight, but he did not have the coin in his purse."[3] He did not seem to miss it.

An eighteenth-century farmhouse and vineyard in Carroll County became the wellspring of the Singletons' hospitality and scholarship. The devoted couple were childless—so the whole Hopkins community was taken in as family. In the spring, wine would be chilled outside; in the summer, the bumper crop of vegetables would appear at the Hopkins YMCA; in the fall, at harvest time, Charles Singleton would teach *Paradiso* with red-stained fingers. The grapes that he and his beloved wife Eula had grown were bottled and sold under the label "Est! Est!" after the Montefiascone wine region; it was the only wine made in Maryland. Everyone would be invited to a harvest festival, where graduate students would stomp on grapes and Eula would make vast cauldrons of spaghetti. In his classes, his stories would sparkle in Tuscan or English, and his lengthy citations would flicker from French to Italian to English from memory, without hesitation.

The Girards spent many happy days with the Singletons on the farm, including forays on the little pond with the tiny boat that had been named "Le Bateau Ivre," after the Rimbaud poem of that name.

"I *had* to love Johns Hopkins," said Freccero. After all, he said, Singleton was there—and Singleton was everything. Although the New York City boy had learned Dante on his immigrant grandfather's lap, staring at the images of *The Inferno,* Dante wasn't in Freccero's crosshairs as an area of academic study until, as a graduate student, he heard Belgian literary critic Georges Poulet's talks on Dante, which "totally seduced me,"[4] he later admitted. Poulet, the author of the four-volume *Studies in Human Time* and at that time head of Johns Hopkins's Romance Languages department, encouraged Freccero's new direction. He was widely considered Singleton's intellectual heir, a closeness that nurtured and then wounded him.

Freccero is proud of his working-class origins, and allows himself another excursion in a highly digressive conversation. He told me about a long-ago exchange with a French-born professor. "From what class are you?" he was asked. "Why, the very lowest," Freccero answered. The Frenchman was genuinely perplexed. "Your achievement, how do you explain it?" Freccero scoffed at the memory, then was thoughtful. *"People are afraid that all people are equal."* The words would haunt me later, as I studied the chapters of Girard's first book.

Freccero recalled Girard's other friendships, including the volatile and energetic young graduate student, and later colleague, Eugenio Donato, who would have an important role in Girard's life. Although initially Gossman's graduate student, he quickly attached himself to Girard. "Donato loved him tremendously. He was a passionate guy," recalled Freccero. Donato was born in Cyprus, of an Italian father and an Armenian mother, and raised, at least during his early years, in Alexandria. He spoke a broken Italian and French and a potpourri of other languages, none of them perfectly. He had no Mother Tongue, really. For Girard, Donato was a link to the intellectual world in Paris from which Girard was estranged—Girard was "not a guy to go out to the café all night and shoot the breeze," said Freccero. But Donato was precisely such a person, and in that way he increased Girard's recognition and reputation.

Macksey also recalled Donato as "a junior person in a very senior department," but one who was a game changer nonetheless. Donato was teaching classes on Claude Lévi-Strauss, Jacques Lacan, and structuralism very early.

"René was developing as René, and Eugenio was developing as an interpreter of these people," he explained. "As the French say, he 'had a nose.' He knew where the cooking was taking place." Even Donato's histrionic, operatic side was an asset. "I found him a wonderful colleague. His enthusiasms were contagious. He had more villains in stock—that was fun, too."

"Eugenio was polemical. René was never polemical. He understood the role of good academic battles, which René never did. To have Eugenio as a younger colleague was important," explained Macksey. "He and René were very close. Eugenio was richer for having René in his life, and René's life was richer for having him."

As always, Freccero added emotional insight and nuance to the portrait. He reminded me of what I had already observed—beneath the warmth and courtesy, Girard's cool and measured nature keeps everything in proportion. Yet in friendship, he has often been attracted to people of passionate nature—Freccero and Donato among them. "Eugenio loved René so fiercely," said Freccero. "Girard loves everybody, but there are no great loves in his heart. If there were any, Donato comes close." The collegial love fests were inevitably unequal. Freccero, who freely admits he was smitten, found that Girard "is the least needy person I have met."

"What one seeks in a love is some sign of one's uniqueness, and you don't get that from René. He loves you—but don't get excited; he loves many others, too."

■   ■   ■

The problem with attempts to describe Girard's work—including this one—is that they are less rhetorically commanding and confident, less elegantly pugnacious and provocative, less witty and wise than Girard's own writing, which serves as a sharp Toledo blade piercing reader expectations. Others have written shelves of books about his work—and yet if an interested person should come to me asking how to approach Girard's oeuvre, I would refer him or her to *Deceit, Desire, and the Novel* rather than secondary sources and interpreters.

The prominent Marxist theorist Lucien Goldmann is a case in point. His labored discussion of Girard's first book in *Towards a Sociology of the Novel*[5] offers an intriguing comparison with the works of Hungarian literary historian and critic György Lukács. For Girard, as well as for Lukács, "the novel is the story of a degraded search (which he calls 'idolatrous') for authentic values, by a problematic hero, in a degraded world."[6] But from there we wander into the weeds of abstraction.

By contrast, *Deceit, Desire, and the Novel: Self and Other in Literary Structure* remains practical, lucid, and focused on the novels at hand and what they reveal about human nature.

At the heart of the book is our endless imitation of each other. Imitation is inescapable—it's how we learn, it's why we don't eat with our hands, it's why we communicate beyond grunts. When it comes to metaphysical desire—which Girard describes as desires beyond simple needs and appetites—*what* we imitate is vital, and *why*, and can be a symptom of our ontological sickness. While he did not coin the word "mimesis"—Erich Auerbach predates him, along with Aristotle and even Plato—certainly much of its usage in our contemporary culture comes from René Girard.

The "Romantic lie" Girard attempts to dismantle is the myth of personal autonomy, the "authentic self" so dear to thinkers from Rousseau onward. The hero wants something, and it is really "he" who wants it—unaffected by others, as if he were not also a slave to public opinion and the approbation of friends and family. Girard saw an inevitable third in these transactions—the one who modeled the desire, who taught us to have it.

Central to the novels he examined is the protagonist who aspires to freedom but is not free at all, since he (or she) worships the "mediator," living or dead, whose desires the characters adopt as their own. "The object is to the mediator what the relic is to a saint,"[7] Girard wrote. Julien Sorel adores Napoleon, and keeps the emperor's memoirs hidden under his mattress; Emma Bovary worships the fashionable ladies in Paris, and takes lovers in imitation of them.

"Even the most passionate among us never feel they truly are the persons they want to be," he explained later in a Stanford essay. "To them, the most wonderful being, the only semi-god, always is someone else whom they emulate and from whom they borrow their desires, thus ensuring for themselves lives of perpetual strife and rivalry with those whom they simultaneously hate and admire."[8] We want the object because we believe it will make us akin to the admired rival, a false god we come to fear and hate as well as revere and emulate. Rivalry becomes obsession, enduring even after the *objet du désir* has been knocked out of the tennis court.

Wagner's *Ring Cycle* provides one example: "The gold is *nothing*, clearly, since it's the ray of sunshine that alights on it and transfigures it. And yet the gold is *everything,* since it's what everyone is fighting over; it's the fact of fighting over it that gives it its value, and its terror,"[9] Girard explained in an interview.

Girard describes two kinds of mediation. In "external mediation," the mediator exists outside the world of the hero, and remains a remote idol—the stories of Amadís de Gaul for poor Don Quixote, or, the knightly tales for the *Inferno's* Francesca da Rimini. These forms of imitation are delusional enough, but they are unlikely to foster conflict and violence by their very nature. All hell breaks loose, however, in internal mediation where the mediator is alive and within the sphere of the hero, and hence capable of resistance and reciprocity. Imitation turns into rivalry, and adoration alternates with hatred. The protagonist must "rescue" the beloved from the antagonist, or kill the king to attain the throne that he feels rightfully belongs to him. Or she longs for the admiration of the clique that mistakenly extols the rival, and not her—she deserves tenure, or the Pulitzer Prize, more than the other. Eventually, the rivalry is so strong that the coveted object disappears—the shuttlecock is batted into the bleachers, so to speak—and the rivalrous doubles resemble each other more and more in their mutually destructive "Spy vs. Spy" antics—all the while insisting that it's their differences that set them at odds.

"The romantic is a prisoner of the Manichaean opposition between Self and Others and thus always works on one plane only. Opposite the empty and faceless hero who says 'I' is the grinning mask of the Other. Absolute exteriority is opposed to absolute interiority."[10] For that reason, "The romantic work is a weapon aimed at others."[11] From these apparently straightforward observations flow so much else. The book, ostensibly a case study of five authors, reaches beyond literature to talk about our psychology and the cultural problems of our world, including fashion, advertising, manners, propaganda, and intellectual fads.

Deceit, Desire, and the Novel already bears Girard's signature writing style—formal yet engaging and approachable, erudite, incisive, and masterful—it's the book that would make his reputation. I found the book rather addictive, though *Library Journal* called it "a highly complex critique of the structure of the novel," and added a warning: "As may be expected, the interpretations are highly psychological, the argument philosophical, and the intellectual footwork, dazzling; but for the reader, the going is slow, and conviction, grudging." [12]

For many, however, it was a revelation. "You can always trust a Frenchman to view the world as a ménage à trois," wrote Andrew Gallix in *The Guardian,* writing about Girard's theory of mediated desire. "Discovering *Deceit, Desire, and the Novel* is like putting on a pair of glasses and seeing the world come into focus. At its heart is an idea so simple, and yet so fundamental, that it seems incredible that no one had articulated it before."[13]

Deceit, Desire, and the Novel does a deep dive into a handful of authors—Cervantes, Stendhal, Proust, Dostoevsky, Flaubert—and into a few works in particular (principally *Don Quixote, The Red and the Black, The Possessed,* and *Remembrance of Things Past*). These authors, Girard claims, not only saw the mimetic disease in themselves, but found the antidote. While it's far more than a case study, those not already familiar with the five authors he studies are likely to be left out in the cold. Although he claims "all" great literature is constructed this way, in fact the subset he considers is small and focused. He makes no attempt to shoehorn everything into his theory—and he's making larger points about our culture, at least as important as his literary reflections.

How much was Girard cherry picking? And was the genre he was critiquing already exhausted before he set pen to paper? Literary fashions change faster than human nature, after all. French literary critic Walter Strauss asked the question in *Comparative Literature*:

Professor Girard clearly aligns himself with the antiromantics, and consequently rejects all modern nihilism; indeed, his remarks on contemporary writing tend to be hostile (though often perceptive). I am afraid his quick dismissal of Nietzsche prevents him from carrying his valuable explorations beyond Proust into the 'age of suspicion.' But precisely here I would wish that the study had dealt with Kafka and possibly Beckett; does not the entire process of mediation, and with it the possibility of 'vérité romanesque,' totally collapse with Kafka? And is there not in Kafka and in Beckett an urge to surmount desire, or to renounce it? The sheer force of Professor Girard's convictions prompts me to raise these questions, not in the spirit of cavil, but in the spirit of homage to the splendid achievement of the critical intelligence exemplified by this book.[14]

However, he overlooks how Girard dealt specifically with Beckett, as well as Camus and Sartre, in one of his final chapters; their protagonists, he argued, are often modern incarnations of the Underground Man, in whom metaphysical desire is even more successfully buried under a false cloak of autonomy. "Many superficial resemblances can be traced between Dostoevsky and other recent fiction. In both there is the same hatred of Others, and the same radical disorder, the same 'polymorphism' in the collapse of all bourgeois values."[15] Kafka is discussed half a dozen times throughout *Deceit, Desire, and the Novel.*

Closer to home, Johns Hopkins's distinguished existentialist philosopher and theologian Ralph Harper in the *Journal of Religion* tackled the spiritual implications of Girard's work. Given how much these issues were to preoccupy Girard in future years, Harper is worth quoting at length:

> He suggests that all five novelists were participants in the 'death of God' drama of our civilization. Not only is it true that the heroes of the novels imitate each other rather than Christ, the real point is that they imitate while pretending to believe that spontaneity, autonomy, and originality are the new values of emancipated man. And each in his own way has discovered—however consciously is another matter—the false promise of metaphysical autonomy and therefore has felt it necessary to take desire—imitate someone else—in order to go on pretending that God is really dead and man god. And so when we remark on the absurdity of mediated desire, we are really noticing the pathos of metaphysical disappointment.

He concluded, "To be made uneasy by this thorough analysis is probably one of the consequences of the pervasiveness of the disease, which Girard calls contagious, and a testimony to the psychological and metaphysical acumen of the author of this fascinating book."[16]

A new author could not have asked for more. In the years since, many have misunderstood Girard, sometimes, it seems, almost intentionally. Let's take a moment to lay to rest some of the charges: Some have accused Girard of being doctrinaire, applying his elixir too universally. Yet most French intellectuals do precisely that when establishing their theories; they have to assert a case strongly to be heard at all in the clamorous world of French letters. Is Girard's work any more didactic than Sartre's heavy-handed *Critique of Dialectical Reason,* for example? In Girard's work, there may be less of a "formula" than meets the eye, in any case. Girard's bold, declarative language disguises how much he is often weaving together his ideas as he writes, with his own inventive genius in the ink. "René is brilliant enough to find reasons," Macksey said to me. "Usually great men focus on one idea—he's had several, and he has the genius to glue them together."

Another misconception has offered ready kindling for his critics: Girard is certainly not insisting that mimetic desire is the only dynamic at work in human relations, though one could certainly get that reading in some of his less careful passages; nor is he arguing that the biological drive for food and shelter is mimetic. He made it clear that he has concerned himself, largely, with the human endeavors where mimesis *is* at work. As he himself said, novelists, playwrights, and archaic religion "are inevitably concerned with rivalry—conflictual mimetic desire, which is always in the way and is a huge problem for living together—doesn't mean it is the only thing there is."[17]

He added that "writers are obsessed with bad, conflictual mimetic desire, and that's what they write about—that's what literature is about. I agree with Gide that literature is about evil. That doesn't mean evil is the whole of life. I hear this question all the time: 'Is all desire mimetic?' Not in the bad, conflictual sense."[18]

Nor is Girard denouncing mimetic desire, which he sees as unavoidable, and often desirable. Even "bad" mimetic desire, he said, is a doorway, and intrinsically good, "in the sense that far from being merely imitative in a small sense, it's the opening out of oneself."[19] If so, then mimesis is not the problem, and that takes us one step back into perhaps more metaphysical territory, since "the degradation of the fictional world is the result of a more or less advanced ontological sickness,"[20] as Goldmann writes. What is ultimately sought is vertical transcendence, not horizontal fixation. Why the resistance to Girard's ideas, which can so easily be found in our daily lives as well as in our literature—and not least of all, engraved on our own hearts?

"People are afraid that all people are equal." Those words of Freccero haunted me, for a reason: in a sense *Deceit, Desire, and the Novel* could be studied from that particular angle, from the fear we have that our terrestrial gods are false and, ultimately, just like us. The insistence on our radical differences grows louder, more strident, even as "technical progress is wiping away one by one the differences between men."[21]

·   ·   ·

Deceit, Desire, and the Novel weaves together many of Girard's impressions
from Avignon reading, which would stay with him for the rest of his life—the
mimetic monkeys of Kipling's *Jungle Book* seem to hover in the background,
as well as the images from the children's edition of *Don Quixote*, and Proust
figures prominently throughout.

However, the more immediate inspiration for *Deceit, Desire, and the
Novel* was Stendhal, and particularly, the article Girard had written in 1954
defending Stendhal against attacks by Paul Valéry.[22] "I'd noticed that in
writers like Stendhal and Proust the same geometry governed human relations even though they were describing different worlds," Girard explained.
"Then I found the same forces at work in Cervantes, Shakespeare, Molière,
Marivaux, Dostoevsky, Joyce, and so on. Not to mention cases that are almost
too obvious like *Carmen* over which we throw the hypocritical veil of 'bad
taste' . . . When works of art are so hugely successful, there are profound
reasons for it."[23]

Other influences were in play. Some have pointed out the tie with Sartre's
notions of *mauvaise foi*, the bad faith that causes people under social pressure
to adopt values, manners, and social roles that run counter to their authentic
selves. Man is "condemned to be free," wrote Sartre, and such people deceive
themselves into thinking they have no freedom, and so fail to act authenti-
cally, which in turn gives rise to envy, jealousy, and *ressentiment*.

Girard said the three writers who most fully grasped the role of mimetic
desire were Shakespeare, Dostoevsky—and Dante.[24] Dante wrote that envy
was the root of evil, though Dante scholars pass over the topic lightly. Lectures
on love, detached from self-interest, occur throughout Dante's masterwork.
The Florentine poet also understood that good can come from imitation. He
presented role models via allegorical tableaux and visions offered in the *Pur-
gatorio*. In *Paradiso,* Dominic and Francis of Assisi, founders of somewhat
rivalrous orders, praise each other in lovely line after line.

As a lover of Proust, Girard would see at once that Dante had created
the template that Proust was to follow in *À la recherche du temps perdu.* The
Commedia is an attempt to arrive at a place from which the poem, which the
reader has just finished, can be written. Dante the pilgrim must become the
Poet who has been with us from the beginning of the work. Dante undertakes

a journey to the limits of vision to find a place outside time and space where he will judge not just his neighbors and his society, but most of all himself. Many authors have imitated the recipe since—for Dante and Proust, however, it was clearly more than a gimmick or a shopworn narrative convention, but part of a spiritual quest that involved suffering, self-renunciation, and a kind of resurrection. The author steps out of the paper prison he has created—Dante in poetry, Proust in the novel, and, in a surprising twist, Girard in the literary study that had absorbed him.

Girard admitted years later that he approached *Deceit, Desire, and the Novel* "in the pure demystification mode: cynical, destructive, very much in the spirit of the atheist intellectuals of the time."[25] He had been one of them, after all. It would not be the way he finished the book; the border between the two psychological lands is misty, and it is not always evident where one country leaves off and another begins.

In a sense, he was not discovering mimetic desire so much as discovering other authors' discovery of it. And as he explained later, he began to undergo the process he had depicted in his authors—as if he had stepped into the book he was writing, and inadvertently become one of the characters he was observing and describing. He said the last chapter is the one he had redrafted later, for reasons that we will explore in the next chapter. With those final pages of *Deceit, Desire, and the Novel*, we step into the world he is about to abandon. As he himself pointed out, "Every novelistic conclusion is a beginning."[26] The impression appears to have been as strong as the moment when Pinocchio is kissed by the fairy and becomes a real little boy.

Leo Spitzer had been one of the few who read the manuscript and responded to Girard, offering a helpful suggestion about Girard's kinship with phenomenologist Max Scheler's *Das Ressentiment*—Girard had read the book a few years before, but hadn't made the connection with his own work. He adopted some of Spitzer's suggestions and added an epigraph from Scheler to *Mensonge romantique*: "Man possesses either a God or an idol." Girard elaborated on his chosen epigraph (which doesn't appear in the English edition of his book): "The false prophets proclaim that in tomorrow's world *men will be gods for each other*. This ambiguous message is always carried by the most blind of Dostoevsky's characters. The wretched creatures rejoice in the thought of a great fraternity. They do not perceive the irony of their own formula; they think they are heralding paradise but they are talking about hell, a hell into which they themselves are already sinking."[27]

The well-meaning Macksey made a suggestion that he would later consider "a *folie*": "I stupidly urged René to send his manuscript to Poulet," he said. "Poulet and René together were two of the knockout people I've known in my life."

Georges Poulet, the one who had inspired Freccero to a lifelong study of Dante, had been the first reader of Macksey's dissertation years before. Poulet had left Johns Hopkins about the time Girard arrived. The phenomenologist literary critic, who pioneered a "criticism of consciousness," was "old guard" by the standards of the avant-garde, and probably to Girard, too. Yet his endorsement would have meant a great deal.

Although Girard wasn't particularly seeking advice, like any new author he was anxious to get early reactions of eminent scholars to his work. After about a month of silence, Girard wrote to ask Poulet again for his response. "The letter came back, he knew it by heart by the time told me," said Macksey. The fifteen-page, single-spaced letter would have been difficult to memorize, though it was apparently memorable.

"It was an intemperate letter," Macksey told me. "Poulet saw in René's work two people he really couldn't stand"—Hegel and Sartre. Poulet had been skeptical of Hegel's wide influence in France, particularly with Alexandre Kojève's renowned lectures, which had influenced Sartre as well. "Poulet might have taken two months and written a much more temperate letter, and then there wouldn't have been anything to talk about." But Girard's impatient prodding had provoked a too-hasty response.

Girard later described the letter as "extremely passionate and hostile saying one should not handle literature like that because ultimately it is an intrusion into the life of the author."[28]

He continued: "He hated Freud, and he saw my theory as a variation on psychoanalysis. His letter was very harsh, and could have discouraged a novice. Of course, I knew that Poulet would not like my book and I wanted to have his reaction because my book was in fact a reaction against the kind of aestheticism he represented. I was very conscious that *Mensonge Romantique* would infuriate the critics who saw literature as a 'world of its own', which belongs only to authors, as pure creation, detached from society! Georges Poulet was a prime exponent of this kind of criticism."[29]

Girard claimed to be pleased with Poulet's reaction, but surely his comment is partly emotional self-defense. Macksey seems to have gotten it right: "Frequently when René was hurt or offended or threatened, he could turn it into a joke." And so the Poulet letter became a reliable source of revelry at the lunch table.

.   .   .

The novels discussed in *Deceit, Desire, and the Novel* end without a road map to any future. In *Don Quixote*, Stendhal's *The Red and the Black*, and Dostoevsky's *The Possessed*, the protagonist has seen his delusion and renounces it. Then dies. No wonder critics have found the conclusions of these books unsatisfying, a hasty postscript tacked onto a long letter.

What happens after the last pages? Dante's *Divine Comedy* offers the ultimate ending for all stories, which is no doubt one element in its appeal. In any case, Girard was interested enough in Dante for a seminal essay— "Mimetic Desire in Paola and Francesca," which would be published in French in 1963 as "De la Divine Comédie à la sociologie du roman."[30]

For centuries, the story of Paolo Malatesta and Francesca da Rimini has been heavily marketed as a romantic ideal. George Sand was not alone in attempting to mimic its trappings for her lover—painters painted it, musicians composed music for it. Yet no one before observed how much Dante's famous lovers are drawn into their abyss entirely by imitation. Girard offered his own take on Dante with his anti-romantic theme of imitators imitating imitators in the name of spontaneity: far from a predestined amour, the love is a hysterical, derivative thing born of a book—"One day, for pastime, we read of Lancelot, how love constrained him; we were alone, suspecting nothing." Francesca pointedly names the one responsible for her downfall, and it's not Paolo: "A Gallehault was the book and he who wrote it; that day we read no further in it." In Arthurian lore, Gallehault is the "king from beyond the marshes" who encourages Queen Guinevere and her knight Lancelot in their reckless passion. For Francesca and Paolo, as for so many others, literature becomes the imaginary map for their desires, and for that reason the essay is sometimes called "By Literature Possessed." (In Boccaccio's telling of the same story, there are other mimetic elements—Paolo is pointed out to Francesca by others; in Dante's version, Paolo stands in his brother's stead at the betrothal ceremony.) The two lovers who are dupes to their book are, in a sense, Dante's own rebuke to his younger self. He had once idolized love and the poetry of love, which had inspired and straight-jacketed him.

It is all Girard ever wrote on Dante, but the influence of his Dantisti friends glows through the pages like sunlight through amber. The man who often cited the absence of evidence as indirect evidence—the dog that didn't bark in the night as a kind of proof—has plenty of patterns of evidence in his own life. He told me that he didn't write more on Dante because he had the era's first-rate Dante scholars around him, so it seemed redundant; he reasoned that he would never excel them, and so bypassed a mimetic imbroglio. Yet when he said categorically "all desire is a desire for being,"[31] well, at least for this reader the influence of Dante (as well as Hegel and Heidegger) on his thinking was apparent. It's one short step to the Florentine's notion that all sin is a form of distorted love. The thinking is the same, if the objective is arguably different—and only arguably, because Girard was about to undergo a powerful conversion to a religion that equated God with love, and with ultimate being. Dante's spiritual pattern would hold in other ways during that tumultuous time, too.

Girard was sitting squarely within the center of the Dante circle—a newcomer to this immense tradition. He knew two of the Dante scholars of his era who had been singled out by critic Harold Bloom as two vertices of "the celestial trinity of Dante interpreters"—Singleton, the presiding deity of the department, and then his brilliant pupil Freccero (and later Girard knew their pupil, Robert Harrison, who would be a cherished friend and ally at Stanford). In a telling moment, Freccero said that the two had intended to co-author the essay "By Love Possessed," but the Dante scholar had stepped aside. Said Freccero: "You don't collaborate with Jeremiah. You just show up and take notes."

.   .   .

Girard would see a similar pattern in Camus. It would occur not in a single masterpiece, but in the long journey between *L'Étranger* and *La Chute* (*The Fall*). In a 1963 essay, "Camus's Stranger Retried,"[32] he would trace Camus's spiritual trajectory, along the patterns he had described in *Deceit, Desire, and the Novel,* between the French author's early *L'Étranger* and late *La Chute*. The essay earned a $1,000 "best essay" award from the Modern Language

Association—important early recognition from the American academy, and one that pleased Girard enormously.

Girard took a dim view of Camus's early protagonist, that blank and aimless "modern hero" Meursault: "The life of this hero is objectively sad and sordid. The man is, indeed, a derelict; he has no intellectual life, no love, no friendship, no interest in anyone or faith in anything. His life is limited to physical sensations and to cheap pleasures of modern mass culture."[33] Camus portrayed Meursault as an existential innocent, simply because he experiences himself so, despite shooting an Arab in cold blood. Often readers (and Girard, too) overlook a brutal ambush and beating of a Moorish girl, which Meursault enables for his seamy friends. Hundreds of high school teachers in the 1960s and 1970s tried to follow Camus's lead, teaching the story from what they presumed to be the author's avant-garde point of view, which Girard rightly terms "nihilistic individualism."[34] But as Girard argues, "A work that is against everything in general is really against nothing in particular and no one actually feels disturbed by it."[35] Girard sees in Camus's Meursault a direct line that extends from Rousseau's *bon sauvage* into the present, all part of the "Romantic Lie," a bad faith attempt at authorial self-vindication, a way of punishing *les autres*. One could even argue that Camus's ostensible stand vis-à-vis *les autres*—the guilt of the "judges" against the innocent Meursault—is the author's naive rejection of the "the spirit of the crowd." But his novel hides perhaps a greater truth: our interconnectedness to each other, our common humanity. The romantic adheres to that truth, if only in a backhanded way: he always casts a sideways glance on the others, to see the effect he is making: "The romantic does not want to be alone, but *to be seen alone*."[36]

Girard reveals the "structural flaw" in *L'Étranger*: without the murder, there would be no trial and no judgment, so the pity Camus tries to extort for his hero, along with his judgment on the crowd, rings hollow. His execution has nothing to do with his behavior at his mother's funeral, his personal qualities, his putative spiritual innocence, or anything besides the undisputed fact that he has committed a murder. "If, at the most crucial point in this sequence, *Fatum* is suddenly brandished, or some other deity, as vague as it is dark, we must note this sudden disregard for the rational course of human affairs and take a very close look at the anti-social message of the novel. If supernatural necessity is present in *L'Étranger*, why should Meursault alone come under its power? Why should the various characters in the same novel be judged by different yardsticks? If the murderer is not held responsible for his actions, why should the judges be held responsible for theirs?"[37]

Camus's writing is persuasive. We trust Meursault's story of himself as a lost child of the sun, rather than the bourgeois mediocrity that Girard exposes. Perhaps Camus himself hadn't sorted out the truth about Meursault, nor separated it from himself; "I was poised midway between poverty and sunshine," he wrote in 1937, describing his impoverished childhood in French Algeria. Girard doesn't consider the possibility that Camus was *intentionally* presenting us with a thoroughly unreliable narrator, whose statements should no more be taken at face value than Humbert Humbert's. If so, he's hardly alone. Generations have taken the same road, including the high school teachers who assigned the wrong book. We should have read the more insightful *La Chute*, in which Clamence, the lawyer who champions "victims" of the law against unjust judges, discovers his own questionable motives and shady character, and comes to see himself as self-righteous and self-deceiving. "The confession of Clamence is Camus's own, in a broad literary and spiritual sense," wrote Girard. The author's characters are no longer self-justifications, but alter egos for his own psychological states as he realizes the truth of his situation. "The author, tired of his popularity with all the *bien-pensants* of the intellectual élite, found a witty way to deride his quasi-prophetic role without scandalizing the pure at heart among the faithful."[38]

Girard admired the existentialist author, as a man and writer. "Most people ignore the fact that Albert Camus was the first one to react against his own cult,"[39] he wrote. He compares *La Chute*'s conclusion with the final redemption in *Crime and Punishment*. As with the other books he discusses in *Deceit, Desire, and the Novel*, the fiction is the story of the author repudiating his past works and deeds. "Progress in matters of the spirit is often a form of self-destruction," Girard reminds us; "it may entail a violent reaction against the past."[40]

In *La Chute*, "The real question is no longer 'who is innocent, who is guilty?,' but 'why do we, all of us, have to keep judging and being judged?' It is a more interesting question, the very question of Dostoievski. In *La Chute*, Camus lifts trial literature back to the level of this great predecessor."[41]

·   ·   ·

In the era of New Criticism, when the life of the author was off limits, René Girard had made a bold statement: What is going on in the soul of the writer is the business of literature.

Perhaps no novelist makes that case as powerfully as Dostoevsky, who would become the subject of another book for Girard, one that is often overlooked, thanks, in part, to a complicated publishing history. Its publication fell between *Deceit, Desire, and the Novel* and the book that marked a signal change, *Violence and the Sacred*. The monograph was first issued as *Dostoïevski, du double à l'unité* by Plon in 1963, but didn't appear in English until 1997, as *Resurrection from the Underground: Feodor Dostoevsky*.[42]

"From *Notes from the Underground* on, Dostoevsky is no longer content to rehash his old certainties and to justify himself in his own eyes by continuing to take the same point of view about others and about himself," Girard wrote. "He exorcises his demons, one after the other, by embodying them in his novels. Nearly each book marks a new conversion, and this imposes a new perspective on the perennial problems with which he deals."[43] Girard points out again and again how we imitate those we wish to resemble, hoping to "fuse" ourselves with the other, whom we love and loathe, as they alternately fascinate and frustrate us. We are addicted to our obstacles, and go "underground" to hide the derivative nature of our lives, even from ourselves.

When the English translation was released in 1997, one of Girard's former graduate students from Johns Hopkins, Andrew McKenna, reviewed it, focusing on the poisonous nexus of "pride and self-hatred that wracks the conscience of Raskolnikov in *Crime and Punishment*, who doesn't know whether his murder of an old pawnbroker places him above or below humanity."

Similarly, "Ivan Karamazov cannot determine if he is responsible for the murder of his father, who inspires in him a hatred that he turns on himself at the peril of his own sanity, as he hallucinates the burlesque taunts of a sycophantic devil 'made in his own image and likeness,'" McKenna wrote. "Where 'meaning is furnished by others in a world devoid of objective values,' we find rival doubles everywhere, and this ubiquitous contest divides us against both ourselves and others. In such late works as *The Brothers Karamazov*, Dostoievsky presents clearly the need to discard the Manichean image of some gruesome fiend thwarting our nascent good will, the conceit with which Enlightenment philosophy and its step-child utilitarianism disguised a deluded narcissism. Instead we have to see the devil, 'liar and father of lies,' as old Karamazov cynically calls himself, in the role of others as they tempt and seduce us with the desires that they model for us and that they necessarily oppose when we try to imitate them."[44]

.   .   .

Avignon and family had been his bedrock, but even bedrock gives way to time and erosion. Joseph Girard was dying of prostate cancer. He was a recognized figure, and not just regionally. His decline was chronicled by his old school, the École des Chartes in Paris: "In recent years, as he approached eighty, Joseph Girard's activity fell off. He walked with more difficulty. From time to time he returned to the Palace, but he could no longer climb the stairs to his office; he sat at the door, chatting with the guards, watching the stream of visitors without troubling himself about what was going on. He often revisited the past, if only in the echo of his memories. In June 1961, he underwent an operation which went badly, despite all the care that surrounded him . . . little by little he left us."[45]

Joseph Girard was *in extremis* when Girard received the telegram. "When he was called, he went," said Macksey. "He couldn't be sure he would arrive in time, or that his father would be conscious." The most moving account, however, was from Freccero, who spoke with Girard after his return: On his hurried arrival to the Avignon family home, Girard tried to speak to his father, but he couldn't understand what the dying man was saying. Slowly, he realized his father had reverted to speaking in Provençal, the ancient language of the region.

Girard fils had a chance to be with Girard père in the final days, and father and son had a kind of reconciliation, with his anti-clerical father receiving the last sacraments. On 7 May 1962, he was "taken into the affection of his own," in the traditional phrasing of the obituary.

The bigger and more unexpected blow occurred the following year, with the death of Girard's youngest brother, Antoine, in 1963. I remember discussing this with Girard, as the day dwindled into evening, and he was silhouetted against the fading light in the elegant living room:

> He was a very late child of my mother. He was the fifth one. It was a very
> sad story. He always was a difficult child. He was the only one of these five
> children who had a problem with his studies. And he finally killed himself.

Because of problems with his studies?

    Yes, yes. He had considerable problems. . . . It's very difficult, you see, because I was already in America when he killed himself. I don't really know for sure, you know. . . . His whole life he had problems—with his studies, and with social relations, his fellow students. Finally, he committed suicide.

    Throughout, Girard intimated that this was the brother he didn't know well—the difference in age, his distance from Provence. I would learn later that Girard often softened the past this way, after thick scar tissue had formed over the psychic wound. The circumstances were ambiguous—he appears to have thrown himself in front of a tram: "I think René thought of it not as a suicide but as a kind of *folie*," recalled Freccero. "I felt it was a big deal. You can't be blasé about your brother's death."

    But Marilyn Yalom recalls a reaction that was far from detached or philosophical. The Yaloms' professional peregrinations had taken them to Hawaii and then Stanford, where she remembers completing her thesis at Stanford's Green Library. She had not seen Girard for three years at the time she flew back to Baltimore to defend her dissertation and suddenly he was not there; he had flown back to France to meet the family crisis. It was a disappointment for her, but the circumstances were a "terrible, terrible blow to René," she recalled.

    Joseph Girard had been such a strong, guiding hand behind Girard's development, one wonders whether his disappearance from the scene the year before had hastened the crisis. "The family always feels guilty in such cases, if it couldn't help," René Girard once said. "Whether he was the scapegoat of the family, to be honest, I haven't given it enough thought. After all, now that I think about it, maybe that's actually typical."[46]

    I ran across an enigmatic passage in an unsigned preface by the editors, from *To Honor René Girard,* tracing Girard's personal journey with the novels he studied in *Deceit, Desire, and the Novel,* and his search for truth in the greatest literature: "The novels were not however to be used instrumentally, as if they were some less-than-reliable data base, but rather read in their own terms, as revelations of a truth beyond statistics, arrived at through considerable personal suffering."[47] Sometimes I thought that the same terms would hold true for Girard himself.

.   .   .

The high-spirited daily or near-daily lunches at the faculty club or around Baltimore continued. The group assembled, mostly from Romance Languages, with reinforcements occasionally from the English Department. "He was a major figure at Hopkins in the humanities—and even among the scientists. Everybody knew who René was," said Gossman.

The Scotsman recalled with some chagrin how they had mocked their predecessors, including an eminent one, the great Hopkins scholar Henry Carrington Lancaster (1882–1954), author of *A History of French Dramatic Literature in the Seventeenth and Eighteenth Centuries*. Gossman came to regret it.

He learned a little humility as a result of being perhaps overly influenced by Girard's rising star. Gossman called his own first book, a study of Molière, an exercise in chutzpah, on Lancaster's former turf. "I paid virtually no attention in it to any of the positive facts he had spent his life establishing and took scant account, in general of any scholarly literature," he later wrote. "I missed out on a great deal as a result and now think of this book as deeply flawed. But it was in the spirit of the department of which Girard was the leading light and it was generously (too generously) received as a breath of fresh air in seventeenth century studies—which I suppose to some extent, historically, it was."[48]

"Slowly, my dizzy high spirits subsided, and I began to worry about the seriousness of the approach I had joined in promoting. I was also disturbed by the charismatic aura around Girard. All of us, young faculty and graduate students alike, longed for his attention and approval. It seemed to me that we were becoming slavish imitators, automatically applying Girard's celebrated principle of 'désir triangulaire' to everything and increasingly incapable of independent judgment and criticism."

He continued: "I had also begun to find his intellectual style troubling. It seemed to be excessively assertive, contemptuous of other possible points of view, insufficiently respectful of the complex objective world of both texts and history, and indifferent to argument and discussion. The trick was to simply pronounce clever or provocative things that had a certain intellectual plausibility or attractiveness without taking the time to ground them solidly. Possible objections and counter-arguments were not entertained. I decided to step back a little."[49]

He was, however, the kind of person who *would* step back. "Lionel at times could be very Scottish," said Macksey; he tended to see the world in "straight, moralistic terms, sometimes more of a historian, unlike the other people." Macksey insisted that there was never a chance Gossman would be anyone's acolyte. "He was standing apart, always a bit skeptical—too Scottish for flamboyant gestures. His attitude was complicated, not entirely disinterested." Yalom recalls the history a little differently, too: a sibling rivalry had emerged between Freccero and Gossman for René's approval and affection—but Gossman, like Yalom herself, was Jewish and something of an outsider not only by nature but by heritage. The affinity between the two colleagues from the French and Italian cultures was bound to be stronger.

Gossman, too, told me that his feelings were complicated, and he was apologetic and a little defensive. He, too, loved Girard—"everybody loves René," as Freccero had said. "It was not about him personally, but about my need to withdraw a bit," Gossman explained again. "I was as upset as anybody else." Everyone has contradictions—and both Gossman and Girard and everyone else in their lives are not exceptions.

He felt his "modest declaration of independence"—not opposition but merely re-gathering himself—was seen as betrayal by some of his colleagues, including his first PhD student, Eugenio Donato. Yet, Gossman wrote, "I simply wanted to withdraw, find a space of my own."

In any case, Girard would soon be swamped by bigger influences and bigger egos, and he would come to know firsthand the destructive influence of powerful personalities on thought and society.

.   .   .

The takeaway from Girard's landmark book: We live derivative lives. We envy and imitate others obsessively, unendingly, often ridiculously. "All desire is a desire for being," he said, and the being we long for becomes wrapped up in a person, who becomes idol and eventually rival, locked in an impossible conflict for an object, an honor, a promotion, a lover, or the esteem of others, which is in itself a shorthand for a bigger battle with bigger forces, which Girard would discuss in his subsequent books.

We all find it easy to critique the mimetic desires of others, but our own snobbishness and sensitivity to public opinion usually escape our notice. We wish to conceal our metaphysical emptiness from others, in any case, and from ourselves most of all.

Girard stopped short of direct self-portraiture—so did Proust, and Stendhal, and Dostoevsky in their fiction. He was never given to confession and dwelling on himself, yet occasional admissions emerge in interviews, such as the conversations with Michel Treguer in the 1990s: "It must be admitted that I probably displayed some mimetic demagogy in the way I expressed myself. . . . Remnants of avant-gardist jargon are sprinkled through my books." He admitted—too harshly, I would say—that the time-honored virtues of patience, faithfulness, obedience, and modesty eluded him: "We're terribly lacking in those virtues. I'm too much a man of my era to possess them myself, but I revere them. Indeed, nothing seems more conformist or more servile to me these days than the hackneyed mythology of 'revolt.'"[50]

What happens when you yourself become the idol? Girard, too, was increasingly finding himself the target of mimetic envy—and at this point, perhaps, still enjoying it. Freccero remembers a distinguished eighteenth-century scholar grabbing Girard by the shoulders and announcing, "Just for fifteen minutes, I'd like to be you!"

CHAPTER 7

Everything Came to Me at Once

Midway in the journey of our life I found myself in a dark wood, for the straight way was lost.

—Dante Alighieri, *Inferno*, Canto 1, trans. Charles Singleton

René Girard had reached the traditional midway point of life—thirty-five years old—when he had a major course correction in his journey, rather like Dante. The event occurred as he was finishing *Deceit, Desire, and the Novel*. I've circled around an event that was pivotal in Girard's life. Let us return to it now.

Dante's "dark wood" is a state of spiritual confusion associated with the wild, dangerous forests. Three beasts block his path; the leopard, the lion, and the wolf represent disordered passions and desires. Dante's conversion begins when he recognizes that he cannot pass the beasts unharmed. Girard experienced his "dark wood" amidst his own study of the disordered desires that populate the modern novel. His conversion began as he traveled along the clattering old railway cars of the Pennsylvania Railroad, en route from Baltimore to Bryn Mawr for the class he taught every week. While reading and writing as he chugged along between the cities, he underwent what in today's clinical and somewhat prissy modern jargon are called "altered states"—and they apparently continued with more or less intensity for several months.

Girard's conversion is no secret, but what's less commonly understood is that it was born in an experience that he has spent his entire life trying to explain. "Conversion experiences" don't always lead to a change in religion; and not all conversions are rooted in an altered state—but for Girard, the two went hand in hand. The watershed marks Girard's transition from being a clever, up-and-coming lit critic to something far more profound. It was something no one could have anticipated, least of all himself. "Conversion is a form of intelligence, of understanding,"[1] he said; it's also a process, in addition to an event, and as such would absorb him for the rest of his days.

Girard himself was somewhat reticent about the gaudy nature of such a claim. "I have never spoken about my conversion, because it seemed to me difficult, embarrassing, and a topic too dangerous to be approached,"[2] he said in 1990. He then qualified, "The word 'dangerous' is excessive. What I meant is that my Christian faith is impeding the diffusion of the mimetic theory, given that academics today feel the obligation to be anti-religious and keep religion at bay."[3]

It happened this way: "In autumn 1958, I was working on my book about the novel, on the twelfth and last chapter that's entitled 'Conclusion.' I was thinking about the analogies between religious experience and the experience of a novelist who discovers that he's been consistently lying, lying for the benefit of his Ego, which in fact is made up of nothing but a thousand lies that have accumulated over a long period, sometimes built up over an entire lifetime."

He found that he was undergoing the same experience that he had been describing in his book. "The religious symbolism was present in the novelists in embryonic form, but in my case it started to work all by itself and caught fire spontaneously," he said. He never explained what, exactly, he means in this cryptic sentence—events that happen outside time and space are very difficult to describe within it. However, he could no longer have any illusions about what was happening to him, and he was thrown for a loop: "I was proud of being a skeptic. It was very hard for me to imagine myself going to church, praying, and so on. I was all puffed up, full of what the old catechisms used to call 'human respect.'"[4]

One senses considerable caution in his explanation. Maybe he'd given up trying to decipher what was so easily misunderstood by almost every-one—including the Irish priest in Baltimore to whom he turned for his first confession since childhood. His experience changed everything, but perhaps the first thing it changed was *Deceit, Desire, and the Novel*.

Sandor Goodhart, the friend and colleague who had daily conversations with Girard a decade later, described to me the impact on *Deceit, Desire, and the Novel,* and how it changed the way Girard viewed the writers he discussed in that work. Goodhart recalled his own education and the rationalizations that were offered to dismiss deathbed conversions in literature: "It was always presented as 'Writers say this, but they're saying it because they're afraid they're dying, blah, blah, blah—so we can't really take it seriously.'" Girard told Goodhart that he had felt the same way. "But then suddenly, his own personal experience suggested to him that something serious was taking place in these works." Girard began to reconsider the conclusion of the novels he was writing about, and in doing so, he made a more earnest attempt to reach these authors on their own terms. His own life had given him the evidence to do so.

He rewrote the conclusion, and apparently rewrote other passages in the otherwise completed work, weaving his new understandings into the whole. The authors, he saw clearly, were describing how they were being freed from their own mediated, "triangular" desires. With that new understanding, they *became* their stories in a new way, with a wisdom previously inaccessible to them. The emergence from prison to freedom was the basis for the major novels he was reading, by Flaubert, Stendhal, Cervantes, Dostoevsky, Proust. The emergence from prison to freedom, and a little more besides.

Even the shelves of books he eventually wrote couldn't tell the whole story. It was just the beginning. The novels he described in *Deceit, Desire, and the Novel* were two-dimensional, flat on a page, but the only possible response he could have was to live out the same narrative in his four-dimensional life through time—just as the authors he had been writing about had done, after finishing the last pages of their own novels. *That* was the ending after the ending.

Girard's friends were incredulous. Macksey confessed that he was so accustomed to the French being anti-clerical that he was taken by surprise. John Freccero made the same assumption: "He was very interested in Sartre, Albert Camus. He was much, in a French way, a leftist, really—nothing

Roman Catholic about him." Nevertheless, Freccero claimed he saw the roots of the invisible tree, including the influence of Madame Girard in Avignon, and the Provençal years generally, perhaps beginning with that proud, first communion photo. The seeds were sown, waiting for the watering can, waiting for what "seemed a historical moment" to Girard. "The rest of us could see it coming," Freccero told me.

This would have been news for Girard, who described himself as a reluctant convert. Freccero recalled a conversation with Nathan Edelman, a French Jew, "who was certainly very touchy about Christianity. He said something to Girard, very lightly, about moving to the right politically and socially. Girard said, 'Nathan, you cannot believe it, but I have been kicked into a change of religion.' His experience with the spiritual was like a kick externally. Something he was forced into." It usually occurs like that, Freccero added. People imagine lightning bolts, "but it doesn't work that way for most conversions. It sneaks up on you."

The external kick kept on kicking. More precisely, the revelation *became* his work: "Everything came to me at once in 1959. I felt that there was a sort of mass that I've penetrated into little by little. Everything was there at the beginning, all together. That's why I don't have any doubts. There's no 'Girardian system.' I'm teasing out a single, extremely dense insight."[5]

If his words are to be taken at face value—why shouldn't they be, really?—he had the glimmerings of all the future phases of his work, from imitative behavior, to the nature of desire, to scapegoating, to lynching, to war, and ultimately to the ends of the world, all in this intense period of several months. This should not be taken as a claim of divine imprimatur on his oeuvre. His intellectual work led him to his electrifying encounter, and not vice versa. Nevertheless, for the one who experiences this kind of mental acceleration, the experience is persuasive, penetrating, and unforgettable—as it was for his fellow countrymen René Descartes, Blaise Pascal, and Simone Weil.

As unlikely as it may look to outsiders, I suspect that this experience explains his occasional impatience with objections, his eagerness to hurry along to the next phase of his work. He had, to some extent, a whole map of knowledge that needed to be drawn, defined, and interpreted. It also illuminates the extent to which he has been a visionary as much as a scholar, and perhaps sometimes a visionary at the expense of being a scholar. A close colleague, Jean-Pierre Dupuy, a leading thinker about technology, society, and nuclear deterrence from Paris's École Polytechnique and Stanford, pointed out that Girard could be slapdash, he could be disinterested in the critical questions his work raised, and, in his eagerness to move on to the next phase of his work, he wasn't concerned that translations of his major works were problematic.

Girard appears to have experienced what has been called an "intellectual vision," typically unaccompanied by Technicolor imagery or thunder or any visual component at all. Such an experience can last more than a year. Its enduring souvenir is a sense of inner poise and direction. Oughourlian put it this way: "He explained meeting with Whoever"—in other words, his own meeting on the road to Damascus. "This is very important. It explains much of his psychology. He has a certainty and quietness and peacefulness that doesn't exist in normal people . . . When Moses met God, he was never the same," he explained to me. "If I had an experience of the kind, it would change my life. It's one thing to know about Napoleon, it's another to meet with Napoleon."

History abounds with precedents for such nonrational experiences, including some famous ones—Socrates and Pythagoras among them. I suspect Dante experienced something similar in what is perhaps the greatest conversion story in Western history—and that Singleton's oft-repeated remark that the fiction of the *Commedia* is that it is not fiction is, in fact, the secular scholar's own wishful thinking. The very first canto of the *Commedia* drops a clue: Dante uses the verb "*mi ritrovai*" rather than "*mi trovai*" in the first lines of the *Inferno*. That is, he doesn't say "I found myself" (as most translate it) but rather "I recovered myself," perhaps even hinting that he "came to." He's suddenly, alarmingly "awake" to his perilous spiritual condition, and about to undergo a mind-bending set of experiences in this altered state. His contemporaries seem to have thought so: Boccaccio relates that they saw Dante's singed beard as proof of his infernal journey.

Because Girard rarely discussed his radical encounter, it might be useful to review a few other cases to contextualize what proved difficult to explain in words. It's possible, at least, to illustrate the range of conversion experiences, whether or not they resulted in an actual change of religion. Two more cases, then, this time from the seventeenth century: Pascal and Descartes are both from the period of those mansard roofs of the French baroque that so entranced me in Paris. Both lived during Europe's first "total war," the bloody debacle known as the Thirty Years' War—one at the beginning, the other at the end of that conflict.

As a young soldier, Descartes had a series of visions on the night of 10–11 November 1619 that would change his life. While billeted in Neuburg an der Donau, Germany, Descartes shut himself in a small heated room to escape the bitter cold of a lashing winter storm and freezing rain. After he dozed off, he had three troubling visions—just like Ebenezer Scrooge—and determined that they were a divine message. He would spend the rest of his life trying to decipher what they meant. What we call Cartesianism exists because this particular man believed in his dreams. In them, he saw all truths were linked with one another, so that finding one truth and proceeding with logic would crack open the world of science. He would go on to formulate analytical geometry and explore the idea of applying the mathematical method to philosophy. However secular the content of the dreams appeared, his first resolution afterward was to make a pilgrimage to Our Lady of Loreto. Were they just dreams? Not likely. For most of us, our dreams are insubstantial stuff, and not the basis of mathematics and science.

The genius mathematician credited with inventing the calculator, Blaise Pascal, also experienced a "first conversion" after his exposure to Jansenism, and began to write on theological subjects soon afterward, in 1647. After a "falling away" period, his second conversion occurred on the night of 23 November 1654, after his horses plunged off the Pont de Neuilly and threw him into the roadway. Hours later, between 10:30 p.m. and 12.30 a.m., he said light had flooded his room and, whatever he experienced in the minutes that followed, he afterward wrote a brief note to himself that began "Fire. God of Abraham, God of Isaac, God of Jacob, not of the philosophers and the scholars. Certitude. Certitude. Feeling. Joy. Peace . . . Joy, joy, joy, tears of joy" and concluded by quoting Psalm 119:16: "I will not forget thy word. Amen." He had this document carefully sewn into his coat, transferring it when he changed clothes, as a constant reminder. His major religious works followed—including *Lettres provinciales,* which Voltaire praised as the best book that had yet appeared in French, and the *Pensées,* unfinished at his death.

Long ago, certainly. But a more recent experience by a former Communist might also be illuminating. In spring 1938, the influential philosopher Simone Weil spent ten days at the Benedictine Abbey of Solesmes, and had an entirely unanticipated encounter that was to have a lasting effect in her life. "I had vaguely heard tell of things of this kind, but I had never believed in them," she said. She had never read any mystical works, so the contact was "absolutely unexpected."[6] It began a path that would culminate in her spiritual masterpieces, including *Waiting for God, Gravity and Grace*, and *The Need for Roots*. It would end with a request for a deathbed baptism, one that is still not generally known, and was only revealed decades later by her close friend Simone Deitz, who performed the rite a few months before Weil's death.[7]

Girard recorded his experience not in poetry or mathematics, but in erudite French prose; he challenged, he reasoned, but he also made spectacular intuitive leaps of invention. ("René is brilliant enough to find reasons," as Macksey has said.) In an era where the humanities are no longer our culture's lingua franca, he transmitted his new understanding largely through the social sciences. He pored over ancient texts and studied anthropology, sociology, history, trying to explain what he had understood quickly, over a very condensed period in those months of 1958 and 1959. But the social sciences provided an inadequate vehicle. Trying to explain an experience outside time and space is like trying to describe the three-dimensional Eiffel Tower along a single line. He would turn to altogether different language to explain what he had understood: "Christianity reveals its power by interpreting the world in all its ambiguity. It gives us an understanding of human cultures that is incomparably better than that offered by the social sciences. But it's neither a utopian recipe nor a skeleton key for deciphering current events."[8]

In later years, he would warn against a religion designed to increase the comfort of our lives in a consumer society, prettified by "Christian values," which he said would be akin to having a tiger by the tail. "If I'm right, we're only extricating ourselves from a certain kind of religion so as to enter another, one that's infinitely more demanding because it's deprived of sacrificial crutches. Our celebrated humanism will turn out to have been nothing but a brief intermission between two forms of religion."[9]

But the story all began in those tumultuous months before the spring of 1959. It would lead him to promulgate not a tame-dog Christianity, but one for the twentieth and twenty-first centuries, a Christianity that could reveal and respond to civilizations born in repeated, imitative violence, in a world driven forward by envy, competition, and strife.

.   .   .

Let us return to *Deceit, Desire, and the Novel,* and how Girard described the effect his personal revolution had on that first pivotal book:[10] "I started working on that book very much in the pure demystification mode: cynical, destructive, very much in the spirit of the atheistic intellectuals of that time." He continued: "I was engaged in debunking, and of course recognizing mimesis is a great debunking tool because it deprives us moderns of the one thing we think we still have left, our individual desire. This debunking is the ultimate deprivation, the dispossession, of modern man. The debunking that actually occurs in this first book is probably one of the reasons why my concept of mimesis is still viewed as destructive. Yet I like to think that if you take this notion as far as you possibly can, you go through the ceiling, as it were, and discover what amounts to original sin."

A radical debunking can bring one to the precipice of a conversion experience, or something akin to it. He argued that the great writers he was studying had departed significantly from the original plan for their books, and the final product was startlingly different. He explained:

> The author's first draft is an attempt at self-justification, which can assume two main forms. It may focus on a wicked hero, who is really the writer's scapegoat, his mimetic rival, whose wickedness will be demonstrated by the end of the novel. It may also focus on a 'good' hero, a knight in shining armor, with whom the writer identifies, and this hero will be vindicated by the end of the novel. If the writer has a potential for greatness, after writing his first draft, as he rereads it, he sees the trashiness of it all. His project fails. The self-justification the novelist had intended in his distinction between good and evil will not stand self-examination. The novelist comes to realize that he has been the puppet of his own devil. He and his enemy are truly indistinguishable. The novelist of genius thus becomes able to describe the wickedness of the other from within himself, whereas before it was some sort of put-up job, completely artificial. This experience is shattering to the vanity and pride of the writer.

According to Girard, the author's existential downfall makes a great work of art possible, putting into motion a sort of psycho-spiritual dominoes: the crisis of the characters in the books triggered an existential downfall for the novelists, which now made a different future possible for the man reading them centuries later.

What was true for Cervantes was true for Girard, at one remove. "Once the writer experiences this collapse and a new perspective, he can go back to the beginning and rewrite the work from the point of view of this downfall. The novel is no longer self-justification. It is not necessarily self-indictment, but the characters he creates are no longer 'Manichaean' good guys or bad guys."

Is it so hard to understand? I recalled a recent stint in the garage, rummaging through the boxes of my own yellowing papers and manuscripts. I paged through my proposals that never got off the ground; the rejection letters; the ancient, groveling requests for jobs or favors; the ill-conceived or misguidedly written essays or articles that I wished had not found their way to publication. Enough of this, and the self-loathing and self-disgust overwhelms. If it reaches a tipping point, one is flooded with the realization (and relief) that *nobody cared* about any of these petty triumphs, humiliations, and failures. It was not about me. It was never about me. Among all the black marks against me, these will not figure at all—except to me. Do we not all go through a thousand such deaths in a lifetime, if we're even halfway honest? We might even see a pattern in the madness, the lucky disasters, the unwelcomed opportunities, the lines converging as they rise. Take this realization, and multiply a thousand times in intensity, and it becomes a self-renunciation and conversion of sorts—one that the most secular audience ought to understand.

Girard continued: "So the career of the great novelist is dependent upon a conversion, and even if it is not made completely explicit, there are symbolic allusions to it at the end of the novel. These allusions are at least implicitly religious. When I realized this, I had reached a decisive point in the writing of my first book, above all in my engagement with Dostoevsky." Dostoevsky's Christian symbolism was important for him, particularly Stepan Verkhovensky's deathbed conversion in *The Possessed*, but also the end of *Crime and Punishment* and *The Brothers Karamazov*. "The old Verkhovensky discovers that he was a fool all the time and turns to the Gospel of Christ. This is the conversion that is demanded by a great work of art."

·   ·   ·

Girard referred to his enlightening winter of 1958–59 as an "intellectual-literary conversion"—but it was only the first trip to Damascus. He would have a second journey, more intense than the first, which he would describe in retrospect as an easy bliss.

The two-hour train rides to and from Pennsylvania had initially provided a meditative respite. "I remember quasi-mystical experiences on the train as I read, contemplated the scenery, and so on," he said. The sights were little more than scrap iron and the vacant lots in an old industrial region, "but my mental state transfigured everything, and, on the way back, the slightest ray from the setting sun produced veritable ecstasies in me."[11]

The Pennsylvania Railroad would be the setting for a deeper experience—a second road to Damascus. Initially, it had offered a pleasant and undemanding experience, until he discovered some time later, one morning on the familiar train ride to Bryn Mawr, an ominous spot on his forehead. The doctor failed to tell him this type of cancer was eminently curable. "So to me it was as though I was under a death sentence. For all I knew, I had melanoma, the worst form of skin cancer."

"So my intellectual conversion, which was a very comfortable experience, self-indulgent even, was totally changed. I could not but view the cancer and the period of intense anxiety as a warning and a kind of expiation, and now this conversion was transformed into something really serious in which the aesthetic gave way to the religious."

It was Lent. He was thirty-five years old. He had never been a practicing Catholic. "I will never forget that day. It was Holy Wednesday, the Wednesday before Easter," which would have been 25 March 1959. "Everything was fine, completely benign, no return of the cancer."

In Baltimore, Girard met with the befuddled Irish priest who had a hard time understanding what he had undergone. The Girard children were baptized, with Freccero acting as godfather, and René and Martha renewed their vows, at the suggestion of the priest—Martha is quite firm that they weren't "remarried," as even René sometimes said.

"I felt that God liberated me just in time for me to have a real Easter experience, a death and resurrection experience," Girard told Williams. The consent of the will occurred in what he called the "first conversion" experience. The second conversion gave him urgency, depth, and the endurance to take the next steps of his journey.

He never seemed to doubt that he was right, or rather that whatever happened to him that winter of 1958–59 was right, and it was that understanding that drove his writing. "My intuition comes first, and it leads me toward vivid examples, or burns them into my memory when I happen upon them by chance," he explained. This has led to misunderstanding, even condemnation, among "specialists." Girard admitted, "I'm probably partly responsible for this situation. I'm under the impression that I've never been able to lay out my insight in the most logical, most didactic, and most comprehensible order."[12]

His conversion would be a costly personal decision. It closed off an audience; it alienated potential readers and fans. Yet he never backed away from what he understood, in startling moments of clarity, to be the truth.

.   .   .

The seismic shift of that winter of 1958–59 left some unexpected aftershocks. "Curiously, my conversion had made me sensitive to music, and I was listening to a lot of that," he recalled. "What little musical knowledge I have, about opera in particular, dates from that period. Oddly enough, *The Marriage of Figaro* is, for me, the most mystical of all music. That, and Gregorian chant."[13]

Mozart's comic opera is permeated with themes of enduring love in the face of adversity, love rendered almost supernatural by the music. It also has perhaps the most exquisite portrayal of forgiveness in the entire opera canon when the Countess's merciful *Più docile io sono* opens out to a sublime ensemble. Perhaps it is no coincidence that forgiveness was to become a theme in Girard's writings for the rest of his life. As for the Gregorian chant, Macksey was not surprised by Girard's fondness for the Latin Mass—after all, he told me, Girard was practically born in a museum.

"I am an ordinary Christian," Girard told Williams, anticipating those who would make something grand of his faith and his conversion. Sometimes people did make something grand of it. Some years ago, at the end of an online interview with Girard, someone in the comments section asked if Girard was Catholic. One reader replied a little pompously, "René does worship as a Catholic. Precisely because he is Catholic. I would add that he also worships majestically in a beautiful small Catholic Church near Stanford University attending Sunday Mass celebrated by priests who have not forgotten that the Mass is a true sacrifice."

Girard would have chuckled at such a glorious description. He attended the century-old landmark Saint Thomas Aquinas Church in the back third of the pews, on the left side from the entrance—quietly, and without any commotion or self-importance that might draw attention to himself. It was a Gregorian mass.

Wedding of Joseph and Thérèse Girard in February 1920. Joseph's mother Josephine (née Clerc) is sitting behind the groom and to the left, in black. The groom's brother Pierre and his wife Simone are standing behind him. The white-bearded man is the bride's father, Joseph Gabriel Fabre. The bride's mother, Marie Cécile Émilie de Loye Fabre, is at the right of the bride. The children are the bride's nieces and nephews. Photograph is used courtesy of the Girard family.

Joseph Girard in the 1920s. Photograph is used courtesy of the Girard family.

René Girard sits between his grandmother Josephine Girard at left and grandmother Émilie de Loye Fabre at right in a family portrait from about 1932. His mother, wearing a lace collar, stands behind him. His brother Henri is to the left. The other children are cousins, and the other adults are domestic help. Photograph is used courtesy of the Girard family.

A family outing at Viverols, 1933. The children are René, Marthe, and Henri Girard. Their mother Thérèse is at far right, with her niece, Suzanne Fabre, and a cousin, Alice Fabre, in the back row. Photograph is used courtesy of the Girard family.

A family outing at Viverols, 1933: René Girard (*second from left*) is flanked by his cousin Suzanne Fabre at his left and Alice Fabre at his right, with cousin Jean Fabre in the center of the photo. At right, Joseph Girard holds his daughter Marthe. With its dormant volcano, mountains, maars, cinder cones, and lava domes, the regional landscape is the part of France Girard loved most. Photograph is used courtesy of the Girard family.

René Girard and his brother Henri around 1936 at Viverols, France. Photograph is used courtesy of the Girard family.

René Girard with his sister Marie around 1936 at Viverols, France. Photograph is used courtesy of the Girard family.

René, Marie, Marthe (holding Antoine), and Henri Girard before the war, at the house on Arrousaire. Photograph is used courtesy of the Girard family.

René, Marie, Marthe, Henri, and Antoine Girard at home in Avignon, about 1940. Photograph is used courtesy of the Girard family.

Marthe, René, and Henri Girard at a Gothic window, about 1940. Photograph is used courtesy of the Girard family.

A French woman, her head shaved, is pursued down the streets of Chartres by a jeering mob. She holds the baby she had with a German soldier. The iconic photo, taken by the renowned Hungarian war photographer Robert Capa on 18 August 1944, exemplifies the mob behavior René Girard wrote about. Photograph is by Robert Capa © International Center of Photography/Magnum Photos and is used with permission.

Joseph Girard, Étienne Charpier, his son Jacques Charpier, Georges Braque, Marthe Girard, and Antoine Girard in the Palais des Papes at the Avignon Festival in 1947. Photograph is used courtesy of the Girard family.

René Girard in front of the Palais des Papes during the Avignon Festival, 1947. Photograph is used courtesy of the Girard family.

René Girard marries Martha McCullough on 18 June 1951, in Bloomington, Indiana. Photograph is used courtesy of the Girard family.

H

The bus station in Durham, North Carolina, shows the pervasiveness of Jim Crow laws in the South, 1940. Library of Congress, Prints & Photographs Division, FSA/OWI Collection, [LC-DIG-ppmsc-00199].

The grisly lynching of Thomas Shipp and Abram Smith in Marion, Indiana, occurred only sixty miles from where René Girard would reside seventeen years later. The 1930 crime inspired a poem by Abel Meeropol, which would in turn become the lyrics for Billie Holiday's "Strange Fruit"—perhaps the most durable way a society remembers. Photograph is used with permission of the Indiana Historical Society (P0411).

Martha, Martin, and René Girard in Avignon, 1956. Photograph is used courtesy of the Girard family.

René Girard with his infant son Daniel, 1957. Photograph is used courtesy of the Girard family.

Richard Macksey participates in a 1963 seminar at Johns Hopkins. The polymathic professor organized the seminal 1966 Baltimore conference with René Girard. Photograph is used courtesy of Ferdinand Hamburger Archives, Sheridan Libraries, Johns Hopkins University.

Charles Singleton at his desk at Johns Hopkins about 1950. The leading Dante scholar of the last century was an inescapable presence at Johns Hopkins, and the Girards spent many days at his eighteenth-century farmhouse and vineyard in Carroll County. Photograph is used courtesy of Ferdinand Hamburger Archives, Sheridan Libraries, Johns Hopkins University.

John Freccero was Charles Singleton's protégé and a leading Dante scholar in his own right. He became a lifelong friend of René Girard's and eventually helped bring him to Stanford. Here, Freccero is visiting Mason Hall at Johns Hopkins in 2008. Photograph by Jay VanRensselaer/homewoodphoto.jhu.edu is used with permission.

Martha Girard with sons Martin and Daniel in Bandol, France, 1960. Photograph is used courtesy of the Girard family.

In 1960, Joseph Girard at René and Martha Girard's home, Les Cailloux, in Villeneuve-les-Avignon, across the Rhône from Avignon. Photograph is used courtesy of the Girard family.

René Girard holds a seminar on the ideas that would eventually become *Violence and the Sacred* at the University of Buffalo in spring 1971. Photograph by Bruce Jackson is used with permission.

Raymond Federman, René Girard, and Albert Cook at a party at the home of Provost John Sullivan in Buffalo, New York, 1974. Photograph by Bruce Jackson is used with permission.

Albert Cook and René Girard enjoy a party at Arts and Sciences provost John Sullivan's home in Buffalo, New York, 1974. Photograph by Bruce Jackson is used with permission.

René Girard prepares for his reception into the Académie Française at the Girards' Paris apartment in December 2005. Photograph is used courtesy of the Girard family.

René Girard and his brother Henri celebrate his reception into the Académie Française in December 2005. Photograph is used courtesy of the Girard family.

Fellow Académie Française *immortel* Michel Serres called Girard the "new Darwin of the human sciences." Here, Serres at Stanford in 2009. Photograph is used courtesy of L.A. Cicero/Stanford News Service.

René Girard outside the Stanford Faculty Club, June 2006. Photograph by Ewa Domańska is used with permission.

René Girard at Half Moon Bay, California, 25 August 2009. Photograph is used courtesy of the Girard family.

René Girard shows Jorge Montealegre Buire, the Spanish Consul General of San Francisco, the edition of *Don Quixote* he had read as a child, as Martha Girard looks on. Spain honored Girard in a ceremony at his son Daniel Girard's home in Hillsborough in January 2013. Photograph is used courtesy of the Girard family.

CHAPTER 8

The French Invasion

ZORBA: Why do the young die? Why does anybody die?

BASIL: I don't know.

ZORBA: What's the use of all your damn books? If they don't tell you that, what the hell do they tell you?

BASIL: They tell me about the agony of men who can't answer questions like yours.

ZORBA: I spit on their agony.

—Michael Cacoyannis, screenplay for *Zorba the Greek*

The conference has been called "epochal," "a watershed," "a major reorientation in literary studies," "the French invasion of America," the "96-gun French dispute," the equivalent of the Big Bang in American thought.[1]

To hear the superlatives, one would have thought that "The Languages of Criticism and the Sciences of Man" symposium held at Johns Hopkins for a few frantic days from 18 to 21 October 1966 was the first gathering of its kind ever held. It wasn't, but it did accomplish a feat that changed the intellectual landscape of the nation: it brought avant-garde French theory to America. In the years that followed, René Girard would champion a system of thought that was both a child of this new era and an orphan within it. He was at once proud of his role in launching the symposium, and troubled by some of its consequences. Let us consider what happened during this watershed autumn.

The event itself was René Girard's inspiration. He had assumed the chair of the Romance Languages Department from Nathan Edelman the year before, and became one of the triumvirate who brought the symposium together. Another was that brilliant figure who has been somewhat overlooked in American intellectual history—the restless, quicksilver Eugenio Donato. The third, Richard Macksey, was a co-founder of the new Humanities Center. Girard, however, was the senior member of the group, and the one with international connections.

"He already had some visibility. And yet he wasn't so senior that he had offended too many people in Paris, which was significant," said Macksey about his colleague. "René was more aware of issues of civility than we were. He was older and more established." Noting the heavyweight names of those who came to Baltimore, Macksey added that he thought the symposium had a big impact on his French colleague. "René, as a young person, was deeply influenced by this—although he might deny it." (Girard was two months shy of his forty-second birthday at the symposium; Macksey was thirty-five.)

At that historical moment, "structuralism" was the height of intellectual chic in France, and widely considered to be existentialism's successor. Structuralism had been born in New York City nearly three decades earlier, when French anthropologist Claude Lévi-Strauss, one of many European scholars fleeing Nazi persecution to the United States, met another refugee scholar, the linguist Roman Jakobson, at the New School for Social Research. The interplay of the two disciplines, anthropology and linguistics, sparked a new intellectual movement. Linguistics became fashionable, and many of the symposium papers were cloaked in its vocabulary.

Girard never saw himself as a structuralist. "He saw himself as his own person, not one of the under-lieutenants of structuralism," said Macksey. Yet structuralism would have had a natural pull for Girard, who was already moving away from literary concerns and toward more anthropological ones by the time of the symposium. Indeed, in this as in other matters, he was indebted to the structuralists. His own metanarratives strove toward universal truths, akin to the movement that endeavored to discover the basic structural patterns in all human phenomena, from myths to monuments, from economics to fashion.

Given structuralism's interdisciplinary bent, the symposium included representatives of both the humanities and the sciences. It brought together leading French intellectuals from an array of disciplines and interests—over a hundred thinkers from nine nations at the standing-room-only event. The conference was not designed just to bring a range of disciplines together to talk, but rather to teach them *how* to talk through this new intellectual architecture, which had its own language, its own way of writing and thinking. The structuralists were committed to the map they had discovered to order all knowledge; they believed it would lead its practitioners to the universal truths they were trying to access.

Lévi-Strauss couldn't attend in person, but he gave his blessing to the summit. Since so many of the speakers and participants were from France, the event was bilingual, which added a continental élan to the proceedings.

France has always prized its intellectuals, and a philosopher in Paris can achieve the status of a superstar even today. Jacques Lacan, the celebrity among the group, was keenly sensitive to the prestige of what would be his first American appearance. The French doctor had been called the most controversial psychoanalyst since Freud. Lévi-Strauss, Barthes, Foucault, and Julia Kristeva had attended Lacan's renowned seminars at one time or another. With their mutual interests in imitation, rivalry, and the nature of desire, Girard may have felt a natural interest about meeting Lacan in person.

The other symposium speakers, besides the troika of organizers, included Roland Barthes, Lucien Goldmann, Jean Hyppolite, Charles Morazé; Georges Poulet, Guy Rosolato, Nicolas Ruwet, Tzvetan Todorov, Jean-Pierre Vernant, Neville Dyson-Hudson, and the young, thirty-six-year-old Jacques Derrida. Hegelians, existentialists, social scientists, and literary theorists of all stripes rubbed elbows with the newest thinkers from the Continent.

With a brand new Humanities Center, Johns Hopkins had an incentive to put on a high-powered intellectual show, and the support of the center's founding director, Charles Singleton, gave the symposium an added luster. A Ford Foundation grant gave them "just enough gunpowder to make the cannon go off," said Macksey.

Only in the New World could such a meeting occur—certainly not in Paris, with its rivalries, tensions, and tectonic shifts. "The odd thing about it is, this struck me at the time even, these folks would not have gotten together under any circumstances in Paris under the same roof. There were enough lines already drawn in the sand, or drawn in blood, or whatever. So, a neutral ground," Macksey explained.

The symposium was intended to be a crowning achievement for structuralism, but here's the surprise: it signaled its end instead, as the movement slid into post-structuralism, so smoothly and effortlessly that the leading structuralists tend also to be the leading post-structuralists—Lacan, semiotician Roland Barthes, philosopher Michel Foucault, among them. The dark horse, Algerian-born Derrida, delivered the very last paper of the symposium, challenging the work of Lévi-Strauss and impishly skewering the structural weaknesses in the towering edifice the maestro had built. The paper, still a much-read classic of French theory, made the young philosopher's reputation in America and everywhere else. America, not France, would become ground zero for the "deconstruction" he introduced.

Everyone afterward sensed that there had been a metamorphosis. "It wasn't clear whether it was a wedding gown for structuralism in America, or a winding sheet for structuralism in America," Macksey told me. "Did we know what had happened? No, but there was a sense."

·   ·   ·

In my conversations with him, Girard was consistently contemptuous about "la peste," describing it as a kind of star thistle that had taken root across the United States and proved impossible to eradicate.

"When Freud came to the USA, he said, as he approached New York: 'I'm bringing the plague to them'; but he was wrong. Americans digested and Americanized psychoanalysis easily and quickly. But in 1966 we really brought the plague with Lacan and deconstructionism, at least to the universities!"[2] What Girard called "the beginning of the great merry-go-round Americans call 'theory'"[3] started on those few autumn days at Johns Hopkins. It's worthwhile to take a little time to unpack the conference and what it represented, for while Girard is often portrayed as standing alone in a field, he was, in fact, part of this intellectual generation. He was often responding to that cohort and contributing to its thinking, and he was alternately dismayed or inspired by his fellow players over a long lifetime. Does this French invasion sound like ancient history? Let us consider the effects of the symposium on our thinking today, at half a century's distance.

The kind of intellectual tussle the symposium represented could easily fly over the heads of most of the educated American public—and could easily be dismissed as jousting with air. For most, it's hard to understand what the fuss was about—but perhaps that's precisely the point. So much of what we consider as a "given," an objectively "correct" way to think, derives from this generation of mid-century intellectuals and their abstruse philosophical ping-pong matches, however much the heirs may have distorted the more nuanced thinking of these idea shapers. "Post-structuralist" ways of the world have been conflated with the term "postmodern"—a term with more recognition among the general public. By whatever label, the influence of both in our time has been pervasive. Think of the heightened sensitivity to how ideology keeps political and economic power entrenched; think of the way our current sense of history has been splintered into thousands of viewpoints and stories.

Inevitably, ideas were coopted by a cognoscenti that wished to sound clever and up-to-date. A parallel: a Stella McCartney handbag gets applauded in Milan shows, then reproduced in the thousands for customers who find the knock-offs at Bloomingdale's or Macy's. Eventually buyers on a budget find the purse a few seasons later as they paw through the marked-down bin in Ross Dress for Less. Does the Taiwan version have a resemblance to what was paraded on a Milanese catwalk? Sure, but it's far from an original; it doesn't have the subtlety, sass, splash, and dash anymore. Post-structuralism eventually descended to the morass of "relativism" and moral ambiguity—however, to lay that consequence on the shoulders of, say, Derrida, whose positions could be highly principled, misses the point. If you've slapped your ten bucks on the counter, taken home the knock-off handbag, and watched it fall apart in the first seventy-two hours, it's not quite fair to blame that on Gucci or Armani.

Think of it this way: When someone tells you, "That's *your* truth; it's not *my* truth," he is paying homage to the legacy of these thinkers. Though the idea of subjective valuation appears in Nietzsche and others, the post-structuralists took the ball and ran with it. When you are told there is no reality, or when President Bill Clinton defends himself in court by saying,

"It depends on what the meaning of *is* is," he can thank not only Yale Law School, but also Derrida, who advanced the notion that the meaning of a word is not a static thing or even an idea in the mind but rather a range of contrasts and differences in balance with the meanings of other words around it. One edges even closer to the discount bin when one examines how the term "deconstruct" and "deconstruction," so much in the public parlance, especially in criticism, have become synonyms for the more quotidian terms "analyze" and "analysis." When a teenager lazily rebuts your views with, "Yeah, well, that's just, like, your *opinion*"—the response would have been inconceivable a century ago, not only for its impudence, but for its content, such as it is. In the post-structuralist world, there are no absolutes, no great "Truth," no grand historical narratives, only texts to be deconstructed.

Thanks to Foucault, some postmodernists insist that what counts as "knowledge" in a given era is always influenced, in complex and subtle ways, by considerations of power. This idea has given rise to a welter of academic departments and books on post-colonialism, gender politics, ethnic studies, feminist studies. The fissures would deepen beneath the smooth, imperturbable surface of academia for a decade or so before large chunks of the iceberg gave way. Major universities, including Stanford, would reconsider a core curriculum that included an awful lot of dead white men, in favor of literature from Africa or Asia, with more modern works by women and writers of various ethnicities and sexual orientations. Not a bad idea, but one could argue that to love everyone is to love no one, and a curriculum, if not a culture, must be centered somewhere. And, ironically, the thinkers who taught that there are no sacrosanct texts ("It's art if I say it's art") have themselves become sacrosanct, their insistence on plurality the new dogma that it is apostasy to challenge.

The post-structuralist writers also separated history and our "historicity," the latter term encompassing the notion that our history has meaning and purpose, which we interpret and construct as we go along. Our historicity is always up for reinterpretation, and "factual history" may not be separable from our construction of it; we may not even be able to decide reliably what is "meaningful" about our history. (When, exactly, did the Renaissance begin and end? Who decides? Who decides that there was a "Renaissance" in the first place?) Derrida would say that factual history is secondary to our historicity—that is, our interpretation makes the system happen, not the other way around. For example, we "see" constellations in the sky, but they are of our making. Regulus indicates the tail of Leo the Lion for someone who views the sky as a "structuralist." But someone from another civilization might see a bulldozer in the same set of stars. For someone from the red star Antares, the same stars might align in an altered pattern altogether. For Foucault, we have "constellations" of influence and power and meaning. These lines of thinking are a direct attack on the structuralists and modernism in general, as it deconstructs the Hegelian idea of history, which dominated the era and still dominates our historicity—and which had an influence on Girard as well.

"I have always been a realist, without knowing it," Girard said years later. "I have always believed in the outside world and in the possibility of knowledge of it. No new discipline has ever produced any durable results unless it was founded on commonsense realism. This I would say is a principle that has always been verified. I think that the old German idealistic legacy has simply been misleading for the whole European culture," he said, referring to a generation of German thinkers such as Kant, Schelling, and Hegel.

"I'm interested in thinking patterns and I think you have to take the real seriously. Language is a problem, of course, but one that can be resolved. I'm sure that the engineers who managed the flooding of the Nile in Ancient Egypt and agronomists in present-day California, after some initial introduction, would understand each other perfectly. What deconstruction can deconstruct quite well is German idealism, because it is not grounded on *real* premises."[4]

The endpoint of the deconstructive credo may be the Belgian literary theorist Paul de Man's pronouncement that "death is a displaced name for a linguistic predicament."[5] In such cases, sometimes Girard couldn't resist scorn. When he wrote, "Think about the inadequacy of our recent avant-gardes that preached the non-existence of the real"[6]—well, *this* may have been the kind of thing he was considering.

The questions that drove his life were fundamentally different, and little akin to those who were shuffling with the shifting meaning of words, the shifting meaning of meanings. He was moving toward a sweeping teleological *Weltanschauung*, a bold reading of human nature, human history, and human destiny that owed perhaps a little to Hegel. "I think that historical processes have meaning and that we have to accept this, or else face utter despair,"[7] he said in the 1990s. The distance from many of his peers would lengthen with the years. He was so far from moving toward a postmodern notion of history that he would write with haunting certainty at the end of his life, "More than ever, I am convinced that history has meaning, and that its meaning is terrifying."[8]

·   ·   ·

The America that awaited the French when they came to the "Ball-*tee*-more" conference, as they insisted on pronouncing it, would baffle anyone under forty today. Although the 1960s were well underway, most of what we associate with the sixties would not begin until the seventies. This was Baltimore, not Berkeley. The French were still exotic; "Miss Susan Sontag," the future ambassador of French thought to America, was mentioned only twice at the symposium, in connection with her "faintly hysteric ignorance."[9] What did the Americans think of the French? Recall the remarks the Girards heard about "mixed marriages" in Indiana.

Macksey is the last of the troika to be able to speak about the events so many decades past.[10] He shared his memories from his home stuffed with seventy thousand books and manuscripts in English, Russian, French, German, Italian, Spanish, even Babylonian cuneiform (he can read and write in six languages, and laconically noted that his collection includes an autographed copy of *The Canterbury Tales* and a presentation copy of the Ten Commandments). A generous and legendary teacher, he still holds seminars in this spacious landmark home, even though the house is so crowded that a visitor can't walk more than a few feet in any direction without running into a bookshelf. He lives, according to a colleague, on "three hours of sleep and pipe smoke." He writes as prolifically as he reads, publishing fiction and poetry as well as scholarly works. No topic bores him, and his memory is astonishing. Milton Eisenhower, brother of the U.S. president and Johns Hopkins's president at the time of the conference, commented that going to Dick Macksey with a question was like going to a fire hydrant for a glass of water.

Macksey recalled that the program for the symposium was put together quickly, with messages ricocheting around the globe. Girard and Donato were in France during the critical months—the ideal location for recruitment. "I was the most pedestrian of the lot," said Macksey, and the other two pitied him for spending his sweltering summer in Baltimore. The $35,000 grant from the Ford Foundation—a lot, in those days—had come through with unexpected speed the winter before, so the entire event was planned in less than a year, a daunting organizational task before the days of cellphones, voicemail, email, and ubiquitous air travel that could be scheduled quickly.

In addition to scholars presenting papers, the symposium would include a European innovation: "colloquists," who would question and discuss the presentations, and "who would sometimes be standing outside the structuralist wave that was coming in," said Macksey. "We even had some very old people"—by which he meant Hegelians, such as Hyppolite, and perhaps even existentialists. Both camps were influenced by Alexandre Kojève's lectures (as was Girard himself)—"and Kojève was an eccentric Hegelian to say the least." The interlocutors needed to have the intellectual heft to improvise extemporaneous mini-lecture replies that might spur discussion, and also be able to take on the large-scale personalities who were speaking—which put pressure on the organizers to find even more top-notch participants. Paul de Man, who would later be discredited for collaborating with the Nazis' anti-semitic campaigns, was among the colloquists. So were Edward Said, Roman Jakobson, Jan Kott, and others.

"So there was a lot of scurrying around about more people," Macksey said. "René had run into Foucault at a café and—this is secondhand—but he said he was interested in coming. Well, we knew Foucault really was a flake about ever showing, especially if there was going to be bullets flying. I mean, the events of '68, Foucault checked himself into a sanitarium so that he didn't have to make any political statements and stand in the wake of the revolution." Predictably then, Foucault was a no-show. According to Girard, however, Lévi-Strauss was the luminary who had cancelled his trip, creating a black hole in the schedule. Whether Lévi-Strauss or Foucault's failure to appear was the cause, the organizers were looking at an important gap in the proceedings.

Girard was unsure whom to invite, and called Michel Deguy, who had written a long review of *Deceit, Desire, and the Novel* in *Critique*. He tipped him off that Derrida was to publish important essays in the next two years. "That's why we invited him," Girard said. "Indeed, Derrida was the only participant who stood up to Lacan. Moreover, he delivered a lecture that is one of his best essays."[11]

The group had seen Derrida's article in *Critique*, and a few early pieces on different topics, including one on "Freud's Mystic Writing Pad," but he was largely an *inconnu*. "Hyppolite just said, 'I think he would be somebody who would come.' So we got in touch with him, and Derrida, on fairly short notice, said yes, he would come," said Macksey. Hyppolite's voice carried considerable weight: in addition to being "a generous and heroic figure," he had translated Hegel and was considered the dean of Hegel studies in France. The book that arose from the conference, *The Structuralist Controversy*,[12] is dedicated to him. "If Jean Hyppolite said this was a good idea, we were very apt to say yes. It didn't take an awful lot of nerve or reflection to say, 'Yeah, we've read a little bit of this guy and he does sound interesting.'"

"We all knew the real source, who gave the fuse and the explosives for the symposium, and that was a great Hegelian," said Macksey. "What I didn't realize was he wasn't well while the symposium was going on. We corresponded afterward about the texts, but he was terminally ill." Hyppolite would die two years later. As for Derrida, "I hadn't realized that he was going to be the Samson who would tear down the temple of structuralism, really."

The cast of characters was memorable in other ways. Lacan came to the conference early, via New York, where he had made a detour to see the Albert C. Barnes Foundation art collection outside Philadelphia. A graduate student, Anthony Wilden, had trekked to New York for the care and feeding of Lacan, whose English was sketchy, before his triumphal entry into Baltimore. "Lacan was at his best, because he wanted to attract attention to himself alone, and the literature people really felt for him and remained fascinated while the psychiatrists remained indifferent,"[13] said Macksey.

All the guests were housed at the Belvedere Hotel—and it was there that Lacan and Derrida met at last, on American soil. "So we had to wait to come here, and abroad, in order to meet each other!" said Lacan with "a friendly sigh," according to his own account.[14] The mimetic doubles were to have a testy future. According to Élisabeth Roudinesco, a French academic psychoanalyst:

> The following evening, at a dinner hosted by the organizers, Derrida raised
> the questions which concerned him about the Cartesian subject, substance,
> and the signifier. Standing as he sampled a plate of coleslaw, Lacan replied
> that *his* subject was the same as the one his interlocutor had opposed to the

theory of the subject. In itself, the remark was not false. But Lacan then added, 'You can't bear my already having said what you want to say.' Once again the thematic of 'stolen ideas,' the fantasy of owning concepts, the narcissism of priority. It proved too much. Derrida refused to go along, and retorted sharply, '*That* is not my problem.' Lacan was being made to pay for his remark. Later in the evening, he approached the philosopher and laid his hand gently on his shoulder. 'Ah! Derrida, we must speak together, we must speak.' They would not speak.[15]

Lacan was high-maintenance. "He wanted his underwear laundered," said Macksey. "They were silk and he wanted them hand laundered. He wanted this and he wanted that." The Girards remembered the underwear, too. They laughed as they recalled the graduate student who took Lacan's silk shirts and knickers to the laundry. He reported later that when the Chinese managers at the cleaners were warned that they were "fancy" and "special" shirts, they responded by wadding them up and throwing them on the floor, putting the snooty customer in his place, *in absentia*.

Lacan may have strained his hosts' goodwill, but he was easier for the conference organizers in other ways. While most of the participants soldiered through all the days of the conference together, requiring food, chairs, beverages, and amenities, Lacan was conveniently holed up at the Belvedere Hotel writing the paper he was to present, under the patient watch of Tony Wilden, who was assigned to help him translate his inflammatory essay attacking the underpinnings of conventional Freudian psychiatry. "Lacan was trying to prod Tony into writing the paper for him all week," said Macksey. "He was his amanuensis, his cicerone, whatever." Wilden would go on to make a major contribution to Lacanian studies, as well as works on communication theory, ecology, and social interaction. But the symposium tried his nerves, if not his allegiance. As Macksey said, "Tony Wilden put up with a lot."

During the conference, "Tony was calling up here because he realized Lacan had very little English, although he quotes a lot of English, and that he really didn't have a paper," said Macksey. The plan was to circulate the English translations in advance. Hyppolite, among others, had done so. Wilden had urged Lacan to present the paper in French and phoned Macksey, with tentative success. "This was all more difficult when not everybody in the world had cell phones. And he said, 'I convinced him. He's going to do the thing in French. So relax.' So I said, 'Well, you relax.'" Macksey then added diplomatically, "We'll both relax."

Lacan also complained that he hadn't had a chance to meet with the students, which in his unfortunate pronunciation came out as "mate." "Well, of course, because he had been down in the damned hotel he didn't meet with the symposiasts either," said Macksey. "And then he went on about mating with the students for awhile."

"So Lacan enjoyed putting stress on systems, systems frequently being his patients. And he put a lot of strain on Tony—who blew up, of course, at the symposium."

■   ■   ■

On the day of the French invasion, the excitement was palpable. "Well, people were falling out of the windows," said Macksey. "It had an air of improvisation to say the least about it. And of course we had to feed all these characters," he said, adding, "These are all very famous French people, for the most part, they are accustomed to arguing for two hours about where they'll go to lunch." Macksey discussed the caterers, the fine wines served, and the hotel accommodations, but clearly the big show was on the main floor. A closed-circuit broadcast was eventually set up in the new Milton S. Eisenhower Library's lounge to deal with the overflow crowd.

The French psychoanalyst continued his exhibition. "Lacan was clowning around in an extremely calculated and hilarious way," Girard recalled.[16] He threw his arms around the Ford Foundation representative, Peter Caws of Hunter College, as if he were an old friend. "He wanted literally to take over America!"[17]

Girard's own contribution, the first paper in the symposium, was easy to overlook in the drama and pyrotechnics. He added a prophetic note, borrowing from Sophocles's retelling of the Oedipus myth to offer a cautionary tale about those who think they have the copyright on "the truth":

> Tiresias, losing sight of the fact that no God, really, speaks through him; forgetting that his truth, partial and limited, bears the imprint of its true origin which is the heated debates and battles of men as well as the imbrication of converging desires; Tiresias will think he incarnates the truth and he will abandon himself to oracular vaticinations . . . This is the failure of

Tiresias and it might be our own. It is this failure which drags Tiresias into
a painful, sterile, interminable debate with Oedipus. This, of course, should
not be a model for us in the discussions to come. Perhaps it is not fitting
even to mention such a deplorable precedent. But, in matters intellectual
as well as in matters financial, danger and profit always run together.[18]

The sparks began to fly after the next rather uncontroversial paper by
historian Charles Morazé on literary invention. In pages of response to the
presentation, Lacan asked, "Who invents? There would be no question of
invention if *that* were not the question. You consider this question resolved."
He raised "the term *subject* as [something] distinct from the function of
individuality you introduced."[19]

Singleton was not interested in theoretical games; nevertheless, he
generously welcomed the participants, and responded in game, if somewhat
rambling, fashion to Lacan's verbal arcana: "Now, predictably I'm going to
speak about a certain Italian poet. I'm known to think of nothing else or read
nothing else. I'm going to hold to my old habit, use Dante as a touchstone,
and test some of the speculations and assertions made today, including col-
lectivity, social classes, and possibly—though I still have to understand Monsieur Lacan—in-mixing, and so forth. But as far as invention goes, it is in a
sense safe to say that Dante invented nothing . . . in the sense of a problem.
And yet he invented everything. What did he invent? An experience. An
experience that the mathematical symbol does not offer . . . the poetic vision
comes forth in its totality. I think that this question was excellently launched
today in terms of invention. The experience is there to be had by all who
can read the language and prepare themselves to have it. It is repeatable, and
keeps on repeating itself."

"Now this isn't coming close at all to 'signe,' and 'invention de problème,'"
he continued, "it's just suggesting that we are already operating here in terms
of *modern problems*, and just let a plodding medievalist suggest that there
are other historical horizons in which it might be interesting to situate our
thoughts occasionally, as René Girard did in terms of Oedipus."[20]

Poulet had given a fine and generally disregarded paper, and tried to
bridge the chasm that was beginning to open as he responded to Roland
Barthes. "We are a little like people who live in the same building but on
different floors. The difference can be seen in our use of the word *language* . . .

you seem to avoid the word *thought* as if it were becoming rapidly obscene. Nearly every time you use the word *language*, I could replace it by the word *thought* almost without incongruity. I think that if you tried the same exercise, inversely, you would make the same discovery . . . Therefore it seems to me that we are at the same time very close and yet separated by an abyss—an abyss that we could leap if we wanted to."

Barthes politely but firmly refused the hand that Poulet had offered. "I am very touched by what you have said, but I can't really reply because, as you said, there is a separation and, if I may say so, what separates us is precisely language. . . . if I don't use the word *thought*, it is not at all because I find it obscene; on the contrary, it is because it is not obscene enough. For me, language is obscene, and that is why I continually return to it."[21]

A brave new world was dawning, and some tried to get a foothold—or perhaps simply remind some of the participants that they had not reinvented the world. The Polish scholar and theater critic Jan Kott was reeling. "Throughout this colloquium I have had the dizzy sensation that the world is collapsing," he said.[22] Hyppolite's last paper on Hegel opened almost tentatively: "Isn't it too late to speak of Hegel in our age, when the sciences have gradually replaced metaphysical thought?" Macksey sympathized with the great Hegelian: "I wouldn't say he was on the wrong track, he was on the wrong planet." The conference marked the emerging centrality of Nietzsche to modern thought, rather than Hegel.

Thursday evening was to feature two Lacan papers, one by the doctor himself, the other by Guy Rosolato, "who was Lacan's shotgun," said Macksey. Who would go first? The two tussled on arrangements, but finally Lacan had his way and went before his colleague. The title of Lacan's paper was inauspicious: "Of structure as an inmixing of an otherness prerequisite to any subject whatsoever."

Lacan galvanized the audience with a few provocative opening remarks, and then described his obscure musings while holed up in the Belvedere Hotel: "When I prepared this little talk for you, it was early in the morning. I could see Baltimore through the window and it was a very interesting moment because it was not quite daylight and a neon sign indicated to me every minute the change of time, and naturally there was heavy traffic and I remarked to myself that exactly all that I could see, except for some trees in the distance, was the result of thoughts, actively thinking thoughts, where the function played by the subjects was not completely obvious. In any case the so-called *Dasein* as a definition of the subject, was there in this rather intermittent or fading spectator. The best image to sum up the unconscious is Baltimore in the early morning."[23]

The paper was almost incomprehensible because it was not English and it was not French. He had overruled Wilden in the end, saying it would be "a violation of the hospitality rite" to present his paper in French, according to Macksey. Lacan tried to describe how he was rethinking Freud in an impossible mélange of his impenetrable French and his near-nonexistent English, to the confusion of all. He illustrated his concepts with the diagram of a Mobius loop.

Wilden threw in the towel. The public was baffled. The organizers thought they were the victims of "a bad joke."[24]

The interlocutor, the literary theorist Angus Fletcher, was of questionable assistance. Friends had taken him out for several rounds of French 75s, a potent concoction of gin and champagne and lemon juice with a dash of sugar, and Fletcher was the worse for wear.

Fletcher called him out in his first comment: "Freud was really a very simple man," he explained. "He didn't try to float on the surface of words. What you're doing is like a spider: you're making a very delicate web without any human reality in it . . . All this metaphysics is not necessary. The diagram was very interesting, but it doesn't seem to have any connection with the reality of our actions, with eating, sexual intercourse, and so on."[25] At least, those are the heavily edited words from *The Structuralist Controversy*, which don't capture the hysteria and pandemonium (Donato's careful hand would rework this section).

At the event itself, rather than Donato's diplomatic recreation of it, Fletcher's voice had taken on an accusatory tone—"Vous, *vous* monsieur . . ." He attacked in a British-inflected French, while Lacan insisted on replying in his inadequate English. "Lacan was enjoying every bit of this. He was like a Cheshire cat," said Macksey. "Angus just went ballistic."

"I should have been aware, and wasn't, the state that Angus was in. Angus is a very bright guy." Elsewhere in the room, Girard was "trying to climb under the chair, it was so embarrassing," he said. "René felt we owed something to the Ford Foundation, from whom all blessings flow . . . I would watch him. He was the senior member of the troika—at moments, he seemed to be thinking that the wheels had come off and we were rolling downhill." Girard's concern regarding the Ford Foundation was understandable, since "Lacan particularly set Peter [Caw]'s teeth on edge"—perhaps from the moment of the big bear hug.

Macksey felt that the microphone had to be kept from Wilden at all costs. Someone passed the mic to Wilden nevertheless. "At that point Tony lit into Lacan, saying this was your great opportunity, this was your first exposure in the United States. All you had to do was just talk your language and you don't know diddly squat about the English language." Goldmann jumped into the melée, attacking Lacan on procedural grounds as well.

The Structuralist Controversy gives little indication of this discord— remarks were toned down later to reduce the decibel level, and much of the action was between the lines, anyway. According to Macksey, "It got to be about midnight and things were just going on wildly and Rosolato says, 'Oh, he always does this to me. He schedules me to talk right after him and then there's no time.' So Nicolas Ruwet, who is a Belgian linguist, read a paper that I thought was more exact and applied overt structuralism more than most of the people who were participating had done. But nobody paid attention to that paper. Alas."

Back at the Belvedere, Lacan started calling everyone in Paris—Lévi-Strauss and Malraux among them—giving his version of the events. Eventually, he would run up a $900 phone bill from the hotel. "People in Paris thought a small revolution had occurred," said Macksey. But the revolution would take place the next day.

Enter Derrida for the final paper of the symposium on Friday. "You realized fairly early that Derrida was, well, now everyone uses this term, but even then, he was an intellectual terrorist. He had better manners than many French academics. But there was an element of disruption, obviously," said Macksey.

"Of course, that was the stick of dynamite under the meeting. If he had come in earlier in the week it might not have had quite the impact that it did. But he was there at the end."

Derrida's paper was a tour de force, with an abundance of the italicized terms and wordplay that would later irritate those who couldn't keep up with his verbal antics, and who certainly didn't take them seriously. His paper, which he had written in ten days, suggested there was no reality apart from the name we give to it at any moment. Structuralists presupposed an origin and center—Derrida saw only a periphery. Language violates the "universal problematic" and the "moment when, in the absence of a center or an origin, everything becomes discourse."[26] How could a structuralist study the "structure" of a text if it lacked a center or any organizing principle? He set out the program for deconstruction, suggesting not that we abandon the familiar philosophers, but that we read them in a new way. He advocated substituting signs for one another, freed from any tyranny of the center.

"Here or there I have used the word *déconstruction*, which has nothing to do with destruction. That is to say, it is simply a question of (and this is a necessity of criticism in the classical sense of the word) being alert to the implications, to the historical sedimentation of the language which we use—and that is not destruction," he said.[27]

And yet it was destruction—everyone knew it, and Derrida would, through the years, be criticized for it. He saw the structure that the structuralists saw, but he showed where it falls apart. The overarching structure isn't primary, it's secondary—a result rather than a cause. Structuralists saw language as a pure system. Derrida was showing that it is impure and jumbled. We're inevitably mired in a flawed system.

Hyppolite had presented a long series of comments and queries, and then asked what he said would be his last question. It wasn't. He ventured two or three more and then, finally, he asked Derrida to define structure, without the use of algebra.

"The concept of structure itself—I say this in passing—is no longer satisfactory to describe that game," said Derrida. "So I think that what I have said can be understood as a criticism of structuralism, certainly."[28]

What would halt chaos? What would stop a free fall? In a long roundabout way, Hyppolite asked him where he was going with his line of thought—in short, what was he driving at? "I was wondering myself if I know where I am going. So I would answer you by saying, first, that I am trying, precisely, to put myself at a point so that I do not know any longer where I am going."[29]

Game over.

.   .   .

It was over but it wasn't over. The crowd had dispersed, the chairs and rubble cleared away, the trash emptied, but there was a curious coda with Lacan among the American psychoanalysts. "Friday, he wanted to meet with America," said Macksey.

At the end of the week, Lacan asked to meet with the Baltimore psychoanalysts, so there was a final excursion after the conference was officially over. "We had disconvened, except for Lacan 'mating' with students," recalled Macksey, and so the ever-genial host made arrangements to take Lacan to Sheppard Pratt, a leading psychiatric hospital in Towson, a northern suburb of Baltimore.

"The guy who had just arrived as the director [Dr. Robert Gibson]—I think he felt that he had been mugged. I explained, 'This is a very eccentric psychiatrist. He wants to meet with American psychiatrists.' And he said, 'Do I have to read him?' I said, 'No, just hospitality.'"

Macksey accompanied the French doctor to the lavish seminar dinner— he recalled "seas of shrimp and abundant food." After some socializing, the guest of honor rose to speak to the assembly.

"Lacan got up and finished by insulting everybody there in various ways. His topic was the length of a psychoanalytic session—and of course Lacan was notorious for having sessions that only lasted five to ten minutes, and some that lasted three hours. Anyhow, he managed to provoke outbursts there that were at least as loud in decibels as the ones that he had provoked Thursday night."

One eminent psychoanalyst long associated with the university, Sam Novey, had had enough. "Sam got up and said sort of to nobody in particular but to the audience in general, 'I know a schiz when I see one,' and walked out. Others just quietly walked out. A few others made little speeches. Lacan was enjoying every minute of it."

•   •   •

The participants in the conference regularly use hyperbolic expressions to describe it—blood, bullets, dynamite, gunpowder, terrorism, Samson pulling down the pillars, and so on.

On an intellectual level, however, the earth really had shifted beneath everyone's feet. One person knew it. Macksey described how Poulet was stopped on the campus by a colleague who wanted to know how the symposium was going. "We just heard a paper that destroyed everything I stand for, but it was a very important paper," he replied. Said Macksey, "I cherish that little anecdote. It showed that Poulet wasn't a fool. He knew what was happening." Did the others understand the importance of the Derrida paper? "A number of people did, but a number of people didn't."

Let's consider, for a moment, the many ways Derrida's paper pulled out the stakes that supported the structuralist tent. Structuralists on the whole accepted the existence of a "reality," some material, human, or socioeconomic facts beneath their ideas; post-structuralists questioned that very notion, emphasizing that the gulf between "ideas" and "reality" is constructed through discourse. If any "reality" exists, it may be worlds apart from our perception of "truth." For structuralists, systems were all—they emphasized the importance of systems in structuring our worldviews, our sense of ourselves, our thoughts. They sought "universal truths" through structures that bind people together. Post-structuralists had given up that search, and instead focused on difference and on the individual reader or speaker operating within a structure. Rather than seeing coherent systems, they saw incoherence and a mushrooming plurality of meanings.

The structuralists' eagerness to uncover hidden patterns and structures within culture began to seem contradictory and problematic, their language tainted by authority and entrenched academic rituals. Many structuralists began decamping to the post-structuralist tents. Yet the line between the two was often blurred—after all, both emphasized language, but structuralism's fatal flaw (according to post-structuralism) is that it "privileged" one point of view, however grand and overarching, over another, which is choice, not truth. Post-structuralism had swallowed structuralism, acknowledging its quest for structure and order, but exploded into *bricolage*, using found things to make something new (think collage in art, remixing in music). The year after the symposium, in 1967, Derrida published three audacious books that were new volleys in his war on structuralism, which was still trendy in French intellectual circles: *Speech and Phenomena*, *Writing and Difference*, and his masterwork, *Of Grammatology*.

Derrida discovered America in the way Girard had nearly two decades earlier, and none of the pieces went back together in quite the same way—for him or anyone else. Derrida quickly became a superstar with international speaking engagements and even film gigs. He proselytized in West Africa, South America, Japan, and even the U.S.S.R. He would become the most frequently cited authority in papers submitted to the Modern Language

Association, and his influence and his centrality were inescapable, the new
orthodoxy. "America IS deconstruction," Derrida would crow.

In the following decade, Johns Hopkins would be a hotbed for post-
structuralist thought and thinkers. Derrida returned to teach at Johns
Hopkins several times. Lucien Goldmann, Georges Poulet, Michel Serres,
Emmanuel Levinas, Roland Barthes, and Jean-François Lyotard also made
guest visits. Literary critic Paul de Man, who began his long and fruitful
association as the herald of deconstruction when he met Derrida at this symposium, moved from Cornell to Johns Hopkins. He told Macksey, "'I'm so
comfortable at Cornell and happy, but I feel I should get into the fray.' Well
he got into the fray and a couple of bombs exploded."

"It was a time of enormous intellectual ferment, much of it the work
of French thinkers and writers," wrote Gossman. "As phenomenology and
existentialism were challenged by structuralism and structuralism in turn
by 'post-structuralism,' we in the French section of the Romance Languages
Department found ourselves in the role of mediators between our colleagues
in the other disciplines and the French *maîtres penseurs* to whom we had
direct access and whose aura illuminated us too to some extent. Curious
physicists and puzzled English professors looked respectfully to us to provide
explanations of the latest trends. French in those years was an extraordinarily
lively discipline at the very center of the Humanities."[30] Americans who had
been insulated from Continental fashions, Girard explained to me, did not
see that this tsunami was an enthusiasm posing as truth, a vogue that would
pass—as existentialism was passing, as structuralism was beginning to pass.
Today, in the second decade of the twenty-first century, post-structuralism
is no longer cutting-edge. The *au courant* literary scholars are now absorbed
in such innovations as Franco Moretti's data-crunching modes of literary
analysis, the digital humanities, or combining evolutionary psychology and
brain science to determine how we may be hard-wired for fiction-making,
aesthetic appreciation, and the like.

An important element in "la peste," and one not commonly remarked
upon, is that American and British students don't have the grounding in
philosophical discourse that their French, and often European, counterparts
do. In France, for example, philosophy is formally taught at the high-school
level; at best, an American student gets a little bit of Plato's *Republic* and
Machiavelli's *The Prince* in political science classes—nothing from the most

recent half millennium. A reasonably educated Frenchman has the vocabulary for abstract philosophical discussion, and can tinker with these concepts
in a way most Americans cannot. Author Jean-Paul Aron wondered how any
student who did not have Plato, Hegel, Husserl, and Heidegger downloaded
into their mental software could appreciate Derrida's restless and sophisticated oeuvre. How, he wondered, could they understand his "enigmatic
work"? He added, "Some powerful ideas, swiftly vulgarized, had to satisfy
their [i.e., the students'] appetite."[31]

That's one reason avant-garde French thought took the country, east to
west, like smallpox among the natives. No natural immunities existed in a
nation new to the feverish intellectual fads from Europe. French thinkers
were a hot ticket, and the trendy new scholars could name their price. Academic departments were "ruining themselves to attract the Parisian stars in
order to be one up on their neighbors."[32] The French swelled with pride at
the success of their boys in Baltimore (not a single woman had been on the
program).

Todorov, Genette, Julia Kristeva, and others took to the road to spread
the gospel. "There were heartrending lexical conversions: at Madison, at
Minneapolis, at Ann Arbor nobody wrote about Flaubert anymore: they
'read' him. Columbia . . . was captured and soon it was Yale's turn: Yale,
which under the masterly direction of Henri Peyre had become the frontrun-
ner in French studies in the United States." Irvine, at that point one of the
lesser University of California schools, became the "aerial bridgehead uniting
theoretical France and American universities."[33]

.   .   .

One French scholar had a different take on Derrida's triumph—and Girard's
attitude toward it. "We knew and understood each other much better than
the Americans did," said Jean-Marie Apostolidès, an Auvergne-born scholar,
playwright, psychologist, and colleague at Stanford. "Derrida could cheat
people and take himself as a god. He could not cheat us."

Apostolidès is an engaging and flamboyantly off-the-wall character,
apparently unfettered by the need to please his colleagues; he seems to relish
making sweeping, provocative remarks as he nears his retirement. So perhaps I should have been less startled when he insisted Derrida was Girard's
mimetic double. Seeing Derrida's success "transformed René. He thought

'Why not me?'" said the *provocateur*. "It's definitely what convinced René to transform his public image into something stronger."

After all, Derrida had managed a spectacular, American-style self-reinvention. The Algerian-born thinker had failed to make a mark in his first adopted home. "He was humiliated—belittled and passed over in France," Apostolidès said, "probably because he was arrogant." Apostolidès continued calmly, emphatically: "Derrida's obsession was success. He tried to place his spoon everywhere in America. . . . He had no success in France. He was a little humiliated Jew and he wanted revenge. He took America as his field for revenge."

Benoît Peeters, the Derrida biographer, visited Apostolidès for his research, and the Stanford scholar thinks the author presented a creditable, if somewhat whitewashed, view of the philosopher. Not surprisingly, his own frank criticisms didn't appear in the six hundred–page book. "He did not present Derrida as totally cynical," said Apostolidès, dismissing Derrida as a hypocrite, especially in his image as a "great feminist": "It's a big, big lie if you know his private life," he said. "He was fucking women everywhere in America." The silence, he said, is out of deference to Marguerite Derrida, the widow—and also because many of Derrida's women now have prominent academic roles.

This was hardly a secret, however, despite his remarks. Even Peeters noted euphemistically, "Derrida had an irresistible desire to seduce. And if he almost never spoke of his relationship to women, this was because his obsession with secrecy was greater in this area than in any other. But many people knew that 'the feminine' was, for him, always in the plural."[34] Part of his cachet and influence in America, no doubt.

The theatrics of Baltimore raise another important point, and one that's emerged since. To put it bluntly: How much was pure sham, pure preening and ego jousting? At times, the mimetic rivalries and derivative desires seemed to be a showcase for the very principles *Deceit, Desire, and the Novel* describes.

The American philosopher John Searle excoriated Derrida, insisting,

> You can hardly misread him, because he's so obscure. Every time you say, "He says so and so," he always says, "You misunderstood me." But if you try to figure out the correct interpretation, then that's not so easy. I once

said this to Michel Foucault, who was more hostile to Derrida even than I am, and Foucault said that Derrida practiced the method of *obscurantisme terroriste* ... And I said, "What the hell do you mean by that?" And he said, "He writes so obscurely you can't tell what he's saying, that's the obscurantism part, and then when you criticize him, he can always say, 'You didn't understand me; you're an idiot.' That's the terrorism part."[35]

Not everyone, of course, agrees with this reading—though many have criticized Derrida for his byzantine writing, with its italics, its phrases in phantom quotation marks, and its dizzying wordplay. Girard himself clearly felt respect, as well as dismay, for his colleague. Girard himself, although distressed by the deconstructive frenzy Derrida wrought, clearly had respect for his colleague as well. In particular, he wrote and spoke admiringly of Derrida's early essay, "Plato's Pharmacy," which anticipated his own insights in some respects.

To some extent, Searle's criticism reflects the porous divide between analytic and continental philosophy, and the former still dominates the American intellectual landscape and our public discourse. Speaking very roughly, analytic philosophy focuses on analysis—of thought, language, logic, knowledge, mind; continental philosophy focuses on synthesis—synthesis of modernity with history, individuals with society, and speculation with application. Anglo-American philosophy has emphasized the former; mainland Europe the latter. Searle is aligned with the analytic camp; so is linguist and philosopher Noam Chomsky, one of America's leading public intellectuals.

Chomsky called Lacan a "total charlatan" posturing for the television cameras, charging that "there's no theory in any of this stuff, not in the sense of theory that anyone is familiar with in the sciences or any other serious field. Try to find in all of the work you mentioned some principles from which you can deduce conclusions, empirically testable propositions where it all goes beyond the level of something you can explain in five minutes to a twelve-year-old. See if you can find that when the fancy words are decoded. I can't," he said.[36]

Searle's and Chomsky's critique is part of the American opposition that began in the 1980s, continuing the philosophical school of "American pragmatism" that looks for ideas to deliver some intellectual payoff. American pragmatists have been called "the plumbers of philosophy"—they attempt to solve problems, not provide elegant and clever descriptions of problems.

Perhaps questions should be practical, too. Sometimes a single naive question can bring down an entire edifice of thought. Let me extend a few naive questions, then, in that spirit: How is a philosophy embodied in the man who espouses it? What is a philosophy that does not change a man—not only what he says, but how he lives? How does a man's being—the sum of his knowledge, experience, and will—"prove" his knowledge? Can we ever devise a philosophy, even a theory, wholly apart from who we are, and what we must justify? These questions were raised in earnest when Heidegger's affiliation with the Nazis, and later Paul de Man's complicity with them, were revealed. What does the test of time show us about the merits of an idea? However heated the arguments in the Parisian coffee shops, in the end, decades later, they would become systems of thought characterized by wordplay, mind games, and a noncombatant's flexibility, charm, and elasticity—all delivered with an ironic wink. And what of Girard?

.   .   .

Girard had already begun to define himself in opposition to the prevailing winds. In the wake of his intense conversion experience, he seemed to be picking up the torch from older French thinkers, such as Blaise Pascal or Simone Weil—people who weren't afraid to use the word "God" without irony.

With the abandonment of grand narratives, the fans of deconstruction found little meat in Girard's development of a totalizing theory, which bridged so many disciplines. It was a game of musical chairs that left Girard and a few others standing and bewildered.

Invisible fingers were already scribbling "Mene, Mene, Tekel, Upharsin" on the walls. Said Girard, "At that point, I felt at Johns Hopkins as alienated as in Avignon with my post-surrealistic friends. One year later deconstruction was already becoming fashionable. I felt uncomfortable with that fashion. That's the reason why I went to Buffalo in 1968."[37]

Donato followed him to the State University of New York at Buffalo, continuing his long and tempestuous relationship with Girard—"the tempest was on Eugenio's part," said Martha. This was the beginning, not of a rift, for they remained close friends, but the first bumps along their long road together. Donato, with his passionate nature, had fallen under the spell of post-structuralism. Martha laughed as she recalled Donato telling them that he was going to make a speech. "He said, 'It's going to be wonderful. No one will understand a word I am saying.'" He was only half joking.

Within a few years, "Derrida was being thrown in René's face," according to Martha. When confronting these contrary headwinds, she explained, "René's reaction is not to stand and fight, but to say 'You don't want me,'" and depart. Freccero had already left for Cornell—"you can get buttermilk anywhere," he had told me by way of explanation—after a painful estrangement with Singleton, who had regarded him as a son. Girard would write much about double-bind mimetic relationships of mentor and protégé, but Freccero only said, "If I was weaker, it would not have happened. If he was softer, it wouldn't have happened." The lunchtime clique was breaking up.

This was not everyone's view. Gossman, when I spoke with him decades later, was astonished at the very idea that Girard had felt alienated, and said it didn't correspond with his own perceptions of Girard's power and sway in Baltimore. "When he left, we were stunned. What were we going to do now?" His predecessor as chair, Nathan Edelman, was "wonderful, but a quiet, gentle guy. He didn't throw his weight around. He was happy to let René run the show"—so Girard's departure would leave a vacuum.

"Why was he going to Buffalo, dammit? What a place to go! We felt we had been sort of abandoned." Yet Gossman, too, would leave Johns Hopkins for Princeton in 1976, for many of the same reasons. The Johns Hopkins students "all imitated Derrida like crazy . . . They would borrow phrases and whole modes of speech. I didn't know if they understood what they all meant." French vogues had discouraged students from speaking in class; they feared that they were not à la mode. He found the students at Princeton, farther from the epicenter, were livelier and less inhibited, and his teaching acquired new vigor.

I wondered if Girard's departure indicated, once again, how he was more sensitive to slights than he sometimes let on, despite some of his more pugnacious attitudes—if so, it would have been a considerable handicap in a field of postmodern thinkers who seemed to enjoy the fistfights almost as much as the glory. However, it could be that Girard simply practiced what he preached. I asked him once what to do if one found oneself a scapegoat, or at least the target of malice. "You just leave," he said.

.   .   .

The hurricane left town, but Macksey is still dealing with the correspondence from the event, half a century later. The scholar, now an octogenarian, told his interviewer, Bret McCabe: "I got correspondence, and I should have done this this week and I haven't—people keep writing who are addicted to one or another of the players." I'm afraid my correspondence had contributed to the backlog.

At one point, the elderly scholar began looking for a light for his trademark pipe, and asked his guest if he had a match handy. They began shuffling through the mountains of papers, looking for one, and McCabe waved a matchbook he'd found. "No, they're empty." Then he caught the script logo of a Swiss tobacconist on the box. "They're Davidoff. I haven't had Davidoff since Jacques Derrida was here."

CHAPTER 9

Le Système-Girard

Everyone is guilty, yet not completely responsible.

—René Girard

The impetuous young doctor from Paris had made a wild miscalculation. On an impulse, he flew to New York City to meet René Girard in January 1973. "I didn't know how to contact him. I was crazy," he said. These were the days, he reminded me, before Google, smartphones, and email.

The eager psychiatrist was Jean-Michel Oughourlian—before the books, the titles, and the Paris apartment in the sixteenth arrondissement. He was, back then, working in the laboratory of pathological psychology at the Sorbonne, among other appointments. And although he had a brief internship at Johns Hopkins's hospital about the time of the famous Baltimore conference, there's no reason his path would have crossed Girard's then. After all, during his stay at Hopkins, *Violence and the Sacred* hadn't yet been published, on either side of the ocean—and that was the book, published by Grasset in 1972, that propelled the journey. "I read it once, twice, three times, four times," he said.

And then he boarded a plane. All he knew was that Girard was supposed to be a professor at the "University of New York." He would find him.

After he left the busy American airport, he appealed to a family friend in the city for further assistance. The friend, who sold kitchens for hospitals and other institutions, didn't know how to find the professor either, but together they consulted his resourceful secretary. An hour later, she learned that he wasn't in New York City, but rather in Buffalo, and that Oughourlian would need to take another flight to upstate New York, nearly four hundred miles away. The doctor was flummoxed, not having understood the size of the state or the dispersal of its state universities. His earlier stint in Baltimore apparently hadn't given him a strong sense of the vastness of America—or, he would soon learn, the extremities of its weather.

The persevering secretary got a phone number. They called, but Girard was in class. When they returned from lunch, they were able to talk to Girard by phone at last. Girard's reaction was understandable: "Who are you? I don't know you." Oughourlian gave his elevator pitch: "I think your hypothesis could revolutionize and change completely psychology and psychiatry." Oughourlian was, in particular, defining his own ideas about how individual psychology affects and is affected by others, working on a concept they would eventually call "interdividual psychology."

Girard demurred again. "I'm in French literature and comparative literature," he explained, worlds away from psychology and psychiatry. He added that his current interests were developing along the lines of ethnology and biblical texts. Moreover, a flight to Buffalo was impossible: he was looking out at a landscape buried in more than six feet of snow and no airplane would be able to land. He made a counteroffer: "I'm coming to Paris in April. I promise I'll call you."

It may have been a noisy time in the world, but Buffalo seems like a quiet interlude in Girard's life, from 1968 to 1976—and in a way it was. Yet his productive sojourn next to the Great Lakes, with the return to Johns Hopkins that followed it, was to see the publication of two of his best known and most provocative books, *Violence and the Sacred* and *Things Hidden since the Foundation of the World*.

He would also form new and lasting friendships: among them an important one with Michel Serres, who would call him "the Darwin of the social sciences" and eventually sponsor his election to the prestigious Académie Française; his first graduate student at Buffalo, Sandor Goodhart, who would go on to become a professor of English and Jewish Studies at Purdue; and finally the disappointed man who returned to Paris that winter.

Oughourlian would eventually become a conduit for bringing Girard's mimetic ideas into the hard sciences, as well as one of his interlocutors for *Things Hidden*. But first there was the book for which Girard is perhaps best known, *Violence and the Sacred,* the work that inspired the impulsive trip across the Atlantic.

·   ·   ·

The six-foot snowbanks on Lake Erie paint a picture of the State University of New York at Buffalo as a cold and forbidding backwater, but that would be far from the truth. In the shifting academic hierarchies of postwar academia, Buffalo was suddenly the hot new intellectual hub. The postmodern literary critic Leslie Fiedler, author of what some considered the decade's most important book on literature, *Love and Death in the American Novel*, was recruited to be part of the all-star team of the English Department. So was Lionel Abel, the Jewish American playwright, literary critic, and essayist who had written *Absalom*. He had won an Obie, but more importantly, Sartre had called him the most intelligent man in New York City.

Other prominent names joined the team: novelists John Barth and Raymond Federman, poets Robert Creeley and Robert Hass. The addition of René Girard to the English Department was a bigger surprise: all the Frenchman's books were written in his native tongue.

"For at least a decade, the UB English department was the most interesting English department in the country,"[1] recalled Bruce Jackson, who joined the faculty in 1967. "Other universities had the best English departments for history or criticism or philology or whatever. But UB was the only place where it all went on at once: hot-center and cutting-edge scholarship and creative writing, literary and film criticism, poem and play and novel writing, deep history and magazine journalism." A constant flow of visitors guaranteed intellectual circulation and fresh air, whether the guests stayed for a day or a year. The department had seventy-five full-time faculty teaching everything from literature and philosophy to film and art and folklore. "Looking back on it from the end of the century, knowing what I now know about other English departments in other universities in those years, I can say there was not a better place to be."

The legendary architect behind the effort was Prof. Albert Cook, who was determined to create a department of leading stars and critics. Jackson described him as "a man in constant motion, forever talking or reading or writing. . . . He was a presence . . . He never seemed to change. Other people got older, paunchier, balder, slower, but Al Cook was always Al Cook. He transcended the physical. He was medium height, big in the chest, always scheming. Al was my idea of what Odysseus looked like."[2] By the time he recruited Girard, he had already finished his three-year term as department chair but was still a guiding hand and go-between in recruiting academic luminaries.

Few places could have been as ideal for Girard. He had carte blanche to write and teach whatever he wanted, and the course load was relatively light. "He also said he was glad to break out of being a Frenchman teaching French and have closer ties with other departments, as he did with English at Buffalo," Martha explained. "René was always getting offers. The Buffalo one came with a chair as University Professor." Not least of all, perhaps, it was far away from intellectual fashions and the structuralist and post-structuralist crazes. Derrida and Foucault came to lecture, to be sure, but Foucault couldn't stand Buffalo, which Girard may have regarded as a kind of recommendation for the place.

"I loved Buffalo," Girard told me. More than Johns Hopkins? "In some ways, yes," he answered. Girard arrived on the campus in 1968, and Eugenio Donato followed him the same year.

.   .   .

Donato started it. A few years earlier, the brilliant deconstructionist had encouraged Girard to read some of the cutting-edge thinkers from the Continent, which led to the 1966 symposium. Then he began recommending the great twentieth-century anthropologists—Émile Durkheim, Bronisław Malinowski, Alfred Radcliffe-Brown, and others. Girard later explained that, beginning around 1860, anthropologists, particularly English anthropologists, were documenting the last archaic peoples and their religious institutions before the modern world absorbed them. They were doing so, he said, "in a manner which is incomparable."[3] This direction would take him to sacrifice, scapegoating, archaic religions, and the astonishing conviction that religion was not the cause of violence, as generally supposed, but rather, in early societies, the solution to it.

The new shift in Girard's interests surprised everybody. When he finished *Deceit, Desire, and the Novel*, everyone thought his next book would pick up where the earlier work concluded, with hints at his growing preoccupation with themes of conversion and redemption.

It didn't. *Violence and the Sacred* soared in an entirely new direction. His new work took on Sigmund Freud, ritual, violence, and sacrifice. He didn't return to Christian themes until *Things Hidden since the Foundation of the World*.

A great man's career often has a moment where he passes off the radar screen of his peers, moving into places that no longer send reassuring blips back to observers. If so, this may have been such a point for Girard—or perhaps not a point at all, but a line marking a vanishing trajectory.

"He was supposed to come out with *the* book," Freccero recalled. "When you read *Violence and the Sacred*, and look back at the cocktail parties and Proust . . ." Freccero paused, and then thought a moment. "He's very Dantesque. He abandons one line of thought and you haven't understood where he's going and then—aha! *that's* where he's going."

Donato started it? Perhaps. But Goodhart recalled a slightly different origin for Girard's new direction. "He said, 'Let's assume that these writers—Flaubert, Dostoyevsky, Stendhal, and Cervantes—are really to be taken seriously. Let's take them seriously, and take their deathbed conversions seriously. Then, how are we to understand that?'" The questions took Girard back to ancient texts—such as Sophocles's *Oedipus*, the subject of his 1966 symposium lecture.

"The reading of culture through literature led him to the reading of culture through Greek tragedy. The reading of culture through Greek tragedy led him to the reading of culture through anthropology. *That's* how he got to anthropology. He got there through the reading of Greek tragedy. That opened, for him, the door to anthropological reading." Euripides, Aeschylus, and Sophocles, especially *Agamemnon* and *Oedipus,* brought him to rituals and sacrifice. Inevitably, these themes took him back to the Bible as well. Hence, Donato's suggestion fell on kindling that had already been prepared for the flick of a match. It lit an intellectual fire that the wind would sweep into a direction no one had foreseen.

Girard had already given intimations of his new direction when he spoke about Oedipus at the 1966 symposium, and the landmark event itself had continued the line of thought and fueled more insights: "He realized that the Continental thinking, the fad for structuralists or for post-structuralists, focused upon difference," Goodhart recalled. "It did not focus upon the breakdown of difference, or what he called the crisis, or this concept that he named 'undifferentiation.'" In French it's *indifférenciation,* a word Girard brought into play to describe this process of societal breakdown. One could argue that the differences and tensions at the symposium were practical demonstrations of the principles he was attempting to describe, as Continental differences melted on an American playing field, and the participants vied to distinguish themselves from each other, each seeking a crown in the new epoch.

To these accounts, we must add a third: toward the end of his career, Girard put a slightly different slant on events, casting himself as more a solitary figure than he actually had been. "When I moved from literature to anthropology, I did it totally on my own," he said. "During that period, I probably read more books than at any time before or after—I was mainly concerned about the religious and the sacrificial elements. As a matter of fact, I never stopped reading books from the viewpoint of sacrifice."[4] These years were, as he said, "the most hyperactive period of my life I have known, at the end of the 1960s, when I alternated between elation and depression in the face of what I was trying to construct."[5]

Girard's forays into uncharted territory made waves in the department. Goodhart recollects his first encounter with Girard as a first-year graduate student in the spring of 1969, at the popular lectures that were held in the department. Girard was a regular speaker—on this particular day, the lecture was titled "Literature, Myth, and Prophecy." According to Goodhart, "He opened with a sentence that went something like the following: 'Human beings fight not because they're different, but because they're the same, and in their accusations and reciprocal violence have made each other enemy twins." Goodhart was riveted to his chair for the hour or so that Girard spoke.

He called his wife immediately after the talk, wildly explaining that he'd just heard a talk that had revolutionized his mind, giving him a new understanding of everything he thought he knew. His mind was in a swirl, and he was reeling. He attended every lecture afterward. He became Girard's first Buffalo graduate student and later his research assistant. His first service was a humble one: he remembers Girard bringing him chapters of *Violence and the Sacred* for copying and sending to the publisher. They spoke daily.

He wasn't the only one impressed. Girard began holding informal seminars for a small circle of students and faculty who were interested in his ideas. For the first semester, Girard gave lectures on his own work, featuring Oedipus, Lévi-Strauss, Dostoyevsky, and the Hebrew Bible, with a bit of the Gospels, too. The group included Goodhart and other future associates, such as Josué Harari and Cesareo Bandera. It was an early harvest; the publication of *Violence and the Sacred* would draw a larger following in the years to come.

The unsigned preface from a Stanford book published the 1980s, *To Honor René Girard*, traced his unexpected journey: "No one at the time, perhaps least of all Girard, could have perceived what was to be the next stage in the development of his thought, although in retrospect the progress of his attention from the individual to the group seems to have been almost inevitable—one might say that this temporal paradox, the inevitability of the unexpected, is precisely what defines his work as an oeuvre. In *Violence and the Sacred*, some of the same mechanisms that were revealed to be operative in the Proustian salons were traced out on a vast anthropological scale, with the addition of a theory of sacrifice that enabled Girard to define religion in pre-legal societies as the realm of controlled violence."[6]

.   .   .

With *Violence and the Sacred*, René Girard would present all human history as a crime thriller, in which the murderer escapes undetected, and the private investigator—in this case, Girard himself—is left only with hints and clues. Human society as a whole is guilty and complicit, hiding the body, and lying about what happened and how. The world's religions and mythologies are the fibs it tells, both revealing and camouflaging what happened. Who benefits? The murder is what gave birth to the society in the first place: its generative event.

"When we describe human relations, we lie," Girard told me. "We describe them as normally good, peaceful and so forth, whereas in reality they are competitive, in a war-like fashion." That simple message is at the heart of *Violence and the Sacred*. Although mimetic desire does not become a theme until the sixth chapter, it underlies this book and all his future books and interviews. In *Violence and the Sacred*, the connection between imitation and violence was inextricably forged.

The link was straightforward: desire, being imitative in nature, spreads contagiously. Hence, society carefully regulates marriage and property, for example—matters likely to trigger envy and imitation, which proliferate and therefore threaten the society as a whole. One woman, not necessarily the most attractive in a village, inspires the desire of one man, then two, then by contagion all. The process accelerates as it spreads. One parcel of property becomes valuable chiefly because it is wanted by all factions—think of the history of Alsace-Lorraine, or Jerusalem.

In what he called a "mimetic crisis," differences melt as people, in their escalating rivalry, begin to resemble one another more and more. As a rule, customs and laws prevent people from converging on the same objects and symbols—whether the distinctions derive from carefully preserved caste systems or social laws as complicated as those found in Leviticus—but these begin to collapse in a mimetic contagion. Think of our own society's annual Black Friday free-for-alls, which dissipate by Saturday morning, leaving wreckage and even death in their wake. Where tensions are longstanding, however, the situation deteriorates into cycles of vengeance. In Dante's Florence or Shakespeare's Verona, each retaliation triggers a new one. A once well-defined, differentiated society deteriorates into all against all.

Increasingly, one person or one group appears to be responsible for the whole trouble. The mimetic contagion moves from desire to the targeting of a specific victim. The selection of a scapegoat—the person or group accused of causing the societal breakdown—is not random. The scapegoat is typically an outsider—a ruler or foreigner, a woman, or people of an ethnic, racial, or religious minority—someone who has little or no capacity for retaliation and thus will stop the cycles of vengeance. Suddenly the war of all against all turns into the war of all against one. The individual or group has no chance against a mob convinced of the guilt of the accused.

I thought of this in recent years, as long-simmering racial tensions erupted in riots in the second decade of the new century, notably in Baltimore, where Girard spent so many years, and where octogenarian Dick Macksey was still ensconced in his big house with tens of thousands of books. Each in a series of deadly incidents could be preempted only by a guilty court verdict, regardless of the evidence in the particular case at hand, regardless of the appropriateness of the charge, and regardless of the courtroom standard of guilt beyond a reasonable doubt. Repeatedly, clamorous voices insisted that one individual, usually a policeman, must be "made an example," "must pay"—and pay, it was sometimes said, not for behavior in a particular moment in a particular place, but for all injustices, over the last century or two.

The scapegoat can be killed, exiled, or otherwise isolated or punished—and suddenly, for a while, there's peace. No one wants to see him or herself as a murderer or unthinking participant in mob violence. Unanimity is important. Everyone must throw a stone. Nobody commits the murder, because everyone does. The outcome is pinned on some sort of inexplicable fate, a combination of circumstances, or divine will. The victim is first perceived as guilty, then as a savior, a god, responsible for the return of the peace that had been interrupted. Oedipus the regicide is deified at Colonus, and in Euripides, the ambushed Helen of Troy becomes a celestial object in the night sky. Those who lived through the 1960s will remember the kitschy portraits of the martyred John F. Kennedy that were sold even in drugstores and at roadside stands after the assassination, and also the instant deification of Martin Luther King on his death, with more portraits to adorn the makeshift home memorials of the worshipers.

When the seasons roll round again, or the problems resume, a society reenacts the rite with a real or symbolic victim. One need only witness the archaic glee of our violent sports and reality TV shows, where drama is cultivated and scapegoats regularly provided, to realize that the sacrificial impulse is still at work. An archaic society repeats the process to enlist divine support, through reverence or propitiation. "I contend that the objective of ritual is the proper reenactment of the surrogate-victim mechanism; its function is to perpetuate or renew the effects of this mechanisms; that is, to keep violence *outside* the community,"[7] Girard wrote. "They are striving to produce a replica, as faithful as possible in every detail, of a previous crisis that was resolved by means of a spontaneously unanimous victimization."[8]

These rituals, he argued, are the foundation of human societies. The calls of "We have burned a witch!" yield to "We have burned a saint!" and a fractured France becomes a united nation with the killing of Joan of Arc. Girard noted that the foundations of a city were sometimes *literally* built on human sacrifice. When Hiel the Bethelite builds Jericho "he laid the foundation thereof in Abiram his firstborn, and set up the gates thereof in his youngest son Segun,"[9] in a passage widely interpreted as a reference to human sacrifice. The victim may become the worshipped guardian of the city, as well as the reason for its existence.

"Human society begins from the moment symbolic institutions are created around the victim, that is to say when the victim becomes sacred,"[10] Girard explained. Thus, religion mingles with murder, and a guilt so deeply hidden that it is not experienced at all. The culpability of the victim is unchallenged, and becomes part of the ritually repeated story—hence, the tales of medieval Jews slaying Christian babies, or poisoning wells, reveal the pretext and later justifications for massacres, expulsions, and pogroms. The unanimity of the persecutors, their conviction of the truth of their lies, makes them ready accomplices for concealment. The stories that have come down to us are theirs, not the recollections of the murdered victims.

"The community is both attracted and repelled by its own origins. It feels the constant need to reexperience them, albeit in veiled and transfigured form," Girard wrote. "By means of rites the community manages to cajole and somewhat subdue the forces of destruction. But the true nature and real function of these forces will always elude its grasp, precisely because the source of the evil is the community itself."[11]

In short, violence is the secret soul of the sacred. The real purpose of sacrifice is not to appease transcendent beings. Rather, it is to ensure the survival of a people. This is a truth the society cannot bear to look at directly.

Girard told me that our judicial system is the modern antidote to the mob, with its cycles of accusation and vengeance, its contagious fears and ritual denunciations—and on the whole it works. It has the authority to impose a final punishment of its own—vengeance stops at the courtroom. He once reminded me that the very act of sequestering juries in the United States protects our justice system from contagious thoughts and retaliatory violence—throwing each juror on his or her own reasoning powers and the law, away from the fury and passions of the mob. "You isolate them. You want the people not to see other people and be influenced in mob directions," he told me. "Intelligent democracies can last only if they are aware of the mob and take great precautions against it, but these precautions are not always effective."

Similarly, the American constitution requires the agreement of the majority in two houses of Congress, breaking mob momentums. "The Communists, for instance, are always in favor of only one house of representatives, not two, because it's easier to manipulate," he told me. "If there were three, you could never do anything." Has the formula become less reliable in the modern era? The modern world is constantly threatened by mob aspects, Girard said, and that trend may write the future of our story. But *Violence and the Sacred* appeared in 1972. Television was still relatively new in that era, and the Internet was decades away from its chimerical birth.

.   .   .

In *Violence and the Sacred,* Girard also took on Freudian thinking, replacing it with the more streamlined theory of mimetic desire. Above all, he pared down Freudian psychoanalysis, which had been a house constructed of jerry-rigged additions: "As I kept going, I discovered the explanatory power of mimetic desire, even in specifically Freudian domains like psychopathology. The argument's elegance remains a fundamental criterion: you suddenly see that there is a single explanation for a thousand different phenomena."[12] The "Oedipus complex," for example, can be explained in terms of mimetic rivalry—that is, Oedipus wants his mother because his father does; so can Freud's "death drive." According to Girard, "He contents himself in some sense with adding an extra drive. This motley assemblage inspires awe in the credulous, but if it can be simplified, we have to simplify it."[13] In this light, "unconscious" motivations are another invention to hide the true origin of desire in the mimetic drives of the collective.

"Just as Girard's theory is 'beyond structuralism,' so it moves beyond Freud to develop a model which is more comprehensive and totalizing than the Oedipus complex,"[14] Carl Rubino wrote in *Modern Language Notes,* reviewing the French edition of the book.

Not everyone was thrilled with Girard's radical revision. One critic wrote that he "everywhere shows his contempt for psychoanalysis and delights in the superiority of his own hindsight to Freud's flawed foresight."[15] Not true. Freud came very close to the mimetic system, Girard argued, but his own theories are much more than a stripped-down version of Freud. In fact, Girard was swimming against the tide when he said, "Everyone seems intent on covering *Totem and Taboo* with obloquy and condemning it to oblivion," yet Freud was too close to Girard's own work for him to fail to give him his due:

> He was the first to maintain that all ritual practices, all mythical implications, have their origins in an actual murder. Freud was unable to exploit the

boundless implications of this proposition; in fact, he seemed unaware of the truly vertiginous implications of this idea. After his death, his discovery was summarily dismissed . . . Far from handling his ethnological material like a clumsy amateur, Freud accomplished such a feat of systematization that he himself was thrown off balance. He was unable to formulate the hypothesis that would do justice to his discovery, and no one after him had the vision to perceive that such a thing was even possible.[16]

He gave *Totem and Taboo* a new prominence and a new twist, but with important reservations: "Little by little it became apparent to me that psychoanalytic suspicion didn't go far enough. Freud's sham 'radicalism' ceased to impress me,"[17] he said in an interview years later. He turned the Freudian model on its head, yet follows in its footsteps, going further than Freud in formulating a complete origin of culture.

.   .   .

Violence and the Sacred is a dense, closely reasoned text, passionately argued and of immense scope. It is unified by its search for understanding violence, in myths, rituals, ancient literature, history. As well as its unorthodox readings of the Greeks and of Shakespeare, it includes in its compass Heraclitus, Sir James Frazer, Hegel, Freud, Georges Bataille, Dostoevsky, Friedrich Hölderlin, Lévi-Strauss, Jean-Pierre Vernant, and Derrida. It considers the elaborate sacrificial rituals of the Ndembu, the Dinka, the Chukchi, the Sioux and the Swazi, and many others in its sweep. *Phi Beta Kappa* called Girard's hypotheses "powerful, well sustained, contestable, perhaps monumental"—nonetheless, it claimed the essay is greater than its hypotheses.[18] The book was called deliberately unfashionable in its approach, and faulted for its "shrill, polemical stance."[19] Well, he had heard that criticism before when *Deceit, Desire, and the Novel* was published.

Critics were bewildered, antagonized, daunted, and intrigued. The book was called "fascinating and ambitious," "a magnificent performance," and "insistently and intentionally scandalous."[20] Rubino wrote that *Violence and the Sacred* is "a truly formidable book, one which is filled with *der Ernst des Begriffs* and which therefore demands our serious attention. How does one 'sit down to review' such a book? *La violence et le sacré*, like *Phenomenology of Spirit* itself, is a book that demands many serious readings; it does not call for reviews, which too often become, for both writer and reader alike, mere devices for bypassing the real subject matter, while combining the semblance of seriousness and exertion with a dispensation from both."

Rubino continued: "Girard has written a truly Hegelian work which, like the *Phenomenology* itself, provides an account of the totality of human culture. It is therefore natural to expect that his book will be subject to the same kinds of attack which have been aimed at the *Phenomenology,* and it is also natural to expect that the book will come through those attacks as well as its predecessor has."[21]

The book was predicted to cause arguments among anthropologists, psychoanalysts, philosophers, lit students, structuralists, and post-structuralists alike. And so it did. Over the years, social scientists had become suspicious of grand theories of the *Golden Bough* variety. They accused Frazer of not contextualizing his findings, cherry-picking myths and rituals to fit his paradigm. The subsequent overreaction meant that anthropologists became perhaps too obsessed with all the details of a particular culture, and unwilling to make any comparisons or generalizations at all. The particularized studies, one after another, offer no overarching perspective, with each researcher having his own handkerchief-sized turf. Those who had clipped their own wings reacted predictably to the literary critic who had taken to the clouds.

Cultural anthropologist Victor Turner, whose work Girard had cited, objected to Girard's approach more categorically, although he had been on a parallel path in his study of rituals and conflict: "Anthropologists must cleave to some empirical findings even though they might limit Girard's most plausible speculations. He bases too much of his thesis on literature and too little on ethnography and human biology. There is no physiological evidence that man possesses an aggressive instinct," he wrote. "More plausible is the view that aggression is a consequence of frustration and that many frustrations arise from the order of society. This perspective is an important alternative to Girard's theory since, if it is correct, human beings outside the patterned arrangements of roles, statuses, and hierarchies should be less frustrated, less prone to violence than those crimped by social obligations."[22] One rather wonders if he had read the book, in which Girard argues that frustrations arise from thwarted desire, and are therefore effect as much as they are cause. In any case, where would one find hermits outside any "patterned arrangements of roles, statuses, and hierarchies"?

Anthropologists demanded field studies, empirical findings, and decried "a dearth of direct evidence."[23] But, Girard replied, how do you do fieldwork on events that happened centuries ago, or that happened over a period of millennia, especially if the participants were, at the time, at pains to conceal their proceedings? How do you collect "direct evidence" for myths? Isn't ancient literature itself an artifact and some of the best primary documents anyone could hope to find for a people's life and thinking? As far as empiricism, Girard's work cited the work of many researchers around the world, documenting some of the last societies untouched by modernity.

One critic asked how we can take seriously Girard's claim of the systematic concealment of evidence. One wonders why that required a stretch of imagination in the Vietnam and Watergate eras, with their falsified body counts broadcast daily on the network news, the revelations of missing tapes, and the public lies. Surely the best evidence is within ourselves, which is why the book rings true for so many readers. *We* conceal the evidence, *we* tell the story in a way that exonerates ourselves. Every single day. We have no reason to believe our forebears were any different. God questioning Cain on the whereabouts of his brother, or Adam on explaining why he munched the fruit, or Nathan tricking David into the confession of his murder of Uriah— isn't much of our talk an attempt to defend ourselves, deflect blame, conceal at least as much as reveal? If we're honest, isn't this the story of our lives?

Victor Brombert, whose Jewish family had fled several totalitarian advances in Europe, saw the truth of it, concluding in *The Chronicle of Higher Education*:

> Nonetheless, the book has a haunting effect, and reveals a resolutely independent mind. On the genesis of myth, the bridge between myth and rite, collective obsessions, and the predicament of modern society that seeks ever greater numbers of sacrificial victims in a desperate effort to restore the efficacy of a lost sense of ritual, René Girard has much to say. The book will strike only the superficial reader as pessimistic. . . . A period that has known variations of unprecedented mass violence, and specifically the Nazi frenzy directed against the Jew as scapegoat, cannot afford to neglect René Girard's contribution. *Violence and the Sacred* is an important book.[24]

■   ■   ■

Most scholars were critiquing René Girard's ideas from comfortable arm-chairs in an academic setting. Robert Hamerton-Kelly, the learned South African theologian and ethics scholar who was Girard's friend and colleague, offered a reality check from another quarter. He described a long, strange letter Girard received in the 1980s, telling about the murder of a man in the Msinga District of Zululand, South Africa.

The murdered man had been the director of church-related food relief and other social work in the district. His widow, Creina Alcock, described in the letter how he had died in an ambush while returning from a peace confer-ence he had brokered among fighting clans. Once the treaty was signed, one clan quickly got its guns and ambushed another clan on its way home. Creina Alcock's husband was killed. She was left to raise two sons and carry on his work.

"In the period after the ambush, accusations of witchcraft abounded and women were burned in their beds. Creina Alcock stayed on in the midst of this eerie mayhem in her compound of beehive-shaped huts on a promon-tory overlooking a dry riverbed on which many of the interclan shootouts took place," Hamerton-Kelly wrote.

> She tells of sinking into a deep depression after the murder of her husband, of losing the will to live, and of, nevertheless, persevering, chiefly because she had to defend her women servants against the witch burners.
>
> One afternoon, in the library of the University of Natal at Pieter-maritzburg, where her father had been a professor of classics, she came upon *Violence and the Sacred,* took it down, and began to read it. As she told Girard in her letter, that reading was the beginning of her journey up out of depression and back to life. She said that as she read, she realized that there was someone out there in the real world who understood what was going on in Msinga, that the death of her husband and her ongoing experience of violence was not just a weird nightmare, that she was not going mad, but, on the contrary, that there are anthropological categories with which to interpret these violent phenomena, that the phenomena are 'normal' abnormalities, and that no one here is crazy, except perhaps those who would deny the symptoms of a sacrificial crisis. Discovering that there is a theory that covers her experience persuaded her that she remained, despite the strangeness, a member of the common human race.[25]

.   .   .

René Girard was a theorist, but one with a complicated relationship to the very notion of theories, which tend, as he pointed out, to be engraved in marble. He wished his own work not to be taken as a foolproof formula, but as a working dynamic in human society.

"When I say that my mimetic anthropology is a series of hypotheses I truly mean it, and the so-called 'système-Girard' which is attributed to me, even in the introduction to the French paperback edition of my books, exists primarily in the mind of those who have no firsthand experience of the dynamic force of the mimetic theory," he explained in an interview. "They see my work as something static, a bunch of dogmatic propositions about the way things are. I do not recognize myself in their summations of my views. This does not mean I am not serious about my work. Just the opposite. What should be taken seriously, however, is the mimetic theory itself—its analytical power and versatility—rather than this or that particular conclusion or position, which critics tend to turn into some creed which I am supposedly trying to force down their throats. I am much less dogmatic than a certain reading of my work suggests."[26]

Girard had a skeptical relationship vis-à-vis theory and had doubts about its future. Elsewhere in the same interview, he ridiculed it as a vogue: "If a Rabelais shows up at the right time, he will do hilarious things with our current scholasticism and in particular with our use of the word 'theory.' My anticipation of this future—I am old enough to have seen several literary fashions—makes it easy to understand why I prefer not to define myself as a theorist. The word 'theory' has been so fashionable in recent years that, in the near future, it will sound horribly dated and ridiculous. The next generation will wonder what impulse could move so many people to go on endlessly writing the most convoluted prose in a complete void of their own making, disconnected not only from the reality of their world but from the great literary texts, of which recent theory has been making a shamelessly parasitic use."[27]

Yet in the end Girard *was* a theorist, and ferocious in defense of his theories (Freccero called him "a Jeremiah" in that regard). He welcomed the snowballs. He told me, "Theories are expendable. They should be criticized. When people tell me my work is too systematic, I say, 'I make it as systematic as possible for you to be able to prove it wrong.'" Our conversation continued:

I like your comment, "Without a theory, facts don't mean anything."

But this is very important for scientists. People in the human sciences—you know, the sciences of man—are always saying that theories are not scientific, and so forth. Of course, but without theories, there would be no science. As a matter of fact, the danger today is precisely that there are many facts without theory, and the incompleteness of science is often due to the lack of theory to connect the facts.

Can you give an example?

Well, for instance, the arrival of Einstein is not the arrival of something *factual*. There have been verifications of Einstein's theories, showing that light made curves, and that sort of thing. But all Newton took a different shape in Einstein. The reason Einstein is true is not mostly because of this factual verification, but because it gave a new significance. If a theory explains more facts than a previous one, it's a good one. Period.

.   .   .

If an eagle had swooped beneath the rainclouds of a summer storm in Buffalo, looking down over the city's university, it might have spied a Quonset hut on the southern side of the Buffalo campus, as the rain pounded insistently on the corrugated steel roof. And if its eyes had by some sort of wizardry pierced the metal, it might have observed two huddled men underneath, earnestly talking about Shakespeare.

Despite the lavish blank check Cook had been given to make the Buffalo English Department a world-class showcase for academic innovation, it was housed in two spartan, overcrowded Quonset huts labeled "Annex A" and "Annex B" (although they weren't "annexed" to anything)—little more than sheds, really. "Annex B" may be remembered, among other things, as the place where Girard encountered Shakespeare. The catalyst was Sandy Goodhart, and he remembered the rain that was the backdrop to their conversations.

Girard's interest in the Bard was initially sparked by watching a film of *A Midsummer Night's Dream*—but which version? Colleagues cite both Max Reinhardt's 1935 classic with Olivia de Haviland, Victor Jory, Dick Powell, James Cagney, and Mickey Rooney, using Felix Mendelssohn's famous score, and Sir Peter Hall's 1968 Royal Shakespeare Company production, which premiered on American television screens on 9 February 1969. Goodhart said it was the earlier film, yet Martha, who of all people ought to know, said it was the later film. If so, we might be able to date Girard's interest in Shakespeare to that very day. Hall's shoestring budget production is a trifle dated now, with its hippie fantasy of the fairy kingdom, whose scantily clad denizens are painted green. The lighting is so uneven that you often cannot be sure whether day or night is intended. Yet the acting is stellar, featuring many performers who were not famous then but would become so in the succeeding years—Diana Rigg, Helen Mirren, Ian Holm, Ian Richardson, and Judi Dench (who, as critics carefully noted, was clothed in little more than a half-dozen tiny leaves). Above all, the cast breathed fresh air into old forms. The performers embraced a new naturalness and abandoned tired stage conventions.

In short, the film was something of a revolution. Peter Hall's use of the hand-held camera, usually seen as a stock ploy to generate suspense for horror films, gave the film an artless, jittery, you-are-really-there effect—especially in the play's most psychedelic and otherworldly settings. The lost and befuddled love-struck quartet became increasingly muddy and unkempt in the forest—anticipating the spirit of Woodstock, which would occur later that year.

However, the text was Girard's primary inspiration, although that text had been delightfully repackaged for a new era. Witness Helena's idolatry toward the bosom friend who has distracted her lover and becomes a mimetic model and rival:

> My ear should catch your voice, my eye your eye,
> My tongue should catch your tongue's sweet melody.
> Were the world mine, Demetrius being bated,
> The rest I'd give to be to you translated.
> O, teach me how you look, and with what art
> You sway the motion of Demetrius' heart.

Martha recalled that René spent a decade writing and thinking about Shakespeare—not a strategic choice in the world of academia, but the Stratford playwright intrigued him, and as always, Girard followed his nose. It was the longest he had ever spent on a book. Martha said that René, in those days, had given the impression that the English bard had been reaching out to him through the centuries, almost as if he were receiving help from the other end. Her remark would be echoed years later, by Benoît Chantre, when speaking about Girard's relationship with the military theoretician Clausewitz.

"His discovery of Shakespeare really was a discovery," recalled John Freccero—certainly it was so for Girard himself. Shakespeare is so deeply immersed in his language and his times that he can remain a forever closed book to the foreign speaker—Girard had previously considered him little more than "an Anglo-Saxon Racine," according to Freccero.

Early on, Goodhart sensed Shakespeare's affinities with Girard's work, and made a persuasive presentation on *Othello* in Girard's seminar in Annex B—at that point, it was to be his dissertation topic. The talk was so well received it spilled into two sessions. "*Othello* was extremely important for both of us," Goodhart recalled. Afterward, Girard approached him and said, "You've convinced me that Shakespeare really is as important as Cervantes and the others. If I had known about Shakespeare before, I would have included him in my book."

Goodhart told me he was grateful that Shakespeare had not found his way into the pages of *Deceit, Desire, and the Novel,* otherwise *A Theater of Envy: William Shakespeare* would never have been written. The fervent, brilliant work is a refreshing and exuberant take on Shakespeare. Nevertheless, the book tackles Shakespeare from only one vantage point—Girard's own theories, of course.

A Theater of Envy is the only book Girard conceived and wrote in English. It is unlike anything else he had written, and clearly born from an enthusiasm and the power of a new love. In the introduction, he apologizes for the lopsidedness of the whole affair. James Joyce is somewhat awkwardly positioned in the middle. *A Midsummer Night's Dream,* not surprisingly, takes up nearly a quarter of the book. He regarded that play, in particular, as "Shakespeare's first mature masterpiece, a veritable explosion of genius."[28]

It is tempting to think of *A Theater of Envy* as a one-off *divertissement*— but that would be a mistake and more than a little dismissive. It is a striking book, and perhaps Girard's most neglected effort, combining his literary preoccupations with a complete unfolding of his ideas on desire, mimesis, and sacrifice, in a way that is spirited and iconoclastic. That said, it has not fared well in the world. Although it was first published by Oxford University Press in 1991, the book is now available only through St. Augustine's Press in Indiana, in an edition with a fragile binding that dries and splits, and pages that turn yellow within a few years. That's too bad, because the volume makes Girard's ideas more accessible to most educated English speakers and therefore had the potential for bringing a whole new audience to his work. While readers today may not be familiar with Dostoevsky's *The Possessed* or Cervantes's masterpiece beyond the barest outlines, they will still know *Hamlet, Julius Caesar,* and *Othello.* And from these examples, *Le Système Girard* can be reconstructed from scratch, without resorting to anthropologists or postmodern thinkers.

Shakespeare and Girard. There is much to connect the two writers, separated by centuries and a mother tongue. Shakespeare openly confronts that most taboo of vices, envy, "the astringent and unpopular word"[29] that represents the besetting vice throughout the Bard's plays. Shakespeare also anticipated the Girardian concept of mimetic crisis, which the playwright calls a "crisis of degree," when social distinctions melt and chaos ensues. Shakespeare's repeated use of themes of covetousness and scapegoating, whether in comedy (Helena and Hermia alternately blame each other for alienation of affection) or in tragedy (Othello longs for Cassio's *savoir faire,* so he becomes a rival), or in the arresting motif of sacrifice and ritual in *Julius Caesar,* most clearly stated by Brutus:

> Let us be sacrificers, but not butchers, Caius.
> We all stand up against the spirit of Caesar;
> And in the spirit of men there is no blood:
> O! then that we could come by Caesar's spirit,
> And not dismember Caesar. But, alas!
> Caesar must bleed for it.

Girard found Shakespeare's history plays less pertinent to his themes, which is rather surprising. The plays resound with mimetic crisis, as kings fall and usurpers grab power, all in quest of the "hollow crown" as a mimetic *objet du désir,* which would seem to place them squarely within the Girardian realm. Shakespeare was keenly aware of the "the canker vice," "that monster envy" that causes ambition, selfishness, and conflict. The Bard's "sacred kings," victims readied for sacrifice (for example, Richard II, Henry VI), underscore the message of *Violence and the Sacred.* Although he was indifferent to the histories, however, Girard found "something radically new, a more humane and even religious note" in Shakespeare's late romances—works that are often overlooked by critics and theatergoers alike, even today.

The book, although written in English, was first published in a French translation and won Frances's Prix Médicis in 1990. However, Girard's understandable slips proved fatal to the critical success of the book in English. As a foreigner and a newcomer to Shakespeare, he often projects his own previous misconceptions of the "Anglo-Saxon Racine" onto others, in such passages as this one: "Shakespeare is more comical than we realize, in a bitterly satirical and even cynical mode, much closer to contemporary attitudes than we ever suspected."[30] Shakespeare's trenchant humor and bitterness are no surprise to centuries of Shakespeare lovers, even allowing for the stark differences in what each era considers "funny." (For example, the playwright's love of puns and peripheral figures of fun test the patience of many modern theatergoers.) In a similar vein, Girard writes, "His supersonic insolence is exactly what is needed to rescue Shakespeare from the mountain of humanistic pieties and aesthetic mush under which the 'noble bard' has been buried for centuries"[31]—but surely the vestiges of bowdlerizing were well in the past by the 1960s and 1970s, as the Peter Hall production makes clear. Nobody is crushed by that mountain today.

Thus, not everyone was charmed by *A Theater of Envy*, and Girard gave plenty of reason for offense in a competitive academic field. One unusually hostile review defended the traditional turf: "Arguing from a position of total conviction, René Girard proposes that the complete works of Shakespeare—and, he tends to suggest, the very mind of the writer himself—can be explained, and can only be explained, in terms of the concept of 'mimetic desire,'" Gregory Woods began in *The Renaissance Quarterly*'s blistering attack. The review overlooks the French thinker's obvious aim to describe Shakespeare's work through his own theory, and so misses the point of the book, but Woods summarizes the hostility within the entrenched world of Shakespearean scholars: "This is the kind of lofty criticism that requires few footnotes since it only rarely refers to other critics by name. Girard prefers to lump them all together as the mythological beast 'traditional criticism,' which he attacks at every opportunity. . . . These problems are irritatingly augmented by his habit of saying 'we' when he means 'I', thereby imposing an invented consensus on even his weakest ideas. Although, when castigating politicized critics for bias, he argues that 'undecidability is the rule in Shakespeare as in all great mimetic writers,' throughout the book he himself is preposterously decisive. His reading of any play is the 'correct' one; others are 'incorrect.' This is so reductive that it actually threatens damage to Shakespeare."[32]

It's been a quarter century since *A Theater of Envy* was published, and I think that we can safely say Shakespeare has not been damaged. But the review showed the reasons for the ruffled scholarly feathers. Girard was more interested in exploring his own ideas than he was in negotiating the complicated academic terrain he had wandered onto—and the knives were out. The disdain was not universal, by any means. Other Shakespeare aficionados had a more open disposition.

Goodhart described a colloquium in which C. L. Barber and Girard switched their customary roles—an academic version of the "Lord of Misrule." Goodhart explained that the critic Barber, who had written a "subtle and adventurous book on Shakespeare's use of traditional ritual in his early plays" (*Shakespeare's Festive Comedy*), would discuss Proust, and Girard would speak for the first time on Shakespeare and identity crisis in *A Midsummer Night's Dream*. "The performance that followed was electrifying, and afterward, with the room still abuzz from the *tour de force* to which we had just been witness, C.L. Barber stood up and declared: 'I have been teaching this play for fifty years, René, and you have just explained it to me.'"

Girard's work had that effect on people, Goodhart wrote—"a kind of 'Midas touch' which reorients you entirely towards texts or subject matters with which you have long been familiar."[33]

A Theater of Envy was a daring, perhaps even reckless venture from a professional point of view. Shakespearean studies is a popular and overpopulated field, with tenacious fashions and received wisdom—one not welcoming to the bold and uninitiated. He was, moreover, not a native speaker. Dangerous waters indeed. But perhaps it was a gift of love not only to the English bard, but to the language that had become his own, and to the university that had taken him into its English department during his most prolific years.

·   ·   ·

The cerebral excitement of the two scholars who huddled in conversation as the rain pounded on the corrugated steel above them gives an impression of detachment and intellectual euphoria at Buffalo. That was not the whole story, for these were the years of the Vietnam and Indochina War, as well as an array of social and cultural upheavals. If they didn't seem to affect Girard greatly, it's not to say they didn't affect others at Buffalo. The Girards shrugged off the mayhem when we discussed it—Girard, as always, was in his own intellectual world during those years, and Martha was protecting the calm and orderly environment in which he could work; they were, as always, a no-drama couple. That was not the case elsewhere on campus. Said Prof. Bruce Jackson of the turbulent time, "It touched nearly everything we did: how we taught our classes, the lives of our students, our conversations."

Occasionally someone would ask me where the Girards were in the sixties. Were they attending sit-ins and wearing love beads? Did they march together in Washington? It's not quite as daft as it sounds. Many of their colleagues were doing precisely that, and it's worthwhile to take a few moments to consider what was happening around them at Buffalo, which was an epicenter for change, and the effect it had on their colleagues—and the impact it had on one of them, in particular. This is where the Girards were *not* in the tumultuous 1960s.

The era left perhaps its deepest mark on Leslie Fiedler, who, with three members of his family, was arrested for "maintaining premises for the use of marijuana" on Friday, 28 April 1967.[34] He had been a faculty advisor for a campus group "Lemar" (that is, "Legalize Marijuana"), which triggered weeks of twenty-four-hour police surveillance, ending with a search warrant and the removal of "a quantity" of marijuana and hashish. Fiedler and his wife, his son, his daughter-in-law, and two visiting seventeen-year-olds were busted. Fiedler was found guilty in 1970, with a sentence that included jail time. Multiple appeals later, the decision was finally reversed in 1972. A woman testified under oath that she had planted the illegal substances just prior to the police entering the Fiedler home.

Girard had described Fiedler as the most entertaining and iconoclastic of the Buffalo group, but he was already working under dark clouds by the time Girard arrived on campus: his home insurance had been cancelled by two providers, the University of Amsterdam had reversed its decision to have him as a Fulbright lecturer, and his legal costs were crushing and stressful. His marriage would end about the same time as his exoneration.

Fiedler's trauma was only a hint of events to come. Within a few years, the police occupied the campus to quell anti-war demonstrations. Jackson recalled when hundreds of Buffalo policemen in riot gear occupied the Main Street campus in the spring of 1970. "Tear-gas canisters were fired into stairwells of the old Norton Union so they would enter the circulating air system of the entire building. A Buffalo police official went on one of television news programs and denied firing any tear gas anywhere on campus. . . . I have a photograph of the window over the front door of the Union riddled with holes from the blast of a police shotgun."

At the height of the disturbances, forty-five faculty members who had occupied the university's Hayes Hall for a peaceful sit-in were arrested for criminal trespass. The group, protesting the police excesses as well as the war, staged their protest one Sunday morning when the building was empty of anyone save them. They sat around a table in the president's office. When they were warned to leave, Ray Federman, who was among them, became agitated—he was a French Jew who had been a World War II resistance fighter, and his family had died at Auschwitz. To calm him, the German poet and translator Max Wickert read selections from Kafka's *The Trial*.[35] A quieter member of the group was a young computer programmer and assistant professor of English who had arrived on campus the same time Girard had. J. M. Coetzee would later write about the influence of Girard on his own writing, and would eventually win a Nobel.

The police lifted the "Buffalo 45" out of their chairs, one by one, and passed them out of the crowded office. At the police station, they were fingerprinted and put behind bars for the day. The New York Superior Court eventually overturned their convictions, which could have resulted in a six-year prison sentence, ruling that the university's decision to ban all campus gatherings was unlawful. No harm done—for all except the South African assistant professor of English who lost his green card. Coetzee told an interviewer years later, "In the wake of my arrest, my legal situation as a foreigner in the U.S. simply became untenable."[36] He began writing his first book *Dusklands* (1974) at Buffalo. One of its two stories focuses on the effect of Vietnam on the American psyche; the second describes the colonialist interaction with the South African natives in the eighteenth century. Both stories show an unmistakable Girardian influence.

Although *Violence and the Sacred* was not published in Paris until the year after Coetzee returned to South Africa, he was already familiar with *Deceit, Desire, and the Novel*, which he read while at Buffalo. It changed his views on *Madame Bovary.* They were both, after all, colleagues in the same department, and René Girard was discussing his ideas at the popular lectures in Annex B. Girard's new theories were very much part of the general buzz. Coetzee had a strong interest in the archaic societies of his native South Africa and the precarious brutality of apartheid. He had an interest in historical discourse and historical lies. He also had a unique foothold in postmodern literary culture, and was interested in the theoretical discourses of structuralism and post-structuralism, a conversation dominated by linguists. The 1966 conference that brought French thought to America occurred the year following his arrival at his first American port-of-call, the University of Texas at Austin, where he would receive his PhD in linguistics. It seems unlikely that the younger man of about thirty would not have attended a lecture or two. In fact, one of his colleagues remembers him at one, although the author himself doesn't recall any direct interaction with Girard at half a century's distance. However, he still remembers clearly Girard's impressive physical presence, and that Girard's works had a deep effect on him. Eventually, he would make a more systematic study of them.[37] He must have pored over *Violence and the Sacred,* in whatever country and whatever language the book found him—everyone was.[38]

How do we tell the story of the man who was not in the midst of the worldwide upheaval that dominated his era, and whose life was serene and externally uneventful? We have to go by what he writes, and what others have written under his star. Girard's oeuvre influenced many writers, including Milan Kundera, Roberto Calasso, Karen Armstrong, Simon Schama, James Carroll, and Elif Batuman. Let us examine one of them—Coetzee—a little more closely, for this is a case where we can trace a direct line from Girard's thought to a Nobel author's pen, a man whose novels have, in turn, affected the attitudes, opinions, beliefs, and, on occasion, the actions of others, many years later.[39]

Coetzee often brings a Girardian lens to bear on a world he knew firsthand, rooted in South Africa's racial disparities. "The Narrative Jacobus Coetzee," the second of the two *Dusklands* stories, begins by noting the relationship between the Boer settlers with the Hottentots who are serving them, during an era—the eighteenth century—when many white settlers, under the autocratic rule of the Dutch East India Company, were shifting from the status of established burgher to semi-nomadic trekboer. "Everywhere differences grow smaller as they come up and we go down," the eponymous narrator notes in the opening paragraph. Then he gives a textbook description of mimetic meltdown:

> The days are past when Hottentots would come to the back door begging for a crust of bread while we dressed in silver knee-buckles and sold wine to the Company. There are those of our people who live like Hottentots, pulling up their tents when the pasture gives out and following the cattle after new grass. Our children play with servants' children, and who is to say who copies whom? In hard times how can differences be maintained? We pick up their way of life, following beasts around, as they pick up ours. They throw their sheepskins away and dress like people. If they still smell like Hottentots, so do some of us: spend a winter under canvas in the Roggeveld, the days too cold to leave the fire, the water frozen in the barrel, nothing to eat but mealcakes and slaughter-sheep, and soon you carry the Hottentot smell with you, mutton fat and thornbush smoke.[40]

How can the differences be maintained? They can't. Only Christianity, says Jacobus, makes the difference. The narrator says, "We are Christian, a folk with a destiny." Destiny, of course, requires time. The Hottentots, by contrast, are trapped in the present—"it is pointless to ask a Bushman how old he is, he has no conception of number, anything more than two is 'many,'" and of course to count is to master time. The narrator himself is "a hero of enumeration. He who does not understand number does not understand death." Wandering the unexplored interior of South Africa, abandoned and alone, Jacobus too gets reduced to the state of his adversaries—losing his boundaries in the wild. All senses but sight become numb in the vacuum of impressions, with only death as a marker of time and meaning. He defends his "difference" with a massacre of the natives who had humiliated him.

Violence haunts Coetzee's work, here described in visceral detail, but with the author's mandarin, clinical, even chilly detachment. The narrator of the first story of *Dusklands*, "The Vietnam Project," is as fascinated by ritual and violence as Jacobus is. In his words, "The instrument of survival in the wild is the gun, but the need for it is metaphysical rather than physical."

"No more than any other man do I enjoy killing; but I have taken it upon myself to be the one to pull the trigger, performing the sacrifice for myself and my countrymen, who exist, and committing upon the dark folk the murders we have wished. All are guilty, without exception. . . . Who knows for what unimaginable crimes of the spirit they died, through me? God's judgment is just, irreprehensible, and incomprehensible. His mercy pays no heed to merit. I am a tool in the hands of history." This, from the author who is a committed vegetarian and advocate for nonviolence.

Coetzee dares to take his thinking to a place where few will follow: to our use of animals as the ultimate scapegoat, which dates to the day when Abraham sacrificed a ram in place of his son Isaac. In that regard, as in many others, he has been controversial. In Coetzee's Booker Prize-winning *Disgrace*, a discredited academic strikes out into the veld, echoing the trekboer's journey—others have also noted its echoes with the author's swift and unpleasant departure from Buffalo. Unable to defend his daughter from rape, the professor becomes an assistant at an animal shelter, with a new understanding of the country people he had previously despised. The author's Conradian journey inward in the quarter century between *Dusklands* and 1999's *Disgrace* had shifted his outlook: the later book is suffused with a severe and godless mercy, unwarmed by Girard's Christianity—and yet, Coetzee's consolation may sometimes be enough.

Coetzee takes the side of every outcast, of each broken, discarded, and abandoned scapegoat of our world—and in that sense, he and Girard are kinsmen. Certainly Coetzee's tempered words had guided me on a similar painful journey, the same one his protagonist encounters at the end of *Disgrace*:

> So on Sunday afternoons the clinic door is closed and locked while he helps Bev Shaw *lösen* the week's superfluous canines. One at a time he fetches them out of the cage at the back and leads or carries them into the theatre. To each, in what will be its last minutes, Bev gives her fullest attention, stroking it, talking to it, easing its passage. If, more often than not, the dog fails to be charmed, it is because of his presence: he gives off the wrong smell (*They can smell your thoughts*), the smell of shame.

I thought of them as I carried my own beloved dog to her *lösen*—the German word for "solution"—after fourteen years, the amiable black lab I had owned since puppyhood reached the day when she could no longer walk and, despairing, would no longer eat. I recalled Coetzee's words as I carried her in my arms, like a lamb, to her death:

"He and Bev do not speak. He has learned by now, from her, to concentrate on the animal they are killing, giving it what he no longer has difficulty calling by its proper name: love."[41]

CHAPTER 10

The Zero Hour of Culture

"It isn't fair, it isn't right," Mrs. Hutchinson screamed, and
then they were upon her.

—Shirley Jackson, "The Lottery"

Girard had not forgotten the impulsive fan who had flown the Atlantic to see him. He had promised to contact him when he arrived in Paris, and he kept his word. "He called. He said, 'I'm at the Rue Jacob in the 5th arrondissement. Why don't you come down tomorrow?" said Oughourlian.

When the doctor arrived at the hotel, however, he couldn't find Girard. He paced the lobby, afraid of a missed encounter, another frustrating delay, after months of waiting. Finally, one of the clerks told him, "But Professor Girard is out on the sidewalk, waiting for someone."

Recollecting the event decades later, he smiled. "I had been looking for an old, gray-haired man with glasses," he said. "Here was an athletic guy, large, with plenty of black hair." The encounter began an exploration for the meaning of the meeting. Each had his own aims. What would these two men, dissimilar in temperament and fields of endeavor, find in each other?

"We started talking. We continued talking till the evening. We decided to work together," Oughourlian said, speaking in his characteristic series of short, declarative sentences. But the future encounters would take place in Buffalo, not Paris. The following year they began their work together at the Cheektowaga Sheraton Hotel.

In truth, *Violence and the Sacred* had left behind an untold story. Girard said his initial intention had been to make it a two-part book: the first part addressing archaic culture, the second part discussing Christianity. Eventually, he decided to cut the part on Christianity—the whole project was taking too long to complete. In *Violence and the Sacred,* mimesis does not become a theme until the sixth chapter. He had wanted to throw the book's emphasis on sacrifice, instead. Colleagues were surprised by what seemed a radical change of direction—the perception partly a result of the way he set out his argument.

Girard hardly stopped to worry about the matter. He was anxious to move on and finish the section of the book he had dropped: "I started to write *Things Hidden* immediately, in 1971, even before the publication of *Violence and the Sacred*. I never stopped working, not even for a single day," he explained. "For me it was really the continuation of my project, because I was still elaborating the same theory. It was a long and hard process because I was obsessed by the apparent impossibility of explaining myself. Not that I had trouble in getting new examples of archaic religion: quite the contrary. What was hard for me was to work out how to juxtapose all these examples and show how they illuminate each other."[1] He was about two-thirds through the effort when he connected with Oughourlian.

The doctor saw that mimetic desire had applications in his own work with drug addiction. He was interested in showing how people are not psychologically isolated in their own heads, but rather bound with everyone else in a dynamic, contingent process of imitation—in short, "interdividual psychology." Together, the two new friends did a long interview that Girard finally concluded was not good enough to publish. Then Girard countered by suggesting the dialogue incorporate the two-thirds of a book Girard had already written. The dialogue became a trialogue when, in 1976, they were joined by another psychiatrist, Guy Lefort, who headed the psychotherapy center of Ainay-le-Château. A tape recorder, always a presence of its own, became a fourth.

The collaboration that began in Buffalo continued in Baltimore, with Oughourlian bringing his wife and child to Maryland, renting a house, a car, and everything else he needed from the literary theorist and author Stanley Fish, then at the beginning of his career at Johns Hopkins. The fancy little sports car did not survive the sojourn unscathed. During a summer shower, it slid sideways into another vehicle—a good thing, since the car barely escaped tumbling down into a ravine, and only wrapped around a tree instead.

Nothing, however, seemed to interrupt their concentration, a crashed car least of all. Girard, as usual, was methodical and disciplined in his habits: "René came every morning. We had coffee and worked till noon. My wife cooked lunch. We worked till evening," Oughourlian told me. "We spent three months working every day."

Reflecting on their relationship, Oughourlian would write years later that Girard had been a master in the same way that Socrates, Plato, and Aristotle had been: "attentive and interested by what the pupil has to offer and offering each time in return an answer of genius, that is to say, an answer at once obvious and unexpected, one that the pupil would never have found by himself but that he recognizes as true and immediately makes his own." He pointed out that a genius is someone who sees what others do not. Everyone has watched an apple fall from a tree, but only Newton responded with the theory of universal gravitation.

Girard gave him two gifts that affected all areas of his life: "an utter irreverence with regard to canonical authors, that is to say, freedom of thought; and lightness, humor, and laughter when approaching the thorniest problems," he wrote. "I have never laughed so much as during the preparation of *Things Hidden,* nor have I ever learned so much."[2]

"Gradually, gradually, gradually," he told me, the book came together. Girard's secretary typed an unwieldy manuscript of nine hundred pages. That was the first draft of *Des choses cachées depuis la fondation du monde,* published in 1978 by Grasset in Paris, later published by Stanford University Press in 1987 as *Things Hidden since the Foundation of the World.* While Girard said he would have finished the book on his own with another year, he was, not surprisingly, thoroughly exhausted, and happy to shorten the labor. He was also eager to clear the backlog of reading and writing, and press on to something new.

"We worked for five full years, which we had fed by exchanges and trips," said Oughourlian. He had been a good partner for Girard—he was provocative and intellectually omnivorous, and those qualities likely endeared him to Girard, as well as helping the collaboration move forward. When Girard told me that Jean-Michel was his best friend, I could certainly understand the reasons for it.

The book would eventually have three sections, focusing on anthropology, the Judeo-Christian scriptures, and interdividual psychology—the last category including reflections on sexuality, narcissism, hypnosis, and psychosis.

As Oughourlian explained to me, "My interest was first to encourage René to clarify his ideas, second, to dare him to talk about the Bible, and finally to dedicate a full third part of the book to interdividual psychology."

.   .   .

Things Hidden would not have been nearly so controversial had René Girard been fascinated by the Koran or the Vedas or the Diamond Sutra. Yet Girard was only doing in a more intensive way what he had done all along: bringing the tools of the social sciences to bear on ancient texts and, increasingly, biblical ones. In the postmodern world, even a truth must be fashionable enough to merit consideration. The distaste and resistance that Girard's theory has sometimes provoked reflects today's postmodern bias against the cornerstone of Western civilization—and the situation was even worse in France.

At the Stanford Bookstore café in his half-hour afternoon break between classes and meetings, Jean-Pierre Dupuy dispatched a large muffin and some sort of high-energy bottled water. Not that he seemed to need the extra energy. As someone closely associated with Girard, he explained to me why he felt his colleague and friend is completely ostracized in French intellectual circles.

He quickly listed three big reasons for the rejection of Girard and what he has to say:

Reason #1: "He believes in God, and he says it." Dupuy said that *laïcité* in France means, in practice, "a public hatred of religion," which makes Girard a jolting departure from the norm. "If a French leader said 'God bless France,' people would take to the streets. It would be the revolution again," said Dupuy.

Reason #2: "He believes in the possibility of a science of man," he said. Post-structuralism, and other "isms," have denied the possibility of knowing truth, or at least devalued it. Therefore in France, he said, "truth is no longer legal tender."

Reason #3: Finally, what he called the last straw: "#1 and #2 are the same reason." That is, "if it's possible to reach the truth, it's because truth is given by God, and the incarnation of God is Jesus Christ."

Notwithstanding Dupuy's assertions, and despite the open professions of religious faith of American politicians, I'm not so sure the situation is very different in the United States, among the *bien pensants* of our own country.

That may be one reason that Girard's work has stronger resonances with Eastern Europe's historical and cultural milieu, where the practice of the Christian religion was often under attack during the Communist era, and where Girard's works had immediate, personal relevance. We value what we pay for, and not just in cash. His works were often smuggled or shared in samizdat editions during the Cold War and had urgent applications for those who read them. Participants in Poland's Solidarity movement, the Czechs' Velvet Revolution, and other anti-Communist resistance said Girard's works were textbook lessons for resisting the violence they saw around them. He inspired them. When I mentioned knowing Girard to leading Eastern European poets Adam Zagajewski and Tomas Venclova, their responses were startlingly identical and instantaneous: then I envy you, they both had said.

Venclova, a freedom fighter and dissident who was forced to leave his native Lithuania during the Communist years, later wrote to me a letter from a uniquely informed point of view: "Violence and scapegoating are the most essential phenomena of human life. Perhaps nobody has escaped them, both as victim and a perpetrator: I know it well from my personal experience, as everybody knows (even if subconsciously or semi-consciously). One may agree with the opinion that the scapegoat mechanism is not the only foundation of religion and human culture, but its substantial role was never elucidated so fully as in Girard's works," he wrote.

He was personally convinced of Girard's idea that the New Testament unmasks the scapegoat mechanism and sacrificial crisis, adding that Christ's work was profoundly misread through the centuries. He was less allergic to the religious dimensions: "Girard's scholarly enterprise may border on metaphysics and mysticism, but I believe this is inevitable for virtually any doctrine which is thought over earnestly and brought to its final conclusions."

Benoît Chantre, in an email from Paris, registered a harsher response to academia in general, and especially in France: "It must be first remembered that the university is, like all institutions, structured by jealousy." Girard's interdisciplinarity, he said, was a slap in the face to academic classifications, rituals, and taboos. "This is also why René chose the United States, where originality is probably more easily respected than in France. In fact, he realized that leaving his first country in 1947, he also left a formidable intellectual clergy."

On both sides of the Atlantic, *Things Hidden* marked the turning point where some followers turned back. They had been lulled by earlier books into believing that Girard didn't take his Christianity all that seriously or that, at least, it was less important than the values that drive most academics in search of reputation. With this book, he came out of the intellectually unfashionable Christian closet. Some supporters felt betrayed—they didn't see it coming and felt suddenly left out. The postmodernist historian Hayden White accused Girard of being medieval and reactionary in a 1978 *Diacritics* article—and claimed that his work had become less science than metaphysics. Serres's review of *Things Hidden* stubbornly refused to mention that the book's central concern is the revelation of Christ. But Girard's new position wasn't designed to make a splash, nor did it include a public relations strategy to minimize the punches he was going to take from critics. He simply moved in the direction of the thoughts that were increasingly preoccupying him.

Those who had been waiting for Girard to state his views, who felt he had been less than candid, were forced at last to drink the glass full strength. The dosage often proved fatal for the interest of those imbued with "the sacred horror vis-à-vis the Bible that characterizes modern humanism and anti-humanism as well,"[3] in Girard's words. However, he had attracted some new fans, too: one colleague told me about a friend who had managed to read around the Christianity in Girard's earlier books, yet was so intrigued after finishing *Things Hidden* that he walked halfway across Paris in the rain to meet interlocutor Lefort—a shorter version of the journey Oughourlian had taken across the Atlantic some years earlier.

Perhaps both fans and detractors were startled by the unsettling change in tone, even though it passed largely unremarked. Unlike *Violence and the*

Sacred, which discussed anthropological findings in cultures long ago and far away, the customs of Tupinambá cannibalism and the myths of the Tsimshians, *Things Hidden* almost compelled a response from the reader, without the comforting authorial scrim of distance. In its pages, Girard criticized his fellow academics, suggesting that "critical thinking is never more than an attempt at personal justification," and described our modern plight this way: "The victims are always there, and everyone is always sharpening his weapon for use against his neighbor in a desperate attempt to win himself somewhere—even if only in an indefinite, Utopian future—a plot of innocence that he can inhabit on his own, or in the company of a regenerate human race." He said that the paradox is strange but quite explicable, since sacrifice is the consequence of the struggle between doubles, "with everyone accusing everyone else of giving in to it, everyone trying to settle his own account with sacrifice by a final sacrifice that would expel evil for good."[4]

His new theories interpret us, as much as the other way around. Not "mankind," but *you* are under the microscope, as he discusses a range of contemporary topics, including psychoanalysis and cultural production. He was not prone to confession, yet passages like the following are necessarily born in self-knowledge. These unaccustomed disclosures may be one of many reasons this book seems to have been the one closest to his heart:

> In effect, desire is responsible for its own evolution. . . . Desire is always using for its own ends the knowledge it has acquired of itself; it places the truth in the service of its own untruth, so to speak, and it is always becoming better equipped to reject everything that surrenders to its embrace . . .
>
> The idea of the demon who bears light is more far-reaching than any notion in psychoanalysis. Desire bears light, but puts that light in the service of its own darkness. The role played by desire in all the great creations of modern culture—in art and literature—is explained by this feature, which it shares with Lucifer.[5]

He continued his reflections on scapegoating, sacrifice, and the beginning of societies: "In effect, our most essential discovery is precisely the zero hour of culture, which is also the hour of sacrifice—the founding sacrifice."[6]

He found new patterns in the Old Testament. Despite the blood and vengeance that pervade these ancient texts, the Jews begin to take the side of the victim—Abel, Joseph, Job, the suffering servant of Isaiah, the psalmist who is surrounded by an angry mob who wish to kill him ("They compassed me about, yea, they compassed me"). Sacrifice is still justified as the need of a jealous God, but defended with less and less conviction. Sacrifice is exposed, but not yet renounced. "No scapegoating outfit will talk about scapegoating," said Girard—yet, he continued, that's precisely what these texts begin to do. "The Gospels are built exactly like a myth with one exception, that a few people secede from the crowd to say: 'It's not true! Stop everything! It's not too late. Stop everything! The victim is innocent!'"[7]

The Crucifixion reveals the sacrificial mechanism in its brutal totality—some of the participants (Pilate, the centurion) voice their awareness of the scapegoating process, even as they participate in it. Jesus's death, Girard argues, is the consequence of the "intolerable revelation,"[8] and further proof of it as well. As we have become aware of and repelled by our propensity for violence—and, more specifically, aware of our rituals of scapegoating and blame—the time-honored "solution" no longer works. When we are aware of how a mirage distorts our vision, it loses its power to sway our interpretation of what we see, even as we still "see" it. But the world is getting better and worse all the time, as Maritain observed; hence, we have the parallel trends of texts pouring forth from persecutors, and our growing ability to decipher these very texts, as their meaning grows increasingly clear. It is a change, he writes, more radical than any humanity has faced in the past, part of the "terrifying and wondrous history of our time."[9]

We may kill as savagely and with greater frequency, but the murders no longer bring peace. We are faced with a stark choice, even as the body count mounts. Girard writes that "if men turn down the peace Jesus offers them—a peace which is not derived from violence and that, by virtue of this fact, *passes human understanding*, the effect of the gospel revelation will be made manifest through violence, through a sacrificial and cultural crisis whose radical effect must be unprecedented since there is no longer any sacrilized victim to stand in the way of its consequences."[10]

The way to break the cycle of violent imitation is a process of *imitatio Christi,* imitating Christ's renunciation of violence. Turn the other cheek, love one's enemies and pray for those who persecute you, even unto death. Love triumphs over violence—eventually. But it may not be the peaceful transition some imagine. "Since they do not see that human community is dominated by violence, people do not understand that the very one of them who is untainted by any violence and has no form of complicity with violence is bound to become the victim. But we must see that there is no possible compromise between killing and being killed." Our blindness is not innocent; humankind has a huge stake in violence and "people fail to understand that they are indebted to violence for the degree of peace that they enjoy."[11]

Nonviolence can become fatal, he argues, if it is not unanimous—if all mankind offers the other cheek, no cheek will be struck, but all must commit themselves irrevocably to the task. "If all men loved their enemies, there would be no more enemies. But if they drop away at the decisive moment, what is going to happen to the one person who does not drop away? For him the word of life will be changed into the word of death." The dynamics of all against one, again, linked to the central Christian imperative to love one's neighbor as oneself: "It is absolute fidelity to the principle defined in his own preaching that condemns Jesus. There is no other cause for his death than the love of one's neighbour lived to the very end, with an infinitely intelligent grasp of the constraints it imposes."[12]

In perhaps his most controversial stance—though controversial only for orthodox Christians—Girard rejected the notion of atonement for sins as a vestige of our sacrificial thinking. The Crucifixion did not represent a sacrificial death, he said, but rather a death to end sacrifice altogether. "It is the murderers who carry on the sacrifices and holocausts that Yahweh no longer wishes to hear of,"[13] he said.

God is not to be blamed, but rather all mankind, and mankind alone. "People are constrained to invent an irrational requirement of sacrifice that absolves them of responsibility. According to this argument, the Father of Jesus is still a God of violence, despite what Jesus explicitly says."[14] Jesus is killed not because God willed it, but because human beings wanted it.

On this subject, however, the winds were about to shift dramatically in Girard's life—in fact, the first strong breeze began to blow a few years before *Things Hidden* was published, when he met Raymund Schwager in Sauveterre, outside Avignon.

.   .   .

Things Hidden since the Foundation of the World sold briskly in France— thirty-five thousand copies in the first six months, putting it second on

France's nonfiction best-seller list. Girard noted that with the paperback edition, the numbers climbed to one hundred thousand. He credited his publisher Françoise Verny at Grasset, who was influential with the media. She regularly had her authors invited to the famous literary television show *Apostrophes*, "and that was two-thirds of her power,"[15] according to Girard, who was interviewed on the show on 16 June 1978. Journalist and economist Jean Boissonat became interested in *Des choses cachées*, and he was another media insider who helped promote the book.

Author Chris Fleming noted that it spurred intense and often heated discussion in the top echelons of the French academy: "Theorists such as Michel Serres, Paul Ricoeur, and Philippe Sollers were all admirers of the work, and, later, other theorists such as the renowned Italian philosopher Gianni Vattimo and the Canadian social and political theorist Charles Taylor expressed—and, indeed, continue to express—more than a token admiration for Girard's project."[16]

The admiration was also mingled with criticism. Existentialist author Ralph Harper, who had praised *Deceit, Desire, and the Novel*, lauded this book, too, with a lyrical essay in *Modern Language Notes*. By and large, he accepted Girard's argument about the fusion between violence and the sacred, with reservations that took Girard to task for some of his more absolute statements (for example, he noted that surely even primitive religions have hymns of praise and transcendence that are not linked with sacrificial ritual). He was swept away by the central contention and overarching vision: "One has only to re-read the *Iliad*, as I myself did recently, to be overwhelmed by its cinematic exhibition of a machine of perpetual vengeance and retribution, with Destiny, the Olympian gods, and men meshed together like gears that are designed for an entropic conclusion. The pervasive note of compassion that runs through the *Iliad* seems to come from another planet, a note sad and pure and still."[17]

Harper, who had written about Kierkegaard, Heidegger, and Proust, was also an Episcopal priest, so he had a natural affinity with Girard's new thrust. He concluded with a meditation on the book's Christian themes: "The book is itself prophetic. Not only does it look at our time as a time of 'gestation,' but it is written in tones of passionate clarity, never fuzzed by meanness of spirit. One may think of Estragon (in *Waiting for Godot*) telling Vladimir, 'All my life I have compared myself to Him,' of the many martyrs for love, and of those like St. Francis or the author of the *Imitation of Christ* who wanted above all to share in a new kind of desire, the love of being as being, the love of neighbor as neighbor, and therefore as well, of God as God. Violence has yet to meet up with enough men and women who refuse to handle the machine of vengeance. History, however, records enough instances of people who turned aside from violence for us to believe that the Gospels' Kingdom is not utopia."[18]

Author and screenwriter Frederic Raphael had written in both the *Sunday Times* and *New Society* to praise the book, noting that Girard's corpus was "of magisterial breadth." He admitted that he wasn't a likely enthusiast for its point of view, but wrote that he was "left uneasily conscious that even his rehabilitation of the ontological argument is of a rare sophistication." Girard described Jesus, who is "the existential evidence for God," as neither Jew nor Christian, belonging to no church and founding none, "but His divinity derives from His having existed, against all the odds, and in speaking a language beyond human range."[19]

Things Hidden since the Foundation of the World signaled a new direction in other ways, external to the book itself. In the future, it would attract more and more theologians to his ranks, a move that hurt his reception in the wider world, though he didn't seem to care much. He lost interest in the avant-garde players and the academic politics and lobbying; letters went unanswered. "He's not interested in correspondence and lobbying and academic politics," anthropologist Mark Anspach, one of Girard's frequent collaborators and interlocutors, told me. "He said he had a letter once from Foucault but he doesn't know what happened to it. It got lost when he moved or something. What can you do with someone who lost a letter from Foucault, right?" Although Girard wanted as broad an audience as possible—who doesn't?—he was first and foremost going his own way. He welcomed fellow travelers, but was usually unruffled by defections.

Literary theorists, anthropologists, and psychologists were shortsighted when they dismissed him out of hand because of their neuralgic reaction to his religion. They had much to learn from him, and religion was no barrier to understanding much of his work about the causes of human violence, what lies behind human competition, why we desire what we do, and the need for "vertical transcendence," however defined. Moreover, Anspach, an atheist himself, told me that you don't have to accept Christianity to recognize the importance of its message for Christian culture and civilization. "Just from a social science point of view that should be obvious," he said.

Goodhart, who is culturally Jewish though not observant, never felt that what Girard had to say didn't apply to him, too. While he respected Girard's Christianity, he firmly pointed out, "René never made the cross central. He never made it the entry ticket."

.   .   .

One of Italy's leading intellectuals, Roberto Calasso, would write in *The Ruin of Kasch* that René Girard is one of the "last surviving hedgehogs," using the typology Isaiah Berlin derived from Archilochus's precept, "The fox knows many things, but the hedgehog knows one big thing."[20] It's a somewhat misleading comment, for contrary to Calasso's assertion, Girard wrote about more than the scapegoat. It is only one concept in a whole edifice of thought, unified by a lifetime's effort. Calasso is certainly correct, however, in the sense that Girard's "expertise" is the system of thought he developed— Girard would claim that it was his downfall, telling me, "I'm a specialist of the mimetic theory, but the mimetic theory is my creation, you see? You're not supposed to have your own theory in the academic world. You cannot theorize about literature and sociology in the manner I do. The mimetic theory—they would tell you it's a gimmick, maybe."

The daring and the confidence rankled critics. Even some allies had qualms. The title of *Things Hidden since the Foundation of the World* rubbed many people the wrong way. It was often read not as a Gospel reference,[21] which it was, but rather as bolstering the imagined grandiosity and theatricality of the author. It was the first of his books in a Q&A format, and some felt the interactions were stilted. All the interlocutors marvel at what the master has said, and the conversation is a false tussle. While *Violence and the Sacred* had been a voyage of discovery for Girard and his readers, as he retraced his own steps on the journey, *Things Hidden* was exposition. It was a clearer presentation of his theories, perhaps, but some found it dogmatic, in an era when that word had acquired a heavy stigma.

Yet some of the critics were admirers, too. Years later, French philosopher and anthropologist Lucien Scubla raised interesting questions—some off target, some spot on—and others expressed legitimate reservations about the brand of Christianity René Girard promulgated in *Things Hidden*.

Far from confounding sacrificial logic, Scubla pointed out that if "Christ is indeed the lamb of God who takes away—who *takes away* and not who *reveals*—the sin of the world,"[22] then the crucifixion is indeed a sacrifice, and, with the last supper, can be read in a sacrificial light. And contrary to Girard's claims, he maintained that "nothing truly indicates that Girard's 'revelation' would require God to intervene in history."[23] One is left with the feeling that there is a lot more to Christianity than non-violence, that Girard is making one appetizer into the entire restaurant menu—for emphasis and effect, perhaps, but at the expense of the whole. Scubla wrote: "To be sure, if Christianity is the true religion it doubtless has to distinguish itself from all other religions; but if it no longer has anything in common with other religions, is it still a religion?"[24] The last point is witty, but Girard was not one to cling to the word "religion."

Surely Scubla knew this, as he concluded: "But we will not pretend any longer to believe that René Girard is unaware of all this. All those who have had the opportunity to converse with him have been able to appreciate his extreme modesty and know that he never fails to point out the partial and lacunary character of his research and his results. 'There is reason to believe,' he writes at the end of *Des Choses cachées,* 'that very important aspects elude us which will one day be brought to light.'"[25]

·   ·   ·

Things Hidden since the Foundation of the World began at Buffalo, but concluded at Johns Hopkins. Why return? "He always had a fondness for Johns Hopkins, especially in his earliest days there," explained Martha. Truth is that he was "restless," she added, and would continue to be.

It was a triumphant return, in any case: "René Girard has had an *annus mirabilis* last year, by any academic standard," James Bready wrote in the *Baltimore Sunday Sun*. He caught Girard between terms on Johns Hopkins's Homewood campus, where the professor was tied up with correspondence before his trip to France the next day. In Paris, he would supervise the annual crop of graduate French students who would study at the Sorbonne through April. Beardy suggested, "Maybe French television will be pestering him to do further talk shows. Maybe Grasset, his publisher, will be dangling a big advance in the hope he lets it have his next book, too—his study of *Troilus and Cressida*, and encirclement of all Shakespeare, perhaps? Or, who knows, maybe Professor Girard will be homesick for the United States, where his wife and children are."

Whatever waves he made in intellectual circles, the attention Girard received from the mainstream press was infrequent—he couldn't boil his thoughts into the kind of soup most editors wanted, so the long feature from books columnist Bready in the *Baltimore Sunday Sun*[26] was most welcome: Girard enjoyed battling with the academic circles, but he never forgot the importance of reaching a wider public. The attention was just another small reason to celebrate.

It had indeed been an *annus mirabilis*, or rather a duration of good fortune after he had been lured back to Johns Hopkins in 1976 with a high-level deal that included an appointment to Richard A. Macksey's Humanities Center. In addition to *Things Hidden* in France (which would be published in English by Stanford University Press in 1987), Johns Hopkins University Press had just published in 1978 *To Double Business Bound,* a collection of ten essays, seven of which had been written in his adopted language, English. Yet another first for him, and he was pleased with the book. "I think it is a beautiful object," he wrote to the Johns Hopkins University Press.[27] By that time he was back on campus as the James M. Beall Professor of French and Humanities. The book of essays was selected by *Choice* as one of the outstanding academic books of the year, along with *Violence and the Sacred,* published in English at last. In 1979, he became a member of the American Academy of Arts and Sciences.

"Yet Girard comes on as an optimist—imagine, what heavier sin could a man commit, in the judgment of a modern fin de siècle doomsayer?" Bready asked. The article documents the sort of misunderstandings that would dog Girard for years: "For Girard projects a civilization in which covetousness is indeed finally phased out. Violence nowhere, sacredness everywhere. Where Pascal thought to open an avenue to the almighty via the purity of mathematics, Girard discerns a psychosocial route, and he finds it in Judeo-Christian thought." Girard, he wrote, finds transcendence and reasonableness "in a theory of the victory of divine love." Girard did nothing of the kind, really.

Occasionally, he would mention that he was still teasing out the insights that had occurred in one tight ball of perception in the winter of 1958–59. Girard explained it this way: "The people who complain about not finding this or that in my books are the same, as a rule, who ridicule the excessive

ambition of *le système-Girard*. What they mistake for an encyclopedic appetite is the single insight that I pursue wherever I can recognize it and which is
too alien to their way of thinking for them to perceive its singleness."[28]

And although the *Baltimore Sun* article would conclude that Girard had
at last settled down, with Martha as a reference librarian at Johns Hopkins
(she had gotten a degree for librarian work at Drexel University while they
were at Bryn Mawr), their older son Martin in Pittsburgh, and Daniel and
Mary at Cornell and Boston University, respectively—the truth is that he
was "restless," as Martha had observed. Macksey recalls that on his return to
Johns Hopkins, the family lived a block away from campus on Bishop's Road.
He remembers passing by the house in the early morning, when Girard was
already at work, "playing Wagner at 200 decibels."[29]

He still considered other offers—in a decade, Freccero would start working to bring him to Stanford. But by the late 1960s, West Coast universities
were already trying to lure him away. After returning to Maryland from a
Pacific visit, Martha remembers the Avignonnais professor looking out pensively at a peaceful, snowy scene in Baltimore. "I wouldn't trade this for all of
California," he said with conviction.

CHAPTER 11

Lotus Land

Human revolutions happen for men, for things, or for opinions: all are
cemented by blood.

—Revolutionary Jean-Paul Rabaut Saint-Étienne, beheaded on 5 December 1793

René Girard was in late middle age when he arrived at Stanford and
assumed the imposing title of Andrew B. Hammond Professor of
French Language, Literature, and Civilization—the tag he would hold
until his retirement in 1995. By now, his corpus was in place and his scholarly reputation secured. He had established a steady routine and prodigious
output.

Certainly his schedule would have made him at home in one of the
more austere orders of monks. His working hours were systematic and adamantly maintained. "You couldn't get up in the morning and *not* see René
at his desk," Martha recalled. He began his day in the night, at about 3:30
a.m.—half an hour earlier, even, than Gandhi had—and worked till noon
or so, then took a walk or relaxed for a while. More work, or classes and
meetings with students, followed in the afternoon. The network news, every
night—that was a daily ritual. He explained to me that he preferred working

at home, and given his schedule and his companionship, it's no wonder. Buffalo, Baltimore, Palo Alto. Under such circumstances, what difference would a change of locale make?

Perhaps a great deal. California is an alien Lotus Land. Those who were not born to it never become thoroughly accustomed. The former republic of California is more a world than a state, unless "state" is taken to mean a condition of mind, rather than an organized political community. It has trees thirty feet across and waterfalls a thousand feet high, and two thousand species of plants found nowhere else on earth. California is separated from the rest of the continent by a mountain range and uniquely borders Mexico and faces Asia. For centuries, early mapmakers portrayed it as an island—that's still the way California sees itself, and how others see it, too, forever floating off the mainland. It's ground zero for latter-day hippies and for Hollywood, for cultural trends and technological gadgets. It's also a place of profound alienation. Californians are impersonal and friendly at once.

Natural beauty and sunshine often mitigate the need for fellow humans. Martha never entirely adjusted. She leveled the usual accusation at California—it's shallow and unsociable—but, as she also observed, human interaction can be easy to avoid where space is abundant, nature lavish, and the weather allows hikes, swims, and jogging almost year-round. It was a tough transition after the human warmth and conviviality of New York and Maryland. But people tend not to leave California; it enters one's bones without one's permission.

For Girard, California would have been somewhat reminiscent of his birthplace—a Mediterranean climate with plenty of sun, abundant wine and olives, and lemon trees in the enclosed interior courtyard at the front of their Eichler home. "I always thought this would be the best place," he told Martha, the winters of Buffalo and Baltimore long forgotten.

And so it would become Girard's final home, from 1981 into the twenty-first century. He would continue elaborating his theories in such books as *The Scapegoat* (1982 in French; 1986 in English), *Job, the Victim of His People* (1985; 1987), and *I See Satan Fall Like Lightning* (1999; 2001), as well as in interviews, for example, *When These Things Begin* (1994; 2014) and *Evolution and Conversion: Dialogues on the Origins of Culture* (2004; 2008), and in essays, such as *Oedipus Unbound: Selected Writings on Rivalry and Desire* in 2004. His last book, *Achever Clausewitz,* or *Battling to the End* in

English (2007; 2010), would take his work in a new direction, bringing his understanding to bear on modern European history. But by the time it was published his productive life was all but over.

The university town of 1981, when the Girards arrived, was a world of coffee shops and bookstores, and it had at least a few comfortable restaurants that could be considered old haunts, in a climate that made *al fresco* dining a year-round occasion. It has since become the high-tech capital of the world, the heart of Silicon Valley, with large Verizon, Apple, and T-Mobile outlets on University Avenue, along with a Whole Foods temple a few blocks away. Parking requires an aggressive, half-hour search on the small-town streets that were never meant for the traffic they now bear. The new face of wealth is no longer dour silver-haired investors with Lincoln Continentals, but rather twenty-somethings in t-shirts and sandals, who vote Democratic and very green, spend $20,000 on bikes, and order their lattés with soy milk. They would really rather be robots. Meanwhile, the city is encircled by Latino and black communities of the unincorporated areas of Menlo Park, Redwood City, and East Palo Alto, populated by service providers, who drive pickup trucks with rakes and shovels and lawnmowers to cut lawns and landscape gardens, just as their wives arrive at homes more quietly with buckets and mops. The social differences and distinctions are firmly in place, even reinforced by growing inequities. People with comfortable five-figure incomes can no longer afford Palo Alto, but scatter towards San Mateo or San Jose when work is done. At 5:30 p.m. each weekday, they jam the highways in both directions. That is the city. But the university?

"Stanford University is so startlingly paradisial, so fragrant and sunny, it's as if you could eat from the trees and live happily forever. Students ride their bikes through manicured quads, past blooming flowers and statues by Rodin, to buildings named for benefactors like Gates, Hewlett, and Packard," wrote Ken Auletta in a 2012 *New Yorker* article. "Everyone seems happy, though there is a well-known phenomenon called the 'Stanford duck syndrome': students seem cheerful, but all the while they are furiously paddling their legs to stay afloat."[1]

Stanford had long been nicknamed Leland Tech, but as it became a high-tech wonderland, the humanities began to feel the pinch in a more acute way. During Girard's time at Stanford, enrollment in the humanities would drop from about a third of the students to a percentage in the mid-teens.

Humanities majors plummeted from 20 percent to 7 percent in the year prior to Girard's death.[2]

With its growing preoccupation with technology, engineering, and science innovation, Stanford was an odd place for Girard, but it was to have some surprising ramifications for his work. Meanwhile, he was joining a department that had some oddities of its own.

.   .   .

Girard was the first superstar hire, and he was coming into a department where star power was deeply resented. The department was a chaotic place, a house divided, with large and sometimes obsessive egos. With the new configuration of faculty, the power lines ran between the department's two preeminent figures—Freccero in Italian, and Girard in French. Serres would join them as a full professor in 1984, becoming a third corner in a triumvirate.

Henri Peyre took notice, in faraway Yale, with updates from Stanford's top-notch Mallarmé scholar, Robert Greer Cohn, who was one of his many frequent correspondents. "How is René Girard doing? Has he quite a following at Stanford? Has he drawn students to literature?"[3] Peyre asked on 18 October 1982. If only he knew, but not only literature. Girard was attracting more and more interest from the social sciences, sociology, psychology, history, philosophy, religious studies, and eventually theology. He was, moreover, building on the base that had developed over the decades in Baltimore and Buffalo. Within a few years, Peyre would be mollifying the same correspondent, who had written a "wrathful, indignant" letter about "what is happening in our profession and what is ruining the humanities at Stanford." Peyre continued to admonish and console: "The drowning, stifling of literary values into a potpourri of pseudo-sciences is nothing less than an assault against not just tradition, but intelligence & honesty. One wonders what students trained in that manner will turn into. I like & esteem Serres, & some of Girard's books: both are very gifted persons; but also outrageously partial and dogmatic. There should be room in a department for other approaches than theirs & for sheer enjoyment of beauty. Do not allow yourself to become bitter and to indulge polemics if it turns into self-destructiveness. What you say, represent & write is far too valuable for that, & it will outlive the obscurist & verbose theories of those who at present disagree with us."[4]

Peyre was not alone in the confusion of what, exactly, Girard was doing with "pseudo-sciences." Girard was, to use that overworked term, *sui generis*. Shortly after his arrival at Stanford, he protested in words that may have added to the confusion: "No. No, I am not a philosopher. You see, philosophy sometimes wanders off into abstract speculation. I work with what is.... I have been asked to make recommendations, political, economic, to point to a suggested course of action, but I will not do that. I have insights of a certain kind, you understand, from my reading, my research, my thoughts which have grown and been shaped over time—it takes me a long time to write—but it is not safe ground for me to make suggestions. I let others derive those from what I can present to them in my writing."[5]

.   .   .

Girard's debut at Stanford was marked by another remarkable symposium, though not as paradigm-shattering as the 1966 "The Languages of Criticism and the Sciences of Man" in Baltimore. The 1981 event that he organized with Jean-Pierre Dupuy, "Disorder and Order," triggered no earthquakes, but was nevertheless called "a daring encounter between humanists of many countries and scientists with unconventional views not only on the diverse conceptions of disorder and order in their various disciplines, but also on the often illusory nature of the cultural fragmentation that affects us and from which we all suffer."[6]

At the time, "interdisciplinarity" was the new buzzword, but the symposium tackled it with refreshing innovation and depth, exploring the connections that linked domains previously held to be separate—Serres had spoken a year before of a "Northwest Passage" between them, a route that is uncommon, narrow, hard to find, and often impassable.

During the symposium, Nobel prize-winning scientist Ilya Prigogne and Nobel economist Kenneth Arrow volleyed ideas with Girard, and so did Ian Watt, Henri Atlan, Isabelle Stengers, Cornelius Castoriadis, Michel Deguy, Heinz von Forster, Francisco Varela, and others. William Johnsen, a Joyce and Woolf scholar, later wrote: "Even sport doesn't provide an adequate metaphor for the way ideas flew around the room. Everyone and everything levitated."[7] Girard's champions were on hand, too. Oughourlian, in particular, gave a provocative talk in which he reclassified various forms of mental illness using mimetic theory.

For Girard and Serres, the symposium marked another chapter in a lifelong conversation. The friendship was one of Girard's most enduring memories from Buffalo. Serres would be an influential fellow traveler, eventually becoming one of the most prominent public intellectuals in France with a weekly radio spot that reached millions. "The respective *styles* of Girard and Serres are very different, yet they agree on the competitive and combative character of the intellectual climate of the second half of the twentieth century," Johnsen wrote. Their camaraderie represented a significant departure from the "dominant intellectual *styles* of enmity."[8] Typically, Girard homed in on human social relations, and Serres brought in arguments from the natural sciences, with human behavior only one element among many, and not necessarily the most interesting. At the symposium and elsewhere, it was a mutually rewarding dance between the hedgehog and the fox.

Johnsen documented the reciprocal influence over the years: Girard is an invisible presence throughout Serres's *La Naissance de la physique* (1977), as Serres openly acknowledges. In Serres's most Girardian work, *Rome: Le livre des fondations* (1983), he retold the myths of Rome's sacrificial beginnings *à la Girard*. In turn, Girard acknowledged his debt to Serres for pointing out the passages in Pliny that he used to develop his reasoning in *The Scapegoat*. Johnsen compared their literary interplay to a Japanese *renga*, a poem whose authorship alternates.[9]

Both men brought considerable luster, not just to the symposium, but to Stanford as well. Robert Harrison, speaking much later, as chair of the French and Italian Department, noted that for the last 150 years, Western philosophy has limited the role of philosophers, discouraging them from synthesizing, speculating, or constructing overarching meta-narratives. The idea of the *grand récit*, the sweeping narrative, is distinctly non-postmodern, perhaps even non-modern, the "yes we can" of an older concept of the philosopher, he said. Girard and Serres belong to a vanishing breed and were unclassifiable even in France, and represented an affirmation that "philosophers can—even in our time—tell the *grand récit*." Harrison, a friend to both, added that they belong to a generation of grand *philosophes* and French master thinkers. Both of them come from a tradition that thinks big and bold.

"France rewards boldness—always has."¹⁰ And for the moment, high-tech Stanford did, too.

·   ·   ·

Girard may have been the first high-power hire, but he was not, in the mind of the department chair, going to be the last. At this juncture, Jean-Marie Apostolidès reenters our conversation. The French literary scholar, playwright, and psychologist had been recruited from Harvard to be the chair of the French and Italian Department in 1987, the year *Things Hidden* was published in English.

His return to Stanford was the stuff of academic dreams: the West Coast university doubled his Harvard salary—he still brags that *Time* magazine had called him to ask about it, since it was the highest salary in America in the literature field. It was a big paycheck, and he had proposed a big ambition. "My own concept was to have a department with big names and only big names . . . to create huge visibility." He wanted to create an all-star team of French intellectuals with international standing, "of having all the faculty like René," he told me. Once settled in, he was obligated to implement the program he had proposed.

When a foreign object strikes a power line, sparks can fly and fires may start. Apostolidès said his dream clashed with another plan, already afoot in the department. Girard was a man with a vision, too, and he and Serres had attempted to bring to Stanford some of the up-and-comers who were aligned with Girard's research interests, Apostolidès told me.¹¹ According to Apostolidès, that was the plan, and he was the department chair who blocked it. Others recalled a department where there was already resentment and jealousy of Girard, and a chair who was divisive and inflammatory. But again it suggests—who could really doubt it?—that Girard learned about mimesis and power dynamics firsthand, from his own failures and frustrations. His theories did not arise from nothing, an inspiration from the ether that took shape in that magnificent head after he had inhaled the air. Nor were the insights of 1959 a substitute for experience; rather, they provided a context to help him make a coherent whole of the puzzle his own reading and experiences would offer. At any rate, it didn't dampen the respect and admiration Apostolidès had for his colleague, many years later.

The friction may have had a mimetic edge. Apostolidès, too, was interested in anthropology, and was intrigued, in particular, by the relationship
between words and blood, and his insistence that words only become "real"
when blood is spilt for them—when we met he was working on a philosophical and psychological study, *Of Ink and Blood: The Writings of Theodore
Kaczynski;* he is also the author of 1999's *L'Affaire Unabomber.*

He said that Girard represents "the last in the school of École Française de
Sociologie," an influential and exceptional group of researchers that formed
around Durkheim and Mauss in the late nineteenth and early twentieth
century. Its adherents applied ethnographic representation to contemporary
social phenomena, and were preoccupied with the sacred, sacrifice, ritual,
social cohesion, and collective movements. "I would place him as the last representative of that frontier between sociology and psychology," Apostolidès
told me. "For the rest, he is in line with Georges Bataille."

Apostolidès resigned as chair in the mid-1990s, unable to make peace in
a difficult department. He is still on the Stanford faculty, and said he has had
a good and productive life since. Happy? Sure. As he said, what more could
he want?

.   .   .

Marci Shore, who teaches European cultural and intellectual history at Yale,
brings light to dark corners of history, philosophy, and ideology with such
books as her poignant and provocative *The Taste of Ashes: The Afterlife of
Totalitarianism in Eastern Europe* (Crown, 2013) and her forthcoming *Phe-
nomenological Encounters: Scenes from Central Europe.* She teaches Girard's
theories at Yale, with an especial focus on *Violence and the Sacred.*

It is cheering to see such an acclaimed scholar presenting Girard's work
in an Ivy League classroom; however, we must remember that Shore is a tenured faculty member. At the foot-soldier level, making Girard's corpus the
subject of one's teaching, thesis, dissertation, or book can be risky. Girard's
contentions have not always been welcomed by academe, and his proponents
have explored other avenues to make his work better known.

Mark Anspach had taken on some of the biases early as an undergraduate
at Harvard (he received his degree in 1981). He had read *Things Hidden* and
proposed a senior thesis on aspects of Girard's corpus. When they met years
later, Girard told him that he was the first to do a thesis on his work without

having been his student. With approval from Harvard, Anspach worked day and night on his thesis, a passion as well as an obligation.

His finished thesis was torpedoed by one of the faculty referees, who didn't object to his approach or method, but objected to Girard as the topic. "He said this guy's ideas are dotty. That word stuck in my mind—you know, 'dotty.' It was dotty," Anspach recalled. He protested, in vain, that the thesis topic had already been approved, and it was unfair to fault it later.

Those who want to pursue the lines of thought Girard had opened through his books, articles, and lectures face an obvious problem: A more general audience would require them to recreate Girard's system of thought from scratch at each presentation. How could one move forward and refine a system of ideas without having to explain and explain and explain everything from Square One again? "Girardian" meetings, publications, and websites gave those who were determined a first audience for their work, and one that would not have decided, *a priori,* it was "dotty." How else could they talk to each other? How, to use that overworked word, could one create a synergy?

In 1981 the Dutch Girard Society was born in Amsterdam. The Colloquium on Violence and Religion (COV&R) was founded at Stanford in 1990. The Association pour les Recherches Mimétiques began in Paris in 2005. In 2007 three groups—Theology and Peace, the Raven Foundation, and Peter Thiel's Imitatio—were launched. Others groups were founded in Australia and South America.

Peter Thiel, billionaire cofounder of PayPal and author of the bestselling *Zero to One*, was perhaps the most surprising champion to come forward during the Stanford years. He had been a Stanford student of Girard's in the late 1980s, when Thiel was an undergraduate majoring in philosophy. "One of these ideas that was starting to percolate in the underground, was that there was this very interesting professor with a different account of the world; it was out of tempo with the times, so it had a natural appeal to a rebellious undergrad," Thiel explained in a 2009 Imitatio video.[12] "I suspect that when the history of the twenty-first century is written, circa 2100, he'll be seen as one of the truly great intellectuals."

A self-described gay libertarian, and the face of a new, young generation of wealth, he also invests in research to dodge death and retool the human body to live forever. His "Imitatio," a project of the Thiel Foundation, underwrites research on Girard's theories and has brought a different kind of energy to Girard's brainwork in the humanities and social sciences. Inevitably, it has also raised academic eyebrows. In academia, high-tech wealth and entrepreneurship tend to be out of sync with scholarly endeavor, except in the realms of science and engineering. They tend to be seen as crass, even though crass is the very nature of the capitalistic enterprise that drives Silicon Valley and underwrites places like Stanford. While these high-tech partnerships might seem odd bedfellows for Girard, he's been a longtime risk-taker, too. As Freccero once pointed out, "He's always been around people willing to be entrepreneurs. He's an intellectual loner—Jeremiah or John the Baptist."

Author and journalist Joseph Bottum made an even-handed assessment of the trade-offs, noting that Girard had been transformed into a sect in America, as had Leo Strauss, Ernest Becker, and Eric Voegelin, attracting disciples, translators, and proselytizers. "To some extent, the transformation may have had a good effect, releasing Girard from the ghetto of literary criticism and pointing him in directions he needed to go," he wrote. "But this development may have had an unhappy effect as well, over-extending his thought and yet simultaneously narrowing it into a 'Girardian System.'"[13] Were these organizations, in effect, institutionalizing, reifying something that must remain fluid and open? Sometimes it seemed so.

In another sense, they also failed to prepare his allies for speaking to the uninitiated—I heard an anecdote about a literary scholar who, at a conference on an American author, cited no authority in the discussions *except* Girard. "I think one problem with Girardians too is often once they become Girardian, they just quote Girard," said Anspach. "That turns people off—rightly, I think—because it's not like Girard is the only person who's ever said anything interesting."

There were other issues that made a fuller integration into academic settings problematic. With his out-of-the-closet Christianity and his growing preoccupation with theology, Girard's stock had taken a dip in academic circles. As theologians became interested in his work, the critical mass of his enthusiasts shifted. A lot of assumptions were made at conferences where ministers would chat about how much Girard's work changed their pastoral practice. Sometimes they were accused of proselytizing, and sometimes the accusations were on the money. Anspach, who describes himself as Jewish and atheist, said that he met newcomers who said it was their first conference—and it would be their last—for precisely that reason.

In short, those who wished to study and promote Girard's theories faced some tough questions. How much should one bend to accommodate cultural gatekeepers and opinion leaders? The attempt to do so is itself a mimetic phenomenon. These arbiters can keep their power and status as arbiters only by withholding. Their rejection, in bipolar mimetic fashion, can send one careening into the opposite, a cloistered tradition of "Girardianism." What's the answer?

Perhaps it's unrealistic, in today's world of consumerism and mass marketing and branding, to stick with the small, quiet, one-on-one personal "aha!" that Girard has always emphasized as an entrée to his work. To my eye, the man in the middle of the efforts grew increasingly pleasant and passive as the efforts about him grew more elaborate and ingenuous. But the "aha" still happens, and it still works.

In 2004, social and political philosopher Jean-Pierre Dupuy was attending a conference in Berlin when he was confronted at a café by a man who asked, "Why did you become a Girardian?" He responded in a beat, "Because it's cheaper than psychoanalysis."

The story was told to me by eyewitnesses, but Dupuy himself dismissed it with a Gallic shrug and an Italian saying, "Si non è vero è ben trovato." The American equivalent might be Ken Kesey's dictum, "It's the truth even if it didn't happen."

Later I found this passage, in which Dupuy describes his encounter with Girard in a way less flippant than the purported remark in the Berlin café. The director of the influential journal *Esprit*, Jean-Marie Domenach, had urged him to read *La violence et le sacré* in 1975. He read it reluctantly and "was impressed but not especially moved by my reading of Girard's book."

That year he met Paul Dumouchel, a French-Canadian philosopher living in France who told him to stop whatever he was doing and read *Deceit, Desire, and the Novel*. "I did so and it was the shock of my life. That reading immediately had on me the effect of a ten-year psychoanalytic cure," he said. "The shock was initially more emotional than intellectual. I was stuck at the time in a series of personal problems, bad relationships and the like. I discovered that they were sheer instances of general rules governing the human condition. I had thought I was alone in hell and I discovered that everyone was located there one way or another."[14]

Dupuy includes the anecdote in an essay that is about Girard and his other passion, the philosopher and social critic Ivan Illich—after all, Girard is not the only one who has said anything interesting, as Anspach noted. Sometimes things are better seen slant-wise. Hence, Dupuy has taken an indirect route to integrating Girard's theories into public forums, frequently with what appears to be little more than a casual aside from a podium. At speaking events, Dupuy often brings Girard's thought to bear on the subject at hand—a Stanford panel on nuclear deterrence with California Governor Jerry Brown comes to mind, as does a public conversation with philosopher Slavoj Žižek on God. These efforts have placed Girard within a range of wider, novel contexts not usually associated with him, giving his thought a hearing among new audiences. More behind-the-scenes work included a meeting with business magnate George Soros and discussions with the prominent French economist and journalist Bernard Maris, who was murdered in the Charlie Hebdo massacre on 7 January 2015.

Robert Harrison has also found new audiences for Girard in much the same way, sometimes via iTunes and his radio show "Entitled Opinions." One example: when I mentioned Girard's name in conversation at a recent gathering of women writers, the face of a prominent left-wing journalist and former *Mother Jones* editor lit up. She'd heard about Girard by listening to Harrison's two-part interview with him in 2005.

.   .   .

Simone Weil wrote that the Gospels offer a theory of humankind before they present a theory of God—in short, an anthropology before a theology. Girard followed suit, although his radical interpretation of the Christian message left him vulnerable to claims that he had poured a new wine into the old bottles of a reductive gnosticism, preaching the salvific power of an illuminating knowledge.

He wasn't preaching anything, however. The books from his Stanford years—in particular, *The Scapegoat*, *Job*, and *I See Satan Fall Like Lightning*—largely reflect his increasing preoccupation with a close reading of Biblical texts, which he thought revealed the truth of human existence. His was not, however, an attempt to create a Third Testament. "I'm a realist, you know," he claimed. "I think that texts talk about reality and real events."[15]

The Scapegoat (published as *Le bouc émissaire* in 1982) opens with Girard's dissection of *The Judgment of the King of Navarre* by Guillaume de

Machaut, a mid-fourteenth-century French poet. In the narrative, catastrophes beset the poet, yet the very real Black Death is jumbled with improbable and natural events, cities destroyed by lightning, people knocked over by a rain of stones. The Jews were to blame—they had poisoned the public water, too—and at last God exposes the crime: "Then every Jew was destroyed, some hanged, others burned; some were drowned, others beheaded with an ax or sword. And many Christians died together with them in shame."[16]

Girard's classic study of this "persecution text" confirmed his earlier conclusions. The persecutors "are too naïve to cover the traces of their crimes ... They do not suspect that by writing their accounts they are arming posterity against them."[17] Subsequent chapters explore stereotypes of persecution, myth, violence and magic, leading us to Teotihuacan, the Titans, and Scandinavia. The second half of the book addresses the New Testament, retracing much ground Girard had covered before, but in a more accessible fashion for a new audience, and focusing on a reading of key texts on the beheading of John the Baptist, Peter's Denial, and the Crucifixion.

The volume published almost twenty years later in France, *I See Satan Fall Like Lightning*, seems a sort of bookend to *The Scapegoat*, expanding on the ideas of his earlier works in a shorter format, with a less intensive disciplinary focus on fields that would be a hurdle for the general reader—anthropology or French theory, for example.

While both books were published in France by Grasset, his house since *Deceit, Desire, and the Novel* years before, in the United States his books often had to look for publishers, sometimes Stanford University Press, sometimes more offbeat venues. In France, *I See Satan Fall Like Lightning* was a best-seller. In the United States, by contrast, the book was published quietly by Maryknoll's Orbis Books, with clerics providing dustjacket blurbs.

Dick Macksey, still living on a few hours of sleep and pipe smoke, weighed in on the latest phases of Girard's work, noting that his colleague from Baltimore days is "one of the prophets of our time, a time not notably rich in prophets."

Macksey was "fully aware of the *skandalon* of his raids on alien turf," but gave a different twist to Girard's swift, one-man operation: "It is not unusual to see theories of literary interpretation resurface, retailored and often after a considerable passage of time, in other disciplines," he wrote in *Modern Language Notes*. What is unusual, he noted, is that Girard took on the job himself: "He himself, armed only with strong theories of mimetic desire, violence, and victimage, began to venture—boldly—into the fields that would normally have had to wait for second-generation colonization by practitioners of these other disciplines (anthropology, psychology, philosophy, sociology, theology and scriptural studies)."

Moreover, he continued, these ventures, beginning with *Violence and the Sacred,* "allowed his own thought and models to continue to evolve in response to the encounters. By the time that *Des Choses cachées depuis la fondation du monde* captured an enormous general audience in France, the disciplinary barons of the other fields were, if not subdued, at least mortally engaged."[18]

I See Satan Fall Like Lightning received some important attention (its title, like that of *Things Hidden,* was drawn from a dramatic Biblical passage, this time from the Gospel of Luke), including an entire page in *Le Nouvel Observateur.*[19] In it, the prominent French writer and intellectual Pascal Bruckner observed, "Among the innumerable posterity of Nietzsche, there is a branch that never ceases to surprise us: the Christian branch." René Girard saw that Nietzsche grasped the true revolution of Christianity: its concern for the victims, the "slave morality" that made all men equal. Girard, of course, separated himself radically from Nietzsche when the German philosopher opted in favor of the strong against the weak and for what Girard called "the monstrous mimetic contagion of a Dionysian lynching."

The revolution Christianity brought to our thinking—that is, the moral imperative to protect the weak against the strong—factors into the horror with which the world reacted to the Holocaust. Bruckner noted that the example was all the more pronounced because Hitler massacred victims to promote a master race over the "inferior races," the triumph of the strong over the weak. It was a retrograde motion that reasserted the values of archaic sacrifice, with their scenes of collective hatred and lynching to bring temporary respite and unity to a splintered community—"antisemitism has never had any other foundation, any other function," wrote Bruckner.

In his book, Girard argued that "Satan" is the engine behind mimetic crisis. He is the "principle of darkness," once targeted by the Church, and now largely forgotten as an archaic relic. In Girard's eyes, Satan is the sower of discord: he is the public prosecutor and the executioner, the accuser and the jury foreman, spreading disorder, violence, and hatred wherever he goes.

Satan is the contagion that reduces a population of individuals with distinct traits into a hysterical mob. Satan expels Satan: "The Satan expelled is that one who foments and exasperates mimetic rivalries to the point of transforming the community into a furnace of scandals. The Satan who expels is the same furnace when it reaches a point of incandescence sufficient to set off the single victim mechanism."[20] In the review, Bruckner concludes:

> We admire in this book the blistering way Girard reads the evangelical texts and the myths of ancient Greece, overturning our most entrenched beliefs, throwing down the gauntlet on our most deep-seated prejudices. He shows an attention to detail that is a model of exegesis, transforming the most well-known propositions of the Bible or the New Testament into extraordinary statements. One question still troubles all readers of his work: if Judeo-Christianity represents the fundamental revolution in the history of mankind—alone in denouncing the mechanism's perverse persecution, more so than Buddhism, Islam, or Hinduism—does it follow that we have to convert and obey the teachings of any particular church? Hasn't the doctrine of the Evangelists become the common heritage of us all, through its very first light to the eventual spreading of democracy?
>
> Hegel said Christianity was preparing itself for the conditions for its own demise and that its triumph would mark the end of its reign. Perhaps we have already arrived at that point, as Girard remarks at the beginning of his essay. And this unorthodox Christian, who is obsessed with violence more than love, doesn't he participate in this disenchantment, and is he not, despite himself, one of those debunkers who retranslated the mysteries of the Cross and Passion into the language of reason?[21]

.   .   .

Toward the end of Girard's long life, Sandor Goodhart asked the question many had pondered: "How would you answer people who say you are privileging the Greeks, the Hebrews, the Christians, these various peoples of Western cultural heritage, over other groups?" Were the results he found, in fact, limited to Western history and culture? Girard could easily have responded that *Violence and the Sacred* considered tribes in Africa and Indonesia, Polynesia and Brazil, and that *The Scapegoat* had an entire chapter on Teotihuacan. He had taken a different route, however. A series of lectures at the Bibliothèque Nationale de France considered the Vedic tradition, and eventually became a small book of about a hundred pages, *Sacrifice*.[22] He also discussed Hinduism briefly in response to Goodhart's question, in the Q&A interview that would be among his last.[23] The Vedas were an ambitious subject to take on, and one that would likely confound many educated Hindus. Yet it went some way to answer critics who faulted him for considering too narrow a context—though given the scope of *Violence and the Sacred*, that was a flimsy charge in the first place.

As often occurred, Girard's comments in interviews tend to be more qualified than the rhetorical flourishes in his books. In his interview with Goodhart, he made a surprising turn—one that Roberto Calasso, a lover of the Vedas, would have applauded. He replied to a question about "privileging" the Judeo-Christian tradition by attributing the perception to a misunderstanding, and saying he did not wish to privilege the Bible absolutely. India's scriptural texts say everything about sacrifice that he had said: "They tell you about the victim as a solution to the violence. They tell you everything." He found the same patterns of dissolving social distinction, mimetic crisis, even lynching, for example, with the Rig Veda story of Purusha, who is murdered, dismembered, and eventually divinized.

India came close to the truth, but not close enough. Its ancient texts stayed within the sacrificial framework and its mythic constructs. Within these texts, the scapegoat mechanisms "remain undeciphered and inseparable from the sacrificial illusion."[24] Nevertheless, the Upanishads have an "anti-sacrificial thrust, where sacrifice is regarded as murder and rejected"—that is, before Hinduism returned to more archaic notions of sacrifice. In some of the Upanishads, he noted, "they don't give up the word sacrifice, but they say that sacrifice should be purely interior."

Buddhism, flowering on Hindu roots, also fell short, and so did Islam. Buddhism opposes sacrifice. "At the same time, one has to recognize that Buddhism, in the territory where it dominates, has not eliminated earlier forms of sacrifice to the same extent that Christianity has. Neither has Islam. Islam remains compatible with certain forms of animal sacrifice, which are acknowledged."[25] In Judaism, the sacrifices stopped with the Roman destruction of Jerusalem (according to Josephus, over a million Jews were slaughtered) and the Second Temple within it. The end of the Temple marked the end of traditional Jewish culture and rituals—many rites could only be performed at the temple in Jerusalem. One could argue that this is not a renunciation of sacrifice so much as an adaptation to necessity.

With his book *Sacrifice,* Girard is clearly wading in the shallows of a very deep ocean—he acknowledged as much, adding that much more scholarship is needed. The Upanishads were written and compiled from around 1200 B.C. to A.D. 500, and it is difficult to generalize, as he does, that they were written "at the time of great Jewish prophets,"[26] without specifying which of the range of texts we are considering. Moreover, he acknowledges that he is not working from original Sanskrit texts, but rather from *La Doctrine du sacrifice dans les Brahmanas* by Sylvain Lévi (1863–1935), the dedicatee of the book. Future translation of his books into Asian languages will attract new audiences and, it is hoped, new scholarship.[27]

Meanwhile, Girard managed to give a sly dig to the usual charges of his "Western ethnocentrism," which has become a weapon against anthropology itself, and he did so with his customary panache: "Nothing is more praiseworthy than mistrust of ethnocentrism. How could it fail to threaten us, when all modern anthropological concepts come from the West, including that of ethnocentrism—a charge that is brandished by the West alone, and against itself exclusively?" "Mistrust of ethnocentrism is more than legitimate," he continued, "it is indispensable, and yet we must not make of it the prehistoric bludgeon that false progressivism and false radicalism made of it in the second half of the twentieth century. The notion of ethnocentrism was made to serve a poorly disguised anti-intellectualism that reduced to silence the most legitimate anthropological curiosity. For several years the frenzy of 'deconstruction' and demolition sustained an intense excitement in research that today has collapsed, killed by its own success."[28]

■   ■   ■

I had not forgotten Apostolidès's comment about Georges Bataille, the bad boy of French theory, who is still a dark and important presence in that rarefied realm of thought.

Both Bataille and Girard were fascinated with sacrifice and its rituals, grounding their thought in such nineteenth-century anthropologists as Durkheim and Frazer. However, for Bataille, sacrifice was not symbolic or theoretical, not an archaic ceremony abandoned sometime after the Aztecs. It was human and literal. The secret society Bataille formed in the 1930s, Acéphale, had as its emblem a headless man.

We can't be entirely sure what happened within Acéphale—it was a secret society, after all—but the rumors were that Bataille and his confrères tried to recreate a human sacrifice with a very real decapitation. Bataille volunteered himself as a victim, but his colleagues balked—so volunteer victims could be found, but the potential perps got cold feet. In an interesting turn of events, no one was willing to be an executioner—no one was willing to throw the first stone, so to speak. The "new religion" Bataille had hoped to create in his homemade petri dish failed before the first cells began to multiply. Risible, perhaps, yet Bataille nevertheless attracted some fellow thinkers who are today revered: Walter Benjamin and Theodor Adorno among them.

Girard made a single reference to Bataille in *Violence and the Sacred*, as another thinker who, like him, understood that prohibitions held back the tide of violence—a realization Freud had considered briefly, but discarded. Bataille formulated the understanding "with great precision," according to Girard: "To be sure, Bataille is primarily inclined to treat violence in terms of some rare and precious condiment, the only spice still capable of stimulating the jaded appetite of modern man"—rather as Sartre did, in *Critique of Dialectical Reason*. Girard continued: "Yet on occasion Bataille is able to transcend the decadent estheticism he has so fervently espoused, and explain quite simply that 'the prohibition eliminates violence, and our violent impulses (including those resulting from our sexual drives) destroy our inner calm, without which human consciousness cannot exist.'"[29]

Bataille, however, savored the immediacy and intensity of the act of sacrifice itself, rather than its causes and consequences, which had preoccupied Girard. In his efforts to "resacrilize" society, Bataille emphasized the *ritual* of sacrifice, the agonizing death of animal or human, and the psychological states it produces. "The sacred," for him, was an eruption of irrationality and Dionysian power within a world that constantly attempts to create order. The intense moment will not last—it will inevitably be absorbed into conventional, institutional patterns—and hence it must be recreated, again and again, by acts of psycho-spiritual destruction, and often using transgressive sexuality.

The problem with Bataille's solution, rooted in the moment, is not only the impracticality of trying to live that way, always assuming one has the leisure and wherewithal to do so. The moment draws one deeper into the self-absorbed, self-indulgent self, which becomes increasingly reliant on spontaneous combustion moments to create a sense of being.

Bataille was right, however. Annihilation can lead to ecstasy, and not only when the target of annihilation is oneself. He learned that this effect can even be experienced vicariously with figures at far remove, which circumvents the problem of finding volunteer perpetrators. Hence, Bataille was increasingly drawn to rapt contemplation of an unspeakably gruesome photograph of a tortured and dismembered Chinese man, as he might have meditated on an image of the crucified Christ in his seminary days. I couldn't help wondering what the anonymous young Chinese man would have thought of the use of his grisly execution, as a contemplative aid for a man sitting in middle-class comfort in Paris.

However, while Bataille attempted to restore sacrifice, Girard offered a more difficult path that began with the radical renunciation of violence as a solution. Bataille thought nonviolence was an impossible objective, and the best we could hope is to acknowledge and embrace our violence, in a nontheoretical way. Besides, Bataille didn't seem to want the social cohesion that sacrifice offered since he was advocating constant destabilization and disequilibrium, along with the recognition that we are not separate, discrete entities—in short, a constant *indifférenciation* that Girard thought was the source of violence, anyway.

The more I thought, it seemed that Bataille might have more links with Apostolidès himself. Later I asked the Unabomber scholar if he himself had been influenced by these thinkers—in particular, Girard?

He didn't answer at once, and thought for a moment before responding. No, he said, twentieth-century anthropology is soaked in the same issues that preoccupied Girard. "Before René, I was into sacrifice," he said.

But he didn't answer instantly, and I wondered. For a moment, he did, too.

CHAPTER 12

The New Darwin of the Human Sciences

The absolute renunciation of violence is
the absolute renunciation of history.

—John Freccero

On the Stanford campus in the 1980s, at the post office or at the bookstore, I would occasionally cross paths with a remarkable man in his sixties walking intently to his destination. He had the sort of face a film director might type-cast in a movie to play one of the great thinkers of all times, a Plato or a Copernicus. This must have been a marketable asset for a professor of the old school, who made his reputation by means of that large, totemic head, with its dark, deep-set eyes and shock of thick, wavy, salt-and-pepper hair. His sense of purpose was reinforced by a brown leather briefcase, of the professorial kind that disappeared sometime in the era of the laptops, with buckles and straps and usually brimming with papers, letters, and folders.

The face was distinctive and memorable, so much so that I remembered it twenty years later, when I met the professor, by then in his eighties, who was of course René Girard. He had been in my peripheral vision all along, and I had not known it.

I was surprised at his invisibility on his home turf. He would tell me later that few people at Stanford understood what his work was about. In an era that focuses on milliseconds, people like Girard often pass beyond our range of vision. Their accomplishments extend over long lifetimes, not days or months. They pass out of our direct observation, like climate change, or the rising and falling of empires. I wrote several articles to rectify the neglect.

Less than a year after our meeting, he inscribed one of his lesser-known books, *Mimesis and Theory*, "To Cynthia, with all my thanks for her splendid contribution to my scholarly reputation." I wasn't sure I had earned my spurs at that point. He was a charming and engaging companion, and one favorably inclined toward me, for reasons I didn't understand, but it seemed to be one of those lucky turns in my life. A warm and unequal friendship; his deep courtesy kept the inequality from perturbing the conversation.

I saw him whole, as others were beginning to mourn the inch-by-inch waning of the man they once knew. I had no basis for comparison, so I sensed no decline. He was still easily one of the most engaging minds I had ever encountered (a couple Nobelists would be the only possible competition).

He invited me to come back, so the conversations continued informally. "So what shall we talk about today?" he would ask as we settled on the living room couch. Our conversations were wide-ranging, and served as an on-the-ground introduction to the man and his thought. We discussed the formation of crowds, 9/11, his upbringing, religion, political scandals, and the stock market. He offered his friendship, but mostly his time, time, time, sometimes into the early evening. Certainly in an academic atmosphere of bet-hedging, in an era characterized by a fear of commitment and a horror of making strong statements, I found his trenchant wit, frankness, and profound humanity a compelling blend. His restless digging for the deepest human truths, rather than the most fashionable academic trends, spoke to me, too.

He was an indefatigable news-watcher, and conversation tended toward current events. At that time, the scapegoating in the election cycle or the stock-market crash provided ample fuel for his theories. "Yeah, sure. It's always imitative behavior," he said. "In the formation of a crowd, every time you add one, the unity of the mob becomes faster. It has more power and attraction." No one can predict what a crowd will do, he said, unless there is a leader, and there is no leader.

Given that, he marveled at the stability of the United States and its institutions. With the exception of a few intellectuals and government officials, Americans refused to panic—something unimaginable in Europe, he said, where mobs would be rushing the banks to withdraw money. That would be the case a few years later, in Greece.

On another occasion, I asked him to elaborate upon a comment he had made in the press recently: "The West should really start thinking about whether it really has principles, whether they are Christian or purely consumerist." He replied with a chuckle, "Well, they are consumerist, but they are not going to be for long, because there is not going to be anything left to consume."

He embraced the French tradition of reason, yet he had been called a prophet—the latter certainly true if "prophet" is defined as someone deeply rooted in the past, keenly observant in the present, and therefore prescient about the future. Even in his most "prophetic" moments, however, he always attempted to ground his perceptions in that chilly virtue reason, in thinking and expression that was graceful as a syllogism. The Dreyfusard father, the Chartist training, and the whole French Enlightenment haunted even his most visionary moments.

His affection was of the kind that had boundaries, and was not territorial or possessive. Yet his great serenity of spirit was marked by a passivity that puzzled me. I wondered, at the time, whether it was age, or the recognition of the futility of all oppositions, doubles, fighting, and rivalries. Nevertheless, he was a compelling presence, and a persuasive one, despite the absolutes ("never," "always") that infuriated his foes. He would still make arch and satirical jabs at his critics, but in a quiet living room on the south side of the California campus, much of the sting was gone.

On several occasions, he mentioned the change the centuries had brought to the word "sacrifice." In archaic societies, he explained, it invariably meant the sacrifice of others. Only with the Christian era, he said, did *sacrifice* come to mean the sacrifice of oneself.

.   .   .

During the Stanford years, an expanding group of people formed their research interests around Girard, in the realm of politics, economy, nuclear deterrence, as well as the fields in which his work was already recognized.

But some colleagues had an interest that was less observable and not linked to a disciplinary specialization. I sought them out to round out a picture of Girard as a man, as well as a thinker.

At Stanford, Hans Ulrich Gumbrecht, universally called "Sepp," joined the ranks of Girard's aficionados somewhat reluctantly. He admitted that he used to think it was "relatively tacky and cheesy" to admit how much he admired him—"not because he doesn't deserve it, but because oftentimes it's a replacement for really knowing his work. What makes for the difference of his work, the difference of his intellectual temperament and style?"

The scholar is another formidable presence on the campus: he's a widely recognized public intellectual in Europe and also South America, and his books have been translated into twenty languages. The C.V. of the erudite German (he came to America in 1989) is daunting and his conversational style at times affably pugnacious. He is an amiable bulldog whose warmth and generosity are apparent in the first few minutes chatting in his dark and cozy book-lined office (a ladder in a corner helps him reach the uppermost shelves, and three extra bookcases have been wheeled into the small room to accommodate the overflow). He wasn't embarrassed to say that he finally came around to open admiration for Girard's "coherent and edgy" work: "I'm not a Girardian, but it's one of the more important thought systems around."

The word he associates with Girard is *Gelassenheit*, one of those forbidding German compound words, in this case borrowed from Meister Eckhart and the Christian mystical tradition, but given new life by Heidegger. Gumbrecht defines it as a "Let-It-Be-ness," which accepts things in their uncertainty and their mystery.

Yet Girard aroused such fierce animosity. An East Coast professor abruptly turned and walked away at Dostoevsky scholar Joseph Frank's memorial service when I mentioned Girard. (John Freccero once told me, "Their hostility is part of his great charisma.") Another scholar of my acquaintance found him to be a sinister character, and felt his deep eyes were, she said, sucking the soul out of her during conversations.

Gumbrecht matched my anecdotes with a story of his own. At the Stanford Faculty Club, he recalled pointing out Girard to the late German literary theorist Wolfgang Iser, who said, "The physiognomy confirms the violence of his theory." Gumbrecht laughed then and now at the thought, explaining to Iser that he'd gotten Girard all wrong. He is still puzzled at the misconception, and pauses a moment. "That's a very strange charge," he mused, observing how it comes uncomfortably close to the notions that fostered Nazi eugenics. "These are very very strange confusions that happen around great minds. The unpleasantness of what he's describing becomes confused with the man himself." Then he dismissed the subject. "I hate weird projections," he said.

He preferred discussing the oeuvre of René Girard: "It has intellectual power to irritate you in productive ways, to derail normal trains of thought. That's the trademark of grand intellectuals." Girard has been relentless, he said, in teasing out a few profound, generative ideas, beginning from a primary intuition decades ago. That lifelong intellectual feat is rare in our era.

His trail is difficult for others to follow, precisely because as his ideas evolved, "coherence becomes internally more and more complex" in a way that can't be copied or replicated. I had often thought that myself—the daedal edifice of Girard's thought seems to be unfolding from the life of its creator. His psychological engine is at the heart of it, and so it cannot be fully understood from without; therefore it's inimitable.

"He's convinced to the point of self-irony about being right," so much so that he didn't need to get into "stupid intellectual cockfights," Gumbrecht said. He suggested that Girard's oeuvre may undergo an eclipse, as so many strong buildings of thought have done. Even Karl Marx seems a bit démodé now, while he nevertheless remains "a great German classic coming out of German idealism." He was confident that Girard, too, will remain a great and towering figure, and his work will last, since "there's great intellectual life in the roots that exist." He added, "Despite the intellectual structures built around him, he's a *solitaire*. His work has a steel-like quality—strong, contoured, clear. It's like a rock. It will be there and it will last."

He rises to end our short interview, but invites me to come back. He said that talking about Girard is a "sublime pleasure."

John Freccero, too, seemed to find talking about Girard a sublime pleasure, but one laced with doubts and self-doubts about words said and those that remain unsaid. As I left his light-filled Palo Alto home for the last time, he handed me a Stanford festschrift, *To Honor René Girard,* published five years after Girard came to California. Pay particular attention to the preface and the postface, he instructed me. The introductory and closing essays are not signed. Are they by him? He wouldn't say when I asked. I assumed so. I heard his voice as I read it later, at home. Though the passage was somewhat long, the summary is astute and eloquent, and he clearly wished it to stand for him:

> Girard's penetrating analysis of modernity, his diagnosis of 'civilized' violence, his lucidity in the face of ideological justifications, these are all facets of a work which reverberates a genuine concern for integrity. If Girard's voice is able to touch, to alert, at times to irritate so many, it is because it questions all compromises, indulgences and prejudices alike. If his message sounds so definitive, it is because Girard takes nothing for granted. Paradoxically, because it represents one of the clearest and most limpid articulations of humanistic responsibility in today's world, Girard's thought lends itself to many a conflicting interpretation and misconception. An alarmist for some, a prophet for others, here perceived as a propagandist, there as a totalitarian, for most Girard remains essentially a theoretician. However erroneous, these diverse interpretations are probably the best tribute, and certainly the most convincing testimony, to a supremely fecund and brilliant mind.
>
> True, Girard's work is both acclaimed and disclaimed by an astonishing variety of schools and disciplines. The fact that politicians, lawyers, economists, scientists, theologians, anthropologists, writers and experts from all horizons scrutinize and respond to Girard's insights, is in itself a recognition of its power. For the profound resonance of Girard's voice echoes its fundamental simplicity. It speaks of dignity and substance beyond the confinements of suspicion and fear. It inspires and motivates a renewed examination of the roots and ramifications of humanistic thought.[1]

.   .   .

In our conversations, Girard said he had been mulling about writing a book on ecological issues—another indication of his turn toward the sciences, though on his own terms. It began, as other auspicious turns in his life did, with Oedipus. And it would turn on the confusion, from ancient Thebes until now, between what is natural and what is man-made.

As far back as *Violence and the Sacred*, Girard had been questioning the plague that devastated Thebes. Like Machaut's *Judgment of the King of*

Navarre, he found natural and unnatural elements were jumbled in the telling of the story. What, exactly, was going on? Even if Sophocles had in mind the famous Athenian plague of 430 B.C., "he clearly did not mean to limit his reference to one specific microbiotic visitation. The epidemic that interrupts all the vital functions of the city is surely not unrelated to violence and the loss of distinctions."[2] According to the oracle, the infectious presence of a *murderer* is the reason for the disaster. The murderer is unnamed and only presumably singular. The cries of the chorus for sacrifice mix metaphors of disease with more warlike images. The infection and the onslaught of reciprocal violence are one and the same. "The process by which the three protagonists are each in turn tainted with violence corresponds to the progress of the disease, always quick to lay low those who would contain it,"[3] Girard wrote. Human hardship (in this case, a blight on crops, cattle sickening and dying) may precede or follow community panic and violence, culminating in a search for a single culprit to blame.

The word the Greeks used is ambiguous. The "plague" in Sophocles and Thucydides is usually *nosos.* According to classics scholar Frederick Ahl, "The meaning of *nosos* may also be extended into a political metaphor." In Book 5 of *The Republic,* Plato portrays the conflict among the Greek states "not just as civil wars but as themselves a kind of *nosos,* 'sickness': 'in such a situation Greece is sick.' Many in Sophocles' audience may have shared Plato's view that the internecine wars among Greeks are 'the ultimate sickness' (*nosêma*) of the *polis.*"[4]

"The plague is primarily violence, people killing each other," Girard explained in his interview with Goodhart. "Many myths tried to disguise that crisis behind natural disasters, and one very common theme at the beginning of myth is the plague. But we know very well that in archaic societies they do not distinguish the plague as a disease." He added as an aside that the distinction occurred only in the sixteenth century, which would give an additional twist to Machaut's narrative.

For Girard, these so-called plagues bear witness to a sacrifice gone wild, and to a monster in the community that craves more and more victims. As the body count mounts, sacrifice no longer restores peace, and it becomes naked violence itself. "And the whole community then goes haywire; you have a crisis that seems to be impossible to cure, because the more you turn to prohibitions and sacrifice, the more violence you have."[5]

The years brought another level to his reflections. What is a crisis for man is not necessarily a crisis for nature, and ecological concerns are, at root, human ones. In other words, we define events according to ourselves, and what we call "natural disasters" are really human disasters. The crowded conditions of soldiers turned influenza of 1918 into an international catastrophe. Typhoid and cholera "plagues" are caused by contaminated water and food—contaminated, often, by human society and its by-products. The death rate escalates when *human* help and resources are not available. Drought is only a catastrophe if people thirst or go hungry. Earthquakes are relatively harmless in the world of nature; only human occupation in a stricken area makes them a "disaster." So with tornadoes, hurricanes, tsunamis.

Clearly, Machaut was not the only one to mix natural and man-made disasters so obviously in his narrative. As Girard studied apocalyptic texts, he was intrigued by passages such as this one, in the Gospel of Mark: "And when ye shall hear of wars and rumours of wars, be ye not troubled: for such things must needs be . . . For nation shall rise against nation, and kingdom against kingdom: and there shall be earthquakes in divers places, and there shall be famines and troubles."[6] Why, he asked, are apparently human and natural forces mixed together as if they are the same? Perhaps, in our times, they are. He noted that with climate change and man-made interventions in nature, we are considering whether even earthquakes may have a human cause. The possibilities fascinated him.

Girard was keen to move his work into the other sciences as well, and he thought, in particular, his mimetic theory could join hands with Charles Darwin's evolutionary theories—a quotation from Darwin's *Autobiography* opens each chapter of his late book *Evolution and Conversion* (2004). "I am a Darwinist," he explained. "I believe in natural selection." He noted that Richard Dawkins said that we must explain culture by evolutionary theory, and coined the term "memes" to describe "units of imitation." Following his lead, many evolutionist theoreticians began to discuss culture in terms of *memetics*. "They write many books, but seem to have missed the fact that *mimesis*—the Greek word for imitation—is potentially conflictual, and obviously the greatest source of conflict between nations."[7] Girard had long noted that the mimetic behavior of animals generally doesn't escalate to killing, but rather ends with the defeated male's submission to an alpha male. While animals don't have rituals, however, scapegoating exists among them. A predator will select the slowest, weakest, or merely "different" animal within a herd for killing. So humans, too, select an exceptional victim, distinguished either by an exalted or humble role, by race or ethnic distinction, or by physical defect. Oedipus, for example, is a king, but his name itself means "swollen foot." "The hero who limps is everywhere,"[8] Girard said. Think of the wounded Fisher King. "Difference" often marks defect in evolutionary theory. Survival of the fittest may be an invisible companion process in our scapegoating.

.   .   .

The sustained line of thought that began in *Deceit, Desire, and the Novel* was remarkable on many levels, not least of all this one: the emphasis on imitation in humans was not fashionable when René Girard began his career. Yet within decades convergent claims from research in a wide array of fields would put it at the forefront. Astonishing, too, given Girard's beginning was as a literary theorist, hewing to the close reading of texts, thinking they had a hidden story to tell us.

"My opinion is that he is *the* thinker who brought the most to the human sciences in the twentieth century," Oughourlian explained. By the time I met Oughourlian in Paris, he had been a neuro-psychiatrist at the American Hospital of Paris for decades, so his interest in the discovery of "mirror neurons" in the mid-1990s, and its link with Girard's theories, was much on his mind. It was a vindication, and one that was "incredible in the history of science—the scientific demonstration of a psychological theory."

Mirror neurons are essentially mimesis built into the human brain. They offer a deep-level physiological explanation for why we flinch when someone next to us is struck by an errant frisbee, or why we cry when someone else cries. Oughourlian cited a straightforward example: when one man drinks a glass of water, research has found that the same parts of an observer's brain are activated. "It's a neuroscientific demonstration of the theory of mimetic desire"—the tiniest neural unit of imitation.

Potentially, it could explain empathy, and why we feel we can "read" other people's minds. Some have even suggested that it could explain autism and the evolution of language. One leading neuroscientist, V. S. Ramachandran, called the discovery of mirror neurons one of the "single most important unpublicized stories of the decade."[9]

Dr. Andrew Meltzoff of the University of Washington's Institute for Learning & Brain Sciences was one of the scientists who confirmed the intuitions that had inspired *Deceit, Desire, and the Novel*. Meltzoff, building on Darwin and Freud, showed the tendency of infants to imitate the people in their lives from their first hour. Although Freud, Jean Piaget, and B. F. Skinner had maintained that newborns were social isolates with no ability to connect with others, what Meltzoff found spectacularly contradicted this: newborns put out their tongues to imitate adults, demonstrating a mimetic connection between self and other from birth. In fact, Meltzoff demonstrated that the first type of human relationship was mimetic. He repeated his experiment again and again, with newborns as young as forty-two minutes. "We're a role model for babies from the moment they look up at us and begin to sculpt their own activities according to what they see in the culture around them,"[10] Meltzoff said. This finding shook the world of developmental psychology.

Among Girard's associates, several described mirror neurons as the cutting edge of mimetic theory. However, the news leaves one uneasy. If mimesis is hard-wired into us, along with its attendant violence and enmities, our predicament would appear to be hopeless. Where, in this, is free will, or, with unshakeable resolve, the ability to relinquish our toxic rivalries?

Then I remembered one of Girard's earlier comments: "But I would say that mimetic desire, even when bad, is intrinsically good, in the sense that far from being merely imitative in a small sense, it's the opening out of oneself. ... Yes. Extreme openness. It is everything. It can be murderous, it is rivalrous; but it is also the basis of heroism, and devotion to others, and everything."[11] Girard, as so often happens, takes us one step back, into more metaphysical territory and vertical transcendence.

We don't escape mimesis, we can only observe it—and in observing it, loosen the grip that envy has on us. And while we may be doomed to mimesis, we have, at least, a choice between picking our models intentionally through what Marcus Aurelius called the "ruling faculty," or else letting them happen accidentally, through the mass media, the secondhand idols of our friends, or sibling rivalries. Rebecca Adams asked Girard whether his theory could account for "desire on behalf of the Other—for nonviolent, saintly desire—as an excess of desire rather than a renunciation of desire." Girard responded, "Wherever you have that desire, I would say, that really active, positive desire for the other, there is some kind of divine grace present. . . . If we deny this we move into some form of optimistic humanism."[12]

The phrasing is vintage Girard, in certain moments where he is not sure what his audience will bear—indirect, allusive, as if the subject were a thousand miles away from him. In another interview, about fifteen years later, he expressed the inherent possibilities of mimesis with a different emphasis: "The question is how can the human community form societies, long-term associations on the basis of that form of rivalry that is endless, that goes on forever. And what does it mean? Should we speak here of evil? I don't think so," he said. He urged the use of a scientific language, and then noted that you can no more stop imitating the violence of your opponent than you can avoid imitating the kindness of your friend. "Kindness escalates and turns into what we call love, which obviously animals don't have. But it escalates the other way too, and it turns into deadly violence, which animals don't have either," he said. "But whether you exchange compliments, niceties, greetings, or insinuations, indifference, meanness, bullets, atom bombs, it's always an exchange. You always give to the other guy what he's giving to you, or you try to do so."[13]

Both answers serve as a reminder that mimesis is not only a locked room, it also offers us a key, and a way out.

.   .   .

In 2005, René Girard was inducted into the august Académie Française, an organization founded by Richelieu in 1635, under Louis XIII, and charged with matters of the French language and its literature. He jostled figurative elbows with *immortels* Victor Hugo, Paul Claudel, Alexandre Dumas fils, Montesquieu, Louis Pasteur, Voltaire, Marguerite Yourcenar, even Claude Lévi-Strauss—in addition to his old friend Michel Serres, who had supported his candidacy.

"To have one [member of the Academy] is exceptional enough, but to have two," Harrison said when Girard was elected to the academy as the second in Stanford's twelve-member department (Serres had become a member in 1990). "Sometimes I think the administration doesn't realize the cachet that Stanford has in France and Francophone countries," he said to *Stanford Report*.[14]

At the ceremonies, Girard was presented with a sword and wore the famous green silk waistcoat embroidered with olive tree branches, as stipulated by Napoleon. Girard said he found the elaborate rituals "very bizarre"—not surprising, perhaps, for one who had spent so much time in anthropology. Speaking by phone from Paris, he added, "People make fun of it, of course—the forty *immortels* who are not immortal at all."[15]

The writer and editor Joseph Bottum has a cherished memoir from the event, though he didn't attend: he received a letter from Girard, "in his terrible handwriting."

> He had been put in a side room, dressed in the uniform of an embroidered frock coat, while awaiting his induction. And, exploring the room, he discovered stationery in the drawer of a writing desk.
>
> So, he wrote, he asked himself who would appreciate a note on académie letterhead—and he settled on me. It was sweet and unexpected, somehow both comic and grand. It was a gesture of the kind that René alone, of all the people I've ever known, was capable. A gesture, I've always thought, a century out of its time.[16]

The image of Girard idly looking for something to do as he waited reinforces the image created in at least one other observer, that Girard was not at all swept up by his own apotheosis.

Sepp Gumbrecht also attended the celebrations with his colleagues Jean-Pierre Dupuy and Robert Harrison, as part of the official Stanford delegation, with Michel Serres serving as master of ceremonies. Gumbrecht noted that Serres is the son of a bargeman and staunchly democratic, yet he makes sure people know he's an academician. By contrast, he noticed that Girard, on the occasion of his glory, didn't much know what to do with himself.

He observed Girard was sitting in a chair, a little uncomfortable, a little beside himself, "as if he's done a favor by letting Michel elect him." Gumbrecht noted that Girard had no need of status symbols; he was someone with no ostentatiousness—and no need to impress you with a visible show of his lack of ostentation, either.

"Something that impressed me at first is that he is someone who clearly—and I say this in praise of him—has an awareness of his importance, and takes pride in it," he said. "Some feel it's exaggerated. I don't. At the same time, I couldn't imagine him not treating every other human being as an equal. He doesn't feel the world and its institutions owe anything to him."

Girard may have made light of the occasion ("the *immortels* who are not immortal"), but in another sense he took it very seriously. Each of the forty chairs has a history, and on the death of one, a new member is chosen who aligns with the profiles of the previous holders of the specific chair. As he pointed out in his speech, Girard's was number thirty-seven, a chair that carried the legacies of ecclesiastics and theologians, as well as poets, philosophers, historians, and literary critics. His immediate predecessor was Ambroise-Marie Carré, a Dominican priest and author who had been awarded the *Légion d'honneur* and the *Croix de guerre*.

His address on the occasion eulogized his predecessor—a requirement, but he did so with unusual warmth. Girard noted that Carré had taken a glorious role in the French Résistance, but mentioned this only in passing. The family was disappointed, some said; they had expected the war years to be the substance of his talk. They didn't know Girard, whose speech exceeded those predictable standards. Girard discussed instead Carré's interior life, "the spiritual drama that accompanied him throughout his life." He explained, "His allusions to it are few, fragmentary, and not always easy to interpret. He never told the full story. That's what I will try to do now."

In his family home at Neuilly at age fourteen, the priest's own words described his peak experience. In *Every Day I Begin* (1975), Carré wrote about the illuminating occurrence that took place in his small bedroom: "I felt with incredible force, leaving no room for any hesitation, that I was loved by God and that life . . . there before me was a wonderful gift. Overcome with a happiness that took my breath away, I fell to my knees." Carré called the event "an absolute beginning" and the event brought him "a joy that no other joy could ever surpass."

Girard continued: "Even half a century later, Father Carré could not talk about this evening without reawakening the emotion of the original experience. Generally, in all that we call memory, the traces of the remembered event are just sufficient to prevent forgetting. Here, however, the word remembrance seems, upon reflection, inadequate."

He emphasized the centrality of Carré's vision throughout his life, a wellspring he would return to again and again, finally resigning himself to living in its remembered splendor. It is worthwhile to spend some time considering Carré's experience, for reading between the lines, I wondered if Girard was not describing himself, too, as he delivered his interpretation of Carré's *confessio*.

Girard himself had had such an experience nearly half a century before, though his seems to have been more articulated and urgent. He had spent the rest of his life trying to explain it. Was he, toward the end of his own life, revisiting the powerful episodes of that marvelous Lenten season, with its double conversion? "I believe that Père Carré must not be seen as a religious writer like so many others, or even a mystical thinker, but more radically, as a mystic in the most concrete sense," he said.

He explained that Carré's experience had held the two markers of a "mystical experience," a term he acknowledged would arouse skepticism in his audience. The first is that it occurs without warning, effort, or invitation. The second is the joy that Carré said no other experience would surpass. Finally, Girard said, "the impression it gives of eternity, inseparable from an infinite power of renewal, of an extraordinary fecundity." He added, "The last feature summarizes all the others and it is the intuition of a divine presence."

However, like many spiritual aspirants, Carré had assumed the process of holiness would include more frequent, intense, and prolonged contacts, and he waited with increasing frustration for new mystical experiences that never arrived. He fell prey to emotional bitterness, spiritual ambition and the drought that follows it, said Girard. "The more one familiarizes oneself with Père Carré, the more one realizes that he subordinates all philosophical and even theological reflection to the desire for a personal contact with God."

Although thwarted desire can turn into revolt, Carré bypassed the modern descent to "the anti-Christian nihilism that has spread everywhere in our time." Girard described how Carré fell afoul of those times, in which there is "nothing more scandalous . . . than this old man clinging to an old dream of holiness." A half century after his experience at Neuilly, Carré decided to touch the inner wound of his being. His spiritual center of gravity was always in the past, not in the future or, alas, the present. He began to "poke the embers of the burned-out fire," according to Girard.

"Before his eyes, the Neuilly experience became a radiant sleeping beauty awakening after a long night." In the experience of a timeless moment, the difference between a memory and a new experience vanishes. Carré's later writings return to his childhood experience at Neuilly, and the realization that he himself had turned from God by trying to storm the citadel by his own efforts—"a typically Western and modern ambition," said Girard.

Carré had been drawn to the models extolled in Western society, "men of action, 'achievers,' the 'entrepreneurs,' in the American sense, almost of free enterprise." The canker vice, that monster envy, again—the connection with mimesis was inevitable.

Carré seemed to be a worthy entry into Girard's roster, fitting the formula he established in *Deceit, Desire, and the Novel:* author and character depart the stage with an end-of-life conversion, with a renunciation of the self and its strivings. The author realizes that he has been shadow-boxing—that he and his enemy are the same.

"Instead of making God an Everest to climb, the final Father Carré sees him as a refuge. This is not skeptical humanism, but rather a surrender to divine mercy," said Girard. In the end, it was humility that freed him. And perhaps Girard, too?

Girard habitually deflected attention from himself and redirected it to his ideas. I wondered to what extent, if any, he had used Carré as subterfuge—in the way Dante used a series of "screen ladies" to express his true love freely, without confession—to describe his own spiritual experience in the decades since. How much was Carré expressing in a lifetime of words Girard's own private experience?

Girard's talks on Christianity mostly advanced his own theories, and were not autobiographical. Perhaps his talk "A Modern Mystical Experience" offers a rare window onto the inner life of the man himself, describing his own spiritual struggles through Carré's early glimpse of transcendence, then the spiritual desert that followed, the long journey when you must follow the same faint star in broad daylight.

It was not what the Académie audience had expected that day in 2005. Girard characteristically pursued his own unique thread on Carré's work, tackling an overtly religious theme in a forum that would not necessarily be friendly to it.

Michel Serres's formal remarks came next. The press commented that he delivered them with unusual feeling. He pointed out that today, in word and image, the media is obsessed with human sacrifice, "representing it and multiplying it with a frenzy such that these repetitions return our culture to melancholic barbarism and commit us to a huge regression in terms of hominization." The most advanced technologies, he said, "thrust our culture back to the archaic age of sacrificial polytheism."

He continued with a direct address to his friend and colleague: "You have uncovered the faith behind the crimes of history and understood those perpetrated in the name of God, not in order for you to justify religion but to reestablish the truth, whose criterion is: don't shed blood."[17]

He called Girard a prophet who had reinvigorated literary criticism, history, and psychology. His theories have helped us comprehend the mechanisms of desire and of the competition that shapes our economy; as a result, we have arrived at a more advanced stage in anthropology, the history of religions, and theology. "I name you henceforth the new Darwin of the human sciences," he finally said. It was the first usage of the term, and the tag stuck.

.   .   .

Conversion is a process, not an event. In Girard's case, one pivotal juncture in that process occurred with an admiring letter for *Violence and the Sacred* in the early 1970s. It led to a friendship. He met Raymund Schwager in Sauveterre, outside Avignon, sometime in the summer of 1975. The cordial, insightful letters continued back and forth for more than thirty years.

The friendship is important because, over years, it changed his thinking on one of the more avant-garde aspects of *Things Hidden,* and altered the direction of Girard's life and his work in ways that would draw more critical scorn rather than endorsement from an increasingly secular culture. Although the seed was planted in the 1970s, the fruit of this correspondence would ripen at Stanford.

His new correspondent was a Swiss Jesuit and professor in theology at Austria's University of Innsbruck. He was the first of the Girardian theologians, and Schwager's enthusiasm was infectious, first with his Austrian colleagues, and later with other theologians, who were increasingly drawn to this French theorist's work. Girard felt so strongly about Schwager's book *Must There Be Scapegoats?,* published in German only months before *Things Hidden* appeared in French, that he said it was "really a twin book" with his own.[18] Schwager would eventually be the inaugural president of one of the main Girardian research organizations, the Colloquium on Violence and Religion.

Girard felt even more strongly about the man himself. "I must say on a personal level Raymund Schwager was totally alien to mimetic desire. There never was any spirit of rivalry between us, any race to the finish," he said. "He was totally selfless, the most selfless man I have encountered perhaps. The spirit of research was in him, but totally pure and totally dedicated to the truth of Christianity and to the enhancement of that truth."[19] Certainly Schwager's example was even more persuasive than his words. Bill Johnsen expressed a companion thought to Girard's: "I am tempted to call Schwager an external model, existing on a different plane altogether, innocent of envy, except that this would deny him credit for his noble and invisible accomplishment of facing envy down, and it would neglect his insistence on the necessity of personal conversion in working effectively with the mimetic hypothesis." Johnsen described the "personal conversion" in Girardian terms: "that is, recognizing one's own mimetic entanglements and scapegoats."[20]

Perhaps Schwager's biggest influence was this: Girard retrenched the position he had taken on "sacrifice" in *Things Hidden*.

One theme that dominates their letters is the analysis of sacrifice. Both agreed about the nature of archaic sacrifice, but Girard had taken exception to the Epistle to the Hebrews, finding that its references to Christ's "sacrifice" held the remnants of archaic religion and an archaic relationship to the sacred. Schwager reasoned that although its language was indeed sacrificial in the archaic sense, the author of the epistle found a new and transformed meaning in the word, locating the sacrifice within the self. The believer bears persecution, calumny, and even death, in perfect *imitatio Christi*. The epistle, Schwager pointed out, underscores the difference between the older forms of sacrifice and the one described in the epistle. Jesus was faithful and obedient to the message of nonviolence, Schwager argued.

In a 17 April 1978 letter, Girard reminded Schwager that he was in an academic milieu where literary critics dominate, not a theological one. He suggested that Schwager was better positioned to describe this aspect of mimetic theory, and the theologian took his advice in several books. But there was no going back. Girard later admitted that he had dismissed the Letter to the Hebrews too quickly: "I was completely wrong. And I don't know what happened to me, really, because I was pretty careful not to do that, generally"—that is, he admitted he had "scapegoated" the Letter to the Hebrews, and that he had been influenced by psychoanalysts, "who have some kind of phobia about the word 'sacrifice.'" The epistle deserves careful treatment, he said, and it was the one portion of *Things Hidden* he wished he could amend. "I ask Hebrews to use the same vocabulary I do, which is just plain ridiculous."[21]

He emphasized that changes in the meaning of the word "sacrifice" contain mankind's whole religious history. Hence the word "sacrifice," within a modern church or other religious context, does not have the same meaning it did in primitive religion. "Of course I was full of primitive religion at the time of the writing of the book, and my main theme was the difference between primitive religion and Christianity, so I reserved the word 'sacrifice' completely for the primitive."[22]

In his later years, Girard had occasionally hinted at his own mimetic struggles, his own wish to appear in the avant-garde. His criticism of Christianity, on this particular point but also more generally, had given him a heretical splendor in some circles, though I always thought he had exaggerated their importance and size. But the more this opsimath (I use this term in praise, not criticism) learned and discovered, the more orthodox he became, eventually admitting that three-quarters of what he had said was already in Saint Augustine.[23] Sometimes one needs to be rescued from one's own cleverness. I suspected the encounter with Schwager took away his last desire to be unorthodox, to be more than another person quietly filling a pew on Sunday mornings. In any case, his new stance took him one large step farther away from fashionable intellectual circles and their feverish pursuit of novelty. Girard's close friend Gil Bailie recalls meeting with theologians in Sonoma, sometime in the mid to late 1980s. Girard had just outlined the implication of our cultural and historical predicament, in light of our mimetic crisis and the failure to resolve it, either with scapegoating or peaceful alternatives. "What is to be done?" someone asked. Girard's response was all the more shocking for needing to be said at all in a roomful of theologians: "We might begin with personal sanctity."[24]

It was not an isolated incident. Girard's assessment of our world situation became more dire and apocalyptic with *Achever Clausewitz*. Oughourlian recalled a lecture in Paris during this time, when he responded to another request for a recipe: What is to be done to avert disaster? "Pray," Girard answered.

·   ·   ·

I had followed firsthand the struggles in bringing Girard's last major book, *Achever Clausewitz,* into English. The translation process, as usual with his books, seemed to be a prolonged ordeal. While I awaited the page proofs for the *San Francisco Chronicle* review I would be writing, the title changed several times. Over coffee years later, Johnsen, Girard's American editor, recalled how he hit the right note for the title of the new translation. "Achever" proved untranslatable in the end; the closest translation might be "to finish off," or in this case, "to complete." Both make a clumsy rendering in English. The German translation had been *Im Angesicht der Apokalypse: Clausewitz zu Ende denken,* or "In the Face of the Apocalypse: Thinking through Clausewitz"—cumbersome in English, and obscure for the relatively large number of Americans who know little about the Prussian military theorist. The title that was finally chosen came from Girard and Benoît Chantre together: "Battling to the End."

Johnsen explained the thinking behind their choice: "The English title throws in focus the language in the book about the struggle of violence against truth, a battle longer than the one with Clausewitz." I looked for the passage he referred to, which was used as an epigraph for the French edition, and found it: Girard claimed that the historical configuration we are now facing is "a modality of what Pascal saw: the war between violence and truth."[25] That returned me to Pascal's letters, where I found this passage in the twelfth of his *Provincial Letters:*

> It is a strange and tedious war when violence attempts to vanquish truth. All the efforts of violence cannot weaken truth, and only serve to give it fresh vigour. All the lights of truth cannot arrest violence, and only serve to exasperate it. When force meets force, the weaker must succumb to the stronger; when argument is opposed to argument, the solid and the convincing triumphs over the empty and the false; but violence and verity can make no impression on each other. Let none suppose, however, that the two are, therefore, equal to each other; for there is this vast difference between them, that violence has only a certain course to run, limited by the appointment of Heaven.

"That wonderful sense of mission, of never giving in, battling to the end, is not at all the dumb reading that suggests we are passive before being destroyed," said Johnsen. Both Pascal and Girard represented a search for a "durable position," he explained. "You must never give up fighting for the truth."

.   .   .

On 28 December 2008, Girard was awarded the Modern Language Association's "Lifetime Scholarly Achievement Award" at the annual convention, that year at San Francisco's lavish hotel, the Fairmont. In its citation, the MLA noted he had been "internationally influential in arguing for literary art as verifiable research in human behavior." The praise continued: "Over fifty years, from his first book on the novel to his recent book on politics and war after Clausewitz, he has inspired interdisciplinary research in the physical, biological, and social sciences and the study of religion. His students and readers have found in him a brilliant and gentle colleague, an inspiration to the truth."

Hundreds of people were packed in the neoclassical hall under the chandeliers. Girard's friends were nearby—Johnsen, myself, and his daughter Mary among them. The Steuben glass triangle that was presented to him (inviting associations with his first book, *Deceit, Desire, and the Novel*) was a distinguished bookend to his long history with the MLA, ever since his early "best essay" award more than four decades earlier for "Camus's Stranger Retried."

I had been in one of the chairs, ballpoint in hand, waiting to scribble a few notes on his remarks. The MLA blogger writing about the event noted that "Girard made me laugh when he said that some of the conversations he was hearing in the halls of the conference were identical to those he used to hear back in the 1960s."[26] He advised us to stress the value and utility of the humanities. He left the podium.

Although it is by no means a requirement for the recipients to make a speech, they usually reflect on their life's work or their field of study. Others have simply offered thanks, as Girard did. But I sensed that the audience was momentarily nonplussed, having expected a little more from one of the most articulate lions in the academy. The applause was warm.

Girard's graceful and easy style of podium showmanship was off—I felt so, anyway. And though I didn't know about his series of small strokes that year, or perhaps simply hadn't understood the seriousness of what I had heard, I sensed something was amiss.

CHAPTER 13

Who Asks about the Souls of These Men?

The truth of metaphysical desire is death.

—René Girard

The middle-aged woman from Sérignan-du-Comtat stepped from the shadows into the late afternoon sun of a hot, dry summer day in Provence. She blinked and squinted into the crowd that had gathered outside the door. After nearly two months confined to the house adjoining the cathedral, which had served as a prison, the light would have been bright beyond bearing. From there the soldiers stepped up and hustled her forward through the jostling crowds and into the relentless sunlight.

We don't know too much about her, but this is what we do know: Suzanne-Agathe Deloye was fifty-three years old, born on 4 February 1741, the daughter of Joseph-Alexis Deloye and Suzanne Jean-Clerc, the fourth of eight children, reared a few miles away from Avignon. For the previous two years, she had lived quietly with her brother, teaching grammar, sewing, and the catechism.

On that particular day, 6 July 1794, once again she was brought before the People's Commission. Once again she was accused of being an enemy of liberty, trying to destroy the Republic with fanaticism and superstition, refusing the oath demanded by law, rejecting citizenship, and fomenting civil war. She was asked again to take a mandatory civic oath of liberty as a citizen of the Republic, and once again she refused.

Undoubtedly, she would have recognized the oxymoron—a "mandatory" oath of liberty, required of prisoner on pain of death—and she would have been too shrewd to be fooled by words like "liberty" and "freedom," anyway; after all, the kindly man who was beside her, who had faced the same oath and the same charges, had been imprisoned for nothing more than celebrating mass. Two years before, she herself had been forced from the Caderousse Abbey, where she had been the Benedictine Sister Marie-Rose. The abbey's nine other nuns had been sent out into hardship, poverty, and whatever recourses they had in October 1792. In the end, perhaps that offered more protection than returning, as she had done, to her bourgeois family home of silk makers. That is where the revolutionary authorities had found Suzanne-Agathe Deloye.

The martyred Carmelite nuns of Compiègne were immortalized in Poulenc's devastating and inexorable opera, *Dialogue of the Carmelites*. But for whatever reason, we seem to know less about the executions farther from the center of action in Paris—in Orange, where the Reign of Terror was especially bloody and ferocious. In fact, the nuns were only a serene and courageous subset of 332 locals who were slaughtered in a six-week period there.

Suzanne-Agathe saw to it that the occasion possessed a heroic panache: the historians say that the Abbé Antoine Lusignan and the Benedictine sister had a friendly contest in martyrdom, so much so that it wasn't clear whether the priest maintained the courage of the nun, or the nun emboldened the priest on the way to the guillotine.

At 6 p.m. that day, the forty or so women she left behind in the house by the cathedral would have heard, for the first time, the ominous sound of the drums and the cries of "Vive la Nation!" signaling the first of the executions, telling the sisters that the new friend who had cheered them only a few hours before had had her head severed from her body and lifted to the crowd. They would follow soon enough.

According to Girard, political terrors often weave together two types of violence: collective persecutions committed by a mob of murderers, and collective resonances of persecutions that are outwardly legal and follow judicial forms, but are stimulated by the extremes of public opinion. The

French Revolution provides excellent examples of both. It's unlikely that the superficial legal rituals reassured those who had been hustled through jubilant, jeering mobs that due process had taken its course. One is reminded again of Girard's words about sacrifice gone wild, that there is "a monster in the community, so to speak, and he wants more and more victims."[1]

When Girard assured me on several occasions that the woman known today as Blessed Marie-Rose of Orange was a distant great-aunt on his maternal grandmother's side, I suspected it was nothing more than a self-serving family myth. However, the De Loye family is still in the silk business in Sérignan-du-Comtat, as it has been since 1770 (the first postwar mayor of the city was a Deloye, so the name is still fashioned both ways). Girard's mother, Marie-Thérèse de Loye Fabre, was born a scant century after these events. It would be impossible *not* to be related—in that part of the world, a century is not too long a history to trace when your family has lived in the same region as far back as anyone can recall. To look at a few photos of Sérignon, or nearby Caderousse, is to understand something of the rootedness of place.

Girard said his mother had retold the story to the children, and it seemed to cast a bit of a mystique over his mother's family.

The fact that he mentioned it on several occasions to me also tells us something about an unseen spiritual compass that, to my best knowledge, is unmentioned in other writings about him. Perhaps it is not too fanciful to suggest that Suzanne-Agathe's defiance, to the death, of the regime's "escalation to extremes," her personal "*non*" to coercion and intellectual fashion, are traits that can be passed invisibly through generations, more fixed by repetition and family lore even than the patterns of DNA. In any case, it may explain some of Girard's attachment to this time, this history. Perhaps it's one reason that, at the end of his life, he returned to it in his final book, *Battling to the End*, describing the developments that have brought us to our twenty-first century predicament—the historical point where Girard has left us, departing the noisy stage.

The medieval cathedral of Orange has a chapel commemorating the thirty-two women who were executed. What would be the effect of this violent family history on an impressionable young man—a history not, as for Americans, a continent away, but in the next village?

.   .   .

"There are signs that communities—archaic communities, but even modern communities, all communities—are subject to disturbances which tend to spread to the entire community contagiously, through a form of mimetic desire," Girard explained on Robert Harrison's radio talk show, "Entitled Opinions," in 2005. "If you have two people who desire the same thing, you will soon have three, when you have three, they contaminate the rest of the community faster and faster. The differences that separate them, the barriers to the type of intercourse that mimetic desire produces, collapse," he continued. "Therefore you go toward what I call a mimetic crisis, the moment when everybody at the same time is fighting over something. Even if that object disappears, they will go on fighting, because they will become obsessed with each other. And as that conflict grows, it threatens to destroy the whole community."[2]

Not all "religious" rituals are religious, of course, and in our modern era, secular rituals may carry vestiges of the archaic sacred. The French Revolution offers an illuminating case study of scapegoating and sacrifice, a mimetic pattern that would reverberate through successive centuries of revolutions, world wars, and finally the international terrorism and nuclear disaster that threaten the twenty-first century. Girard would show us how all is prefigured in a society that had just publicly butchered its formerly untouchable king, in a clumsy and therefore agonizingly prolonged ritual in January 1793. Anything had become possible: the washerwoman could become an informant and revolutionary, the carpenter could become an executioner of the once-great and inaccessible. Taboos were gone, and social distinctions, if they hadn't dissolved entirely, were suddenly much more permeable. The scene would play out again and again in copycat revolutions that would convulse the world for centuries to come. Hannah Arendt, observing the effect of atrocities, wrote "that the unprecedented, once it has appeared, may become a precedent for the future."[3] Each atrocity, each act of terrorism, invites repetition, escalation. The murder of children in Norway in July 2011 is followed by the murder of children in Toulouse in March 2013, then the massacre at Newtown, Connecticut, in December of the same year. We no longer are surprised at a school shooting—it has become routine since Columbine.

Modern times may be the setting for the same archaic violence, but we no longer live in archaic societies. The term "victim" has a new and different meaning than it had in Mycenae, where the scapegoats were not considered to be fully human—hence the double potential they had for future deification as well as vilification and death. Modern societies, including the one that executed Suzanne-Agathe, have lost their archaic innocence. Scapegoating can no longer serve as a brake on violence, but escalates it instead, as if to blot out a subliminal sense of wrongdoing by doubling down on the original error. As the scapegoats, one by one, are executed, the victim pool is enlarged with more accusations and more scapegoats, in a process that becomes self-devouring.

The wealthy and privileged Church—which even held the right to levy taxes—was a logical target. Again, scapegoats are not always innocent flowers, but the blame they carry is disproportionate to whatever they, as individuals, may have done, or whatever guilt the group they belong to can reasonably be expected to bear. Nevertheless, the perpetrators home in on them with a single-minded fury and incoherent motives. Suzanne-Agathe had been at the end of a long chain of violence.

It can be said to have started in 1792, the fourth year of the revolution, when rumor was traveling on electric currents of fear, and fear fostered disorder. The Prussian armies were advancing to Paris to restore order to France and check the revolution's plan for European conquest. News of impending invasion brought riots and bloodshed. Three bishops and over two hundred priests were murdered by angry mobs in September 1792—many of them at the Église des Carmes, a short way down the rue de Vaugirard, where Girard had warmed himself over a heater during the German Occupation. According to a British diplomat who witnessed the events, the clergy were "massacred with circumstances of barbarity too shocking to describe . . . the multitude are perfectly masters, everything is to be dreaded."[4]

Beginning on 21 October 1793, all priests who would not take the oath of loyalty (the vow that Suzanne-Agathe had refused) were liable to be killed on sight, along with all who harbored such priests. Priests and nuns figured disproportionately among the thousands of gruesome drownings in the Loire near Nantes between November 1793 and February 1794 (they were the exclusive cargo in the first two nights of slaughter), and religious also figured prominently in the mass executions of Lyon as well. At Rochefort, about eight hundred clergy refused to take the oath and were put aboard a fleet of prison ships in Rochefort harbor, where most died due to abominable conditions. Some have suggested that the ships were, in effect, one of the first "concentration camps" in the world. From concentration camp to genocide:

a quarter of a million men, women, and children were killed in the Vendée region during these years. These residents were not, as often portrayed, backward-looking royalists, but *citoyens* who had enthusiastically supported the 1789 revolution but revolted at the eradication of their religion. The episode ended with "premeditated, organized, planned massacres, which were committed in cold blood, and were massive and systematic, with the conscious and explicit intention of destroying a well-defined region and exterminating an entire people, women and children first, in order to eradicate a 'cursed race' considered ideologically beyond redemption."[5]

In these events, Girard found the roots of our modern era. He described how the consequences of the French Revolution are still being played out in the escalation to the extremes, as military analyst Clausewitz explained with such chilling prescience. "Thus, terrorism would have its roots in the Revolutionary Wars, of which Napoleon's 'regular' army was the ultimate transformation,"[6] Girard said.

What happened? "With a single murder the murderer enters a locked system. He must kill and kill again, he must plan whole massacres lest a single survivor remain to avenge his kin,"[7] wrote the anthropologist Jules Henry in 1941—and he wasn't referring only to the Brazilian jungle that was the setting for his research. What he stated applies as readily to the genocides of more recent times. It was said of one of the French Revolution's most notoriously cruel mass murderers, Jean-Baptiste Carrier, the man who had engineered the Nantes atrocities and the "pacification" of the Vendée, "This frantic wretch imagined that he had no other mission than to slaughter."[8]

Girard added his assent to Henry's analysis: "Violence, which produced the sacred, now produces only itself," he observed. "The fear generated by the kill-or-be-killed syndrome, the tendency to 'anticipate' violence by lashing out first (akin to our contemporary concept of 'preventive war') cannot be explained in purely psychological terms."[9]

The impending foreign invasion aggravated other tensions within the political makeup of the government. Revolutionary parties struggled for the control of France. The factions had briefly reconciled in the National Convention's unanimous condemnation of the scapegoat king, with its archaic accusations,[10] but splintered into factions again afterwards. The revolution, after four years, had not delivered on its inflated promises to fulfill mimetic aspirations ("jam for everyone!"), and the truly impoverished remained hungry ("no bread!"). In that sense, how much does it differ from political promises and advertising slogans today? Propaganda was born in this era.

The mob, driven by needs real and imagined, demanded more. Human sacrifices followed: those who had been seen as obstacles to true "equality" were guillotined; the new system would surely work once they were eliminated. These moves only bred more fear and dissension, and failed to provide the cement of social unity. The revolutionary leaders inevitably turned on each other. The more ferocious Jacobins rounded up and executed the more moderate Girondins after October 1793, launching the Reign of Terror in earnest. More and more victims were needed, more "enemies" found, and the need for "purification" was always external to oneself, requiring that others be sacrificed. The process accelerated when the Revolution's most iconic figure came to the fore.

The Château de Vizille near Grenoble has a terracotta bust of Maximilien de Robespierre. Unlike other portraits that feature stiff clothes, starched white hair, and tightly pressed lips, in this one, his tie is loosely knotted, and the young man appears to disagree with a comment from an invisible someone seated somewhere to his right. His expression is lively and slightly surprised—his eyebrows are raised and his head is turned to offer a rejoinder at the National Convention. His face and its expression are strikingly modern; without the period garb, he could be an undergraduate at almost any university today. The portrait is within a year or two of others, yet it shows a distinct move from classicism to the romanticism that would take hold in the subsequent decades.

One of the architects of the romantic movement, Jean Jacques Rousseau, would greatly influence Robespierre's thinking, well into adulthood. The resultant worldview, naive in the extreme, likely short-circuited self-recognition. Robespierre believed that the people of France were fundamentally good, a fitting clay for shaping a direct democracy. Of course, direct democracy is one short step from the mob. "Terror is nothing else than justice, prompt, severe, inflexible," he declared. His belief in innate goodness didn't prevent him from launching a program that, in less than a year, would kill as many as forty thousand people. Nor did the slaughter stop him from being tagged, in his pursuit of revolutionary virtue, "the Incorruptible."

.   .   .

Mistrust all movements that invent new calendars—a futile effort to restructure time. The Pol Pot regime did it in Cambodia, with a "Year Zero" that celebrated the genocidaire's takeover in 1975, and so did the French Revolution. The "Great Revolution" would be imitated, and was itself a mimetic event—a replication of its quieter American predecessor. Most thinking proceeds by herd instinct—and what we often call "progress" is just the imitative movement of the herd to an extreme.

"The French Revolution was the most amazing event. France was the first of the great countries to turn atheist," Girard had told me. The transition occurred in fits and starts. In autumn 1793, the Jacobin-controlled National Convention adopted a new calendar that abolished the traditional sabbath and established republican holidays every tenth day (*décadi*). Churches across France transformed themselves into Temples of Reason, and the most famous, Notre Dame, witnessed the *Fête de la Raison* on 20 Brumaire, Year II, or 10 November 1793, to the rest of us. Young girls disported themselves in white Roman stolae with tricolor sashes, gathering around a living, costumed Goddess of Reason. They sang a hymn by Marie-Joseph Chenier: "Come, holy Liberty, inhabit this temple, / Become the goddess of the French people."[11]

Robespierre, however, held to a dreamy sort of theism, the kind whose requirements were flexible and vague. He established the "Cult of the Supreme Being," a mildly theistic and civic-minded religion that he had largely invented himself, to the disgust of the more radical Jacobin advocates for the atheistic, anthropomorphic "Cult of Reason." A man-made mountain on the Champ de Mars was the center of worship, and Robespierre declared the truth and "social utility" of his new religion. The political tussle over religion led, through routes direct and indirect, to the execution of the leaders of the "Cult of Reason" in March 1794.

The tables turned again a few months later. On the day following the last of the Orange executions that summer, Robespierre was denounced and declared an outlaw by the National Convention. His fall was swift. Various political factions had their own motives for revenge—the usual cant about "purification" covered most of them, and fulfilled the era's needs for its own brand of political correctness—but one motive united them all: self-preservation, and a fear that they would be next. On 28 July 1794, Robespierre was guillotined with a score of his associates. His cult disappeared, and both rival cults were officially banned by Napoleon Bonaparte with his *Law on Cults of 18 Germinal, Year X.*

"When a society breaks down," Girard wrote, "time sequences shorten. Not only is there an acceleration of the tempo of positive exchanges that continue only when absolutely indispensable, as in barter for example, but also the hostile or 'negative' exchanges tend to increase. The reciprocity of negative rather than positive exchanges becomes foreshortened as it becomes more visible, as witnessed in the reciprocity of insults, blows, revenge, and neurotic symptoms."[12]

In modern times, Girard wrote that "it is because we have wanted to distance ourselves from religion that it is now returning with such force and in a retrograde, violent form . . . it will perhaps have been our last mythology. We 'believed' in reason, as people used to believe in the gods."[13] He was on the mark, especially considering this history.

·   ·   ·

At the time of Suzanne-Agathe De Loye's troubles, a twelve-year-old officer candidate was getting his first taste of battle and bloodshed. The child would grow up to become a general and perhaps the most important military theorist since Sun Tzu. Carl von Clausewitz (1780–1831) would also become a lasting preoccupation for Girard at the end of his life, forcing him to conclude, "The apocalypse appropriate for our time is perhaps no longer Saint John at Patmos, but a Prussian general riding with his friends along the roads of Russia and Europe."[14]

The imminent Prussian invasion that triggered panic, riots, and lynchings never happened. The Duke of Brunswick attempted his march to Paris, but to everyone's surprise, especially that of the Prussians, the forces were stopped little more than sixty miles inside the French border in September 1792. Goethe, who accompanied the troops, described the fateful encounter, and the unspoken dread of an army facing overwhelming power:

> The greatest consternation spread through the Army. In the morning we had been talking of spitting and eating the French. I myself had been drawn into this dangerous adventure by a confidence in our splendid Army and in the duke of Brunswick. Now everyone was thinking again. People avoided each other's eyes and the only words one heard were oaths and

imprecations. In the twilight we assembled and were sitting in a circle. We had not even been able to light a fire as we usually did. Almost everyone remained silent. Only a few men spoke and their reflections seemed illogical or frivolous. At last they pressed me to say what I thought of the events of the day, as my terse comments had often interested or amused our little company.

So I simply said: "From this place and from this day forth commences a new era in the world's history and you can all say that you were present at its birth."[15]

After the dissolution of the royal military forces in 1789, the French army had been little more than an improvised rabble—but something had changed. These French troops had precision, power, and motivation. They formed a new nation, and they were fired up by an *idea.* "Vive la Nation!" cried the French general, raising his sword as Prussian bullets rained around him. "Vive la Nation!" returned an immense human wave. The Prussian army, exhausted and demoralized, retreated before the vast army that had been organized in a few short days. It was, as Goethe had predicted, a new world.

Girard had consistently impressed upon me how universal conscription changed the reality of warfare forever. Thanks to the *levée en masse,* the soldiers that Brunswick faced were not mercenaries and volunteers supervised by aristocrats. In this new era, whole nations mobilized for war, an innovation that brought the entire citizenry into the conflict in a way previously unimaginable. Promotion was offered on the basis of merit and revolutionary zeal, not birth and social connections, thus dissolving another layer of social distinction (before the revolution, more than 90 percent of the officers had been aristocrats; five years later, only 3 percent were of noble birth[16]). "General mobilization is pure madness," said Girard. "The King of Prussia may have been a tyrant, but he did not have the power to conscript."[17] Yet conscription brought about a million men into the French forces, and by the time of Suzanne-Agathe's execution, they formed eleven armies.

Clausewitz would grow up to become an aide-de-camp to Prince August of Prussia. He would fight in five campaigns in theaters between Paris and Moscow, including the humiliating defeats inflicted by Napoleon at Jena and Aeurstedt in 1806. More importantly, he would become an influential military theorist, often quoted for his epigrammatic "War is the continuation of politics by other means," and sometimes for his statement, "War is nothing but a duel on a larger scale." Girard's last book is haunted by another of Clausewitz's preoccupations, the "escalation to extremes." *Achever Clausewitz* (or *Battling to the End* in English) focused on a subject that had preoccupied Girard since his earliest days: Franco-German relationships. Think of those lead soldiers he played with as a boy, reenacting the great battles of the Revolution and Napoleon. Think of his wartime years in Paris, which became the subject of his Indiana dissertation. The Prussian appealed to Girard's taste for the excessive: "Clausewitz, that's serious business! It smells of sulfur—what's more, the Germans don't want to hear anything about him. I'd say he has a sort of dark prestige,"[18] Girard told a French reporter at the time *Achever Clausewitz* was published in 2007.

As he said in his book, "I think Clausewitz stands alone among such theorists because he was at the turning point of two eras of war and bears witness to a new situation with respect to violence. In this regard, his approach is much more profound and much less technical than that of the others."[19]

Girard had sensed immediately that Clausewitz's *On War* was linked with mimesis. Nations imitate each other in violence, in a worldwide one-upsmanship, and in nothing so much as war. The "romantic lie" he described in *Deceit, Desire, and the Novel* appeared again in a military guise. Clausewitz's first chapter suggests, without saying so explicitly, that war has not stopped since the beginning of history, and that tit-for-tat revenge spurs reciprocity without limit—the "escalation to extremes." Terrifying, but then Clausewitz tells us that absolute war never happens, that it's only a theoretical possibility. Man's natural tendency to hedge his bets, postponing commitment, causes his opponent to scale back. This process inevitably short-circuits unchecked and irreversible escalation. Or rather, it used to.

"This is an apocalyptic book," Girard states in his opening paragraph, boldly adding that his book "will become more understandable with time because, unquestionably, we are accelerating swiftly towards the destruction of the world."[20] Girard makes the case that we are living in eschatological times, but not in the way that evokes colorful images of bombs and beasts. The apocalypse, he told me, will prove to be a long holding pen for mankind, in which problems multiply without resolution. War no longer works as a last resort to settle differences—look at Iraq, look at the Israeli–Palestinian conflict—yet we don't know how to make peace, either. "The era of wars is over: war is everywhere now," he said in an interview. "We have entered an era of transition to the universal act. There is no more intelligent policy. We are near the end."[21] Meanwhile, we have the weaponry to bring an end to the human race, and we know it. Apocalypse, therefore, is neither a whimper nor a bang, but a long, nervous stasis.

"Let us dare to say that we, the French and the Germans, are responsible for the devastation that is underway because our extremes have become the whole world. We set the spark to the tinder," said Girard. "If we had been told 30 years ago that Islamism would replace the Cold War, we would have laughed . . . or that the apocalypse began at Verdun, people would have taken us for Jehovah's Witnesses."[22] We are quickly being outscaled by absolutes that were never supposed to happen, if one takes Clausewitz's assurances at face value.

In the aftermath of 11 September 2001, Girard bought the complete French edition of Clausewitz's *On War* and pored over it for the first time. "The further I advanced in my reading of Clausewitz's treatise, the more I was fascinated by the fact that the tragedy of the modern world was laid out in those dense and sometimes dry pages, which purport to speak only of military theory,"[23] he said. He wanted to take Clausewitz's thought to its logical conclusion—to "finish it off," with all the harsher connotations the word "achever" has in French.

He felt a fresh reading of Clausewitz's work demanded a radical reinterpretation of history and a reconsideration of the role of violence within it.

·   ·   ·

Girard described Clausewitz as a textbook case of mimetic rivalry: "He nursed a fierce hatred and prodigious love towards Napoleon: it would be hard to find a better example of mimesis."[24] Clausewitz hated Napoleon, who had destroyed Prussia in one day at the Battle of Vienna in 1806. Yet he felt Napoleon had restored the glory of war, after the eighteenth century's tendency to attenuate it, with more negotiations and maneuvering than actual fighting. Clausewitz began his famous *On War* in 1816, after the French emperor had already been escorted to his final, unhappy exile at St. Helena, a piece of rock nearly 1,200 miles off the west coast of Africa. Britain had an easier time expelling Napoleon than the Prussian theorist did. Clausewitz never successfully evicted Napoleon from his head, where the Emperor lived rent-free even after his lonely death on the South Atlantic island in 1821.

Girard quipped that Clausewitz was the first man to have a Napoleon Complex, but that's not quite true. Clausewitz died in 1831 without finishing *On War*, but the year before, the enterprising Stendhal had published *Le Rouge et Le Noir*. Its protagonist Julien Sorel pores over books about Napoleon and daydreams about him. Sorel reflects the author's own fascination with his Corsican mediator: Stendhal made his haphazard way onto the world stage as one of Napoleon's soldiers, trekking over the St. Bernard Pass, which was immortalized (and deliriously idealized) a year later in the 1801 painting by Jacques-Louis David. Stendhal would begin a later book, *The Charterhouse of Parma*, with these words: "On 15 May, 1796, General Bonaparte entered Milan at the head of that young army which had lately crossed the Lodi bridge and taught the world that after so many centuries Caesar and Alexander had a successor."[25]

But Napoleon had mediators of his own, in an anxiety-ridden conga line of mimesis. "I am Charlemagne," said the emperor, who was obsessed with history. In particular, he was obsessed with his hero's history, looking for coincidences and parallels, and adopting trappings of the Frankish king to show that he was inextricably fused with his external mediator. In David's painting, Charlemagne's name is engraved on the stone below the rearing horse's feet, along with the names of Hannibal and Napoleon.

Mimetic desire in a population yields copies of copies, and in the end, as the contagion spreads, the repeated images become like the hundredth xerox of a hundredth xerox. The chain of mediation doesn't end with either Stendhal, Clausewitz, or Tolstoy's Pierre.[26] Winston Churchill collected hundreds of volumes about Napoleon as a young man, and intended to write a biography, but never found the time. And while visiting the Moscow home of poet Marina Tsvetaeva, I found a small model bust of Napoleon on her desk—one of many ways she idolized him, the symbol of French empire and conquest, the precursor, in some ways, of the totalitarian powers that would destroy her.

Nor was Julien Sorel the only fictional protagonist haunted by Napoleon. Dostoevsky's Raskolnikov cries, "Yes, that's what it was! I wanted to become a Napoleon, that is why I killed her. . . . Do you understand now?"

∎   ∎   ∎

Benoît Chantre apologizes for speaking English like "a Spanish cow"—but no regrets are necessary. His English is quick and fluent, almost the same pace as his French. Only the occasional repetition of a phrase suggests he might need a chance for his words to catch up with his thoughts. We had met several times in California, through the Girards, but this was the first time in Paris. We sat at a small table in a posh café near the Richelieu branch of the Bibliothèque Nationale. Chantre, an editor at one of France's major publishing houses, Flammarion, is a slight, pale man with a strikingly high, domed forehead—he looks the part of a French intellectual, and the appearance matches the man, whose conversations are wide-ranging, intense, intelligent, but also companionable and pleasant—a fortunate combination that appealed to Girard, for they had collaborated together for well over a decade. In return, Chantre gave him his devotion, founding the Association Recherches Mimétiques in 2006, and serving to this day as its president.

As with *Things Hidden*, Girard turned to an interlocutor for *Achever Clausewitz*, in this case, his longtime colleague. "It was putting a full stop to his work; he couldn't do it alone," Chantre explained. Years after its publication, Chantre still becomes animated when discussing the éclat that greeted the book's publication in France. "As a Chartist, René is very excited by history. People didn't know that. All the French press were very enthusiastic," he said. "René had been repeating himself—the same analysis, the same concepts. It was really an enormous surprise to see history."

Chantre paused over his tea in the pretty, light-filled café off rue Vivienne. "He's a great reader—a genius—*lecteur de genie*. A very brilliant reader, able to read quickly, very closely, and very closely identified with the author he is reading. He comprehends it from within the text itself. It's very impressive."

Chantre came to Stanford several times to work with Girard—in 2005, in 2006, and twice in 2007. The methodical schedule echoes what Oughourlian and others have remembered: Chantre lived in the Girard home so the two could begin work promptly at 8 a.m., comparing the French text against the German original, chapter by chapter, interpreting it as closely as possible. They worked every day, all day, stopping only for lunch and dinner.

Girard wrote in his introduction that "Clausewitz was *possessed,* like all the great writers of resentment," but at times the theorist seemed a little possessed himself. "He became, day by day, Clausewitz himself—it was like hypnosis," Chantre said, gesturing with his hands in a way that suggested a kind of mental channeling. "He could see what was really in the text. He's a genius, and a genius reader of Clausewitz."

Little by little, Chantre discovered that this was Girard's attempt to finish off his own work—*achever Girard*, in that sense. He had an appointment with Clausewitz, said Chantre, and the work would confront the central trauma of Girard's youth, the "strange defeat" of France. As they progressed in their work together, "the more I discovered the book I was helping him to write was an autobiography." He was deeply moved at the invitation to share such an intimate adventure.

Girard returned the appreciation, reminding his younger colleague that his Indiana dissertation topic concerned how American public opinion saw the 1940 defeat. "You are letting me bring my work full circle. However, of course it is only now that I understand what was really at stake,"[27] he said. But it's more than irony, surely, that the subject of his dissertation and those miserable wartime years in Paris should return to him at the end of his life, as he again explored the causes of Franco-German friction. He was completing a lifelong journey. As T. S. Eliot wrote, "the end of all our exploring will be to arrive where we started and know the place for the first time."

He now saw clearly that France and Germany were mimetic doubles, locked in rivalry since the time of Clausewitz and Napoleon. "France has not gotten over the conflict that linked it so closely to Germany for two centuries. The last *poilu* [i.e., infantryman] will be buried with great ceremony. We want to keep making heroes out of all those anonymous soldiers."[28]

The Prussian strategist foresaw it all. "Clausewitz sees very clearly that *modern wars are as violent as they are only because they are 'reciprocal'*: mobilization involves more and more people until it is 'total,'" Girard said, contending that history proved Clausewitz right: "It was because he was 'responding' to the humiliations inflicted by the Treaty of Versailles and the occupation of the Rhineland that Hitler was able to mobilize a whole people. Likewise, it was because he was 'responding' to the German invasion that Stalin achieved a decisive victory over Hitler. It was because he was 'responding' to the United States that Bin Laden planned September 11 and subsequent events. . . . The one who believes he can control violence by setting up defenses is in fact controlled by violence."[29] The events of that bright autumn day in 2001 had given Clausewitz an even darker cast. *The aggressor has always already been attacked* and so feels justified. Of course, the aggressor is inevitably "right"; there are always justifications for those who seek them.

The year 1936 made a dark and fascinating case study. Germany re-armed the demilitarized Rhineland and violated the Treaty of Versailles that had ended World War I. The move was a key moment for intervention: "If we had to choose a point when everything hung by a thread, I would say this was it,"[30] said Girard.

On this side of the Atlantic, the German invasion of the Rhineland is usually portrayed as a straightforward act of aggression. However, it was the last move in a complicated Franco-German *pas de deux* in the region after the end of World War I. Initially, Allied forces had occupied the Rhineland, which included the major German cities of Cologne, Bonn, and Aachen. German troops were banned from the region, though the land was politically administered by postwar Germany. When Germany was unable to pay the massive reparations the Allies demanded in 1923, French forces occupied German's most important industrial base in the Rhineland's Ruhr Valley area, further hamstringing German recovery. The French suppressed any civil disobedience or other resistance from the unhappy German residents and encouraged separatist movements for complete independence from Germany. Hyperinflation and unemployment followed; Hitler made his first attempt to seize power later that year. France got very few reparations, though it succeeded in crippling German industry. The Allied forces were scheduled to withdraw from the region in 1935, but did so early, in 1930, under pressure from the Germans. France knew German rearmament was just a matter of time.

Hence, the fatal moment when everything had been hanging by a thread: German troops, in violation of the Treaty of Versailles, marched into the Rhineland in March 1936. France and Britain responded with appeasement, which clearly had a broader historical context, given the postwar tussle and provocations in the region. France's attempt to permanently weaken Germany resulted instead in its own destruction.

"The trend to extremes thus seems to unfold like fate. It is in this sense that warmongering and pacifism are mimetic doubles,"[31] he explained to Chantre. The Germans were poorly armed and could easily have been defeated, Hitler later admitted. "If France had then marched into the Rhineland, we would have had to withdraw with our tails between our legs," the

Führer had said. But a French invasion would have been seen by its powerful allies as a rejection of the Kellogg-Briand Pact of 27 August 1928, in which fifty-seven countries had promised not to use war to resolve "disputes or conflicts of whatever nature or of whatever origin they may be, which may arise among them." France was dependent on the British and the Americans, who had both vetoed intervention. "Intervening immediately would have made it possible to avoid war, but the intervention was impossible owing to France's alliances,"[32] said Girard.

Moreover, Britain believed that Germany was behaving in an understandable manner, since the Rhineland was part of Germany and the Germans were only entering their own backyard. Most thought that the terms of the Versailles Treaty had been harsh, and its stipulations somewhat outdated by the 1930s. Nevertheless, the Rhineland had been a key buffer zone between France and Germany, to ensure nonaggression.

According to Girard, the defender is the one who wants war; the attacker wants peace: "In 1923 the French wanted to keep what they had acquired from victory in World War I: a precarious peace that they were ready to defend at any price and for which they would invade Germany. Their population was already dropping and they became warmongers out of pacifism. Hitler was then in a strong position because he was invaded first. He did not 'invade' the Rhineland by re-arming it, but 'responded' to aggression against his country. Re-arming the Rhineland was his first counter-attack, and it was to prove decisive," he explained. "It was thus the French *desire for peace* that caused the new trend to extremes. Without realizing it, they perpetuated the absurdity of Verdun."[33]

Girard's interpretation of *On War* presented a stark contrast to Raymond Aron's earlier *Penser la Guerre* (1976), a work once considered definitive. Girard maintained that Aron based his argument on the notion that "absolute war" is only a concept. "This introduces an unbridgeable abyss between the concept of war as a duel and real war. He was writing in 1976 and we had just begun the last decade of the Cold War, the era in which politics managed to hold in check a nuclear apocalypse. Aron reflected ideas of his own time, not Clausewitz. Aron stoked the dying embers of Enlightenment rationality, which was certainly admirable, but unrealistic."[34]

Girard attempted to short-circuit Aron's political interpretation and redefine Clausewitz as a thinker. "René was very influenced by Aron and his rationalism—and it was very, very fascinating to discover Aron's clarity being destroyed by René's reading," Chantre told me. "He wanted to prove Clausewitz was not a political thinker, but an apocalyptic thinker."

Political science is useless under the new dynamics of violence, Chantre said. "We have entered an eschatological age, where we can destroy ourselves," and Girard's work could help us understand the future not only of Europe, but of the world.

Girard had constantly advocated the renunciation of violence, but as his aperture widened, the future came to seem more hopeless, and the recipe for either war or peace increasingly futile. Recalling Hegel's optimism for mankind, he said, "The faith in the necessary reconciliation of men is what shocks me most today. I was a victim of it, in a way, and my book *Things Hidden since the Foundation of the World* expressed the confidence that universal knowledge of violence would suffice. I no longer believe that for the reasons . . . I did not see at the time."[35]

As Girard progressed through the interviews that form *Achever Clausewitz*, his interlocutor, Chantre, asked him repeatedly for the answer—for example, about the possibilities of human reconciliation. Girard's reply was grim, given the nature of mimetic conflict and sacrificial crisis: "The primitive scenario of archaic religion gave birth to gods, rites, and institutions, but today it can be nothing more than sinister play-acting, furious violence leading to thousands and even millions of deaths."[36]

Increasingly, however, violence is seen as indispensable to the advent of peace. Girard said that "the escalation to extremes demystifies all reconciliation, all *Aufhebung*. The illusions based on peace-generating violence, when applied to historical reality, will illustrate the madness of the whole enterprise."[37]

Our current methods of nuclear deterrence illustrate his point. "We accept to live under the protection of nuclear weapons. This has probably been the greatest sin of the West. Think of its implications," said Girard. "The confidence is in violence. You put your faith in that violence, that that violence will keep the peace."[38] In that way, we have sacralized violence, and endowed it with peace-giving powers. We stockpile nuclear weapons that we never use, and never intend to use. Our strength is that they are there, and that we do not use them. Of course, the practice spreads, mimetic fashion, raising the international stakes. Other nations, such as Iran, strive to attain nukes—and not only, or perhaps not even primarily, for deterrence. They don't really intend to use them, either. They do, however, wish to emulate the great powers. They want to be members of the elite nuclear club, and to be internationally seen as important. They want prestige and respect. So does everyone else.

·   ·   ·

On 11 September 2001, the entire nation was exposed to an atrocity in real time. "Television makes you present at the scene, and thus it intensifies the experience. The event was *en direct,* as we say in French," Girard said. "You didn't know what was going to happen next. I saw the second plane hit the building not as a replay but as a live event. It was like a tragic spectacle, but real at the same time. If we hadn't lived it in the most literal sense, it would not have had the same impact."[39]

Suddenly, we were propelled into an era in which an assortment of individuals could declare war on a major power, then dissolve and regroup, with no accountability or any fixed affiliation. There was no one, really, to blame—a group of transnational actors backed perhaps by a nebulous group called al-Qaeda, perhaps with the backing of this or that government. Its cause was as hazy as everything else about it. We search in vain for scapegoats: "The Americans made the mistake of 'declaring war' on al-Qaeda without knowing whether al-Qaeda exists at all,"[40] said Girard.

He noted that the world wars had marked a milestone in the escalation to extremes, but 11 September 2001 was the beginning of an altogether new phase: "Today's terrorism still needs to be analyzed. We still haven't grasped that a terrorist is ready to die in order to kill Americans, Israelis, or Iraqis. What's new here in relation to Western heroism is that it's about imposing suffering and death onto others and, if need be, onto oneself."[41]

He would occasionally tell me that since Islam is a seventh-century religion, it may simply be thirteen or fourteen centuries behind the West in its development as a civilization, looking forward to its own versions of the Reformation and Enlightenment—it's a thinking that has gained traction in the years since. I wasn't sure that logic would hold. We aren't in a seventh-century world, after all, and a people can't create its own cultural time zone within a global technology and economy. Perhaps he was simply struggling for rational answers, like the rest of us: "Our vision of history does not take into account the fact that the entire West is challenged and threatened by this. We have to say 'this' because we do not know what it is,"[42] he explained.

Girard insisted that resentment is not the whole story, but it is certainly a good part of it. The Lebanese scholar who was a MacArthur "Genius" Fellow, Fouad Ajami, wrote in the *New York Times* of a generation floundering between Western consumerism and pious tradition, unable to reconcile the up-to-date Western world they craved with the values their upbringing had instilled in them. Mohamed Atta had spent the days before boarding American Airlines Flight #11 drinking vodka and playing video games, while yearning for Islamic purity and a blessing. The quest for purity calls to mind another "Incorruptible" and another Pascal passage: "L'homme n'est ni ange, ni bête, et le malheur veut que qui veut faire l'ange fait la bête"—"Man is neither angel nor brute, and unfortunately he who would become an angel becomes a brute instead." Ajami wrote:

> The magnetic power of the American imperium had fallen across his country. He arrived here with a presumption, and a claim. We had intruded into his world; he would shatter the peace of ours. The glamorized world couldn't be fully had; it might as well be humbled and taken down.
>
> It must have been easy work for the recruiters who gave Atta a sense of mission, a way of doing penance for the liberties he had taken in the West, and the material means to live the plotter's life. A hybrid kind has been forged across that seam between the civilization of Islam and the more emancipated culture of the West.[43]

Dostoevsky's Underground Man is reborn in a new century, with a different cultural baggage. Mohamed Atta, the leader of the September 11 group and the pilot of one of the two airplanes, was the son of a middle-class Egyptian family. "It is staggering to think that during the three last days before the attack, he spent his nights in bars with his accomplices," Girard observed. "There is something mysterious and intriguing in this. Who asks about the souls of those men? Who were they and what were their motivations? What did Islam mean to them? What does it mean to kill themselves for the cause?"[44] The conflicting desires within the men in the cockpit, arising in cultures so far from home in every conceivable way, and exacerbated by the advertising, media, and day-to-day life in our major cities, have split the psychological atom.

Atta and his ilk are new Raskolnikovs, slaves to their own desire, which is contradictory and self-defeating, and so they are determined to destroy the thing they crave and loathe at once. One could also argue that ISIS represents nothing more than the old nihilism with a technological veneer: Areeb Majeed, a twenty-three-year-old from Mumbai who journeyed to Iraq to join ISIS and returned to his homeland, complained: "There was neither a holy war nor any of the preachings in the holy book were followed. ISIS fighters raped many a woman there."[45] Who asks about the souls of these men?

"On September 11, people were shaken, but they quickly calmed down," Girard said to Chantre. "There was a flash of awareness, which lasted a few fractions of a second. People could feel that something was happening. Then a blanket of silence covered up the crack in our certainty of safety. Western rationalism operates like a myth: we always work harder to avoid seeing the catastrophe. We neither can nor want to see violence as it is. The only way we will be able to meet the terrorist challenge is by radically changing the way we think."[46] He added, "The work to be done is immense."[47] He wrote those words more than a decade ago. I'm not sure than any "immense" work has occurred in the years since, or that we understand more today than we did then.

He outlined some questions we need to answer: "For us, it makes no sense to be ready to pay with one's life for the pleasure of seeing the other die. We do not know whether such phenomena belong to a special psychology or not. We are thus facing complete failure; we cannot talk about it and also we cannot document the situation because terrorism is something new that exploits Islamic codes, but does not at all belong to classical Islamic theory. Today's terrorism is new, even from an Islamic point of view. It is a modern effort to counter the most powerful and refined tool of the Western world: technology. It counters technology in a way that we do not understand, and that classical Islam may not understand either."

It's not enough to condemn the attacks, for these defensive thoughts don't indicate a desire to understand. "Often it even reveals a desire to not understand, or an intention to comfort oneself."[48]

∎   ∎   ∎

After 9/11, we promised ourselves "never again." We thought the worst was over, but even as we began to grow accustomed to our new uncertain world, new hells were brewing in lands far away. Time has dimmed the memory of the most calamitous attack on American soil. It's been reduced to an unspoken norm. In a 2008 interview, Girard said that at the time, "Everyone agreed that it was a most unusual, new, and incomparable event. And now I think that many people wouldn't agree with that statement. Unfortunately, in the United States, because of the war in Iraq, the attitude towards 9/11 has been affected by ideology. It has become 'conservative' and 'alarmist' to emphasize 9/11 . . . Yes, I see it as a seminal event, and it is fundamentally wrong to minimize it today," he continued. "The normal desire to be optimistic, to not see the uniqueness of our time from the point of view of violence, is the desire to grab any straw to make our time appear as the mere continuation of the violence of the twentieth century. I personally think that it represents a new dimension, a new world dimension. What communism was trying to do, to have a truly global war, has happened, and it is real now."[49] Thirteen years after 9/11, on a Saturday in mid-November, supporters of a rogue Islamic State hinted at the release of a new video with English translation, which appeared online shortly after midnight.

The executioner, his head covered with a black hood that had only a horizontal slit for his eyes, walked with a dozen or so ISIS fighters, each holding onto a captured soldier by the scruff of his neck. As the fighters walked past a wooden box filled with knives, they each took one. Then the soldiers knelt, the fighters lined up behind them. The executioner in black spoke in a British voice that had become familiar to us from previous video "shows," and he addressed the American president with ritual bravado: "To Obama, the dog of Rome, today we are slaughtering the soldiers of Bashar and tomorrow we'll be slaughtering your soldiers. With Allah's permission we will break this final and last crusade and the Islamic State will soon, like your puppet [British prime minister] David Cameron said, will begin to slaughter your people on your streets."

Unlike in earlier videos, this time they beheaded the unfortunate soldiers in graphic close-ups, featuring both executioners and victims. Afterward, the black-clad spokesman stood before a head on the ground, which was the target of his remarks as he spoke to the camera: "This is Peter Edward Kassig, a citizen of your country." He reminded Obama of a quote by Abu Musab al-Zarqawi, "The spark has been lit here in Iraq, and its heat will continue to intensify—by Allah's permission—until it burns the crusader armies in Dabiq." The video concluded with the Islamic State's signature closing, and if there is a symbol for our era, it may be this: a solitary fighter walking, carrying an immense ISIS flag, with white letters and symbols on a field of black.

This wasn't the first beheading of a Westerner, but the fifth or sixth within a period of months. Once again, Girard had proven a prophet: we have grown accustomed to hooded men beheading Americans on our television screens, on YouTube, in our streets. Genocidaires who used to provoke revulsion now evoke yawns, and we plead our helplessness to interrupt these events, as black-clad strangers market horror to us. It is the new norm, and by the time the reader is taking in these words and holding this book in hand, it will likely have been outscaled by something even more depraved and nihilistic.

•   •   •

Achever Clausewitz had been an intimate experience. Eventually, Chantre and Girard, working closely together, prepared two thousand pages, which they cosigned. Martha said that René was "very happy" with the final product in the spring of 2007.

Several people said *Battling to the End* was more Chantre than Girard, that the interlocutor leaned too heavily on the pen. Some doubted it was Girard's work because it was so dark. However, Martha confirmed that the dark drift of the book was Girard's own. She told me that he kept insisting that the text should be more, not less, apocalyptic. Others said the pages reveal Chantre's writing style, not Girard's. But Chantre told me that the style was indeed his own but the thoughts were Girard's, and that he was in no way the Svengali behind *Achever Clausewitz*. Chantre's comments echoed my own observations of Girard's precision about his own texts: "He rewrote the entire book with me at least four times. Each page was reviewed very precisely by René."

One of Girard's colleagues earlier had said something similar about another of Girard's collaborations, *Things Hidden*, that it was, in fact, the handiwork of Oughourlian. *Au fond*, Girard's nature is deeply passive, but I'm not so sure that he could be putty in anyone's hands. In a juggler's trick, Girard would appear to lose control of something, only to have it circle back to him, more thoroughly in his control than ever.

My own experience working with Girard on a Q&A text occurred well after the period of his collaboration with Chantre, and after a series of strokes had begun to diminish his acuity. Even then, he was nevertheless a meticulous editor of our interview, endlessly revising his words, so much so that Martha had to intervene to help us meet a deadline. He kept wanting to rethink, revise, and revise again. I imagine it was no different with his other collaborators.

Some criticized *Battling to the End* as belonging to a long-established genre, the old man's end-of-the-world send-off. It's a condescending remark, in such a case, and insults the coherence and depth of Girard's convictions, and his final thoughts on his times. In any case, it's a worthy genre, reflecting the inevitable end of each of us, the end Girard was facing, as he looked at the world he would soon leave behind. Staring his own death in the face, he was startlingly at peace.

He would describe the darkest things so lightly, then pause, and with an elegant flourish of his hand, on one of the few occasions I saw him acknowledge his audience at all: "You can tell people so as not to scare them that Girard is interested in the apocalyptic elements in modern thinking. It doesn't mean he's biting his nails all the time waiting for the end of the world. His aesthetic interest is oriented towards that aspect of the modern psyche— so as not to have people feel that I'm totalitarian in my preoccupations, but I can see other things. In a way, putting it between quotation marks makes it more acceptable."

Achever Clausewitz was written up in *Le Monde, Figaro*, and elsewhere, selling twenty thousand in the first three months. "The reception was wonderful," said Chantre. "Every journalist understood that René had written an important historical book," the story of how the Franco-German relationship had built and destroyed modern Europe.

Hamerton-Kelly had told me that the public excitement was so high that reporters had been on the Girard's Paris doorstep every day, and that he had been concerned about Girard's health—an exaggeration, perhaps, but one that gives an indication of how controversial the book was at the time, cited even by then-president Nicolas Sarkozy. Meanwhile, once back in the United States that had been his home for sixty years, Girard walked the Stanford campus virtually unnoticed and unrecognized.

CHAPTER 14

Terra Incognita

. . . As we grow older
The world becomes stranger, the pattern more complicated
Of dead and living. . . .

—T. S. Eliot, "East Coker"

One statement had been repeatedly spray-painted onto a turret in Tübingen, beginning way back in 1981, as an unusually bitter winter warmed into spring. Over the years, the words, in Swabian dialect and usually written in the old Sütterlin script, became a part of the tourist attraction, so no one scrubs off the paint anymore. "Der Hölderlin isch et verrückt gwae" translates roughly into "Hölderlin wasn't nuts."

The insanity of Friedrich Hölderlin (1770–1843), who died in obscurity but who has since become a towering presence in German poetry, had long been accepted—so the idea that he was in his right mind was still a minority opinion. But the cause found an unlikely champion in René Girard. He had never taken much of an interest in poetry, except for a short-lived interest in Saint-John Perse at the beginning of his career. He would finish his life with Hölderlin.

The 1967 French publication of the *Pléiade* edition of the poet's work captivated him—he reread it constantly. "For me, discovering Hölderlin was a turning point," he said. The discovery was linked with that busy period at Buffalo. Again, "I read him during the most hyperactive period of my life I have known, at the end of the 1960s, when I alternated between elation and depression in the face of what I was trying to construct."[1] The oscillations were rather like those experienced by the erratic Hölderlin himself. The enigmatic poet shows up in several of Girard's works, but he made his most stunning cameo in Girard's final book, *Battling to the End*.

I recalled Freccero's observation that Girard's interest in literature isn't connected to the artistry of words. I had paused briefly to see if I could recollect a time when Girard had admired a beautiful line of poetry simply for its music. I couldn't. Girard never admired literature qua literature, for the aesthetics of a passage, Freccero had continued, but rather as a vehicle for the ideas that interested him, the way literature served Freud or Darwin. Macksey more or less agreed, telling me that Girard had his own maverick reading of people—"his Baudelaire is not like others' Baudelaire." Hence, Girard finds an almost religious redemption for Proust, and makes Christian figures of Voltaire and Hölderlin. Even Nietzsche, Girard once said, was saved at the end, in whatever sense he meant that term.[2] According to Macksey, "he goes around baptizing everyone he likes" as converts tend to do, he added. "That's one of the reasons I love him." Girard, as always, is brilliant enough to find reasons for his predilections. Macksey characterized Girard's attitude as, "I like someone so I give him a Girardian medal," but there is more to it than that. Girard did indeed call Proust "a kind of saint," along with Stendhal, Cervantes, and Hölderlin.[3] Given the enormous profit Girard made from the German poet, and that the Hölderlin he described is wholly different from other accounts, I suspected he might be reading his own life into the poet's, and saw Hölderlin's life as a more dramatic and exaggerated pattern of his own.

Hence, the French theorist who had, in his youth, exposed the "romantic lie" pored over the oeuvre of the ultimate lyric poet of German romanticism. The Frenchman haunted by Franco-German relations all his life spent his final years with an enigmatic German poet who had been bound in a tight friendship with philosophers Georg Wilhelm Friedrich Hegel and Friedrich Wilhelm Joseph Schelling.

In a sense, Girard had been led back to the Swabian by his work on Clausewitz, for Hegel, Hölderlin, and the Prussian officer were contemporaries. Their lives had curled around the same dates, notably the Battle of Jena in 1806—that critical year was a turning point. The twenty-six-year-old Clausewitz headed into the disastrous battle where Napoleon would defeat the Prussian–Saxon army, taking the young officer to France as a prisoner of war. Hegel, finishing his *Phenomenology of Spirit,* would lean outside his window and see Napoleon passing, "the world-spirit on horseback": "I saw the Emperor, this World Soul, riding out of the city on reconnaissance. It is indeed a wonderful sensation to see such an individual, who, concentrated here at a single point, astride a horse, reaches out over the world and masters it . . . this extraordinary man, whom it is impossible not to admire." Hegel considered this battle to be "the end of history," as human societies evolved toward a "universal homogeneous state." Meanwhile, Hölderlin was taken by force to his unhappy stay at the Autenrieth Clinic in Tübingen, where he was to be drugged and forced to wear Autenrieth's "facial mask," designed to stop patients from screaming—all part of his treatment. Straitjackets and immersion in cold water within a cage were also part of the clinic's innovative methods. Believing that he was being kidnapped, he attempted to jump from the coach before his arrival.

Hölderlin makes a significant appearance in *Violence and the Sacred,* but by the time Girard spoke to Chantre for *Battling to the End*, his interest in the poet had deepened. His rendezvous with Hölderlin inspires the most lyrical and profound chapter in that astonishing book. The German poet's solitude and self-abandonment, his sense of God's withdrawal from the world, intrigued Girard, along with the opaque and mysterious verse itself. And so the French theorist who had spent much of his life buried in anthropological studies and sociological theories, suddenly and unexpectedly turned to song.

.   .   .

Old age doesn't have many compensations, but the few it has are formidable. Time tells its story, and we get to see how the various tales end. Choice, chance, will, and destiny play their parts, and the final drama is an incomprehensible mystery. We can only watch with wonder and humility, since we have no idea how our own stories will close.

Charles Singleton, the Dante scholar who was Girard's colleague at

Hopkins, went on to achieve every major honor that he could possibly receive. Then his beloved Eula died in 1985. Later that year, he drowned himself in the pond on his farm in Carroll County—the farm that had been the site of so much laughter and so many parties. Another colleague, Eugenio Donato, that sophisticated and quicksilver intellectual, died in 1983 at forty-six, though the news that he also perished by his own hand was not published, and so I heard the story instead from several colleagues. "He kept moving around. He went to Montreal and then was off at Irvine," Macksey recalled. "He said Irvine was the best place in the world to grow roses but it was terrible for human beings."

In 2002, Schwager suggested inviting Girard to a conference on "Religion and Violence," but some doubted that Girard would be strong enough for the journey to Munich, given his age. Two years later, Girard spoke at the October conference, but Schwager did not. He had died unexpectedly of a heart attack during routine surgery the previous February, ending the long association that had been so seminal for the French theorist. In his address, Girard acknowledged his great debt to Schwager. "In a time when the insistence on originality and on one's own approach is valued so highly this was a deeply moving gesture," according to one participant, Roman Siebenrock of the University of Innsbrück.[4]

Even the happiest stories end with a death. Robert Hamerton-Kelly, that colorful, combative, larger-than-life South African at the center of the Girardian landscape and the co-founder of Imitatio, as well as a senior research scholar at Stanford's Center for International Security and Arms Control, left the hustle and tumble of Imitatio's early years and retired to Portland in 2010 with his beloved wife Rosemary. They wished to be closer to children and grandchildren, and, of all things, he rediscovered his joy in singing. Who would have guessed that it would be one of the happiest times in his rather fortunate life? They had just returned home from a splendid week taking in the San Francisco Opera, staying on Nob Hill, when he complained of feeling slightly dizzy and disoriented. He fell into a coma, and never recovered consciousness from the stroke, dying some days later on 7 July 2013. Those who visited him during those last days had the powerful sense that he was exactly where he wanted to be, and he exhaled his last on the final notes of one of his favorite arias, Mozart's "Ruhe sanft, meine holdes Leben" [Rest softly, my dear one].

In his frail condition, Girard had trouble taking it in. "The news about Bob finally penetrated when I showed him the obituaries, but as I think I've already told you, he has never been one to show grief," according to Martha. Actually, she had never mentioned this. It's not the sort of thing she would normally say.

By the spring of 2008 Chantre and Girard were preparing another book together. They had spent hours poring over the Pauline epistles, reading and pondering them together for another book-length conversation. Finally, Girard told him after suffering several health setbacks, "I will no longer be able to work with you." It was the conclusion of a long collaboration. "He peacefully finished his work," Chantre told me.

In my interactions with Girard at that time, he was always a cheerful presence. He repeatedly said that he was happy at last to be working on nothing. To be done. Achever Girard. I took in his deep tranquility—*Gelassenheit*—and it returned me again to the words of Slavic scholar Carl Proffer: "Dostoevsky insisted that life teaches you things, not theories, not ideas. Look at the way people end up in life—that teaches you the truth."[5]

.   .   .

Shortly after the Girards returned from France in early 2009, it was discovered that Girard had suffered a stroke, though his speech and physical capacities were unimpaired. Girard had always feared his mental acuity was waning—as far back as Johns Hopkins days—but now the decline was unmistakable to himself and his circle of friends. At first he was anxious, but as time went on, he began to see this, perhaps, to be as valuable an experience as any other, offering spiritual, if not intellectual, rewards—or perhaps I had imagined this in my recreation of Girard, just as he had recreated Proust and Baudelaire and Hölderlin. The only time his sunny equanimity faltered was when Martha went into the hospital for serious heart surgery in the summer of 2011. He sank into worry and depression; Martha was ill, and that was intolerable. That is part of the story, too—even the long and happy marriages end with a death.

After Martha's return from heart surgery, I visited them later that summer on the patio next to the pool, shaded by foliage and vines. He mentioned earlier that he had embarked on a project to reread old books—he had mentioned the children's novels of the Comtesse de Ségur from his boyhood, and also *Don Quixote*. I asked about how his rereadings had fared. "They did not give the expected pleasure," he said simply.

René could not conceal his concern about Martha, despite everyone's recent apprehensions about his own health. "She is *really sick*," he said to me earnestly, then paused and reflected. "I am *falsely* sick," he finished, with a slight, eloquent flourish of his hand, graceful as an autumn leaf. Martha later smiled and said that was not so; he had been ill, too.

Within a few years, another stroke would leave his speech garbled and unintelligible. It reminded me of Dr. Georg Friedrich Karl Müller's visit with Hölderlin and the poet's incommunicable isolation: "Not a rational word was to be spoken with him . . . I repeated my visits a number of times, but the sickly man appeared to be worse each time, and his speech more incomprehensible. . . . [H]is speech which sounds half-German, half-Greek, and half-Latin can no longer be understood." Except that Girard was unquestionably sane, and with a word or an articulate wave of the elegant hand, would signal that he understood all, however unable he was to participate.

Girard took all with his usual implacable calm, increasingly "checking out" of conversations. Within a month or two, however, his conversation had started to become understandable again. I remember an incident in late June 2014, when he brightened considerably when I asked him about his cherished Hölderlin, recalling his journey to Germany when he received the Dr. Leopold Lucas Prize by the University of Tübingen in 2006. They stayed on the Neckar River that flows by the tower where the poet spent the last decades of his life. Was I the only person to see a parallel with Girard's own last years, as age and illness began to isolate him? It seemed to me, at times, to be a *demonstration* of what he wrote about the German poet, and a kind of seal on his own life.

With his final preoccupations and his last book, he was subjected to the usual dismissive judgments; its eschatological worldview was enough for outright rejection in some quarters. But the dismissal is only definitive if Girard's observations don't hold true. So far, many passages of *Battling to the End* have proved startlingly prophetic. Suppose we really are caught between two worlds: the old world of violence and the new world of nonretaliation and forgiveness that seems beyond us? Suppose we are spending our whole lives in the long waiting room, waiting for the new world to be born? I had asked him about this, but he had answered slant-wise. So I tried again:

So given this long apocalypse you say we're going through, what would you advise?
What do you mean, what would I "advise"?

What do we do?
Nothing.

We just sit it out?
We just sit it out. Yes.

Girard frequently cited the New Testament passages about how, were these times not abridged, "no one would be saved." But saved in what sense? One cannot assume, in Girard's case, he meant the term in strictly a theological context, rather than an anthropological one. In any case, the prolonged historical antechamber he described—two thousand years and counting, which he himself had called "an infinitely long stretch"—would hardly seem to be "abridged." And it's a prelude to who knows what?

He replied, "Well, anyway . . ." then added with certainty. "God is taking care of it. Yes. Yes."

■   ■   ■

Thirty years ago, I spent some time in the small university town of Tübingen, outside Stuttgart, where I was the guest of friends. It was my first stay in Germany, and I was pleased to find one spot on my travels that had not been bombed to pieces during the war, a medieval town that has retained its Grimm fairy tale charm, nestled on the Neckar River.

For Hölderlin, this town was destiny: along with fellow Swabians Hegel and Schelling, he would attend a Protestant seminary, the "Stift," in Tübingen. The three were held in the tight embrace of close friendship until, in a classic mimetic fashion, it dissolved into resentment, recriminations, snubs, demands for explanations, and eventually silence.

That's when Hölderlin went mad—or appeared to. His precarious life was entrusted to a prosperous cabinet-maker, Ernst Zimmer, a working-class intellectual who had greatly admired his poems and prose. So Hölderlin lived with the Zimmer family in a maize-colored tower near the meadows that would figure in his poetry. Everyone craves acceptance, and for

Hölderlin especially, rejection was a bitter diet. Over the years, his intense poems became fragmentary, much revised, and ultimately forgotten.

Hölderlin's choice, if his solitude could be considered a choice at all, harkens all the way back to issues presented in *Deceit, Desire, and the Novel*. Girard had described "conversion" in terms of relationships to others: "Metaphysical desire brings into being a certain relationship to others and to oneself. True conversion engenders a new relationship to others and to oneself. The mechanical oppositions of solitude and gregariousness, involvement and noninvolvement are the result of romantic interpretations."

He continued: "Solitude and human contact exist only as functions of each other; they cannot be isolated without lapsing into romantic abstraction."[6] Stendhal's Julian Sorel finds true, if brief, happiness with the provincial woman who loves him, and it profoundly affects his relationships with others. "He wonders whether Others are as bad as he once thought them," Girard wrote. "When he no longer envies people, when he no longer wishes to seduce or dominate them, then Julien no longer hates them." Raskolnikov, in the conclusion of *Crime and Punishment*, also triumphs over his isolation but he gains solitude. "He reads the Gospel; he recovers the peace which has so long escaped him."[7]

Hölderlin, too, had fallen prey to the vertiginous swings that Girard described as characteristic of Sophoclean tragedy—"if only one were not so periodical!"[8] the poet lamented. In *Violence and the Sacred*, where Hölderlin makes his first appearance, Girard accepted the theories of his madness, a mental state that he contends is driven by mimetic fever. The older poet Friedrich Schiller was the foremost god in Hölderlin's psychological pantheon, to be adored, envied, and propitiated, especially as the younger poet was endlessly ambitious for his own poetic gift. When the god he had made of another drew near, he was in an ecstasy; as the god pulled away, he plummeted to the darkest despair: "in the grip of that Nothing which rules over us, who are thoroughly aware that we are born for Nothing, believe in a Nothing, work ourselves to the bone for a Nothing, until we gradually dissolve into Nothing."[9]

Witness this abject letter Hölderlin wrote to Schiller in 1797, before the worst fell on him: "in regard to *you*, my dependence is insurmountable; and because I know the profound effect a single word from you can have on me, I sometimes strive to put you out of my mind so as not to be overcome by anxiety at my work."[10]

Girard found Hölderlin's use of poetic, mythic, quasi-religious language to describe his swings of emotion to be both deceiving and revealing. "His letters to Schiller lucidly describe the plight of the disciple who sees his model transformed into an obstacle and rival."[11]

In 1807, Hölderlin at last withdrew to his tower. His family refused to visit him and squabbled shamefully over his inheritance. His former friends neglected him, including Schiller, who had sponsored the publication of Hölderlin's early epistolary novel *Hyperion*. Hölderlin's funeral in 1843 was attended by the loyal and kindly Zimmer family. Nietzsche, who understood Hölderlin's importance, complained that he was little known in German lands, nearly two decades after his death.

.   .   .

The life of solitude has become suspect in our society—even though solitude is an unavoidable consequence of consciousness itself. To be alive and aware is to be alone. Today, however, our lives are composed to the constant chatter of YouTube, Facebook, Twitter, Instagram, and their electronic progeny. Increasingly, being private or alone is viewed as anti-social. This particular war is only beginning: for a new generation, accumulated shared knowledge is the new community, and it is considered selfish to hold back. Shame is futile, because everyone is exposed all the time. The revelation of your neighbor's secrets makes you comfortable with your own worst behavior. Conscience is blunted or explained away, and the old taboos vanish, replaced by more questionable and arbitrary ones. Deleting anything has become the new "sin." Utter transparency 24/7 is the new empyrean. However wrong-headed or absurd this philosophy sounds, it increasingly guides our technological inner circles. One is reminded of Girard's warnings about the movement to the herd, the perils of the hive mind—but what if there's no real alternative to it?

A few currents in the opposite direction show that Hölderlin's withdrawal isn't entirely a convention of the nineteenth century. Philosopher Hannah Arendt wrote that the most important conversations are internal, with ourselves as interlocutors; plurality begins with the individual. Perhaps that's why Hölderlin, in his yellow tower, talked to himself all day. At a 2010 Stanford colloquium on Arendt, Harrison claimed that the overwhelming question in the humanities is: "How do we negotiate the necessity of solitude as a precondition for thought?"[12]

"Every place of silence is invaded by noise. Everywhere we see the ravages of this on our thinking. The ability for sustained, coherent, consistent thought is becoming rare in the thoughtlessness of the age," he said.

Not only in the university, but in society at large, everything conspires to invade the solitude of thought. "It has as much to do with technology as it does with ideology. There is a not a place we go where we are not connected to the collective."

Did Hölderlin find relief from the constant thrum of other voices, other desires, in solitude—a chance to commune with his own personal muse without the prod of rivals and critics, whether real or imagined? "Only now do I understand human beings, now that I live far from them and in solitude"[13]—the scribbled note had been found among his papers at the tower. Girard contended that Hölderlin's solitude was not, or not only, the mark of madness. I remembered Girard's own withdrawal, the days in his study on Frenchman's Road, away from the noise and intellectual fashions of an increasingly celebrated university—secluded away with Martha, and silence, and order. I suspected his remarks on Hölderlin were based on his own internal communing with himself. An audience of one.

·   ·   ·

"All that I have written seems like *straw* to me." So Thomas Aquinas had famously concluded at the end of his life, explaining why he could no longer write. And I sensed the same with Girard.

Girard had told Hamerton-Kelly, as an aside, "I never intended to create a 'theory,' these were just ideas I was turning around in my head. But you know Frenchmen. They have to have a theory." Probably he finished with a chuckle. I'd heard the same story from others. I imagined him saying it with one of those characteristic gestures that signaled he was brushing aside a myth, a psychological cobweb.

On my visits to Frenchman's Road, every week or two, it seemed to me that his own conversion was continuing. The cockiness of his earlier years, the desire to make a splash, however superficial or transient such a motivation may have been, were now the discarded ribbon and wrapping around a greater gift: himself, silent and alone in a room. In some of his later published interviews, he had confessed to "academic narcissism."[14] The boldness and bravura were stripped like paint from a chair—leaving in its their wake

a startling simplicity, the fruit of his own *via negativa*. He had been finding new wisdom in old texts, and while he had added an additional layer of
interpretation, it was still a gloss, still not the whole truth, the whole story. At
what point it was the mental peregrinations of an old man, and at what point
something more, I cannot say. Increasingly abandoned by his own faculties,
he seemed to be engaged in a sort of spiritual "escalation to extremes," the 3
a.m. call of the soul.

So I sensed, in his dissolving presence, a great silence, a great interiority
as the years chipped away the inessentials, including, in the end, even his
autonomy and dignity. *Gelassenheit.* One can argue that is easy for me to
romanticize this finale during occasional visits. Nevertheless, his preoccupation with Hölderlin in his last major book may give us an indication of his
state of mind toward the end, during those visits where he contributed little,
especially when a series of strokes greatly impaired his speech and his atten-
tiveness; he would occasionally signal with a gesture or a word or two that
everything was continuing on the inside.

Every week, every visit, for months, seemed to bring a small annihilation of the self. Without ever really losing himself, he became more remote,
more inaccessible, farther away from us. Freccero had once said, apropos of
Girard's fading presence, "You want to grab him by the arms and say 'Don't
go!'" It would not have mattered if I had done so, of course.

He was left with lightness. Italo Calvino reminds us that weightiness
will be with us, always. Lightness is a subtraction of weight rather than the
pursuit of a pre-existing quality of lightness. I felt Calvino's words in those
days, the way Girard's lightness seemed to dominate the gravity of the situation. After one stroke, one that appeared to be a *coup de grâce*, he was silent
and held my hand as I sat by his bedside for an hour. At another point, when
we feared death was near, he was happy to see me, ebullient and playful, as if
this were some sort of crazy game in which he was inviting me to join him.

His solitude was open-ended and mysterious, like poetry—and perhaps
a little like Hölderlin, in Girard's reading of him. "We have to rise to the
nobility of this silence,"[15] he said of the poet, and that seemed to be the note
to which we had to attune our hearing. "To listen to the Father's silence is to
abandon oneself to his withdrawal,"[16] he said.

.   .   .

Was Hölderlin mad? Girard thought not, at least not entirely, and he was not the only one to come to this conclusion. The poet's friend Isaak von Sinclair was an eyewitness who thought the poet's madness was deliberately assumed. Hölderlin received visitors with an excessively formal courtesy, and spent entire days reciting his works, or prostrated in total silence. Girard referred to this as an "interior exile," taking his leave of the "mimetic giddiness" of the world and the poet's own self-confessed "insatiable ambition," which oscillated with painful intensity between glorification and revulsion toward the self.

Hölderlin's poetry had been haunted with pagan gods and imagery, but Girard saw a different pattern behind the appearances: "I see him instead as frightened by the return to paganism that infused the classicism of his time. He is thus torn between two opposites: the absence of the divine and its fatal nearness.... Hölderlin's soul oscillates between nostalgia and dread, between questioning a heaven that is now empty and leaping into a volcano."[17] Yet Girard insisted that these gods had disappeared for a reason: the destabilization of the archaic order with its sacrifices and victimage mechanisms.[18]

But Hölderlin did not linger in the trap he himself had set, for Girard insists "his withdrawal and immense sadness reveal greater lucidity."[19] Hölderlin turned to Christ as "the only one" and gradually withdrew from the world, as Christ withdrew to be with God the Father:

Now silent is
His sign on the thundering heaven. And there is one who stands
Beneath it his whole life long. For Christ lives yet.[20]

The big "G" began to displace the little "g" in "gods." Scholars have speculated endlessly about Hölderlin's allegiances—his unconventional Christianity, his pagan longings. The phenomenologist, theologian, and former student of Derrida, Jean-Luc Marion, asked: "why not admit that perhaps Hölderlin will teach us more about Christianity than the idea that we have of it—and reciprocally, that the Christian mystery will teach us more about Hölderlin than our polemical convictions ever will?" Marion referred to Hölderlin's "explicit" confessions of Christian faith in several letters, and his "strange declaration," as related by Wilhelm Waiblinger: "I am on precisely this point to make myself Catholic."[21] Strange, that is, for someone who, like Hölderlin, had been trained to be a Protestant minister, with pietist tendencies.

Christ is the exit from the cycle, an arrow pointing upward rather than round and round—but the path is through silence and separation. Girard's final understanding was a theological one: that *"one can enter into relations with the divine only from a distance and through a mediator: Jesus Christ."*[22] "It is not the Father whom we should imitate, but his Son, who has withdrawn with his Father. His absence is the very ordeal that we have to go through."[23] Only "positive" imitation, he concluded, puts us at the right distance from the divine. "To imitate Christ is to do everything to avoid being imitated," he said. "Imitating Christ thus means thwarting all rivalry, taking distance from the divine by giving it the Father's face."[24] This solution, this imitation, flips the escalation to extremes into its opposite—and this, he writes, will take us to the threshold of the Kingdom of God, if we can bring ourselves to abandon our "rationalist reflexes." But the breaking of the Kingdom into this world is a scary thing. Perhaps that's why there's so much lightning and thunder in Hölderlin's poems.

Hölderlin of course was neither the first nor last to consider God's perceived abandonment of the universe. Writers from Aeschylus to the radical nonconformist Simone Weil, a thinker Girard admired, thought that only in suffering and abjection can we know the divine. When you are certain that even God has abandoned you, the divine can take possession of your soul.

Weil's position serves as a sort of insurance against kitsch, especially when she insists on the importance of distance, as did Hölderlin: "Distance is the soul of beauty," in her words. Nobel poet Czesław Miłosz added his own gloss to Weil's phrase, which he often repeated: "This sentence of Simone Weil expresses an old truth: only through a distance, in space or in time, does reality undergo purification. Our immediate concerns which were blinding us to the grace of ordinary things disappear and a look backward reveals them in their every minutest detail. Distance engendered by the passing of time is at the core of the oeuvre of Marcel Proust."[25] So Dante, too, torn by the deeply mimetic strife and violence of Florence, exiled and despondent in far-away Ravenna, saw his city as a distant jewel, although one held in dirty hands, and from that perspective he composed one of the world's greatest masterpieces.

Girard repeatedly draws from Hölderlin's perplexing opening to his greatest poem, with the appropriately apocalyptic title "Patmos":

Near is
And difficult to grasp, the God.
But where danger threatens
That which saves from it also grows.

Or later, in the same poem:

Too long, too long now
The honour of the Heavenly has been invisible.[26]

Many of Hölderlin's poems are threaded with this celestial silence—not the effects of a Dionysian longing, but something more austere, more unfathomable, calling to mind St. Paul's "where sin abounded, grace did much more abound." Other passages from his later odes echo the same mysterious theme:

But, if he must, undaunted the man remains
    Alone with God—ingenuousness keeps him safe—
        And needs no weapon and no wile till
            God's being missed in the end will help him." [27]

Undoubtedly, with time hanging heavy on his hands, Hölderlin pondered who he had been, who he was in the present, and what he was soon to become. Weil sometimes wrote of the dismantling of the self, the need to absent ourself from the inhabitation of the created world, a place from which God has withdrawn. Was that the task Hölderlin had taken upon himself?

If so, Girard was in precisely the same position. I enjoyed a pleasant and festive moment with René and Martha at their home in April 2014. He was cheerful and engaged. Such moments were becoming more sporadic, and therefore more precious. Their daughter Mary had just returned from France, and she had brought back a gift from a cousin: a bottle of Muscat de Beaumes-de-Venise, a sweet, fortified wine made in the limestone hills outside Avignon since nobody knows when. Pliny the Elder had praised the Vaucluse Muscat grape, which makes the golden wine we were drinking that day and which St. Louis had taken with him on the Crusades. The first pope to set up shop in Avignon, Clement V, had increased its production for the Palais des Papes. So it was a fitting libation for this son of Provence. It's a charming wine—mild, but strong enough with its alcohol content to be a tongue loosener. Girard spoke of Madame de Staël, who had written throughout the French Revolution and Napoleon's wars.

Martha poured the gold into tiny liquor glasses for the three of us—a late Easter celebration. René's mother, she remarked, liked to have this particular wine for guests, so the wine connected us to long-ago Avignon, to the house on Arrousaire.

Hovering over each visit was the knowledge that it might be the last. When I had recently asked Martha some time earlier how they both were doing, she responded, "I tell him we're in Terra Incognita now."

Terra Incognita, a place where time and chronology had snapped. And, for a while, I moved into Terra Incognita with them, at least intermittently, during my visits, which seemed to blend into each other. It had been a long journey, from that first meeting in the summer of 2007 to that moment, an encounter that had wound through the Bibliothèque Nationale and the Rhône, the sandstone architecture of Stanford and the Palais des Papes. The ancient walls of the Palais came up again in one of our later conversations, as his frailty began to consume him like the flame on a matchstick.

"Someday we will go to it together." He had stated this not as a question, but with firmness, as a command, looking me squarely in the eyes. He said it, moreover, as if the Palais were a few blocks away, rather than across a continent and an ocean, and was pleased when I gently agreed. And in a sense it happened that way, when I finally made the winter trip in the rain and the seasonal mistral. I had felt him in every step of that journey, in a city that had endured through the centuries, where the Palais des Papes was encircled by battlements like a protected chess piece. I felt his presence even as I was spinning out of Avignon in a silver Citroën, swinging around the ramparts on the modern highway that hugs the city.

Hand in Hand

No philosophical thought will master the shift to charity.

—René Girard

René Girard is not a pacifist. That was the word I received from Paul Caringella, a friend and longtime visiting fellow at Stanford, who had been the first reader for this book. He had sent me a quick note of correction to an early draft of this manuscript, which he thought might lead readers to that erroneous conclusion.

I had not put Girard in quite those terms, but once the issue came up, I realized I had made certain assumptions. Given Girard's emphasis on the renunciation of violence and his warnings about the "escalation to extremes," it stands to reason that he would advocate disarmament and pacifism. How could one sanction any participation in the calamity of war, the inevitable atrocities and injustices, the destruction of cities, the "collateral damage" as civilians are pulled into the slaughter, the unstable and temporary peace that follows? "René doesn't belong to any 'ism.' He's not an 'ism' man," Paul later explained. "People of his stature are not going to be put in classifications like that."

He was right, of course; Girard is not classifiably anti-war or a pacifist, but his position is as surprising in this as it is in so many matters, and also a little evasive. I didn't find any clear statements one way or another. However, I did learn of his involvement in a March 1979 roundtable on nonviolent political action with four activists of *Mouvement alternatives non violentes*. Political philosopher Paul Dumouchel, a colleague of Girard's, discussed his quarrel with the roundtable discussion in a 1981 paper published in *Esprit*,[1] after the movement refused to publish his commissioned piece, which it found too critical. He, in turn, found their methods violent for, as he points out, there are a hundred ways to kill a man short of outright murder, and the group backed many of them. Dumouchel offered a very subtle Girardian critique of how nonviolence activists fall into the trap of mimetic conflict.

Dumouchel pointed out that such organizations aim to identify and defend victims, a process that perpetuates the victimage mechanism in a new guise and reinforces rivalries. In other words, by definition they engage in finger-pointing and blame. "I know of no rivalry in which each does not cast onto the other the entire responsibility for making the dispute worse,"[2] he wrote. The emphasis on techniques and strategies cloaks the desire to win—the very craving that must be relinquished, along with the desire for the last word, the caustic rejoinder, and other passive sorts of revenge, such as calumny or gossip, which extend the desire to be right, and to be acknowledged as right. But what philosophy embodies such a total nonretaliation? In a blamethirsty world, where our plight is the fault of the Muslims or the Christians; the left-wingers or the right-wingers; the rich or the poor; the black or the white—who will say, "I take it upon me. It's my fault. I'll take the rap and try to make things right"?

Dumouchel presented the argument, but Girard has spoken, too, about the slippery mechanism of scapegoating and violence: "The Psalms reveal that violent people are not the ones who talk about violence, but that it is the peaceful people who make it speak. The Judeo-Christian revelation exposes what myths always tend to silence. Those who speak of 'peace and security' are now their heirs: despite everything, they continue believing in myths and do not want to see their own violence."[3]

Various organizations claim to identify with the "real victims"—but who would claim otherwise? According to Dumouchel, "The protagonists of all clashes, whether violent or non-violent, think the same. Each always believes that the victims with whom he or she identifies are the 'real victims' and those supported on the other side are 'persecutors.'"[4]

Have we escaped the violence of mimetic cycles? Hardly. We are moving instead into a world where, as Girard says, "persecution is pursued in the name of anti-persecution"—as had been the case during the French Revolution, where the *ancien régime* and wealthy clergy became the first sacrificial victims fed to the guillotine, but only the first. Next, the sacrifice of the sacrificers by a new group of revolutionary perpetrators, promising that these deaths would yield a permanent peace. And as the sacrifices failed to create the desired harmony, as the road to that harmony disappeared behind them, the monster swallowed more and more, and eventually devoured itself. Significantly, Dumouchel finds the nonviolent activists' activities "pregnant with new forms of sacralization."[5]

Dumouchel pointed out that the *Mouvement alternatives non violentes* sees violence as rooted in objects, and their redistribution is the solution. For Girard, while people fight over real objects, the objects are not to blame for conflict. Mimetic desire *precedes* conflict and the objects of disputes. "Every adversary is convinced of the 'objectivity' of the conflict, of the fact that he or she is right," Dumouchel writes. "All believe that they are in conflict with others for excellent reasons; all think that they are always focused on the object that seems to them to be the unique cause of the clash."[6]

Ultimately, Dumouchel sought political solutions, and faulted Girard for seeming to condone inaction in passages such as this one: "from now on this violence has become its own enemy and will end by destroying itself."[7] While Dumouchel writes of Christ as the only "real victim," since "he alone never participated in violence," it's noteworthy that Jesus also ate fish, cursed a fig tree, and turned out the moneychangers. To reduce Christ to his non-violent stance is to diminish him to a first-century Gandhi, who refused his wife life-saving penicillin because he thought the injection would be a form of violence. The thinking indicates that we have begun to idolatrize nonviolence. Dumouchel admits, in the end, "There are no final solutions. There are only practical, in-the-moment responses: political answers."[8]

Of course, there are no pure victims. Each of us oscillates moment-to-moment between innocence and guilt, angel and demon, god and beast, victim and perp. So does that throw us back, helplessly, on passivity and quietism, powerless witnesses to war, confusion, and terror? I wondered. Perhaps any response is piecemeal, particular, happenstance—a rejection of the mob with the stamp of individual choice. The answer is not the Zealots and Masada, but the last human song at the door to the gas chambers.

■   ■   ■

Suppose there is no future, and the revolutionary human sacrifices for a cause occur in a vacuum for a time that will never exist, for progeny that will never be born, and a purpose that will never see fruition, and we are trapped in an endless repetition of "now." Here the implications of Girard's more apocalyptic thinking cross a line difficult for a post-Christian world to follow. We depend on the future to give the present meaning. Our actions are designed to achieve certain ends and create certain affects. If there is no future and no time, then grand gestures are no more important than infinitesimal ones and all choices must be cast in a different light. Stripped of our mediators, we stand on our own.

For example, Clausewitz, even as a twelve-year-old standard bearer who carried the Prussian flag, was far too immersed in a culture of heroism to be able to resist the magnetism of Napoleon. He entered an endless competition with a man he never met, who very likely never heard his name. Clausewitz is psychologically trapped in that moment, like a fly in amber, and it was the great tragedy of his life. But for us?

> GIRARD: Given the inevitability of mimetic models, it seems very difficult to describe a model that would remain rational. From this point of view, it is vain to try to imagine infallible procedures to prevent us from succumbing to imitation. *No philosophical thought will master the shift to charity.* .. Given the extent of its growing control, escaping from mimeticism is something only geniuses and saints can do. Thus we would place in the order of charity a person who went from heroic temptation to sainthood, from the risk of regression that is inherent to internal mediation to the discovery of a form of mediation that we have to call . . .
>
> CHANTRE: Innermost?
>
> GIRARD: Why not. "Innermost mediation" . . . would be nothing but the imitation of Christ, which is an essential anthropological discovery.[9]

To repeat, we are constantly told we live in a post-Christian era, and Girard's resolution of mimetic drama is unacceptable to us—especially since the ultimate *imitatio Christi* is death, not of the jihadi suicide variety, but rather a sacrifice *for* others rather than *of* others, modeled by a tortured and beaten man who died at the hands of a mob. Robert Harrison was one of many who warned me of the public antipathy toward Girard's Christian line of thought, which runs all the way from *Deceit, Desire, and the Novel* to *Achever Clausewitz*. Harrison once suggested that we can pick our own mediators, more intentionally—look at all the mediators offered in *The Divine Comedy*. But the mediators we pick for ourselves tend to pull one back into one's own limited horizons and *vanitas*, and into the imagined glory of the fascinating "other." Even the most external mediation has perils—look what happened to poor Don Quixote. Dante's mediators, in any case, all point back to *imitatio Christi,* an option that, as already noted, is rather short on takers in the post-Christian, post-everything era.

.   .   .

After the death of the eminent Dostoevsky scholar Joseph Frank, another late-life friend, I spent an evening with his widow, the French mathematician Marguerite Frank, sorting through mountains of his papers on the coffee table and floor. From one pile, she plucked out and passed to me a little-known article by Girard, "Dostoevsky's Demons." She had disregarded it because it appeared in a conservative magazine, *The Weekly Standard*, but the literary editor was Joseph Bottum, a friend, and personal regard always meant more to Girard than political persuasion; he didn't, in any case, much care where his work appeared. But Joe Frank had saved it for a reason, so I read it later on that evening. Girard's article ends with the death of Dostoevsky: "He died on January 28, 1881, in St. Petersburg, not long after the publication of *The Brothers Karamazov*. It's there we find—in the passage in which Ivan Karamazov tells the legend of Jesus Christ's returning to the world, only to encounter the Grand Inquisitor—Dostoevsky's most famous analysis of modern culture's repudiation of its religious inheritance in favor of Enlightenment philosophy's narcissistic individualism. And it's there in *The Brothers Karamazov* as well that we find—in the unconditional love the dying Zosima wills—Dostoevsky's answer."[10]

Girard doesn't quote Father Zosima directly, and what I remembered most was the elder's much-cited injunction—"truly each of us is guilty before everyone and for everyone, only people do not know it." Girard's words returned me to Dostoevsky's masterpiece, in the Farrar, Straus & Giroux translation that Joe had recommended. The flaw in "non-violent" movements such as the one Dumouchel described, is that they lead us to fetishize "non-violence," the absence of something, rather than the charity that wants the good of the other as much as for oneself. In that sense, violence itself becomes a kind of scapegoat, a useful way to disguise our hardness of heart even from ourselves. Zosima's words, and Girard's, are not calling us to form committees, but to burst into flame.

When I finally found the passage I was looking for, I realized that I had not remembered rightly. The injunction was in fact from the mouth of Zosima's beloved elder brother, who was dying. Zosima repeats the words later, before his own death. However, the "unconditional love the dying Zosima wills" isn't boiled down to a single, enigmatic koan, useful for generations raised on slogans and advertising; it goes on for pages, a close-to-perfect exposition of *caritas*.

.   .   .

At the end of the *Brothers Karamazov*, Alyosha rallies a group of boys who have witnessed the death of the friend they had viciously tormented and bullied. He exhorts them to lovingkindness, charity, and "memory eternal," even as they carry the child's flower-bedecked coffin to the grave. It's a resolution many have found unsatisfying—a touch of the Boy Scout troop leader about it—but it is with this very passage that Girard concludes his first book, *Deceit, Desire, and the Novel*. The thought takes us all the way back to Girard's beginnings, at his writing desk in Maryland. Girard freely admitted to me that so much of his life was in his head, yet the scene he chose to end his own book shows his unease with a solitary solution to mimesis and violence, a solution "in his head"—feelings Dostoevsky must have shared. Girard hints as much in the last page of that first book: "In the second part of *The Brothers Karamazov* little Ilyusha dies for the sake of all the heroes of Dostoevsky's novels and the communion which springs from that death is Balzac's and Proust's *sublime lucidity* shared by many. The structure of crime and redeeming punishment transcends the solitary consciousness. Never did a novelist make such a radical break with romantic and Promethean individualism."[11]

He continued that line of thought all the way to *Battling to the End*, in which he admitted that individual resistance to the escalation to extremes is futile: "The only way it might work is if it were collective, if all people stood 'hand in hand,' as the song goes. We have to give up this happy automatic escape, which underlies every form of humanism."[12]

"Hand in hand" sounds more than a little dismissive. Yet there are examples of mass movements that exemplify the principles he endorsed. "Hand in hand" isn't a bad way to describe Solidarity, for example, which began as the Eastern bloc's first trade union that was independent and self-governing, in short, not controlled by the Communist government. Within a year, over a quarter of Poland's population, about ten million, joined Solidarity, which had become a nonviolent social movement that used civil resistance to promote workers' rights and social change. Radosław Sikorski, later to become foreign and defense minister of post-Communist Poland, recalled that there was "tremendous hope and a kind of electricity between people . . . suddenly, millions of people felt that they wanted the same thing"—and it was a thing that could be shared, not competed for, not a zero-sum game, or necessarily "against" anyone. Solidarity was more than the absence of a negative: it signaled a new openness of expression and feeling, a euphoric new sense of brotherhood as people gathered in homes and church basements, united by the injunction from a Polish pope, "Don't be afraid."

Ewa Domańska, a professor in historiography at Poznań's Adam Mickiewicz University (she also teaches each spring in Stanford's anthropology department), remembers the days of the rise of Solidarity in Poland, when Girard's work circulated underground, in samizdat editions. As a student, she recalled assigned reading in *The Scapegoat*, and *Violence and the Sacred*, which offered Poles "a concept of power and violence in the framework of totalitarianism." Girard was a mythical figure to them, she said, and "very important in unpacking the mechanism of how power worked."

"Good mimesis" is a promise that hovers over Girard's oeuvre, along with the hints that it might entail collective obligations, as well as private responsibilities. He himself raised the possibility—and raised the stakes—in *Battling to the End*:

> Up to a certain point, we might be in a state of positive undifferentiation, in other words, *identified with others*. This is a Christian love, and it exists in our world. It is even very active. It saves many people, works in hospitals,

and even operates in some forms of research. Without this love, the world would have exploded long ago. . . . It is more than ever up to each one of us to hold back the worst; this is what being in eschatological time means. Our world is both the worst it has ever been, and the best. It is said that more victims are killed, but we also have to admit that more are *saved* than ever before. Everything is increasing.[13]

In later years, Girard increasingly turned to another theme that may not need repackaging in a post-Christian age: forgiveness, a key to breaking the cycles of vengeance. Forgiveness is more than simply "letting go" of grievances, although that is usually a first step—and it is not, as it so often is in our times, a denial of injury or a naive invitation for more harm. It is a transformational and vigilant process that must be renewed daily against the tide of new or ancient resentments, and it must complete itself in an active reaching out to the other, a willingness to try again.

Girard's comments are usually situated within a theological context, so for the general reader, let me cite a secular ally who seemed to be on a parallel course: political theorist Hannah Arendt takes a brave stab at the mysterious and elusive nature of forgiveness in *The Human Condition*, writing that "forgiveness is the exact opposite of vengeance, which acts in the form of re-acting against an original trespassing, whereby far from putting an end to the consequences of the first misdeed, everybody remains bound to the process, permitting the chain reaction contained in every action to take its unhindered course. . . . Forgiving, in other words, is the only reaction which does not merely re-act but acts anew and unexpectedly, unconditioned by the act which provoked it and therefore freeing from its consequences both the one who forgives and the one who is forgiven."[14]

The stakes are high in the nuclear age, but perhaps not entirely unprecedented. Clausewitz may have insisted that the escalation to extremes was theoretical, but it wasn't always so, if one enters the world of ancient texts and takes them at their word, as Girard did. Hindu scripture, for example, offers a sobering tale about the unremitting cycles of vengeance: in the *Mahabharata*, a game of dice escalates to the end of a world, an end accelerated by an absolute weapon that dooms civilization. The pacifism of the Pandava clan only accelerates the downfall of both rival sides in a fratricidal war. The result is the battle that ushers in the Kali Yuga, the black time of avarice, strife, and moral collapse.

.   .   .

I had scheduled a visit with the Girards on Wednesday, 4 November 2015, but fate had other plans. Martha telephoned that morning to tell me that René had died a few hours earlier, at 2:30 a.m. It was not entirely a surprise; we had known the end was close, but it was a shock nonetheless.

While the occasion was a personal blow for those around him, it had an inevitable public dimension as well. The president of France, François Hollande, said in a statement: "He was a compelling and passionate intellectual, a scholar of unbounded curiosity, a brilliant theorist and foundational spirit, a teacher and researcher with an uncommon love for going against the tide. René Girard was a free man and a humanist whose work has made its mark on the history of ideas."

I had always expected he would pass away peacefully in his sleep, an ending so much of a piece with the last year or two of his life. I had already finished writing the last chapters of this book. I told myself that nothing would be likely to change the arc of his story short of a terrorist attack. So it seemed more than a coincidence that his requiem mass ten days later at Palo Alto's St. Thomas Aquinas Church occurred on a dark day of national mourning for France. Paris had suffered a jihadi massacre of 130 people the day before—the biggest attack on French soil since World War II. That additional grief seemed to hover over the grace and gravitas of the *Kyrie* and *Dies Irae*, an unheard note behind the Gregorian chant of the mass. The Paris event was straight out of the *Achever Clausewitz* playbook—and it seemed to be René reaching out to us, saying, see? what did I tell you? please listen.

On the cover of the program, I read the final lines from *The Brothers Karamazov*, continuing the thoughts I had recently written for this postscript. Let these be the last words, then, for me as well as for René Girard: "Certainly we shall all rise again, certainly we shall see each other and tell each other with joy and gladness all that has happened."

Acknowledgments

Prof. William Johnsen, who edits this series for Michigan State University Press, approached me with an unusual invitation at a Berkeley seminar several years ago. I'd already published several articles about my friend René Girard, and Bill liked what I'd written: "I want you to think about a book idea," he said. It occurred to me that there was nothing that wove together the French theorist's life and work, in a way that made it apparent for the average, educated reader how these ideas fit together in a logical sequence, and are not disparate chunks of occasional inspiration within a long life.

This book would not exist without Bill's invitation in Berkeley, but that is only the first of many reasons I owe him thanks. He patiently championed and guided it every step of the way. His editorial judgment was superb, and I was grateful to lose an occasional difference with him, to the book's benefit.

Also very high on the list: my guardian angel and very first reader, longtime Hoover Fellow Paul Caringella, who had confidence in my very rough drafts. His encouragement and friendship kept this project and its author on an even keel. I often trusted his judgment over my own.

Prof. Robert Pogue Harrison's sheltering wing and consistent support earned my enduring friendship and affection, as well as respect. As Paul had recommended me for the Voegelin Fellowship at Stanford's Hoover Institution,

Robert arranged for my years as a visiting writer scholar at Stanford's Division of Literatures, Cultures, and Languages. I owe many thanks to both.

I am also grateful for the financial support of the Earhart Foundation and the Florence Gould Foundation, as well as the personal generosity of author Mary Pope Osborne.

An endeavor of this sort always has plenty of people to thank, and it can be perplexing to figure out how to apportion one's gratitude. Certainly Mark Anspach assisted this effort, not only with his insight as an anthropologist, but with his background as an experienced translator of René's words. Mark saved me from many a misstep, as well as providing comfort and context during this process. Given his corrections and improvements in his selfless, thorough review of my translations, I would blush to call them my own— however, any errors that remain I must answer for.

Prof. Edward Haven offered guidance on the context of French theory more generally, and his filial duty was much appreciated.

Pauline Ducom gave guidance regarding the fine points of René's life at the École des Chartes, and Silvestre Blandine helped with the Girard family history at the Archives départementales de Vaucluse. Guillaume Fau assisted me with the Girard papers at the Bibliothèque nationale de France, at a time when they were still largely uncatalogued and unsorted. I tip my hat to Bret McCabe in the chapter on René Girard's Johns Hopkins years, but I would also like to take the opportunity to acknowledge him here for his prompt and generous help. I would also like to thank Elena Danielson, Linda Bernard, and Josiane Romer, for guiding translations from various languages. And thanks to Julie Loehr, editor-in-chief at the Michigan State University Press, for patience and good cheer during this long process.

The entire Girard family deserve my eternal praise for their forbearance and trust—not to mention assistance and permissions with photos, records, and interviews. Their confidence in me was enormous, and appreciated.

For my friends and family who have put up with my unusual preoccupation these last few years, particularly the journalist Beth Hawkins, whose reading, advice, and moral support were well above and beyond the call of sororal duty, I owe a great deal.

But surely my greatest thanks of all go to a man I was extremely fortunate to call my friend for eight years, René Girard, the dedicatee of this book and the maker of the feast.

Chronology

1923

- On 25 December, René Noël Théophile Girard is born in Avignon, the second of five children, to Marie-Thérèse de Loye Fabre and a notable historian of the region, Joseph Frédéric Marie Girard, curator of Avignon's Musée Calvet and later the city's Palais des Papes, France's biggest medieval fortress and the pontifical residence during the Avignon papacy.

1939

- On 1 September, Germany invades Poland, leading Britain and France to declare war on Germany in retaliation.

1940 and 1941

- Girard receives two *baccalauréats,* the first the one common for all students, the second in philosophy, with distinction.
- In 1941, he travels to Lyon to prepare for the entrance exam for the École Normale Supérieure, the foremost among the *grandes écoles*, but

left after a few weeks. Instead, he prepares at home for entry into the
École des Chartes, a training ground for archivists and librarians.
- On 14 June, the Germans occupy Paris without a struggle. On 22 June,
France is partitioned into an occupied zone and an unoccupied zone
(Vichy France).

1942–45

- In November 1942, the Germans extended their full occupation to the
south of France, with the Italians occupying the small portion of France
east of the Rhône.
- Girard is appointed to be a student at the École des Chartes in Paris in
December 1942, and moves to Paris before his classes begin in January
1943. He specializes in medieval history and paleography.
- Paris is liberated during a military action that begins on 19 August 1944
and ends when the German garrison surrenders the French capital on
25 August 1944.
- On 2 May 1945, the German capital of Berlin surrenders to Soviet
forces. On 30 April, Hitler commits suicide, along with other members
of his inner circle. On 8 May, an unconditional surrender is officially
ratified.

1947

- Girard finishes his dissertation on marriage and private life in fifteenth-
century Avignon, and graduates as an archiviste-paléographe in 1947.
- In the summer, he and a friend, Jacques Charpier, organize an
exhibition of paintings at the Palais des Papes from 27 June to 30
September, under the guidance of Paris art impresario Christian
Zervos. Girard rubs elbows with Pablo Picasso, Henri Matisse, Georges
Braque, and other luminaries. French actor and director Jean Vilar
founds the theater component of the festival, which became the
celebrated annual Avignon Festival.
- In September, Girard leaves France for the United States to teach at
the University of Indiana in Bloomington. He is first an instructor of
French language, and later teaches French literature as well.

1950

- He receives his PhD with a dissertation on "American Opinion on France, 1940–1943."

1951

- Girard marries Martha McCullough on 18 June. They will have three children: Martin on 8 April 1955; Daniel on 3 January 1957, and Mary on 16 May 1960.

1952–53

- Girard becomes instructor of French literature at Duke University for one year.

1953–57

- Girard becomes assistant professor at Bryn Mawr College.

1957

- Girard assumes post of associate professor of French at Johns Hopkins University in Baltimore, where he eventually is promoted to full professor and chair of the Romance Languages Department. While there, he receives two Guggenheim Fellowships, in 1959 and 1966.

1958–59

- While finishing his first book, published in English as *Deceit, Desire, and the Novel,* Girard undergoes two conversion experiences from the autumn of 1958 to Easter, on 29 March 1959. The Girard children are baptized, and René and Martha renew their wedding vows.

1961

- Girard publishes *Mensonge romantique et vérité romanesque* (*Deceit, Desire, and the Novel: Self and Other in Literary Structure,* published in English by Johns Hopkins University Press, 1965), which introduces his theory of mimetic desire.
- He is promoted to Professor of French at Johns Hopkins University.

1962

- Girard's father, Joseph Girard, dies on 7 May.
- Girard publishes an edited volume, *Proust: A Collection of Critical Essays*, with Prentice Hall (Englewood Cliffs, NJ).

1963

- Girard's *Dostoïevski, du double à l'unité* is published with Éditions Plon (Paris), later in English as *Resurrection from the Underground: Feodor Dostoevsky* (Crossroads, 1997), reissued by Michigan State University Press in 2012.

1966

- With Richard Macksey and Eugenio Donato, Girard organizes an international symposium that takes place 18–21 October: "The Languages of Criticism and the Sciences of Man." Lucien Goldmann, Roland Barthes, Jacques Derrida, Jacques Lacan, and others participate in the standing-room-only event. The conference marks the introduction of structuralism and French theory to America; it marks Derrida's debut in America.

1967

- Girard's mother, Thérèse Girard, dies at home in Avignon on 5 February.

1968

• Girard is appointed Distinguished Professor at the State University of New York, Buffalo, in the Department of English. He begins a lifelong friendship and collaboration with Michel Serres. These years also mark the beginning of what will be a lifelong interest in Shakespeare.

1972

• Girard publishes the groundbreaking *La Violence et le sacré* (Grasset), developing the idea of scapegoating and sacrifice in cultures around the globe (published as *Violence and the Sacred* with Johns Hopkins University Press in 1977).

1976

• In September, he returns to teach at Johns Hopkins University as the James M. Beall Professor of French and Humanities, with an appointment to Richard A. Macksey's Humanities Center.

1978

• With the collaboration of French psychiatrists Jean-Michel Oughourlian and Guy Lefort, Girard publishes *Des Choses cachées depuis la fondation du monde* (Grasset), published as *Things Hidden since the Foundation of the World* in English (Stanford University Press, 1987), a book-length conversation in which Girard promulgates mimetic theory in its entirety. The book sells briskly in France—35,000 copies in the first six months, putting it on the nonfiction best-seller list.
• Johns Hopkins University Press publishes *To Double Business Bound*, a collection of ten essays—seven of which Girard had written in English. The book of essays is selected by *Choice* as one of the outstanding academic books of the year, along with *Violence and the Sacred*, newly published in English.

1979

• Girard is elected as a fellow of the American Academy of Arts and Sciences.

1981

• Girard assumes post of inaugural Andrew B. Hammond Chair in French Language, Literature, and Civilization at Stanford University, effective 1 January.

1982–85

• Girard publishes *Le Bouc émissaire* in 1982 with Grasset (published in English as *The Scapegoat,* 1986) and in 1985 *La Route antique des hommes pervers* (*Job, the Victim of His People*, 1987), developing his hermeneutical approach to biblical texts based on premises of mimetic theory.
• He receives his first *honoris causa* from Frije University of Amsterdam in 1985.

1988

• Girard receives an honorary degree from the faculty of the University of Innsbruck in Austria.

1990–91

• Girard publishes *A Theatre of Envy: William Shakespeare*, the only book he conceived and wrote in English. The earlier French edition, *Shakespeare: Les feux de l'envie*, received France's Prix Médicis in 1990.

1995

• Girard receives honorary degree from the University Faculties Saint Ignatius Antwerp (Belgium).

1999

- Girard publishes *Je vois Satan tomber comme l'éclair* (published as *I See Satan Fall Like Lightning* in 2001).

2001

- Girard publishes *Celui par qui le scandale arrive* (published as *The One by Whom Scandal Comes* in 2014).

2003

- A series of lectures at the Bibliothèque Nationale de France considers the Vedic tradition, and eventually become a small book of about a hundred pages, published as *Le sacrifice*, and in 2011 in English as *Sacrifice.*
- Girard receives an honorary degree in arts from the Università degli Studi di Padova in Italy.

2004

- Stanford University Press publishes *Oedipus Unbound, Selected Writings on Rivalry and Desire,* a collection of Girard's essays.
- He is awarded the literary prize "Aujourd'hui" for *Les origines de la culture* and receives an honorary degree from Canada's Université de Montréal.

2005

- Girard is elected to the Académie Française, an honor previously given to Voltaire, Jean Racine, and Victor Hugo. He takes the thirty-seventh chair, vacated by the death of Ambroise-Marie Carré, a Dominican priest, author, and hero of the Résistance.
- The Association Recherches Mimétiques is founded in Paris.

2006

- The University of Tübingen awards Girard the Dr. Leopold Lucas Prize.

2007

- With Italian philosopher Gianni Vattimo, Girard publishes a series of dialogues on Christianity and modernity as *Verita o fede debole? Dialogo su cristianesimo e relativismo* (published in English in 2010 as *Christianity, Truth, and Weakening Faith: A Dialogue*).
- Éditions Carnets Nord publishes his last major book, *Achever Clausewitz: Entretiens avec Benoît Chantre* (*Battling to the End: Conversations with Benoît Chantre* in English, 2010).

2008

- Scotland's University of St Andrews awards Girard an honorary degree.
- On 28 December, he receives a lifetime achievement award from the Modern Language Association in San Francisco.

2009

- On 8 December, Girard receives a *doctorat honoris causa* from the Institut Catholique de Paris.

2013

- On 25 January, King Juan Carlos of Spain awards him the Order of Isabella the Catholic, a Spanish civil order bestowed for his "profound attachment" to "Spanish culture as a whole."

2015

- On 4 November, Girard dies at his home on the Stanford campus.

Notes

CHAPTER 1. INTRODUCTION

1. *À la recherche du temps perdu*, vol. 3 (Paris: Gallimard, Bibliothèque de la Pléiade, 1954), 1032–33, trans. by Richard Macksey, in René Girard, ed., *Proust: A Collection of Critical Essays* (Englewood Cliffs, NJ: Prentice Hall, 1962), 179.

2. Cynthia Haven, "History Is a Test. Mankind Is Failing It," *Stanford Magazine,* July/August 2009, 58.

3. René Girard, "Conflict," *Stanford Magazine* (Winter 1986), 60.

4. Czesław Miłosz, "A Conversation about Dostoevsky," *Michigan Quarterly Review* 22 (Fall 1983): 548.

5. René Girard, "Souvenirs d'un jeune français aux États-Unis," in *René Girard*, ed. Mark R. Anspach (Paris: Éditions L'Herne, 2008), 29. Translation mine.

6. René Girard, *When These Things Begin: Conversations with Michel Treguer*, trans. Trevor Cribben Merrill (East Lansing: Michigan State University Press, 2014), 129.

CHAPTER 2. MAGNETIC NORTH

1. Dante, *Inferno*, trans. Charles S. Singleton (Princeton, NJ: Princeton University Press, 1970), canto 19, 199.

2. René Girard, *When These Things Begin: Conversations with Michel Treguer*, trans. Trevor Cribben Merrill (East Lansing: Michigan State University Press, 2014), 79–80.

3. Alice L. Conklin, Sarah Fishman, and Robert Zaretsky, *France and Its Empire since 1980* (Oxford: Oxford University Press, 2014), 331.

4. René Girard and Mark R. Anspach, "Entretien," in *René Girard*, ed. Mark R. Anspach (Paris: Éditions L'Herne, 2008), 27. Translation mine.

5. René Girard, with Pierpaolo Antonello and João Cezar de Castro Rocha, *Evolution and Conversion: Dialogues on the Origins of Culture* (London: Continuum, 2007), 17.

6. Girard and Anspach, "Entretien," 27. Péguy was the most famous Catholic Dreyfusard, hence an emblematic figure of that "double religion."

7. Girard and Anspach, "Entretien," 22.

8. Girard, *Evolution and Conversion*, 26.

9. Girard and Anspach, "Entretien," 22.

10. Girard and Anspach, "Entretien," 24–25.

11. Girard, *Evolution and Conversion*, 19.

12. The dates of Girard's school records don't always match his memories, especially when one attempts to allow for his periods of ill health, private schooling, disciplinary actions, and other arrangements that haven't always left a paper trail. Martha Girard and I have spent long afternoons going over these periods of his life as if we were trying to solve a crossword puzzle, without being able to reconcile the discrepancies. René Girard could be careless of dates, but I learned to trust his memories. He remembered clearly that this incident took place under the Vichy regime, which raised the stakes considerably.

13. Girard and Anspach, "Entretien," 25–26.

14. Girard and Anspach, "Entretien," 25.

15. Girard and Anspach, "Entretien," 25.

16. Girard and Anspach, "Entretien," 27.

17. The song expressing support for Pétain had replaced the *Marseillaise*, which had been sung at the opening of the school day throughout France.

18. Girard and Anspach, "Entretien," 26.

19. René Girard, "American Opinion of France, 1940–1943" (PhD diss., Indiana University, 1950), 77.

20. Girard and Anspach, "Entretien," 27.

21. Girard, *Evolution and Conversion*, 19.

CHAPTER 3. DARK TIMES IN THE CITY OF LIGHT

1. René Girard and Mark R. Anspach, "Entretien," in *René Girard*, ed. Mark R. Anspach (Paris: Éditions L'Herne, 2008), 27.

2. Girard was appointed to be a student in December 1942, and moved to Paris before his classes began in January 1943. In France, students at the *grandes écoles* are civil servants, paid by the government to study, with the idea that they will eventually work for the state.

3. Girard and Anspach, "Entretien," 27.

4. Girard and Anspach, "Entretien," 27–28.

5. Eugen Weber, "France's Downfall," *The Atlantic*, October 2001, 117–24.

6. Jean-Louis Missika and Dominique Wolton, *Choosing God, Chosen by God: Conversations with Cardinal Jean-Marie Lustiger,* trans. Rebecca Howell Balinski (San Francisco: Ignatius, 1991), 47.

7. Missika and Wolton, *Choosing God*, 54.

8. Missika and Wolton, *Choosing God*, 51.

9. "Paris 1942: La Vie en Rose," *The Independent*, 9 April 2008.

10. René Girard, *The Scapegoat*, trans. Yvonne Freccero (Baltimore: Johns Hopkins University Press, 1986), 13.

11. Rebecca Adams, "Violence, Difference, Sacrifice: A Conversation with René Girard," *Religion & Literature* 25 (Summer 1993): 11.

12. Girard and Anspach, "Entretien," 27.

13. Girard and Anspach, "Entretien," 27.

14. René Girard, *Violence and the Sacred*, trans. Patrick Gregory (Baltimore: Johns Hopkins University Press, 1977), 159.

15. Missika and Wolton, *Choosing God*, 93.

16. Girard, *The Scapegoat*, 15, 16.

17. Antony Beevor, "An Ugly Carnival," *The Guardian*, 4 June 2009.

18. Girard, *The Scapegoat*, 14.

19. Girard, *The Scapegoat*, 21.

20. Girard, *The Scapegoat*, 6.

21. Beevor, "An Ugly Carnival," 14.

22. Missika and Wolton, *Choosing God*, 107.

23. René Girard, with Pierpaolo Antonello and João Cezar de Castro Rocha, *Evolution and Conversion: Dialogues on the Origins of Culture* (London: Continuum, 2007), 20.

24. Girard, *Evolution and Conversion*, 21.

25. Girard, *Evolution and Conversion*, 21.

26. Girard, *Evolution and Conversion*, 21.

27. Girard, *Evolution and Conversion*, 21.

28. Girard and Anspach, "Entretien," 27.

29. Girard, *Evolution and Conversion*, 22.

30. The story has been told to me and others, but perhaps it is described most fully in his interview on Robert Harrison's radio talk show, *Entitled Opinions*, KZSU, 17 September 2005.

31. Girard and Anspach, "Entretien," 26.

32. Girard, *Evolution and Conversion*, 20.

CHAPTER 4. EVERYTHING IS POSSIBLE

1. Marc Bloch, *L'Étrange Défaite. Témoignage écrit en 1940* (Paris: Société des Éditions Franc-Tireur, 1946). Marc Bloch, *Strange Defeat* (New York: W. W. Norton, 1968).

2. Milan Kundera, *The Unbearable Lightness of Being* (New York: Harper, 1999), 75.

3. René Girard, "Souvenirs d'un jeune Français aux États-Unis," in *René Girard*, ed. Mark R. Anspach (Paris: L'Herne, 2008), 29. Translations from this chapter are mine.

4. First published as *Dostoïevski, du double à l'unité* (Paris: Plon, 1963).

5. René Girard, *Resurrection from the Underground: Feodor Dostoevsky* (East Lansing: Michigan State University Press, 2012), 83–84.

6. René Girard, "American Opinions on France, 1940–1943" (PhD diss., Indiana University, 1950), 98.

7. *New York Herald Tribune*, 4 April 1942, cited in René Girard, "American Opinions on France, 1940–1943" (PhD diss., Indiana University, 1950), 73.

8. Rebecca Adams, "Violence, Difference, Sacrifice: A Conversation with René Girard," *Religion & Literature* 25 (Summer 1993): 11.

9. Michel Serres, "Receiving René Girard into the Académie Française," trans. William A. Johnsen, in *For René Girard: Essays in Friendship and in Truth*, ed. Sandor Goodhart, Jørden Jørgensen, Tom Ryba, and James G. Williams (East Lansing: Michigan State University Press, 2009), 14–15.

10. René Girard, "History in Saint-John Perse," in *Mimesis and Theory*, ed. Robert Doran (Stanford, CA: Stanford University Press, 2008), 5.

11. André Malraux, *The Walnut Trees of Altenburg* (Chicago: University of Chicago Press, 1992), 74.

12. Adams, "Violence, Difference, Sacrifice," 14.

13. Quoted in "Souvenirs d'un jeune Français aux États-Unis," in *René Girard* (Paris: L'Herne, 2008), 31. The passage appears in Stuart Gilbert's translation, *The Voices of Silence* (Garden City, NY: Doubleday, 1953), 541. This translation is mine.

14. René Girard, "Souvenirs d'un jeune Français aux États-Unis," 31–32.

15. René Girard, "Souvenirs d'un jeune Français aux États-Unis," 32.

16. René Girard, "Souvenirs d'un jeune Français aux États-Unis," 29.

17. René Girard, "Souvenirs d'un jeune Français aux États-Unis," 32.

18. Susan Heller Anderson, "Henri Peyre of Yale Is Dead at 87; Was Sterling Professor of French," *New York Times*, 10 December 1988.

19. A. Bartlett Giamatti, quoted in John W. Kneller, ed., *Henri Peyre: His Life in Letters* (New Haven, CT: Yale University Press, 2004), xiii.

20. Girard, "Souvenirs d'un jeune Français," 32.

CHAPTER 5. MANKIND IS NOT SO KIND

1. Jean-Paul Sartre, *Three Plays* (New York: Knopf, 1949), 157.

2. Sartre, *Three Plays*, 161.

3. Sartre, *Three Plays*, 185.

4. René Girard, with Pierpaolo Antonello and João Cezar de Castro Rocha, *Evolution and Conversion: Dialogues on the Origins of Culture* (London: Continuum, 2007), 23. He added "my reaction was inevitable: I was a democrat, of course." However, the segregated South of the era was also largely Democratic.

5. René Girard, "Souvenirs d'un jeune Français aux États-Unis," in *René Girard*, ed. Mark R. Anspach (Paris: L'Herne, 2008), 32.

6. Girard, "Souvenirs d'un jeune Français," 32.

7. Maria-Stella Barberi in *Celui par qui le scandale arrive*, trans. Trevor Cribben Merrill (Paris: Desclée de Brouwer, 2001), 190.

8. Personal email correspondence, June 3 and June 4, 2013.

9. Christian Makarian, "Le Sage de Californie," *L'Express,* October 14, 1999.

10. René Girard, *The Scapegoat*, trans. Yvonne Freccero (Baltimore: Johns Hopkins University Press, 1986), 6.

11. One example is Hermine Braunsteiner, who had become the friendly Mrs. Ryan of Queens. Her husband knew nothing of her past as a sadistic and murderous guard at the death camps. "My wife, sir, wouldn't hurt a fly," he said. Or Elfriede Huth of San Francisco, who had become the sweet Mrs. Rinkel, the widow of a German Jewish refugee, a woman who gave generously to Jewish charities.

12. A stunning example: One month after the 2012 death of Florida teenager Trayvon Martin, director Spike Lee took to Twitter and retweeted the supposed home address of George Zimmerman, the man who was later tried and acquitted of Trayvon's murder, to his 240,000 followers. The address, however, actually belonged to an elderly couple completely unrelated to the case, who fled to a hotel following death threats and such messages as, "Let the PURGE BEGIN," and "LETS THROW THE BRO A SURPRISE PARTY! *LOADS GUN*"

13. Jean-Paul Sartre, *Critique of Dialectical Reason*, vol. 1 (New York: Verso, 2004), 438–39. Many thanks to Sandor Goodhart for bringing this passage to my attention.

14. René Girard, *Things Hidden since the Foundation of the World* (Stanford, CA: Stanford University Press, 1987), 176.

15. Joshua Landy, "Valentine's Day" (paper presented delivered at a meeting to commemorate René Girard's work, Stanford University, 15 April 2011), 13: "Incidentally, Girard has not always been entirely honest about the relationship between his religious and other commitments. In order to allay the suspicion that some of his theoretical stances may be driven by his faith, he tells us that he became a Christian because of his discovery of the scapegoat mechanism, not the other way around. Yet *Violence and the Sacred* was published in 1972, some thirteen years after Girard's conversion in 1959. *Deceit, Desire, and the Novel*, which he published in 1961, contained plenty of Christianity but not a single scapegoat." Landy doesn't acknowledge that books published are *terminus ad quem* for a process of thinking, they say nothing about the *terminus a quo*, that is, when the thinking began.

16. René Girard, *Deceit, Desire, and the Novel* (Baltimore: Johns Hopkins University Press, 1965), 199.

17. Robert Doran, "Apocalyptic Thinking after 9/11: An Interview with René Girard," *SubStance* 37, no. 1 (2008): 31. The interview took place in 2007.

18. Flannery O'Connor, "Some Aspects of the Grotesque in Southern Fiction" (1960), quoted in Harold Bloom, ed., *Bloom's Modern Critical Views: Flannery O'Connor* (New York: Infobase Publishing, 2009), 8.

19. René Girard and Milan Kundera, transcript of radio conversation, 11 November 1989, "Pleasure," France Culture. Translation mine. Many thanks to Trevor Cribben Merrill for bringing this interview to my attention.

20. Jean-Michel Oughourlian, *Psychopolitics: Conversations with Trevor Cribben Merrill*, trans. Trevor Cribben Merrill (East Lansing: Michigan State University Press, 2012), 14.

21. Michael Von Schmidt-Klingenberg and Susanne Koelbl, "Der Sündenbock hat ausgedient," *Der Spiegel*, 25 August 1997. Translation mine.

22. Letter from Henri Peyre to Whitney Griswold, 13 October 1954, in John W. Kneller, ed., *Henri Peyre: His Life in Letters* (New Haven, CT: Yale University Press, 2004), 439–40.

CHAPTER 6. THE PLEASURE OF HIS COMPANY

1. René Girard, with Pierpaolo Antonello and João Cezar de Castro Rocha, *Evolution and Conversion: Dialogues on the Origins of Culture* (London: Continuum, 2007), 29.

2. Lionel Gossman, "In the Footsteps of Giants: My Itinerary from Glasgow to Princeton," Princeton University, 2000, 22–23, Gossman papers, American Philosophical Society Library, Philadelphia, PA.

3. Robert Harrison, "The Generosity of Dante's *Divine Comedy*" (Europe Seminar Series, Stanford University, Stanford, CA, 16 November 2011).

4. "Alumni News," *Johns Hopkins Magazine*, June 2008.

5. Lucien Goldmann, "Introduction to the Problems of a Sociology of the Novel," in *Towards a Sociology of the Novel*, trans. Alan Sheridan (London: Tavistock, 1975), 1–17.

6. Goldmann, "Introduction to the Problems of a Sociology of the Novel," 3.

7. René Girard, *Deceit, Desire, and the Novel*, trans. Yvonne Freccero (Baltimore: Johns Hopkins University Press, 1965), 83.

8. René Girard, "Conflict," *Stanford Magazine*, Winter 1986, 60.

9. René Girard, *When These Things Begin: Conversations with Michel Treguer*, trans. Trevor Cribben Merrill (East Lansing: Michigan State University Press, 2014), 14.

10. Girard, *Deceit, Desire, and the Novel*, 146.

11. Girard, *Deceit, Desire, and the Novel*, 143.

12. Bernard Kreissman, "*Deceit, Desire, and the Novel: Self and Other in Literary Structure*," *Library Journal* 91 (March 1966): 1226.

13. Andrew Gallix, "In Theory: Mimetic Desire," *The Guardian*, 8 February 2010.

14. Walter A. Strauss, "Book Reviews," *Comparative Literature* (1 January 1969): 359–61.

15. Girard, *Deceit, Desire, and the Novel*, 258.

16. Ralph Harper, "*Deceit, Desire, and the Novel* by René Girard," *Journal of Religion* 47 (January 1967): 54.

17. Rebecca Adams, "Violence, Difference, Sacrifice: A Conversation with René Girard," *Religion & Literature* 25 (Summer 1993): 23.

18. Adams, "Violence, Difference, Sacrifice," 25.

19. Adams, "Violence, Difference, Sacrifice," 24.

20. Goldmann, "Introduction to the Problems of a Sociology of the Novel," 3.

21. Girard, *Deceit, Desire, and the Novel*, 138.

22. René Girard, "Valéry et Stendhal," *PMLA* 69 (June 1954): 389–94.

23. Girard, *When These Things Begin*, 14.

24. René Girard, "Mimesis, Sacrifice, and the Bible: A Conversation with Sandor Goodhart," in *Sacrifice, Scripture, and Substitution: Readings in Ancient Judaism and Christianity*, ed. Ann W. Astell and Sandor Goodhart (Notre Dame, IN: University of Notre Dame Press, 2011), 40.

25. James Williams, ed., *The Girard Reader* (New York: Crossroad, 1996), 283.

26. Girard, *Deceit, Desire, and the Novel*, 297.

27. Girard, *Deceit, Desire, and the Novel*, 61.

28. Girard, *Evolution and Conversion*, 29.

29. Girard, *Evolution and Conversion*, 29–30.

30. René Girard, "De la Divine Comédie à la sociologie du roman," *Revue de l'Institut de Sociologie* 2 (1963): 264–69.

31. Girard, *When These Things Begin*, 12.

32. René Girard, "Camus's Stranger Retried," *PMLA* 79 (December 1964): 519–33.

33. Girard, "Camus's Stranger Retried," 528.

34. Girard, "Camus's Stranger Retried," 519.

35. Girard, "Camus's Stranger Retried," 526.

36. Girard, "Camus's Stranger Retried," 527.

37. Girard, "Camus's Stranger Retried," 522.

38. Girard, "Camus's Stranger Retried," 521.

39. Girard, "Camus's Stranger Retried," 526.

40. Girard, "Camus's Stranger Retried," 520.

41. Girard, "Camus's Stranger Retried," 532.

42. The translation was published by Crossroad (1997) and later reissued by Michigan State University Press (2012).

43. Girard, *Resurrection from the Underground*, 3–4.

44. Andrew McKenna, "Resurrection from the Underground," *First Things* 83 (May 1998): 44–45.

45. J. de Font-Réaulx, "Joseph Girard: 1881–1962," *Bibliothèque de l'École des Chartes* 120 (1962): 325–29. Translation mine.

46. Michael Von Schmidt-Klingenberg and Susanne Koelbl, "Der Sündenbock hat ausgedient," *Der Spiegel*, 25 August 1997.

47. Stanford French and Italian Studies, *To Honor René Girard: Presented on the Occasion of His Sixtieth Birthday by Colleagues, Students, Friends* (Saratoga, CA: Anma Libri, 1986), i.

48. Gossman, "In the Footsteps of Giants," 25.

49. Gossman, "In the Footsteps of Giants," 25–26.

50. Girard, *When These Things Begin*, 132.

CHAPTER 7. EVERYTHING CAME TO ME AT ONCE

This chapter was adapted and published separately as *Everything Came to Me at Once: The Intellectual Vision of René Girard* (Belmont, NC: Wiseblood, 2017).

1. René Girard, with Pierpaolo Antonello and João Cezar de Castro Rocha, *Evolution and Conversion: Dialogues on the Origins of Culture* (London: Continuum, 2007), 45.

2. Girard, *Evolution and Conversion*, 44.

3. Girard, *Evolution and Conversion*, 44.

4. René Girard, *When These Things Begin: Conversations with Michel Treguer*, trans. Trevor Cribben Merrill (East Lansing: Michigan State University Press, 2014), 129.

5. Girard, *When These Things Begin*, 128–29.

6. Simone Weil, *Waiting for God* (New York: Routledge, 2010), 15.

7. Cf. Diogenes Allen and Eric Springsted, *Spirit, Nature and Community: Issues in the Thought of Simone Weil* (Albany: State University of New York Press, 1994). Deitz explained that her long silence was at the request of Weil's mother, who said, "I don't want anyone to speak of that while I'm living." Hence, Deitz did not repeat the story during the lifetime of Madame Weil, who died in 1965. Emergency baptisms can be performed by anyone in cases where death is imminent.

8. Girard, *When These Things Begin*, 120.

9. Girard, *When These Things Begin*, 120–21.

10. Unless otherwise noted, his descriptions of his two conversions occur in his interview with James G. Williams, "Anthropology of the Cross," in *The Girard Reader*, ed. James G. Williams (New York: Crossroad Publishing, 1996), 283–86.

11. Girard, *When These Things Begin*, 130.

12. Girard, *When These Things Begin,* 127.

13. Girard, *When These Things Begin*, 130.

CHAPTER 8. THE FRENCH INVASION

1. Richard A. Macksey, ed., *The Structuralist Controversy: The Languages of Criticism and the Sciences of Man* (Baltimore: Johns Hopkins University Press, 2007), ix. François Cusset's *French Theory: How Foucault, Derrida, Deleuze, & Co., Transformed the Intellectual Life of the United States* (Minneapolis: University of Minnesota Press, 2008) and Art Berman's *From the New Criticism to Deconstruction* (Urbana: University of Illinois Press, 1988) offer other accounts of this symposium. Also, Richard Jones, "Sing Doo Wah Diddy with Derrida," *Virginia Quarterly Review* 70 (Winter 1994): 7.

2. René Girard, with Pierpaolo Antonello and João Cezar de Castro Rocha, *Evolution and Conversion: Dialogues on the Origins of Culture* (London: Continuum, 2007), 31.

3. Girard, *Evolution and Conversion*, 23.

4. Girard, *Evolution and Conversion*, 28.

5. David Lehman, *Signs of the Times: Deconstruction and the Fall of Paul de Man* (New York: Poseidon, 1991), 93.

6. René Girard, *Battling to the End*, trans. Mary Baker (East Lansing: Michigan State University Press, 2010), 213.

7. René Girard, *When These Things Begin: Conversations with Michel Treguer*, trans. Trevor Cribben Merrill (East Lansing: Michigan State University Press, 2014), 73.

8. Girard, *Battling to the End*, xvii.

9. Macksey, *Structuralist Controversy*, 223.

10. My own conversations with Macksey in this chapter are used along with the notes of journalist Bret McCabe, who generously shared the transcripts from his own interview from the same period, with Macksey's permission.

11. Girard, *Evolution and Conversion*, 32.

12. *Structuralist Controversy* became that rarity in the publishing world, an academic best-seller.

13. Girard, *Evolution and Conversion*, 31.

14. The account is Derrida's, in "For the Love of Lacan," in *Resistances of Psychoanalysis* (Stanford, CA: Stanford University Press, 1998), 50.

15. Élisabeth Roudinesco, *Jacques Lacan & Co.: A History of Psychoanalysis in France, 1925–1985*, vol. 2 (Chicago: University of Chicago Press, 1990), 410, cited in Benoît Peeters, *Derrida: A Biography* (Cambridge, UK: Polity, 2013), 166–67.

16. Girard, *Evolution and Conversion*, 31.

17. Girard, *Evolution and Conversion*, 32.

18. René Girard, "Tiresias and the Critic," in Macksey, *Structuralist Controversy*, 20–21.

19. Macksey, *Structuralist Controversy*, 42 and 43.

20. Macksey, *Structuralist Controversy*, 50.

21. Macksey, *Structuralist Controversy*, 145–46.

22. Macksey, *Structuralist Controversy*, 292.

23. Macksey, *Structuralist Controversy*, 189.

24. Letter from George Poulet to Marguerite and Jacques Derrida, 4 November 1966, cited in Peeters, *Derrida*, 167.

25. Macksey, *Structuralist Controversy*, 195.

26. Macksey, *Structuralist Controversy*, 249.

27. Macksey, *Structuralist Controversy*, 271.

28. Macksey, *Structuralist Controversy*, 268.

29. Macksey, *Structuralist Controversy*, 267.

30. Lionel Gossman, "In the Footsteps of Giants: My Itinerary from Glasgow to Princeton," Princeton University, 2000, 23, Gossman papers, American Philosophical Society Library, Philadelphia, PA.

31. Jones, "Sing Doo Wah Diddy with Derrida," 8.

32. Jones, "Sing Doo Wah Diddy with Derrida," 8.

33. Aron, quoted in Jones, "Sing Doo Wah Diddy with Derrida," 8.

34. Peeters, *Derrida*, 421–22.

35. Steven R. Postrel and Edward Feser, "Reality Principles: An Interview with John R. Searle," *Reason*, February 2000.

36. Noam Chomsky, interview with the radio program "Veterans Unplugged," December 2012, quoted in Mike Springer, "Noam Chomsky Slams Žižek and Lacan: Empty 'Posturing,'" Open Culture, 28 June 2013, http://www.openculture.com/2013/06/noam_chomsky_slams_zizek_and_lacan_empty_posturing.html.

37. Girard, *Evolution and Conversion*, 31.

CHAPTER 9. LE SYSTÈME-GIRARD

1. Bruce Jackson, "Buffalo English: Literary Glory Days at UB," *Buffalo Beat*, 26 February 1999.

2. Jackson, "Buffalo English."

3. René Girard, "Mimesis, Sacrifice, and the Bible: A Conversation with Sandor Goodhart," in *Sacrifice, Scripture, and Substitution: Readings in Ancient Judaism and Christianity*, ed. Ann W. Astell and Sandor Goodhart (Notre Dame, IN: University of Notre Dame Press, 2011), 54.

4. René Girard, with Pierpaolo Antonello and João Cezar de Castro Rocha, *Evolution and Conversion: Dialogues on the Origins of Culture* (London: Continuum, 2007), 27.

5. René Girard, *Battling to the End*, trans. Mary Baker (East Lansing: Michigan State University Press, 2010), 124.

6. Stanford French and Italian Studies, *To Honor René Girard: Presented on the Occasion of His Sixtieth Birthday by Colleagues, Students, Friends* (Saratoga, CA: Anma Libri, 1986), ii.

7. René Girard, *Violence and the Sacred*, trans. Patrick Gregory (Baltimore: Johns Hopkins University Press, 1977), 92.

8. Girard, *Violence and the Sacred*, 94.

9. I Kings 16:34.

10. René Girard, *When These Things Begin: Conversations with Michel Treguer*, trans. Trevor Cribben Merrill (East Lansing: Michigan State University Press, 2014), 25.

11. Girard, *Violence and the Sacred*, 99.

12. Girard, *When These Things Begin*, 106.

13. Girard, *When These Things Begin*, 107.

14. Carl A. Rubino, "On René Girard, *La Violence et le Sacré*," *Modern Language Notes* 87 (1972): 986–98.

15. Peggy Boyer, "After Freud: Sacrificial Crisis and the Origins of Culture," *Salmagundi*, Spring 1978, 138.

16. Girard, *Violence and the Sacred*, 201.

17. Girard, *When These Things Begin*, 14.

18. Earl W. Count, "Reading," *Key Reporter, Phi Beta Kappa* 45, Winter 1979–80, 6.

19. Homer Obed Brown, "Oedipus with the Sphinx: A Review of René Girard's *Violence and the Sacred*," *Modern Language Notes* 92 (1977): 1105.

20. Victor Brombert, "A Fertile, Combative Mind," *Chronicle of Higher Education*, 21 February 1978, 15–16; Seymour Cain, *Religious Studies Review* (April 1979): 124; Brown, "Oedipus with the Sphinx," 1099–100.

21. Rubino, "On René Girard, *La Violence et le Sacré*," 992.

22. Victor Turner, *Human Nature* (March 1978): 24–26.

23. Ninian Smart, "Violence and the Sacred," *Religious Studies Review* (July 1980, vol. 6, no.3),177.

24. Brombert, "A Fertile, Combative Mind," 16.

25. Robert Hamerton-Kelly, "Breakout from the Belly of the Beast," in *For René Girard: Essays in Friendship and in Truth*, ed. Sandor Goodhart, Jørden Jørgensen, Tom Ryba, and James G. Williams (East Lansing: Michigan State University Press, 2009), 170–71.

26. Rebecca Adams, "Violence, Difference, Sacrifice: A Conversation with René Girard," *Religion & Literature* 25 (Summer 1993): 22.

27. Adams, "Violence, Difference, Sacrifice," 15.

28. René Girard, *Theater of Envy* (South Bend, IN: St. Augustine's Press, 1991), 29.

29. Girard, *Theater of Envy*, 4.

30. Girard, *Theater of Envy*, 5.

31. Girard, *Theater of Envy*, 7.

32. Gregory Woods, "A Theater of Envy: William Shakespeare," *Renaissance Quarterly* 47 (September1994): 663–64.

33. Sandor Goodhart, review of *A Theater of Envy: William Shakespeare*, by René Girard, *Philosophy and Literature* 16 (April 1992): 174.

34. "Fiedler Arrested for Marijuana," *Village Voice*, 4 May 1967, 31.

35. Kenneth J. Heineman, *Campus Wars: The Peace Movement at American State Universities in the Vietnam Era* (New York: New York University Press, 1992), 241.

36. Rae Nadler-Olenick, "Cape Town to Stockholm with a Layover in Austin," *The Alcalde*, January 2004, 52.

37. Personal email correspondence, 22 January 2016 and 3 January 2017.

38. One example among many: Mario Biagini, a close associate of the legendary avant-garde Polish director Jerzy Grotowski, told me how he had discovered *Violence and the Sacred* as a teenager in France: "When I read Girard, I discovered . . . a possible exit from the contradictions I was perceiving in and around me. I read then all books I found by him . . . his analysis of the scapegoat phenomenon is still valid and powerful."

39. It is worth noting, however, that Coetzee writes critically of Girard in an endnote to his essay "Erasmus and Madness" in *Giving Offense: Essays on Censorship* (Chicago: University of Chicago Press, 1996, 248): "Girard's grand theory lacks an empirical basis and may even be unfalsifiable." Then he asks: "Was there one single, originary 'event' which was then imitated elsewhere. How was this original event diffused? Or did originary events occur spontaneously everywhere? . . . At another level, Girard's claim to be revealing a single, final truth is precisely the kind of violent act that he describes as occurring in epochs when belief in universal truths is crumbling, and thus provides an example of—indeed represents—the very violence it seeks to transcend." However, Girard himself has occasionally pointed out the hopelessness of finding definitive, empirical basis for events that happened thousands of years ago, in eras that did not collect statistics, and certainly would not gather them on events they were at pains to conceal. Moreover, the nature of desire in a population is diffuse, and does not originate in a single ur-event. We have hundreds, thousands of desires modeled in hundreds, thousands of ways. Each of us has a welter of competing desires—stronger and weaker desires, and contradictory desires—in any given moment. Coetzee's question is akin to claiming we must have the name of Patient Zero before we can be sure a disease exists. As for Girard's theories being a violent act, it's hard to think of any idea promulgated from a comfortable academic perch as a violent act, short of a direct incitement to violence.

40. J. M. Coetzee, *Dusklands* (New York: Penguin, 1985), 57.

41. J. M. Coetzee, *Disgrace* (New York: Penguin, 2000), 142, 219.

CHAPTER 10. THE ZERO HOUR OF CULTURE

1. René Girard, with Pierpaolo Antonello and João Cezar de Castro Rocha, *Evolution and Conversion: Dialogues on the Origins of Culture* (London: Continuum, 2007), 39.

2. Stanford French and Italian Studies, *To Honor René Girard: Presented on the Occasion of His Sixtieth Birthday by Colleagues, Students, Friends* (Saratoga, CA: Anma Libri, 1986), 52–53.

3. René Girard, *Things Hidden since the Foundation of the World* (Stanford, CA: Stanford University Press, 1987), 245.

4. Girard, *Things Hidden,* 440–41.

5. Girard, *Things Hidden,* 304.

6. Girard, *Things Hidden,* 314.

7. René Girard, "Mimesis, Sacrifice, and the Bible: A Conversation with Sandor Goodhart," in

Sacrifice, Scripture, and Substitution: Readings in Ancient Judaism and Christianity, ed. Ann W. Astell and Sandor Goodhart (Notre Dame, IN: University of Notre Dame Press, 2011), 59, 60.

8. Girard, *Things Hidden*, 166.

9. Girard, *Things Hidden*, 134.

10. Girard, *Things Hidden*, 203.

11. Girard, *Things Hidden*, 210–11.

12. Girard, *Things Hidden*, 211.

13. Girard, *Things Hidden*, 231.

14. Girard, *Things Hidden*, 213.

15. Girard, *Evolution and Conversion*, 40.

16. Chris Fleming, *René Girard: Violence and Mimesis* (Cambridge: Polity Press, 2004), 112–13.

17. Ralph Harper, untitled review of *Things Hidden since the Foundation of the World*, by René Girard, *Modern Language Notes* 93 (December, 1978): 1015.

18. Harper, review of *Things Hidden*, 1018.

19. Frederic Raphael, "The Scapegoat Mechanism," *New Society*, 20 November 1987, 28.

20. Roberto Calasso, *The Ruin of Kasch* (Cambridge, MA.: Belknap Press, 1994), 157–58.

21. "That it might be fulfilled which was spoken by the prophet, saying, I will open my mouth in parables; I will utter things which have been kept secret from the foundation of the world." Matthew 13:35.

22. Lucien Scubla, "The Christianity of René Girard and the Nature of Religion," in Dumouchel, ed., *Violence and Truth: On the Work of René Girard*, ed. Paul Dumouchel (Stanford, CA: Stanford University Press, 1988), 169.

23. Scubla, "The Christianity of René Girard," 171.

24. Scubla, "The Christianity of René Girard," 171.

25. Scubla, "The Christianity of René Girard," 178.

26. James H. Bready, "The Systematic Mind of René Girard," *Baltimore Sunday Sun*, 21 January 1979.

27. Letter from René Girard to Jack Goellner, director of Johns Hopkins University Press, 2 October 1978.

28. Rebecca Adams, "Violence, Difference, Sacrifice: A Conversation with René Girard," *Religion & Literature* 25 (Summer 1993): 21.

29. An intriguing article came out of his Wagner phase: "Superman in the Underground: Strategies of Madness—Nietzsche, Wagner, and Dostoevsky," published in *Modern Language Notes* 91 (December., 1976): 1161–85, and included in *To Double Business Bound*.

CHAPTER 11. LOTUS LAND

1. Ken Auletta, "Get Rich U.," *New Yorker*, 30 April 2012, 38.

2. Andrew Yang, "What's Eating Silicon Valley?" *Huffington Post*, 10 January 2016.

3. John W. Kneller, *Henri Peyre: His Life in Letters* (New Haven, CT: Yale University Press, 2004), 910.

4. Kneller, *Henri Peyre*, 997–98.

5. Comments from a free newsletter, Louise Gulda Larrabue, *Memorial Church Times & Eternity*, (4 November 1981), 1.

6. René Girard, foreword to *Disorder and Order* (Stanford, CA: Stanford Literature Studies, 1984), v.

7. William Johnsen, "The Girard Effect," in *For René Girard: Essays in Friendship and in Truth*, ed. Sandor Goodhart, Jørden Jørgensen, Tom Ryba, and James G. Williams (East Lansing: Michigan State University Press, 2009), 116.

8. William Johnsen, "*Frères Amis*, Not Enemies," in *Mapping Michel Serres*, ed. Niran Abbas (Ann Arbor: University of Michigan Press, 2005), 48.

9. Johnsen, "*Frères Amis*, Not Enemies," 41, 48.

10. Cynthia Haven, "Michel Serres, One of France's 'Immortels,' Tells the 'Grand Récit' at Stanford," *Stanford Report*, 27 May 2009.

11. Eric Gans remembers a similar situation at Johns Hopkins: "In 1978 I was called to Baltimore for a visiting professorship that was to be the prelude to a permanent appointment. Girard was attempting to build a team, and had chosen me as his first collaborator. And I let him down. I believe my failure to secure this professorship was a factor in the disaffection that led to his leaving Hopkins a few years later for Stanford, where he remained for the rest of his life." "René Girard, in Memoriam," *Chronicles of Love and Resentment*, 21 November 2015, http://www.anthropoetics. ucla.edu/views/vw500.

12. "Peter Thiel on René Girard," YouTube video, https://www.youtube.com/watch?v=esk7W9Jowtc.

13. Joseph Bottum, "Girard among the Girardians," *First Things* (March 1996): 42–45.

14. Jean-Pierre Dupuy, "Detour and Sacrifice: Illich and Girard," in Goodhart, Jørgensen, Ryba, and Williams, *For René Girard*, 57.

15. René Girard, "Mimesis, Sacrifice, and the Bible: A Conversation with Sandor Goodhart," in *Sacrifice, Scripture, and Substitution: Readings in Ancient Judaism and Christianity*, ed. Ann W. Astell and Sandor Goodhart (Notre Dame, IN: University of Notre Dame Press, 2011), 63.

16. René Girard, *The Scapegoat*, trans. Yvonne Freccero (Baltimore: Johns Hopkins University Press, 1986), 2.

17. Girard, *The Scapegoat*, 8.

18. Richard Macksey, "Brief Notices," *Modern Language Notes* 117 (December 2002): 1152–53.

19. Pascal Bruckner, "Lynchage Satanique," *Le Nouvel Observateur*, November 1999, 64.

20. René Girard, *I See Satan Fall Like Lightning* (Maryknoll, NY: Orbis, 2001), 35.

21. Bruckner, "Lynchage Satanique," 64.

22. The book was originally published as *Le sacrifice* (Paris: Bibliotheque nationale de France, 2003) and later published in English as *Sacrifice* (East Lansing: Michigan State University Press, 2011).

23. Girard, "Mimesis, Sacrifice, and the Bible." Girard's published interviews usually involved much

back-and-forth editing and revisions, and this one is no exception. Hence, Goodhart dates this interview about 2008.

24. Girard, *Sacrifice*, 87.

25. Girard, "Mimesis, Sacrifice, and the Bible," 64.

26. Girard, "Mimesis, Sacrifice, and the Bible," 64.

27. Some has already begun. Cf. Brian Collins, *The Head Beneath the Altar: Hindu Mythology and the Critique of Sacrifice* (East Lansing: Michigan State University Press, 2014).

28. Girard, *Sacrifice*, 2–3.

29. René Girard, *Violence and the Sacred*, trans. Patrick Gregory (Baltimore: Johns Hopkins University Press, 1977), 221–22.

CHAPTER 12. THE NEW DARWIN OF THE HUMAN SCIENCES

1. Stanford French and Italian Studies, *To Honor René Girard: Presented on the Occasion of His Sixtieth Birthday by Colleagues, Students, Friends* (Saratoga, CA: Anma Libri, 1986), 329–30.

2. René Girard, *Violence and the Sacred*, trans. Patrick Gregory (Baltimore: Johns Hopkins University Press, 1977), 76.

3. Girard, *Violence and the Sacred*, 76.

4. Cited in Mark Anspach, introduction to *Oedipus Unbound: Selected Writings on Rivalry and Desire*, by René Girard (Stanford, CA: Stanford University Press, 2004), x.

5. René Girard, "Mimesis, Sacrifice, and the Bible: A Conversation with Sandor Goodhart," in *Sacrifice, Scripture, and Substitution: Readings in Ancient Judaism and Christianity*, ed. Ann W. Astell and Sandor Goodhart (Notre Dame, IN: University of Notre Dame Press, 2011), 48–49.

6. Mark 13:7–8.

7. Girard, "Mimesis, Sacrifice, and the Bible," 41.

8. Girard, "Mimesis, Sacrifice, and the Bible," 63.

9. Lea Winerman, "The mind's mirror," *Monitor on Psychology*, October 2005, 48. See also The Scicurious Brain, "You Want That? Well I Want It Too! The Neuroscience of Mimetic Desire," *Scientific American*, 30 July 2012, http://blogs.scientificamerican.com/scicurious-brain/you-want-that-well-i-want-it-too-the-neuroscience-of-mimetic-desire. The article uses the terms "mimetic desire" and "contagion" without mentioning Girard. A *Journal of Neuroscience* article by Maël Lebreton, Shadia Kawa, Baudouin Forgeot d'Arc, Jean Daunizeau, and Mathias Pessiglione ("Your Goal Is Mine: Unraveling Mimetic Desires in the Human Brain," *Journal of Neuroscience* 32, no. 21 [2012]: 7146–57) explicitly credits the work of Girard for the concepts behind this discovery.

10. Paula Bock, "Infant Science," *Pacific Northwest*, 6 March 2005.

11. Rebecca Adams, "Violence, Difference, Sacrifice: A Conversation with René Girard," *Religion & Literature* 25 (Summer 1993): 24.

12. Adams, "Violence, Difference, Sacrifice," 25.

13. Girard, "Mimesis, Sacrifice, and the Bible," 43.

14. Barbara Palmer, "René Girard to Join Ranks of the 'Immortals' with French Academy Induction," *Stanford Report*, 7 December 2005.

15. Palmer, "René Girard to Join Ranks of the 'Immortals.'"

16. Joseph Bottum, "A Man after His Time: René Girard, 1923–2015," *Weekly Standard*, 23 November 2015.

17. Michel Serres, "Receiving René Girard into the Académie Française," trans. William A. Johnsen, in *For René Girard: Essays in Friendship and in Truth*, ed. Sandor Goodhart, Jørden Jørgensen, Tom Ryba, and James G. Williams (East Lansing: Michigan State University Press, 2009), 10–12.

18. Unpublished interview cited in James G. Williams, "Dialogue on Sacrifice and Orthodoxy: Reflections on the Schwager-Girard Correspondence," *Contagion* 21 (2014): 49.

19. Williams, "Dialogue on Sacrifice and Orthodoxy," 49.

20. William A. Johnsen, "The Girard Effect," in Goodhart, Jørgensen, Ryba, and Williams, *For René Girard*, 117.

21. Adams, "Violence, Difference, Sacrifice," 28–29.

22. Adams, "Violence, Difference, Sacrifice," 29.

23. René Girard, *When These Things Begin: Conversations with Michel Treguer*, trans. Trevor Cribben Merrill (East Lansing: Michigan State University Press, 2014), 133.

24. Gil Bailie has related this story on a number of occasions; this version is from our correspondence. A fuller account is in Goodhart, Jørgensen, Ryba, and Williams, eds., *For René Girard,* 183.

25. René Girard, *Battling to the End*, trans. Mary Baker (East Lansing: Michigan State University Press, 2010), 213.

26. "Academy Awards, Academic Rewards," Modern Language Association Convention Blog, 29 December 2008, http://www.mla.org.

CHAPTER 13. WHO ASKS ABOUT THE SOULS OF THESE MEN?

1. René Girard, "Mimesis, Sacrifice, and the Bible: A Conversation with Sandor Goodhart," in *Sacrifice, Scripture, and Substitution: Readings in Ancient Judaism and Christianity*, ed. Ann W. Astell and Sandor Goodhart (Notre Dame, IN: University of Notre Dame Press, 2011), 49.

2. Robert Harrison, "René Girard on Ritual Sacrifice and the Scapegoat," *Entitled Opinions*, KZSU, Stanford, CA, 4 October 2005, radio broadcast, edited by the author.

3. Hannah Arendt, *Eichmann in Jerusalem: A Report on the Banality of Evil* (London: Penguin, 2006), 273.

4. Oscar Browning, ed., *The Despatches of Earl Gower, English Ambassador at Paris from June 1790 to August 1792* (Cambridge: Cambridge University Press, 1885), 223.

5. Reynald Sécher, *A French Genocide: The Vendée*, trans. George Holoch (Notre Dame, IN: University of Notre Dame Press, 2003), 251.

6. René Girard, *Battling to the End*, trans. Mary Baker (East Lansing: Michigan State University Press, 2010), 66.

7. Jules Henry, *Jungle People* (New York: Vintage Books, 1964), 7, quoted in René Girard, *Violence and the Sacred*, trans. Patrick Gregory (Baltimore: Johns Hopkins University Press, 1977), 54.

8. M. A. Thiers, *The History of the French Revolution*, trans. Frederic Shoberl, vol. 3 (Philadelphia: Carey & Hart, 1843), 69.

9. Girard, *Violence and the Sacred,* 54.

10. As in archaic societies where the sacred king is killed sacrificially after ritual accusations, Louis XVI is murdered for an assortment of non-reasons. His queen Marie Antoinette is even accused of incest with her son, one of the classic charges in archaic scapegoating and sacrifice. "It was a crowd phenomenon ultimately, a huge one. You can read the French Revolution in terms that are not the same, of course, but then you see aspects of this archaic reality that reappear quite suddenly." Girard, "Mimesis, Sacrifice, and the Bible," 54.

11. R. R. Palmer, *Twelve Who Ruled* (Princeton: Princeton University Press, 1971), 107.

12. René Girard, *The Scapegoat*, trans. Yvonne Freccero (Baltimore: Johns Hopkins University Press, 1986), 13.

13. Girard, *Battling to the End*, 119.

14. Girard, *Battling to the End*, 135.

15. Georges Pernoud and Sabine Flaissier, *The French Revolution* (New York: Putnam, 1960), 162.

16. Karen Armstrong, *Fields of Blood: Religion and the History of Violence* (New York: Knopf, 2014), 282.

17. Girard, *Battling to the End*, 139.

18. Élisabeth Lévy, "René Girard: 'La Guerre Est Partout,'" *Le Point*, 18 October 2007. Translation mine.

19. Girard, *Battling to the End*, 1.

20. Girard, *Battling to the End*, xv.

21. Lévy, "René Girard."

22. Girard, *Battling to the End*, xii.

23. Girard, *Battling to the End*, 2.

24. Lévy, "René Girard."

25. Stendhal, *The Charterhouse of Parma,* trans. Richard Howard (New York: Modern Library, 2000), 3.

26. Clausewitz himself makes a token appearance in Tolstoy's masterwork, *War and Peace*, when Prince Andrei hears the "clatter of three horses' hoofs on the road." The doomed aristocrat overhears the strategist dismiss the casualties as insignificant in his conversation with Count Ludwig von Wolzogen, accompanied by a Cossack on the eve of the Battle of Borodinó (New York: Norton Critical Editions, 1966), 863.

27. Girard, *Battling to the End*, 184.

28. Girard, *Battling to the End*, 180.

29. Girard, *Battling to the End*, 17.

30. Girard, *Battling to the End*, 182.

31. Girard, *Battling to the End*, 182.

32. Girard, *Battling to the End*, 182.

33. Girard, *Battling to the End*, 183.

34. Girard, *Battling to the End*, 6.

35. Girard, *Battling to the End*, 44.

36. Girard, *Battling to the End*, 43.

37. Girard, *Battling to the End*, 44.

38. Robert Doran, "Apocalyptic Thinking after 9/11: An Interview with René Girard," *SubStance* 37, no. 1 (2008): 29.

39. Robert Doran, "Apocalyptic Thinking after 9/11: An Interview with René Girard," *SubStance* 37, no. 1 (2008): 25.

40. Lévy, "René Girard."

41. Lévy, "René Girard."

42. Girard, *Battling to the End,* 212.

43. Fouad Ajami, "Nowhere Man," *New York Times Magazine,* 7 October 2001, 19–20.

44. Girard, *Battling to the End,* 211.

45. Lucy Draper, "Would-Be Jihadists' Letters Home Reveal Unhappy, Mundane Life in ISIS," *Newsweek,* 2 December 2014.

46. Girard, *Battling to the End,* 212–13.

47. Girard, *Battling to the End,* 214.

48. Girard, *Battling to the End,* 214–15.

49. Doran, "Apocalyptic Thinking after 9/11," 20–21.

CHAPTER 14. TERRA INCOGNITA

1. René Girard, *Battling to the End*, trans. Mary Baker (East Lansing: Michigan State University Press, 2010), 124.

2. Robert Harrison, "René Girard on Ritual Sacrifice and the Scapegoat," *Entitled Opinions*, KZSU, Stanford, CA, 4 October 2005, radio broadcast.

3. Girard, *Battling to the End*, 132. Elsewhere, Girard has been more explicit about Proust's case: "Others have protested, pointing out that Proust never made any effort to live according to Christian morality and probably did not even believe in God. This biographical fact does not, however, alter the aesthetic one, which is simply that, although Proust was an agnostic, his masterpiece espouses the Christian structure of redemption more perfectly than the carefully planned efforts of many conscientious Christian artists." René Girard, ed., *Proust: A Collection of Critical Essays* (Englewood Cliffs, NJ: Prentice Hall, 1962), 11.

4. Roman Siebenrock, "René Girard with German Theologians, Munich, September 2004," trans. N. Wandinger, *COV&R Bulletin*, no. 26 (April 2005), 4.

5. Czesław Miłosz, "A Conversation about Dostoevsky," *Michigan Quarterly Review* 22 (Fall 1983): 548.

6. René Girard, *Deceit, Desire, and the Novel*, trans. Yvonne Freccero (Baltimore: Johns Hopkins University Press, 1965), 296.

7. Girard, *Deceit, Desire, and the Novel*, 295–96.

8. Friedrich Hölderlin, *Selected Poems and Fragments*, trans. Michael Hamburger (New York: Penguin, 2007), xxxii.

9. Hölderlin, *Selected Poems and Fragments*, xxxii.

10. Girard, *Violence and the Sacred*, 157.

11. Girard, *Violence and the Sacred*, 156.

12. Cynthia Haven, "Hannah Arendt Considered Today: Totalitarianism, Genocide and the Need for Thought," *Stanford Report*, 25 May 2010.

13. From Wilhelm Waiblinger's 1830 essay "Friedrich Hölderlin's Life, Poetry and Madness," translated by Scott J. Thompson. In Hölderlin, *Selected Poems and Fragments*, xlviii.

14. René Girard, *When These Things Begin: Conversations with Michel Treguer*, trans. Trevor Cribben Merrill (East Lansing: Michigan State University Press, 2014), 132.

15. Girard, *Battling to the End*, 121.

16. Girard, *Battling to the End*, 123.

17. Girard, *Battling to the End*, 121.

18. Heidegger, who also had become fascinated with the Swabian poet, expressed a kindred desperation in different words. In a 1966 interview with *Der Spiegel* toward the end of his life: "Philosophy will not be able to bring about a direct change of the present state of the world. This is true not only of philosophy but of all merely human meditations and endeavors. Only a god can still save us. I think the only possibility of salvation left to us is to prepare readiness, through thinking and poetry, for the appearance of the god or for the absence of the god during the decline; so that we do not, simply put, die meaningless deaths, but that when we decline, we decline in the face of the absent god. . . . We cannot get him to come by thinking. At best we can prepare the readiness of expectation." From "Nur noch ein Gott kann uns retten," *Der Spiegel*, 31 May 1976, 193–219.

19. Girard, *Battling to the End*, 121.

20. Hölderlin, *Selected Poems and Fragments*, 241.

21. Jean-Luc Marion, *The Idol and Distance* (New York: Fordham University Press, 2001), 110.

22. Girard, *Battling to the End*, 119–20.

23. Girard, *Battling to the End*, 120.

24. Girard, *Battling to the End*, 122, 123.

25. From Miłosz's introduction to the poetry collection of filmmaker and poet Jonas Mekas, *There Is No Ithaka: Idylls of Semeniskiai and Reminiscences*, trans. Vyt Bakaitis (Newfane, VT: Black Thistle Press, 1996).

26. Hölderlin, *Selected Poems and Fragments*, 241.

27. "The Poet's Vocation," in Hölderlin, *Selected Poems and Fragments*, 83.

POSTSCRIPT: HAND IN HAND

1. Later published as "Violence and Nonviolence," in Paul Dumouchel, *The Ambivalence of Scarcity and Other Essays* (East Lansing: Michigan State University Press, 2014).

2. Dumouchel, *Ambivalence of Scarcity,* 158.

3. René Girard, *Battling to the End*, trans. Mary Baker (East Lansing: Michigan State University Press, 2010), 118.

4. Dumouchel, *Ambivalence of Scarcity,* 159–60.

5. Dumouchel, *Ambivalence of Scarcity*, 160.

6. Dumouchel, *Ambivalence of Scarcity,* 157.

7. René Girard, *Things Hidden since the Foundation of the World* (Stanford, CA: Stanford University Press, 1987), 203.

8. Dumouchel, *Ambivalence of Scarcity,* 169.

9. Girard, *Battling to the End,* 133. Italics mine.

10. René Girard, "Dostoevsky's Demons," *Weekly Standard*, 20 May 2002.

11. René Girard, *Deceit, Desire, and the Novel*, trans. Yvonne Freccero (Baltimore: Johns Hopkins University Press, 1965), 313–14.

12. Girard, *Battling to the End,* 109.

13. Girard. *Battling to the End*, 131.

14. Hannah Arendt, *The Human Condition* (Chicago: University of Chicago Press, 1958), 240–41.

Index

Page numbers in **boldface** refer to the photograph gallery, which is referred to as pages **A–P**.

René Girard (1923–2015) was one of the leading thinkers of our era—a provocative sage who bypassed prevailing orthodoxies to offer a bold, sweeping vision of human nature, human history, and human destiny. His oeuvre, offering a "mimetic theory" of cultural origins and human behavior, inspired such writers as Milan Kundera and J. M. Coetzee, and earned him a place among the forty "immortals" of the Académie Française. In this first-ever biographical study, Cynthia L. Haven traces the evolution of Girard's thought in parallel with his life and times. She recounts his formative years in France and his arrival in a country torn by racial division, and reveals his insights into the collective delusions of our technological world and the changing nature of warfare. Drawing on interviews with Girard and his colleagues, *Evolution of Desire* provides an essential introduction to one of the twentieth century's most controversial and original minds.

Cynthia L. Haven writes regularly for *The Times Literary Supplement* and has contributed to *The Nation, Washington Post, Los Angeles Times*, and many other publications. She has published several books, including volumes on Nobel poets Czesław Miłosz and Joseph Brodsky. She has been a Milena Jesenská Journalism Fellow with the Institut für die Wissenschaften vom Menschen in Vienna, a visiting scholar at Stanford University, and a Voegelin Fellow at Stanford's Hoover Institution.